コンプレックス・エイジ

Complex age
Yui Sakuma

3

C O N T E N T S
Complex age

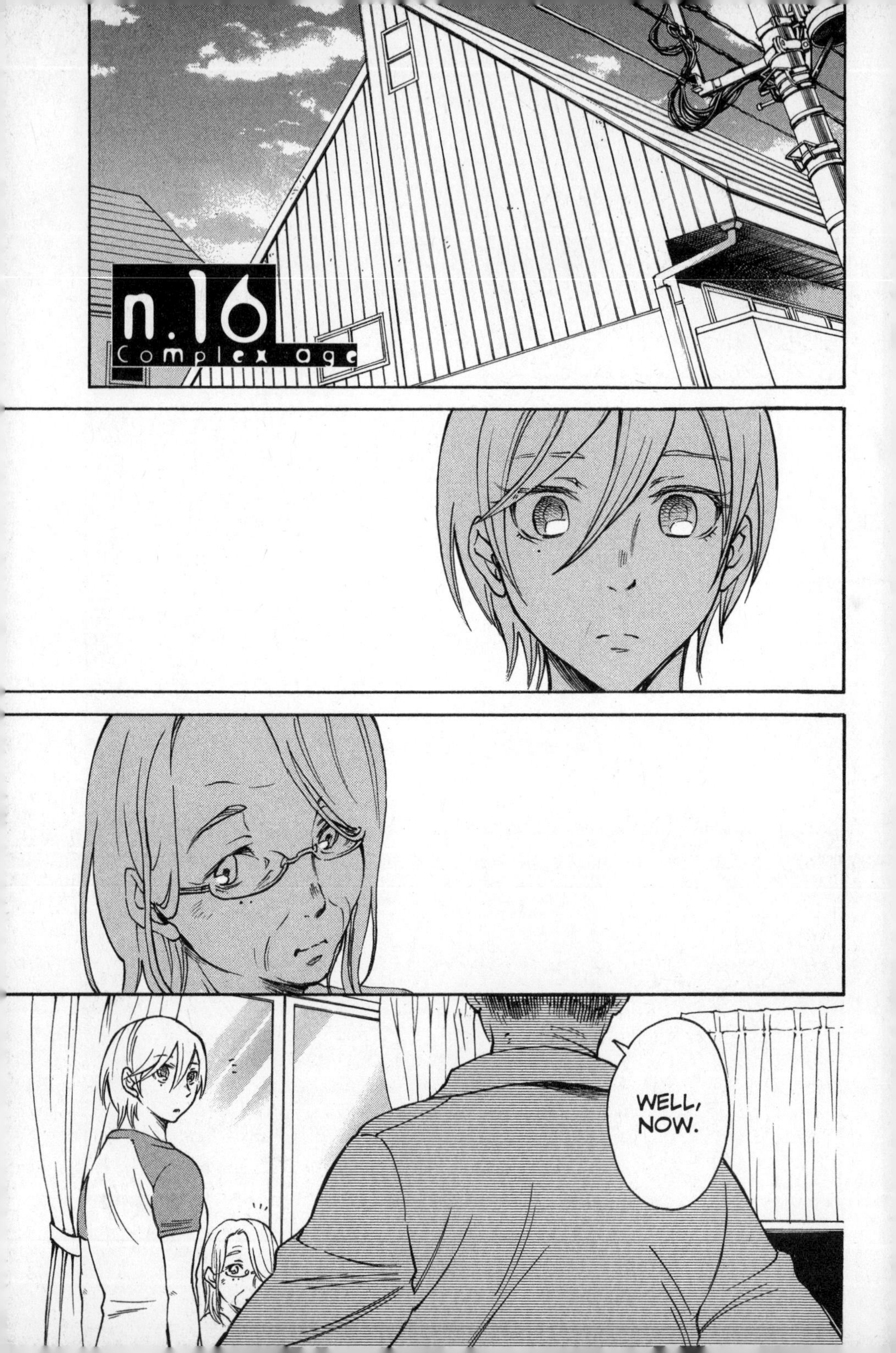
n.16
Complex age
WELL, NOW.

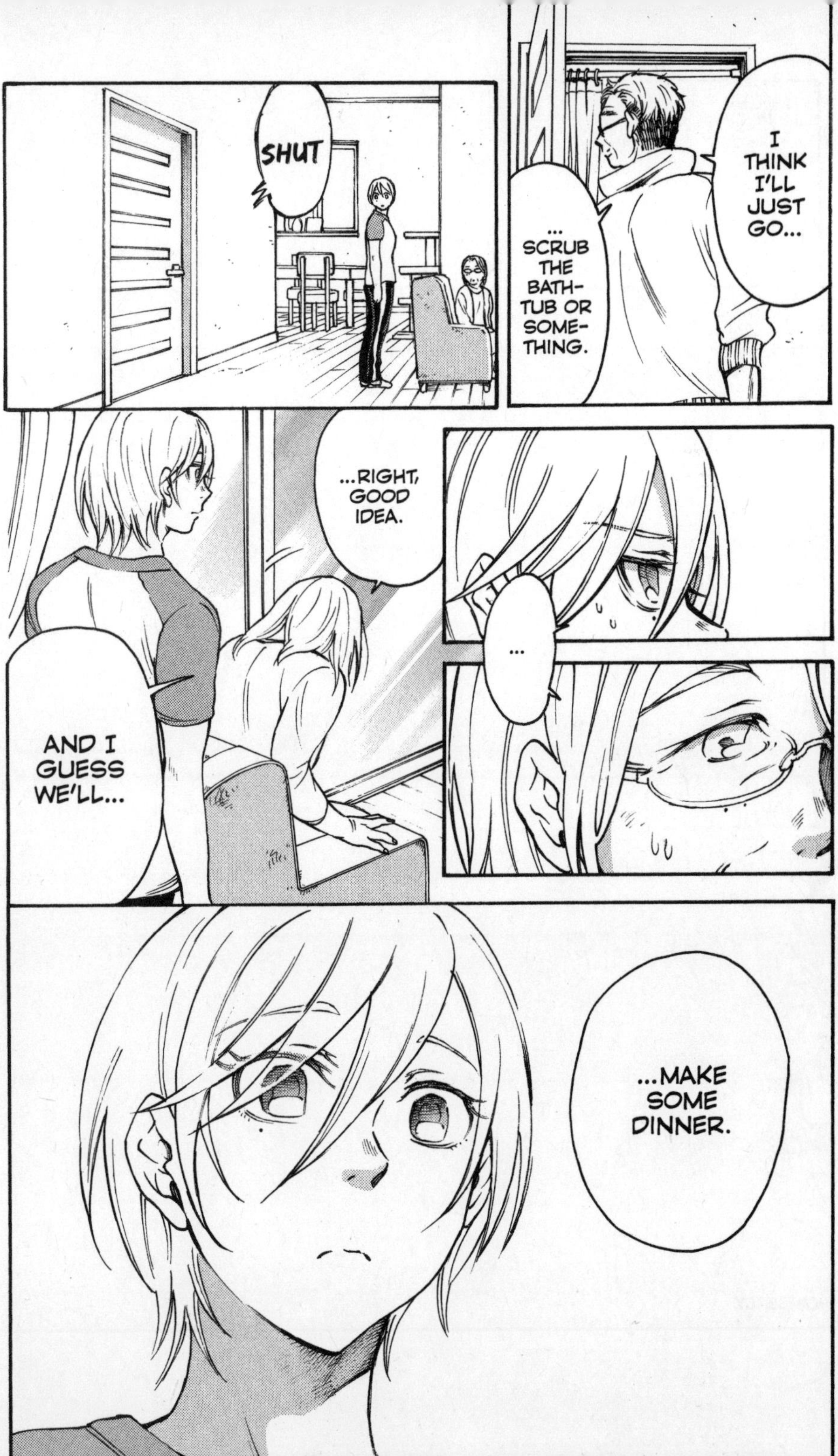
I THINK I'LL JUST GO...
...SCRUB THE BATH-TUB OR SOME-THING.
SHUT
...
...RIGHT, GOOD IDEA.
AND I GUESS WE'LL...
...MAKE SOME DINNER.

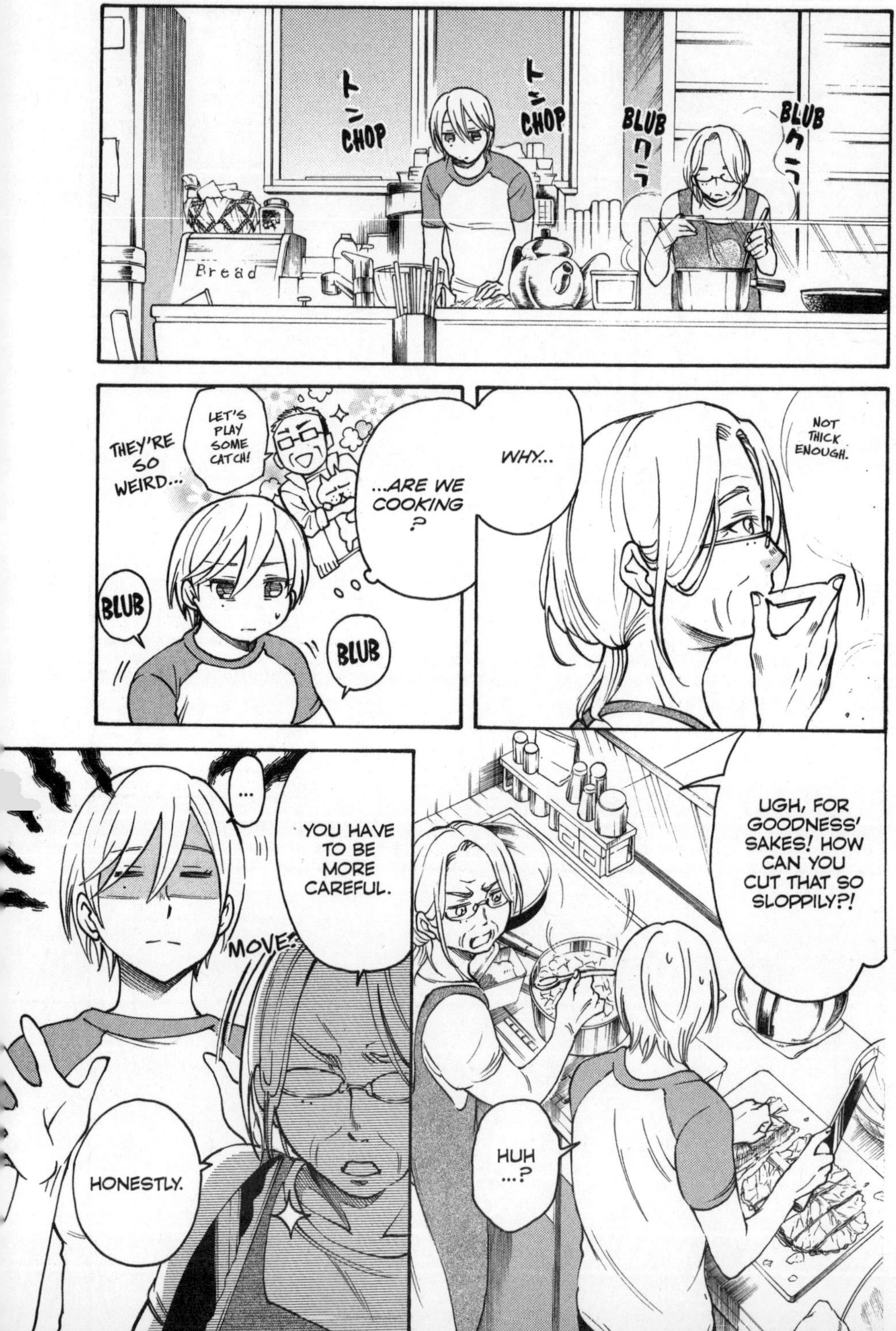
BLUB クラ
BLUB クラ
トン CHOP
トン CHOP
NOT THICK ENOUGH.
WHY...
...ARE WE COOKING?
LET'S PLAY SOME CATCH!
THEY'RE SO WEIRD...
BLUB
BLUB
UGH, FOR GOODNESS' SAKES! HOW CAN YOU CUT THAT SO SLOPPILY?!
HUH ...?
...
YOU HAVE TO BE MORE CAREFUL.
MOVE!
HONESTLY.

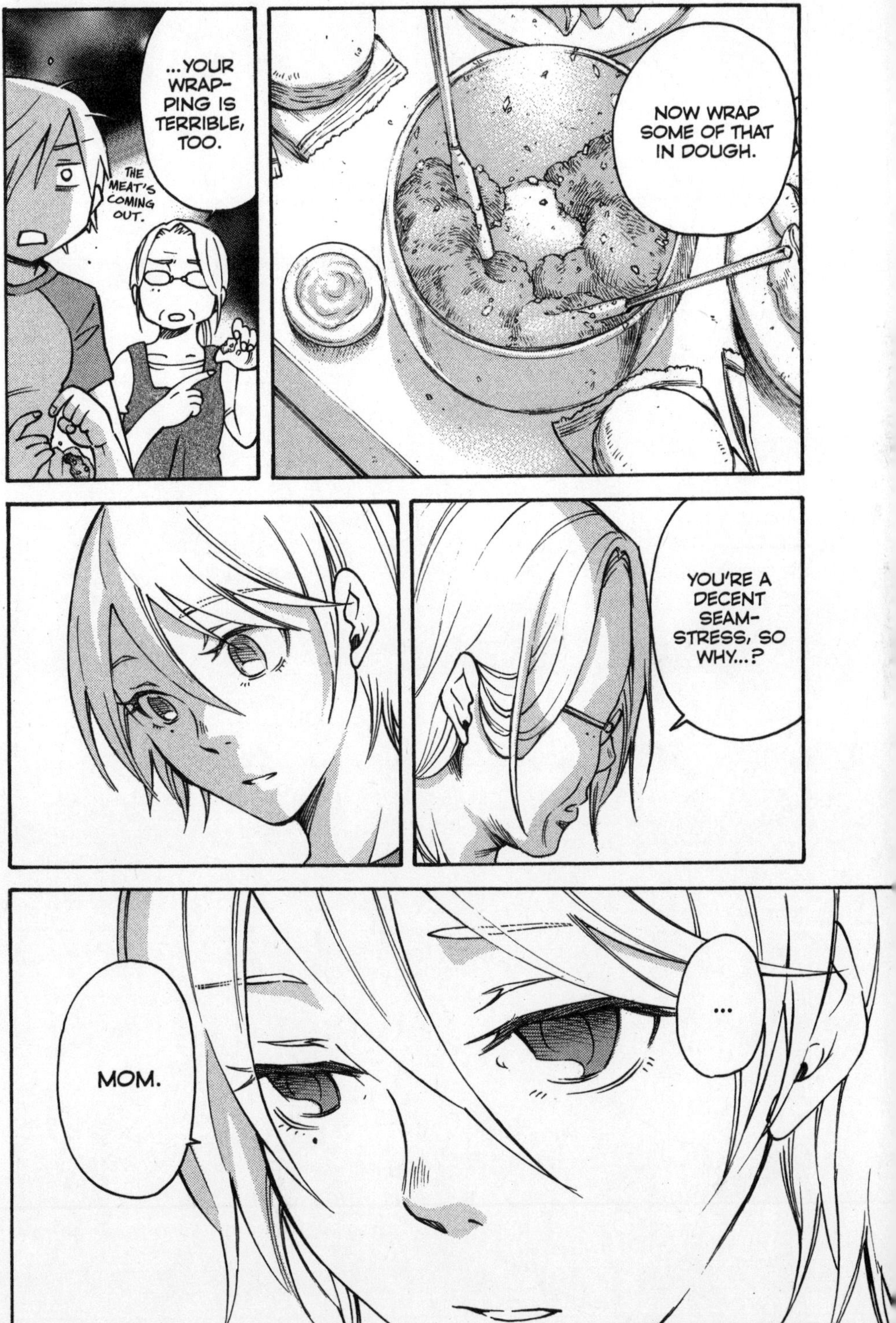
NOW WRAP SOME OF THAT IN DOUGH.
...YOUR WRAP-PING IS TERRIBLE, TOO.
THE MEAT'S COMING OUT.
YOU'RE A DECENT SEAM-STRESS, SO WHY...?
...
MOM.

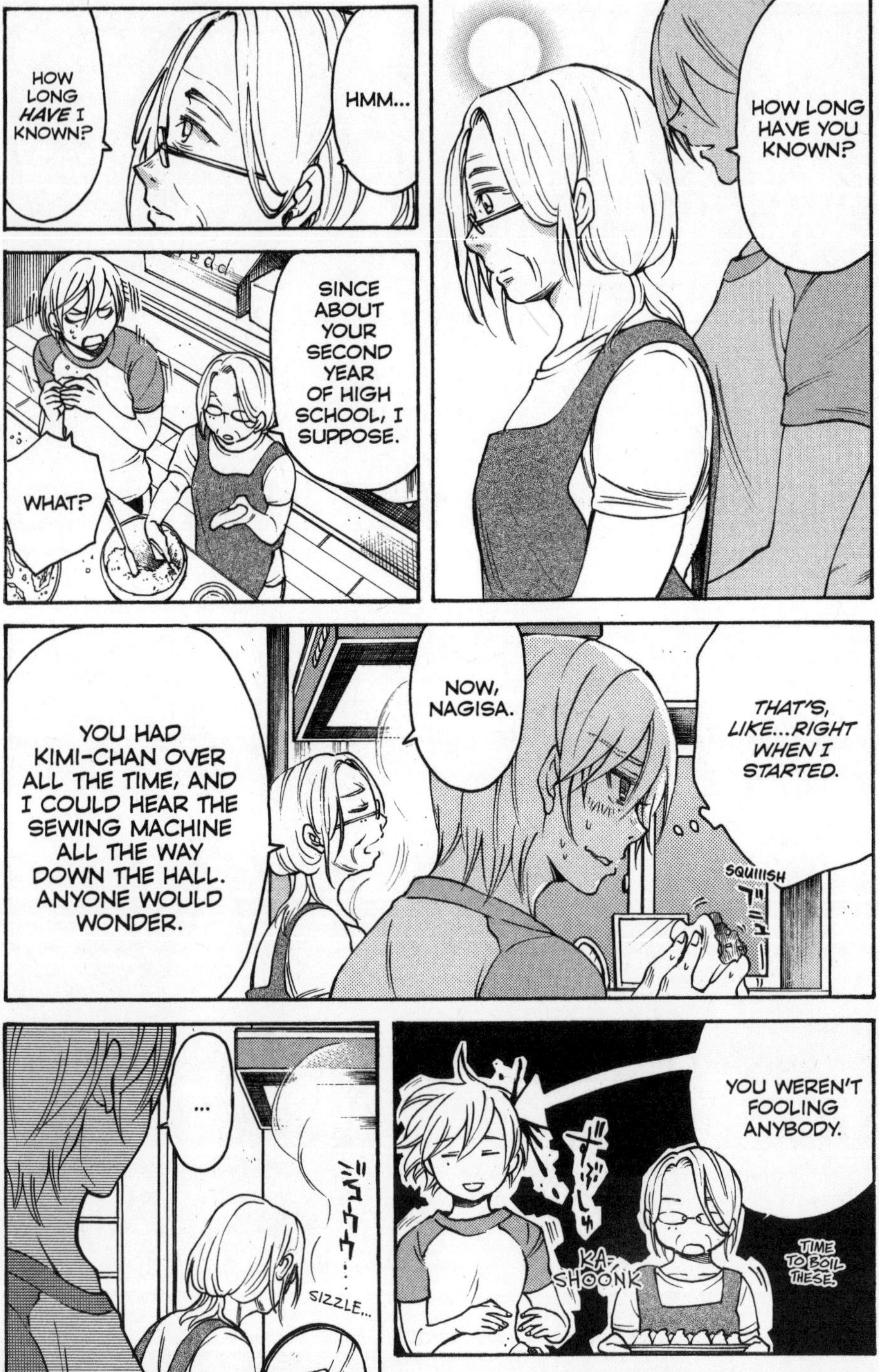
HOW LONG HAVE YOU KNOWN?
HMM...
HOW LONG *HAVE* I KNOWN?
SINCE ABOUT YOUR SECOND YEAR OF HIGH SCHOOL, I SUPPOSE.
WHAT?
THAT'S, LIKE...RIGHT WHEN I STARTED.
SQUIIISH
NOW, NAGISA.
YOU HAD KIMI-CHAN OVER ALL THE TIME, AND I COULD HEAR THE SEWING MACHINE ALL THE WAY DOWN THE HALL. ANYONE WOULD WONDER.
YOU WEREN'T FOOLING ANYBODY.
TIME TO BOIL THESE.
KA-SHOONK
...
SIZZLE...

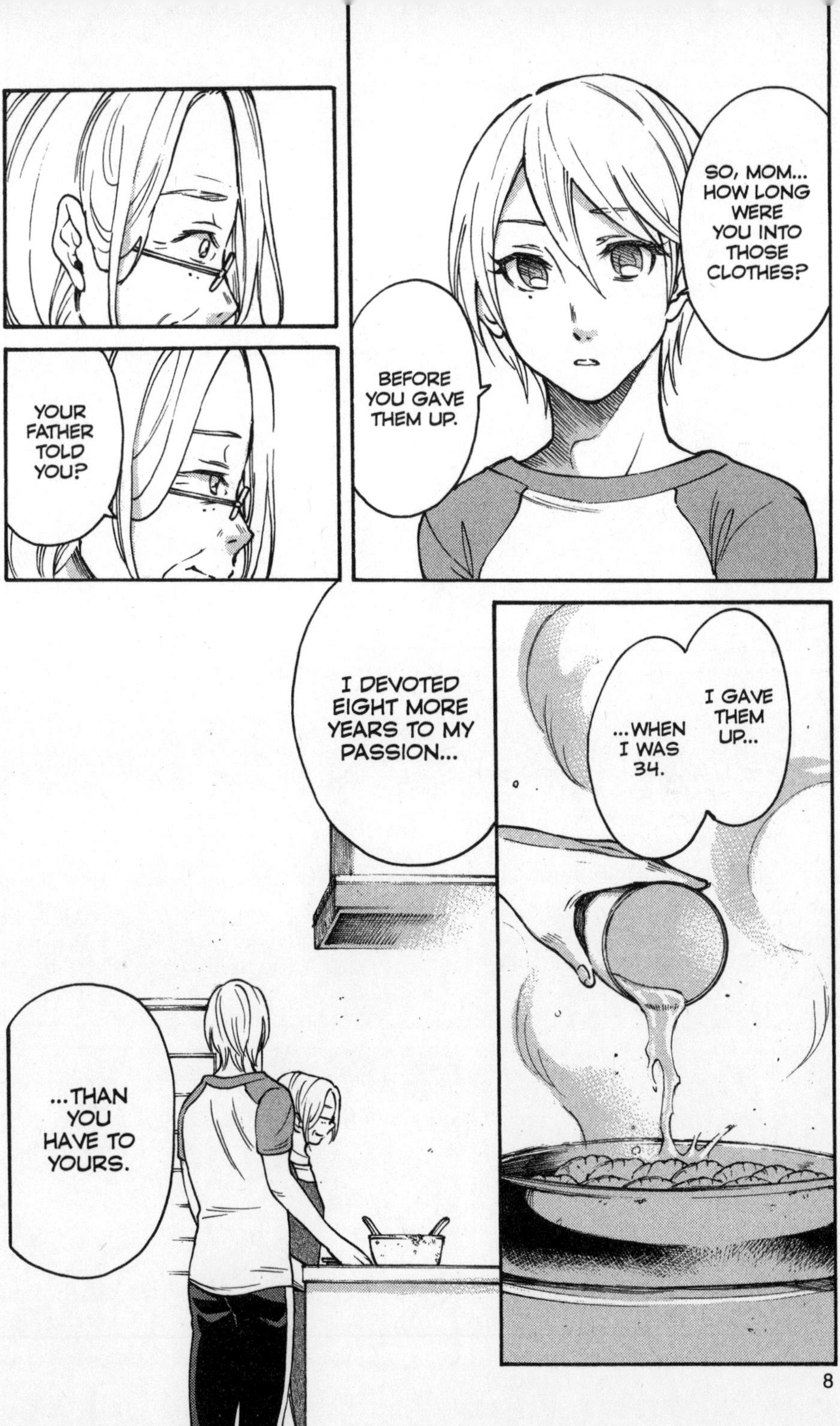
SO, MOM... HOW LONG WERE YOU INTO THOSE CLOTHES?
BEFORE YOU GAVE THEM UP.
YOUR FATHER TOLD YOU?
I GAVE THEM UP...
...WHEN I WAS 34.
I DEVOTED EIGHT MORE YEARS TO MY PASSION...
...THAN YOU HAVE TO YOURS.

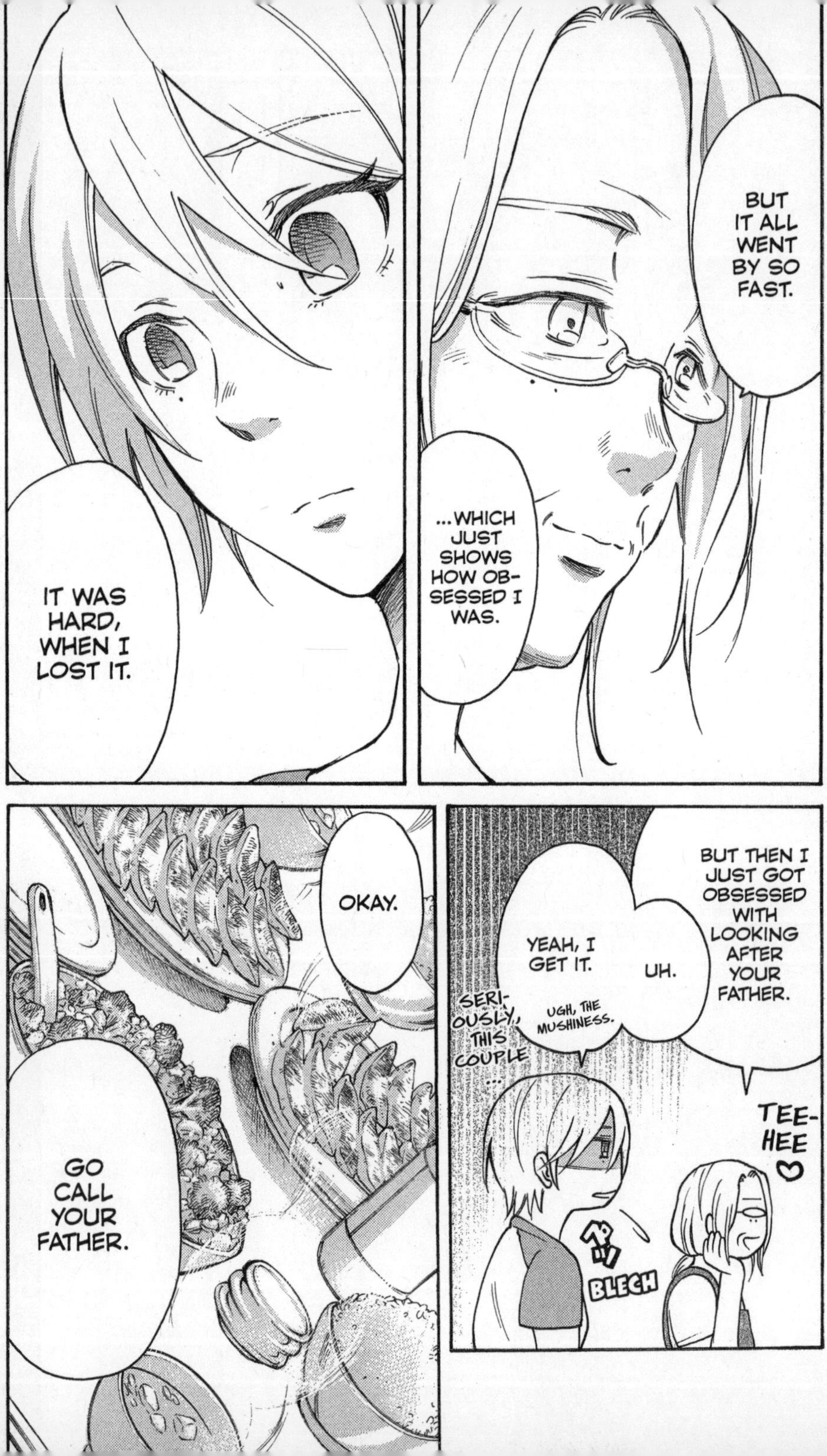
BUT IT ALL WENT BY SO FAST.
...WHICH JUST SHOWS HOW OBSESSED I WAS.
IT WAS HARD, WHEN I LOST IT.
BUT THEN I JUST GOT OBSESSED WITH LOOKING AFTER YOUR FATHER.
UH.
YEAH, I GET IT.
UGH, THE MUSHINESS.
SERIOUSLY, THIS COUPLE...
TEE-HEE ♡
BLECH
OKAY.
GO CALL YOUR FATHER.

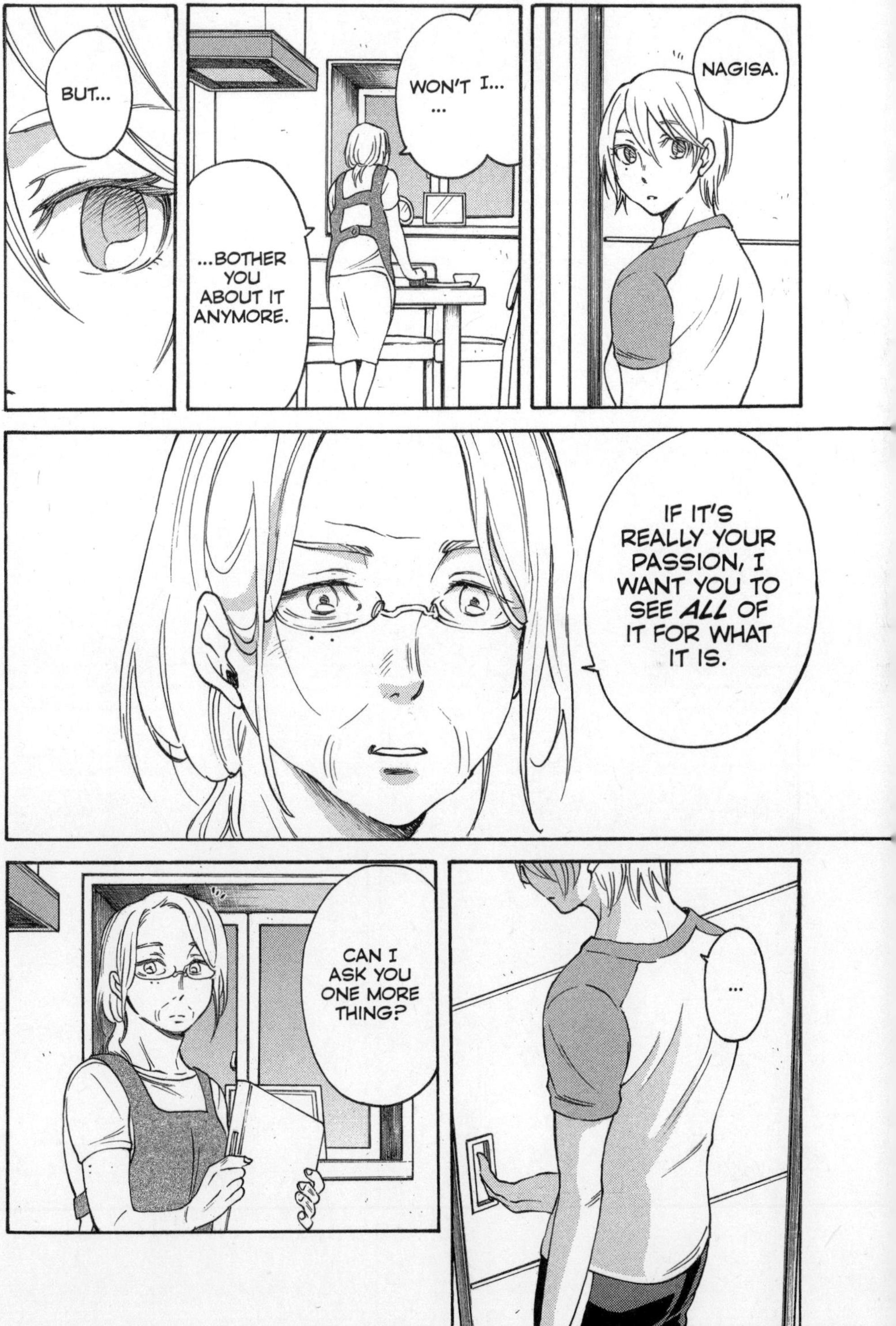
NAGISA.
WON'T I... ...
...BOTHER YOU ABOUT IT ANYMORE.
BUT...
IF IT'S REALLY YOUR PASSION, I WANT YOU TO SEE *ALL* OF IT FOR WHAT IT IS.
...
CAN I ASK YOU ONE MORE THING?

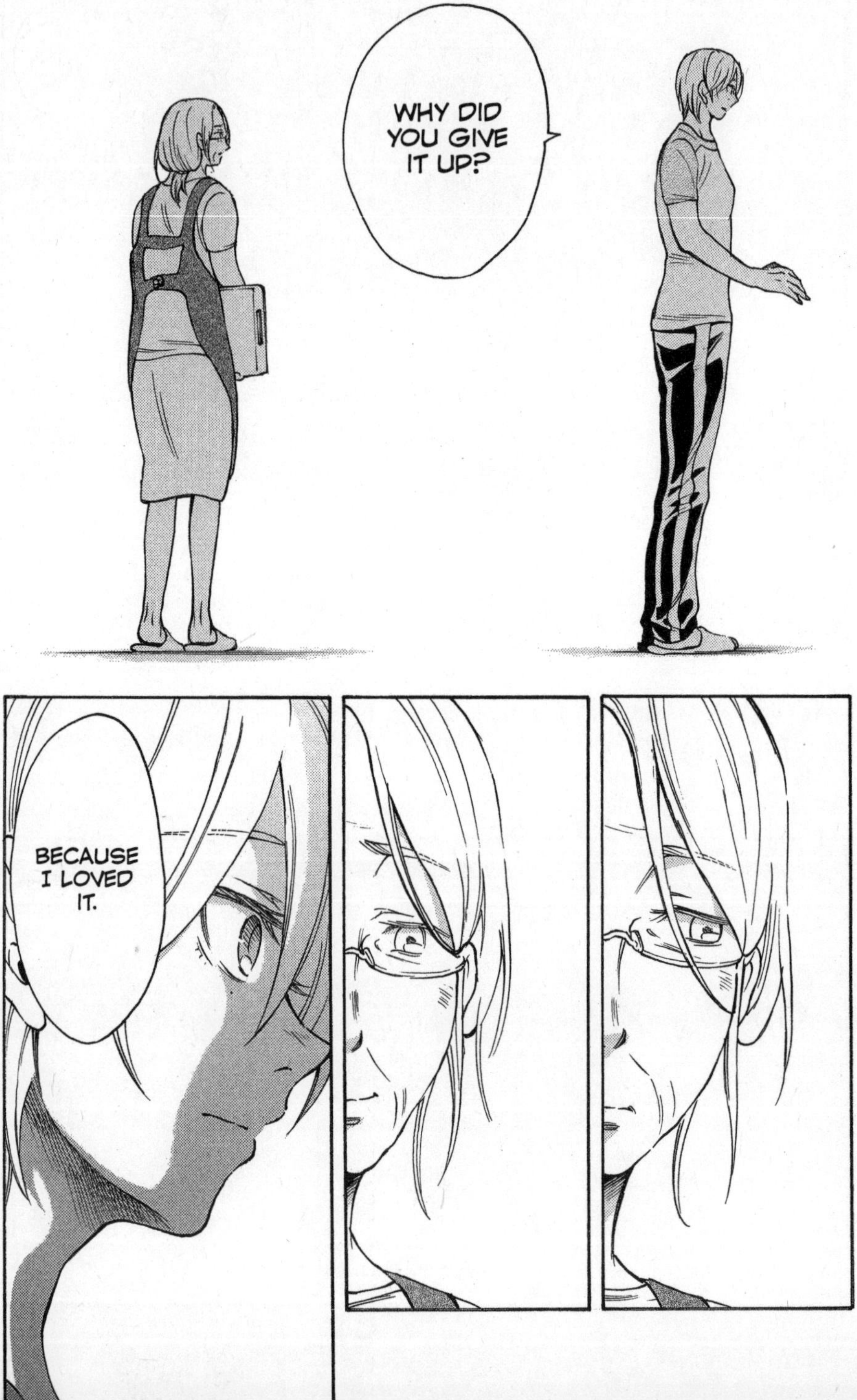
WHY DID YOU GIVE IT UP?
BECAUSE I LOVED IT.

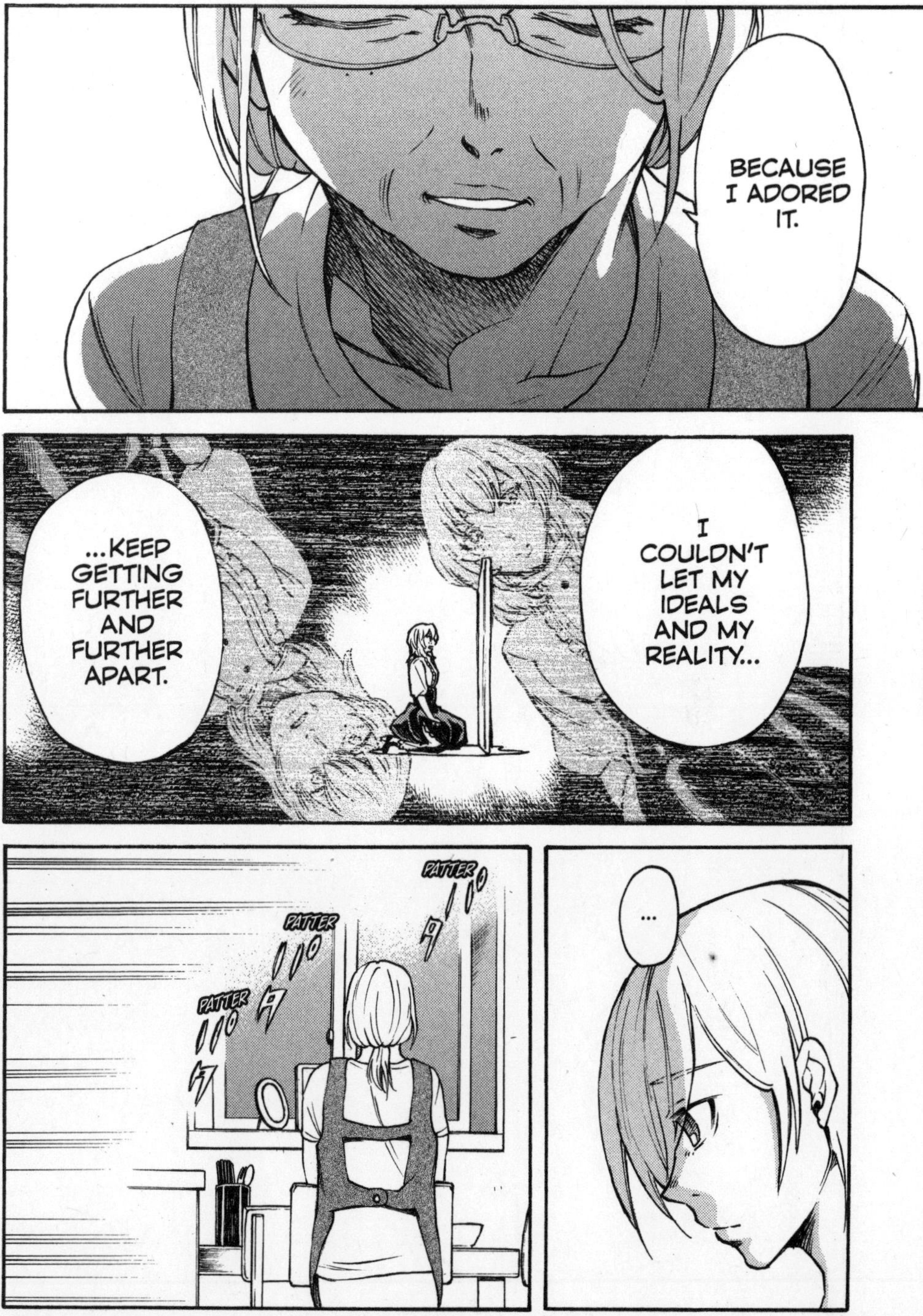
BECAUSE I ADORED IT.
I COULDN'T LET MY IDEALS AND MY REALITY...
...KEEP GETTING FURTHER AND FURTHER APART.
...
PATTER
PATTER
PATTER

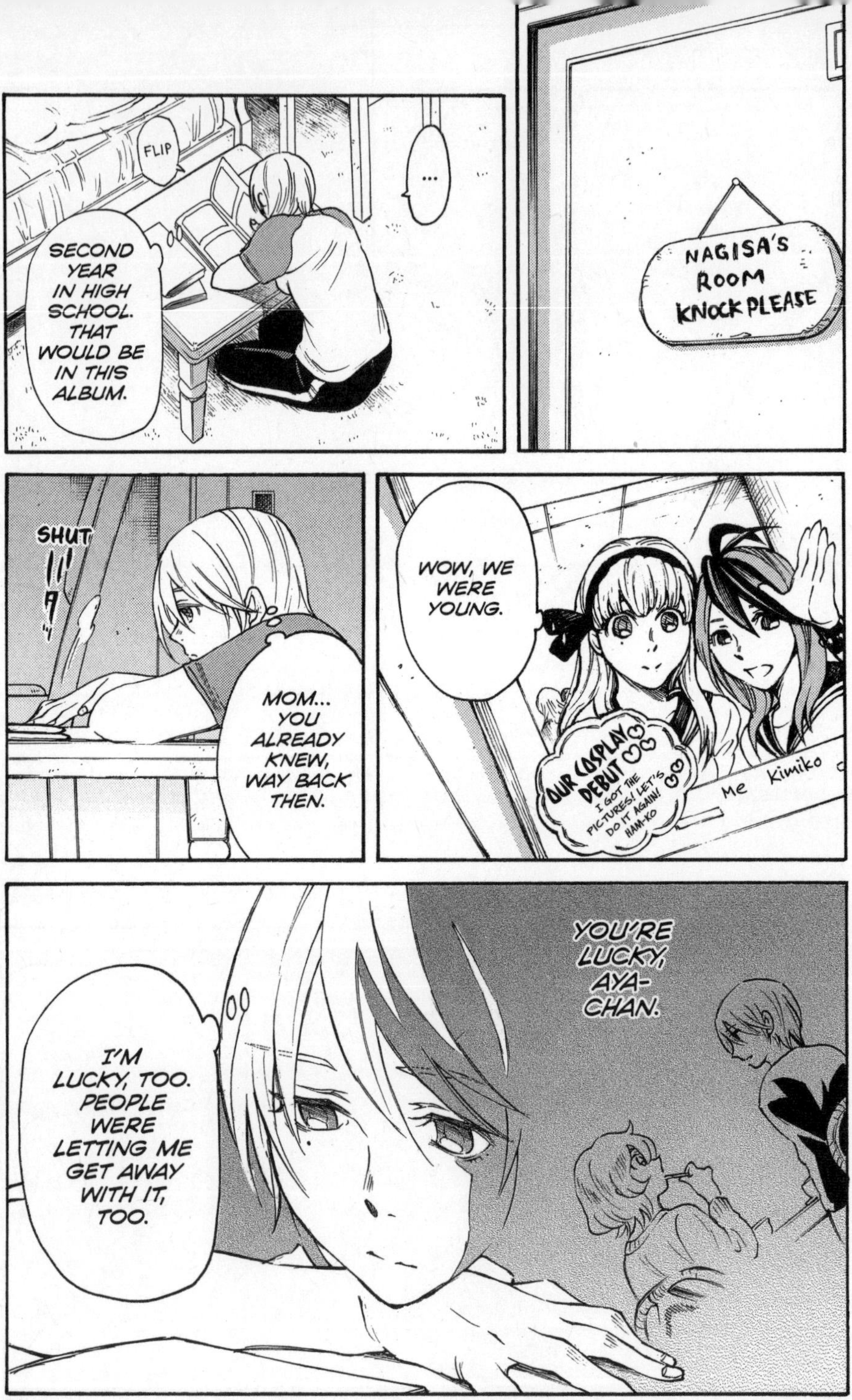
NAGISA'S ROOM KNOCK PLEASE
...
FLIP
SECOND YEAR IN HIGH SCHOOL. THAT WOULD BE IN THIS ALBUM.
WOW, WE WERE YOUNG.
OUR COSPLAY DEBUT
I GOT THE PICTURES! LET'S DO IT AGAIN! HAM-KO
Me Kimiko
SHUT
MOM... YOU ALREADY KNEW, WAY BACK THEN.
YOU'RE LUCKY, AYA-CHAN.
I'M LUCKY, TOO. PEOPLE WERE LETTING ME GET AWAY WITH IT, TOO.

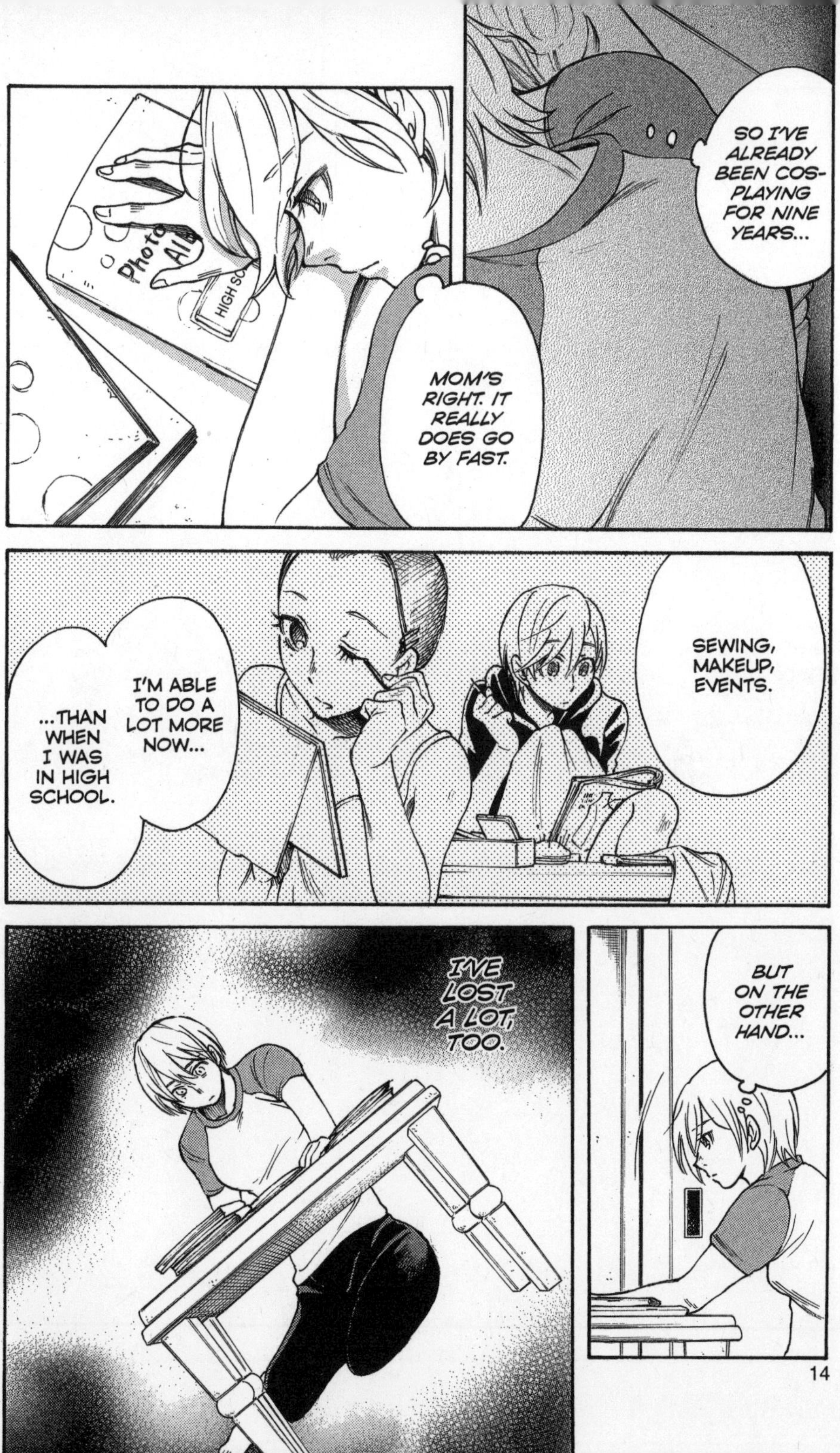
SO I'VE ALREADY BEEN COS-PLAYING FOR NINE YEARS...
MOM'S RIGHT. IT REALLY DOES GO BY FAST.
SEWING, MAKEUP, EVENTS.
I'M ABLE TO DO A LOT MORE NOW...
...THAN WHEN I WAS IN HIGH SCHOOL.
BUT ON THE OTHER HAND...
I'VE LOST A LOT, TOO.

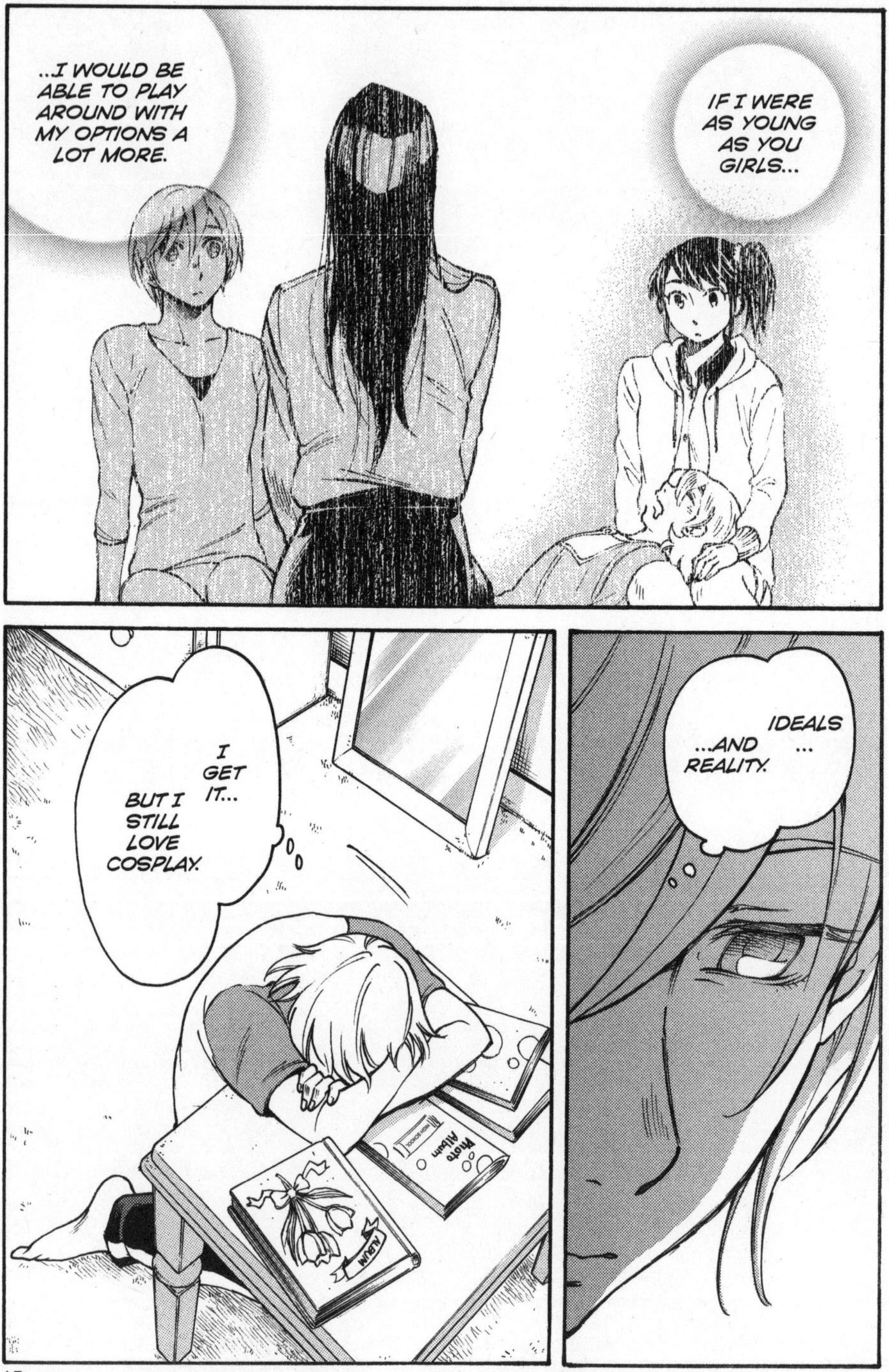
IF I WERE AS YOUNG AS YOU GIRLS...
...I WOULD BE ABLE TO PLAY AROUND WITH MY OPTIONS A LOT MORE.
IDEALS ...
...AND REALITY.
I GET IT...
BUT I STILL LOVE COSPLAY.

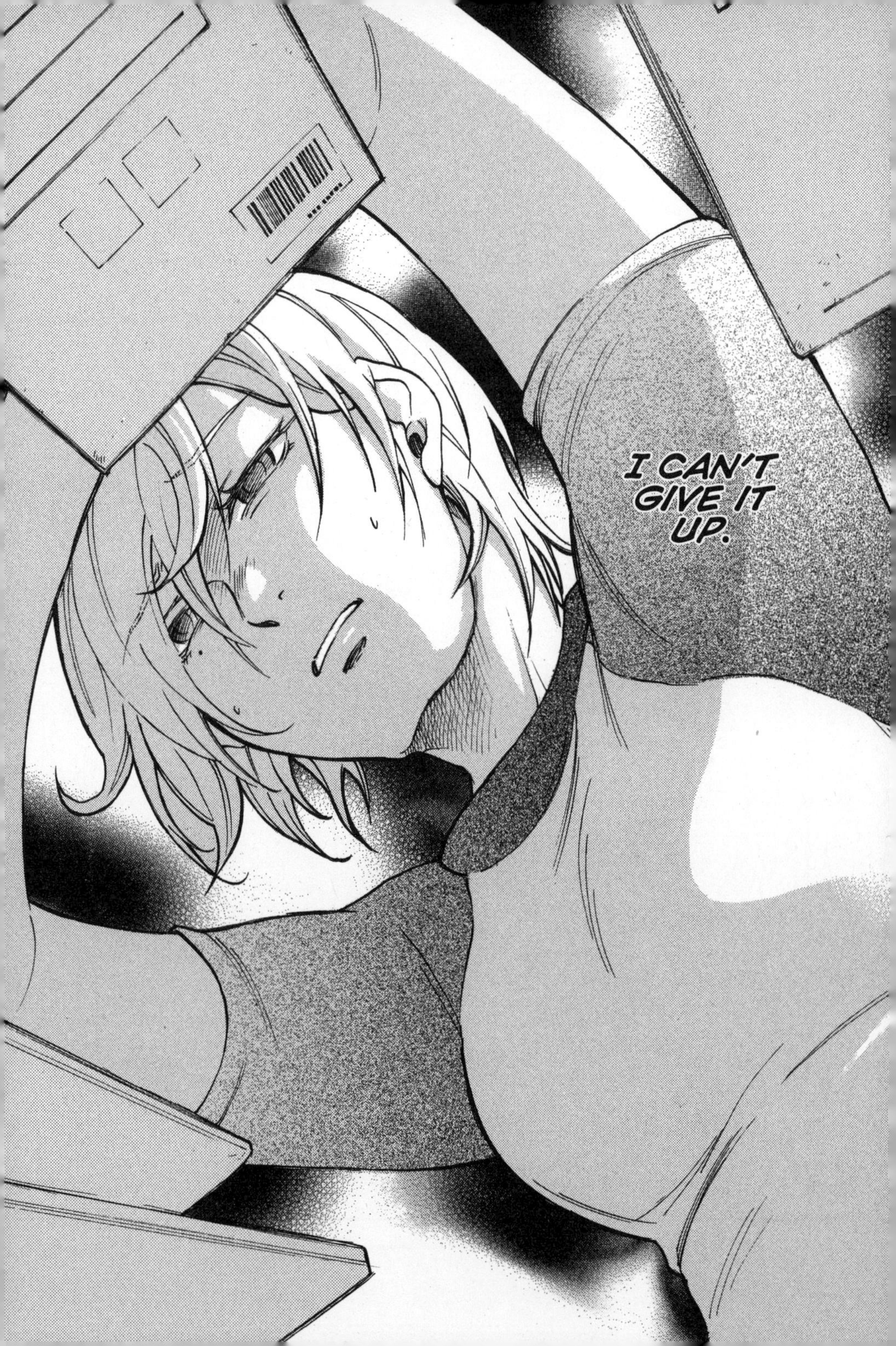
I CAN'T GIVE IT UP.

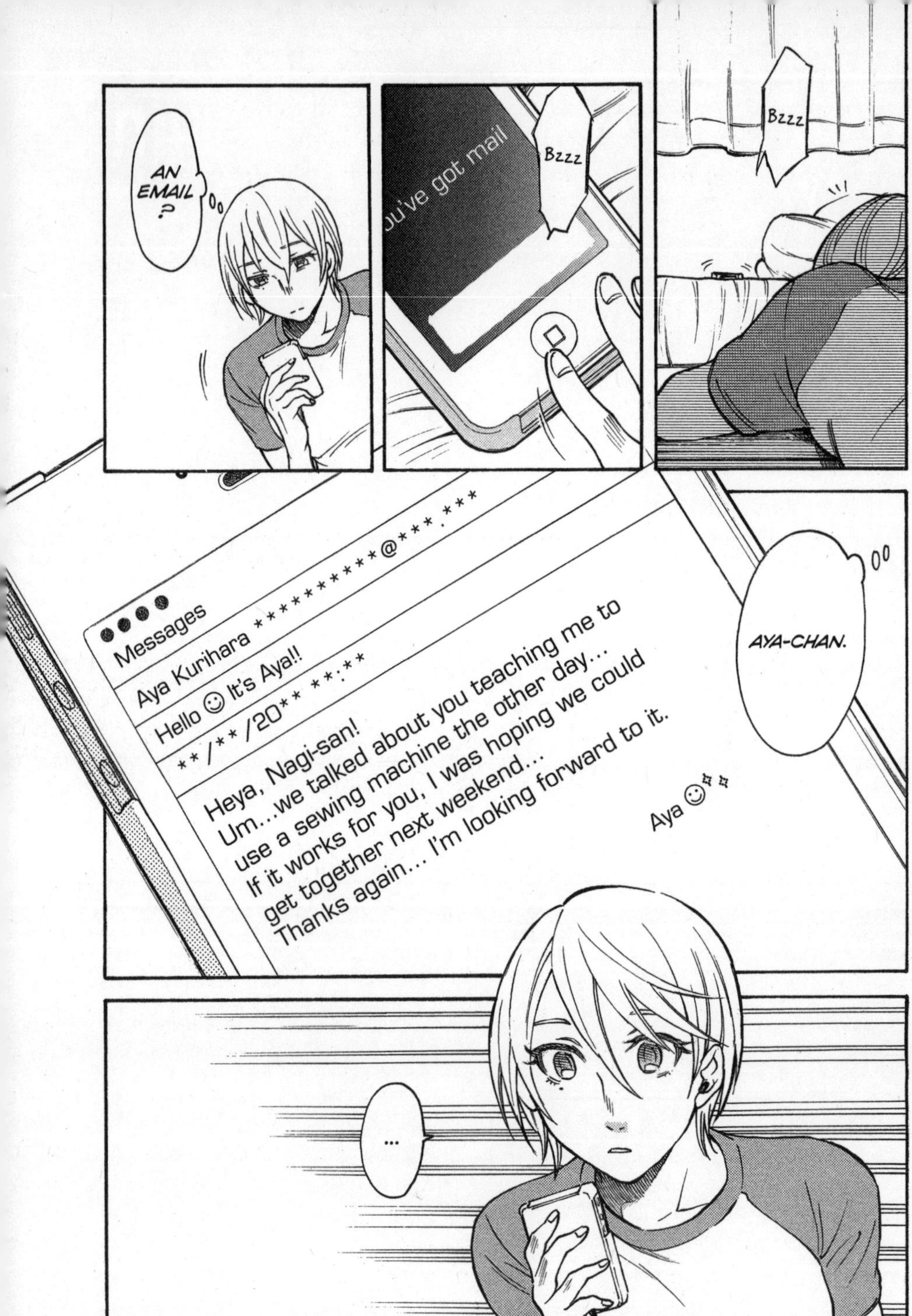
Bzzz
ou've got mail
Bzzz
AN EMAIL?
AYA-CHAN.
Messages
Aya Kurihara **********@***.***
Hello ☺ It's Aya!!
//20** **:**
Heya, Nagi-san!
Um...we talked about you teaching me to
use a sewing machine the other day...
If it works for you, I was hoping we could
get together next weekend...
Thanks again... I'm looking forward to it.
Aya ☺
...

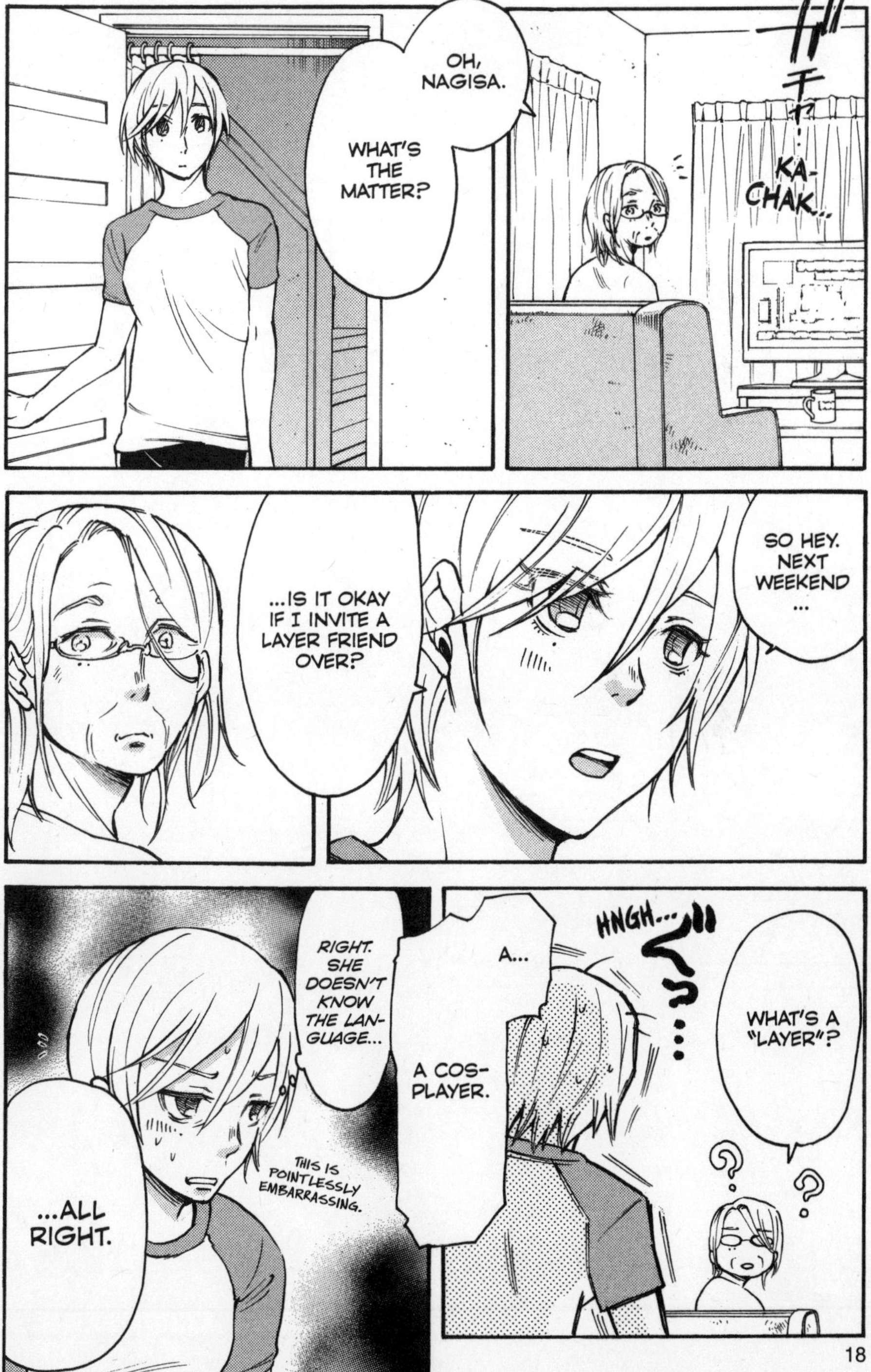
KA-CHAK...
OH, NAGISA.
WHAT'S THE MATTER?
SO HEY. NEXT WEEKEND ...
...IS IT OKAY IF I INVITE A LAYER FRIEND OVER?
WHAT'S A "LAYER"?
HNGH...
A...
A COS-PLAYER.
RIGHT. SHE DOESN'T KNOW THE LAN-GUAGE...
THIS IS POINTLESSLY EMBARRASSING.
...ALL RIGHT.

IF THAT'S WHAT YOU WANT.

The next weekend

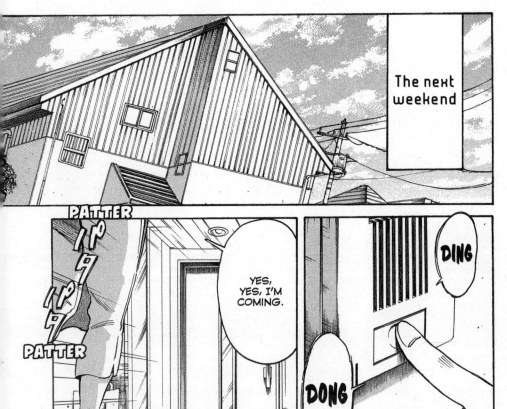

PATTER

YES, YES, I'M COMING.

PATTER

PATTER

DING

DONG
...

19

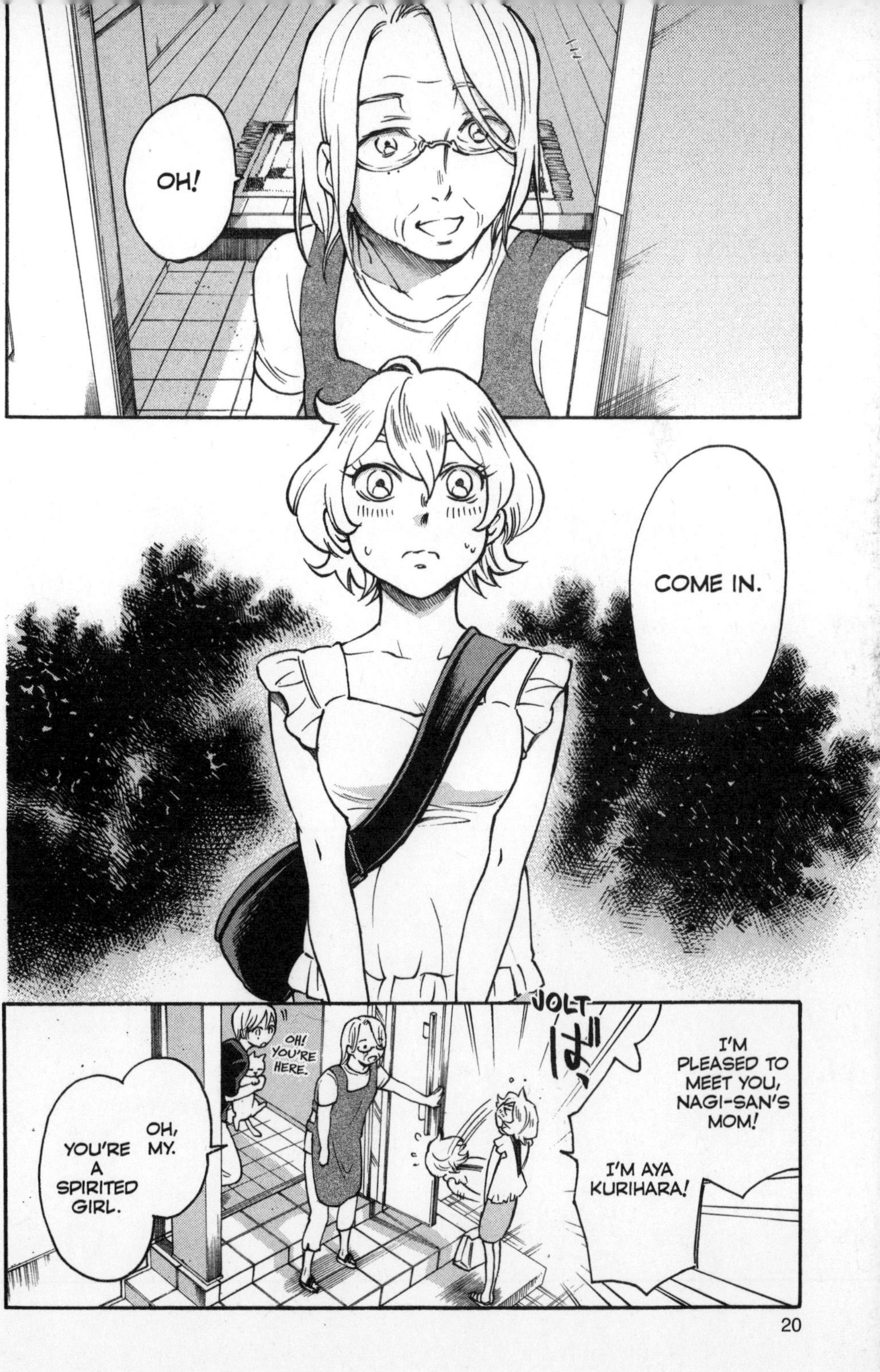
OH!
COME IN.
JOLT
ば
I'M PLEASED TO MEET YOU, NAGI-SAN'S MOM!
I'M AYA KURIHARA!
OH! YOU'RE HERE.
OH, MY.
YOU'RE A SPIRITED GIRL.

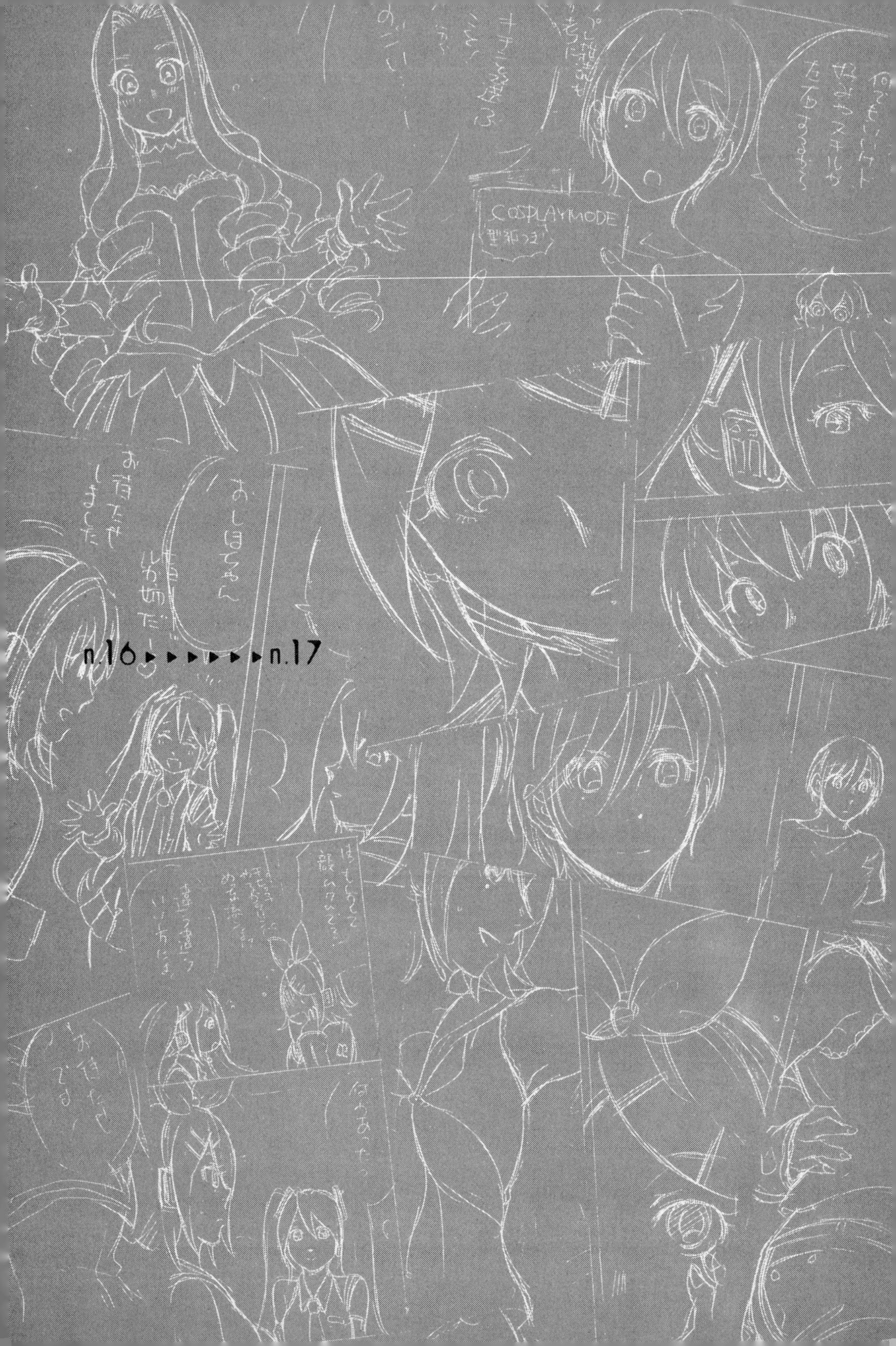
COSPLAYMODE
n.16▸▸▸▸▸▸▸n.17

SPECIAL BONUS

MIKU & FRIENDS COLLABORATION!!

In the series, Nagisa and her friends cosplay the Vocaloids. Here are some bonus illustrations of their costumes!!

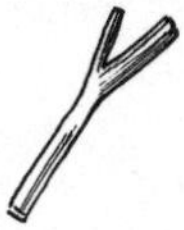

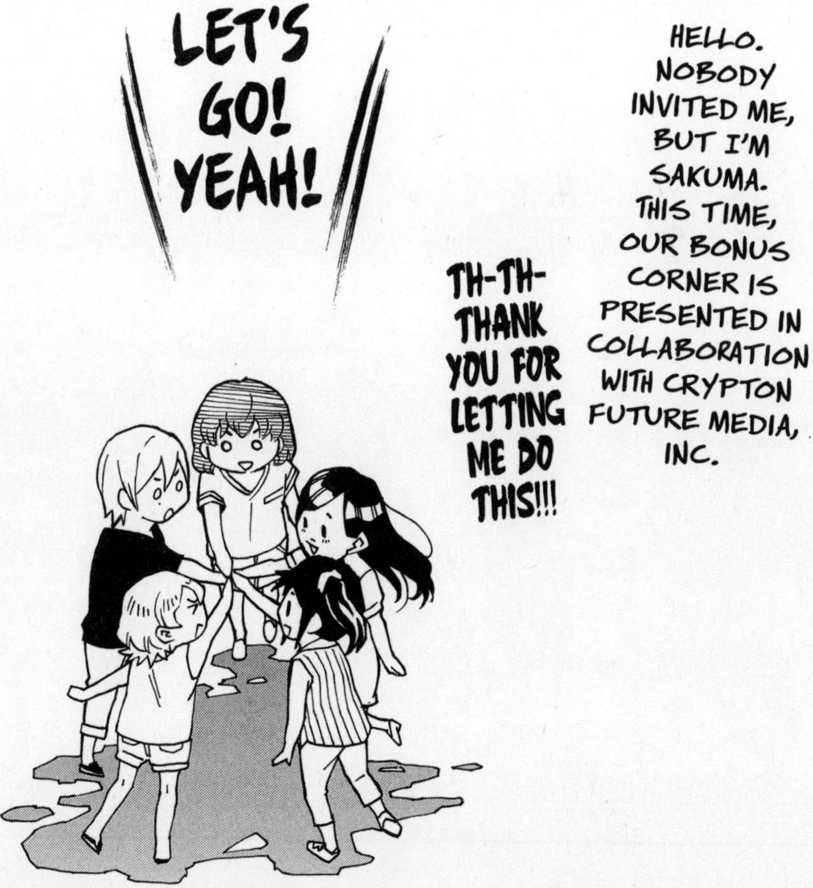
HELLO. NOBODY INVITED ME, BUT I'M SAKUMA. THIS TIME, OUR BONUS CORNER IS PRESENTED IN COLLABORATION WITH CRYPTON FUTURE MEDIA, INC.
TH-TH-THANK YOU FOR LETTING ME DO THIS!!!
LET'S GO! YEAH!

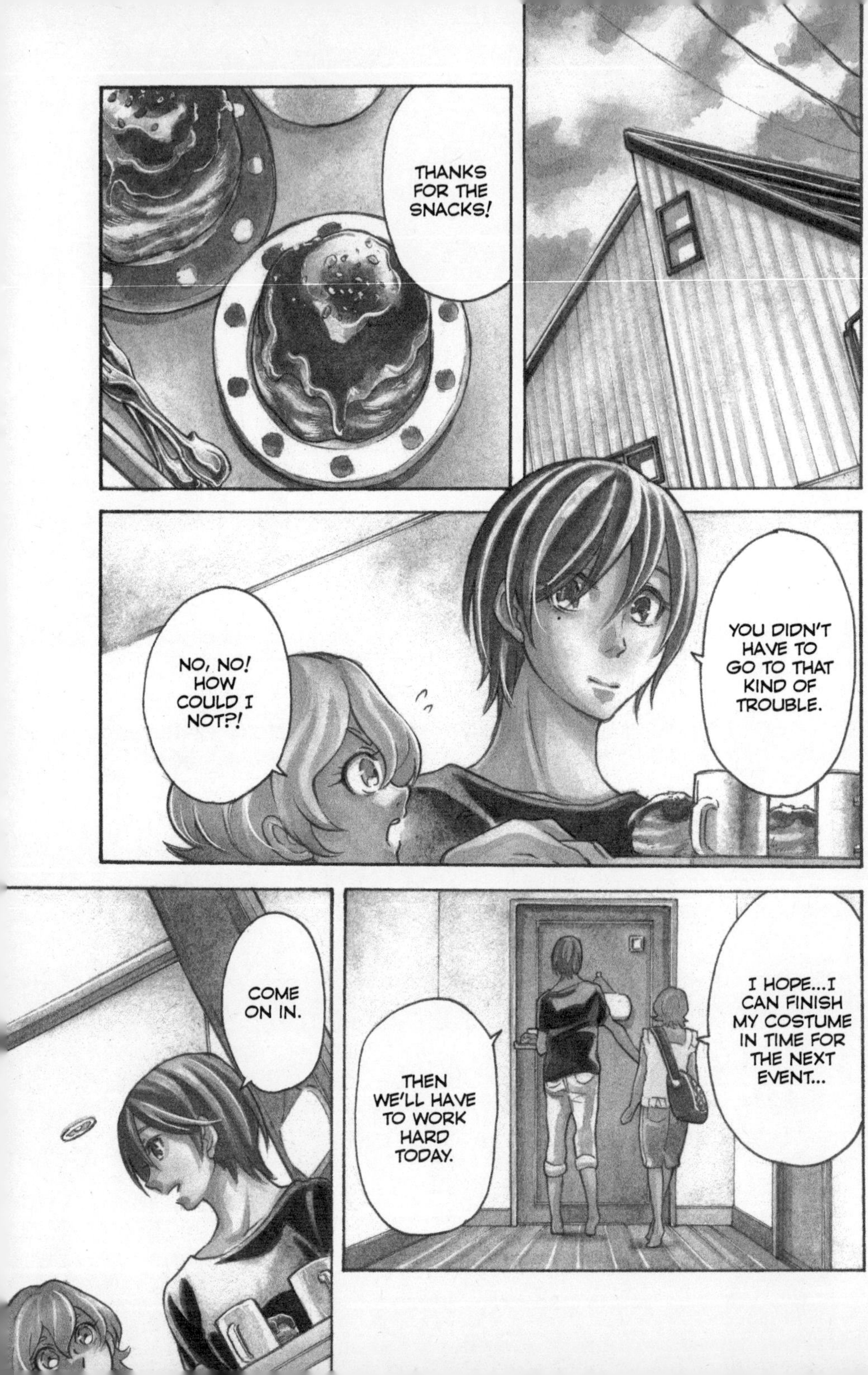
THANKS FOR THE SNACKS!
YOU DIDN'T HAVE TO GO TO THAT KIND OF TROUBLE.
NO, NO! HOW COULD I NOT?!
I HOPE...I CAN FINISH MY COSTUME IN TIME FOR THE NEXT EVENT...
THEN WE'LL HAVE TO WORK HARD TODAY.
COME ON IN.

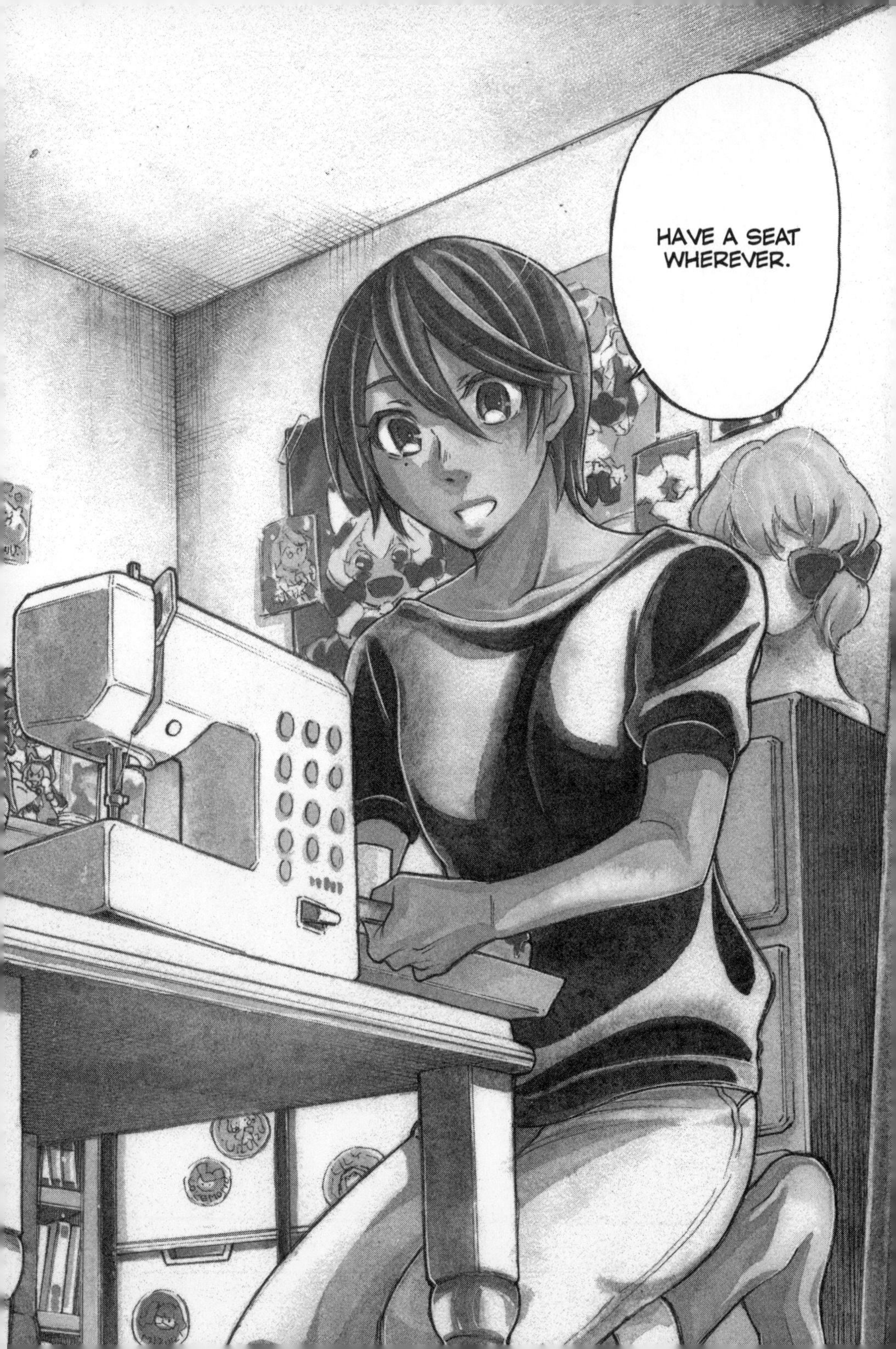
HAVE A SEAT WHEREVER.

n.17
Complex age

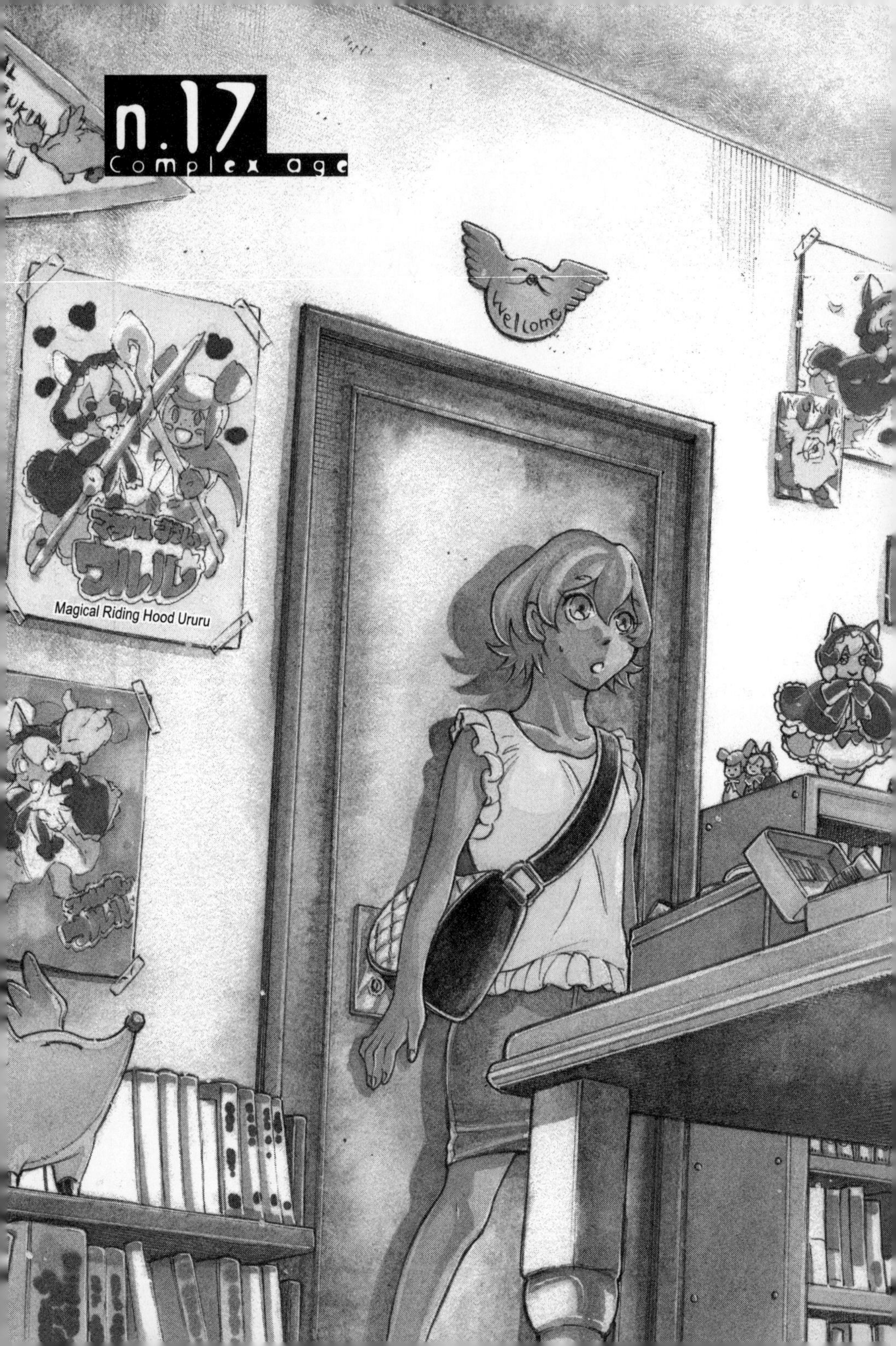
Welcome
Magical Riding Hood Ururu

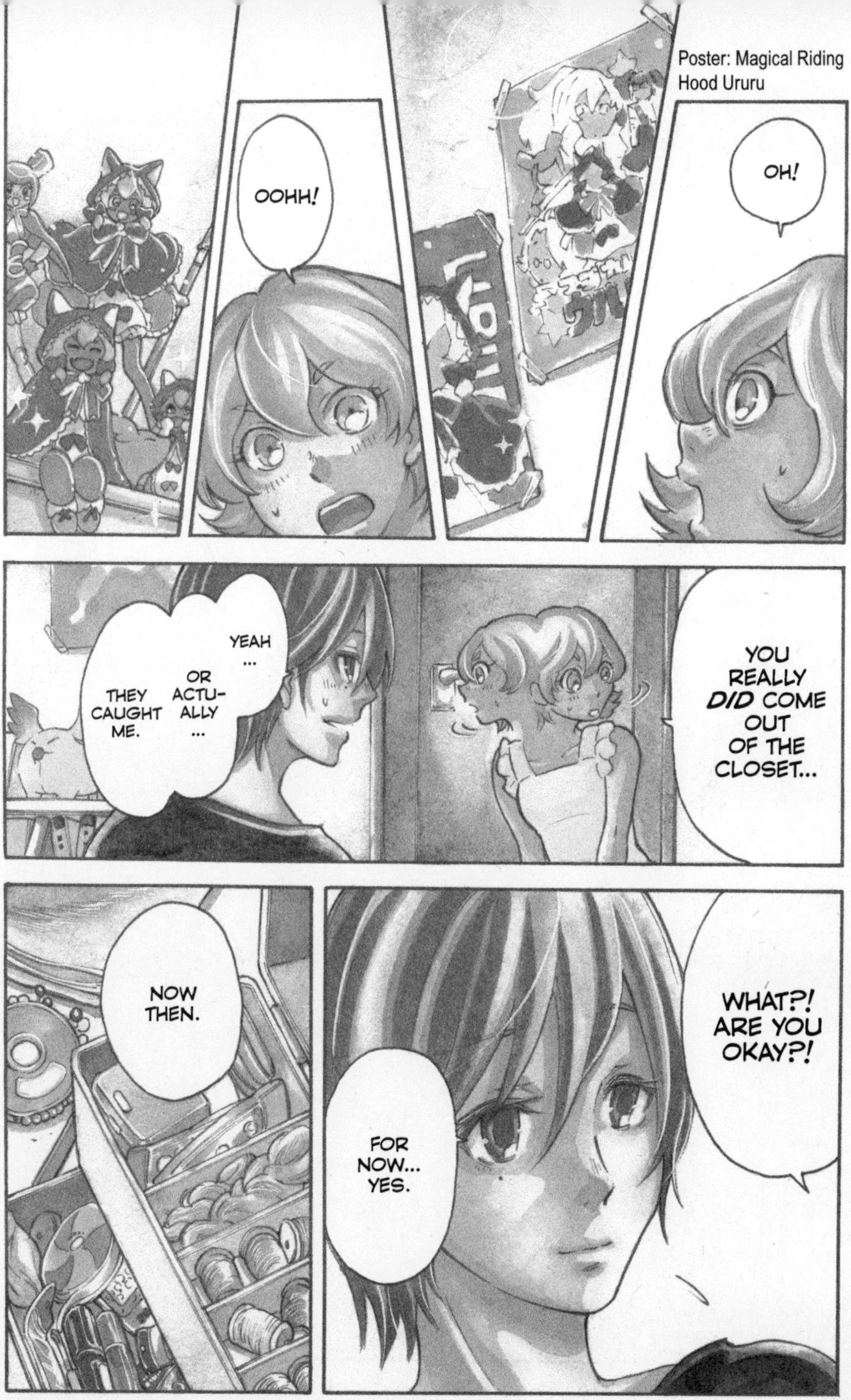
OH!
Poster: Magical Riding Hood Ururu
OOHH!
YOU REALLY *DID* COME OUT OF THE CLOSET...
YEAH... OR ACTUALLY... THEY CAUGHT ME.
WHAT?! ARE YOU OKAY?!
FOR NOW... YES.
NOW THEN.

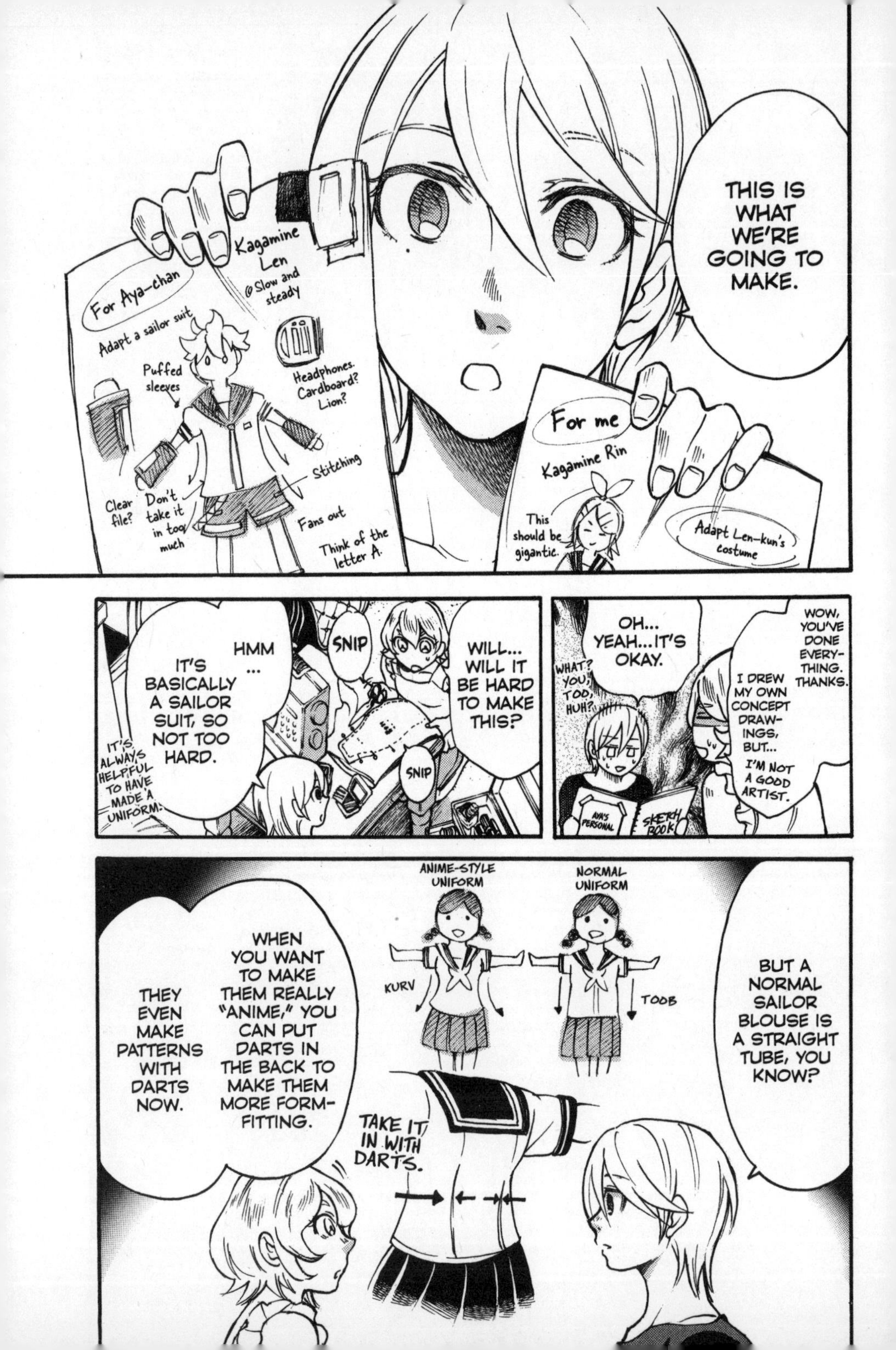
THIS IS WHAT WE'RE GOING TO MAKE.
For me
Kagamine Rin
Adapt Len-kun's costume
This should be gigantic.
For Aya-chan
Kagamine Len
@ Slow and steady
Adapt a sailor suit
Headphones. Cardboard? Lion?
Puffed sleeves
Stitching
Clear file?
Don't take it in too much
Fans out
Think of the letter A.
WOW, YOU'VE DONE EVERYTHING. THANKS.
I DREW MY OWN CONCEPT DRAWINGS, BUT...
I'M NOT A GOOD ARTIST.
OH... YEAH...IT'S OKAY.
WHAT? YOU, TOO, HUH?
AYA'S PERSONAL SKETCH BOOK
WILL... WILL IT BE HARD TO MAKE THIS?
SNIP
SNIP
HMM ...
IT'S BASICALLY A SAILOR SUIT, SO NOT TOO HARD.
IT'S ALWAYS HELPFUL TO HAVE MADE A UNIFORM.
BUT A NORMAL SAILOR BLOUSE IS A STRAIGHT TUBE, YOU KNOW?
NORMAL UNIFORM
TOOB
ANIME-STYLE UNIFORM
KURV
WHEN YOU WANT TO MAKE THEM REALLY "ANIME," YOU CAN PUT DARTS IN THE BACK TO MAKE THEM MORE FORM-FITTING.
THEY EVEN MAKE PATTERNS WITH DARTS NOW.
TAKE IT IN WITH DARTS.

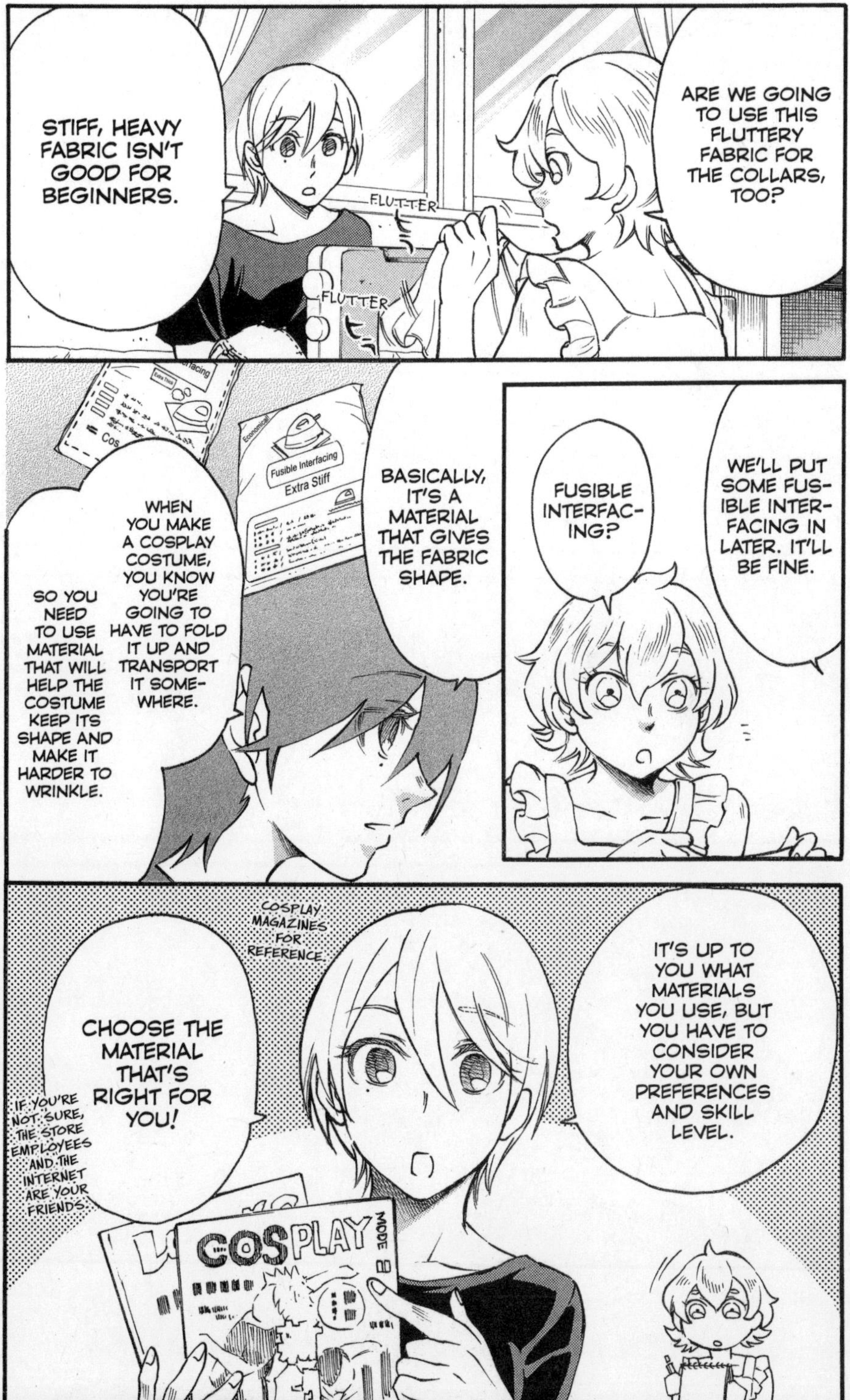
ARE WE GOING TO USE THIS FLUTTERY FABRIC FOR THE COLLARS, TOO?
FLUTTER
FLUTTER
STIFF, HEAVY FABRIC ISN'T GOOD FOR BEGINNERS.
...
WE'LL PUT SOME FUSIBLE INTERFACING IN LATER. IT'LL BE FINE.
FUSIBLE INTERFACING?
BASICALLY, IT'S A MATERIAL THAT GIVES THE FABRIC SHAPE.
Economical
Fusible Interfacing
Extra Stiff
WHEN YOU MAKE A COSPLAY COSTUME, YOU KNOW YOU'RE GOING TO HAVE TO FOLD IT UP AND TRANSPORT IT SOMEWHERE.
SO YOU NEED TO USE MATERIAL THAT WILL HELP THE COSTUME KEEP ITS SHAPE AND MAKE IT HARDER TO WRINKLE.
IT'S UP TO YOU WHAT MATERIALS YOU USE, BUT YOU HAVE TO CONSIDER YOUR OWN PREFERENCES AND SKILL LEVEL.
COSPLAY MAGAZINES FOR REFERENCE.
CHOOSE THE MATERIAL THAT'S RIGHT FOR YOU!
IF YOU'RE NOT SURE, THE STORE EMPLOYEES AND THE INTERNET ARE YOUR FRIENDS.
COSPLAY
MODE

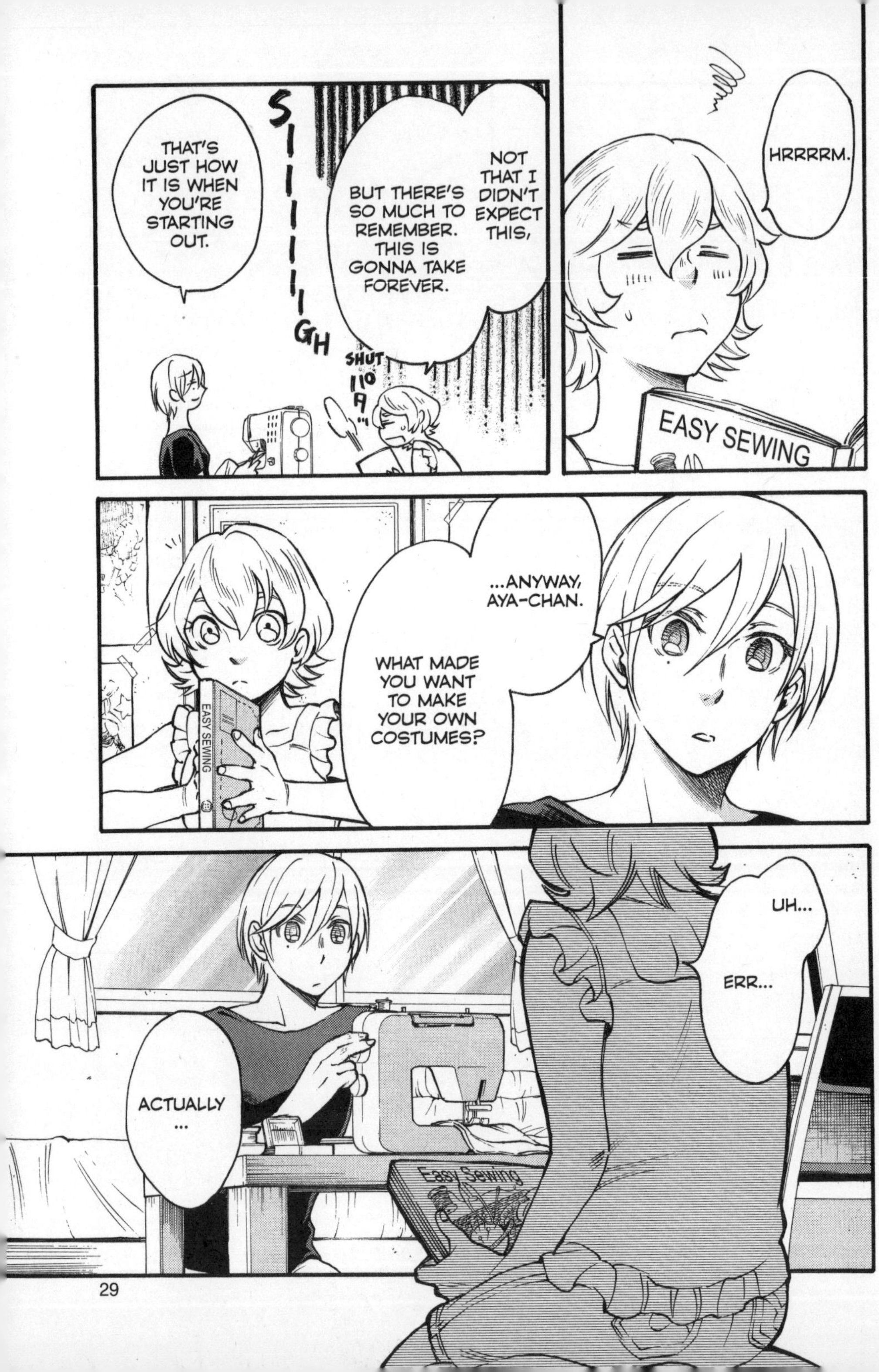
HRRRRM.
EASY SEWING
NOT THAT I DIDN'T EXPECT THIS,
BUT THERE'S SO MUCH TO REMEMBER. THIS IS GONNA TAKE FOREVER.
SIIIIIGH
SHUT
THAT'S JUST HOW IT IS WHEN YOU'RE STARTING OUT.
...ANYWAY, AYA-CHAN.
WHAT MADE YOU WANT TO MAKE YOUR OWN COSTUMES?
EASY SEWING
UH...
ERR...
ACTUALLY ...
Easy Sewing

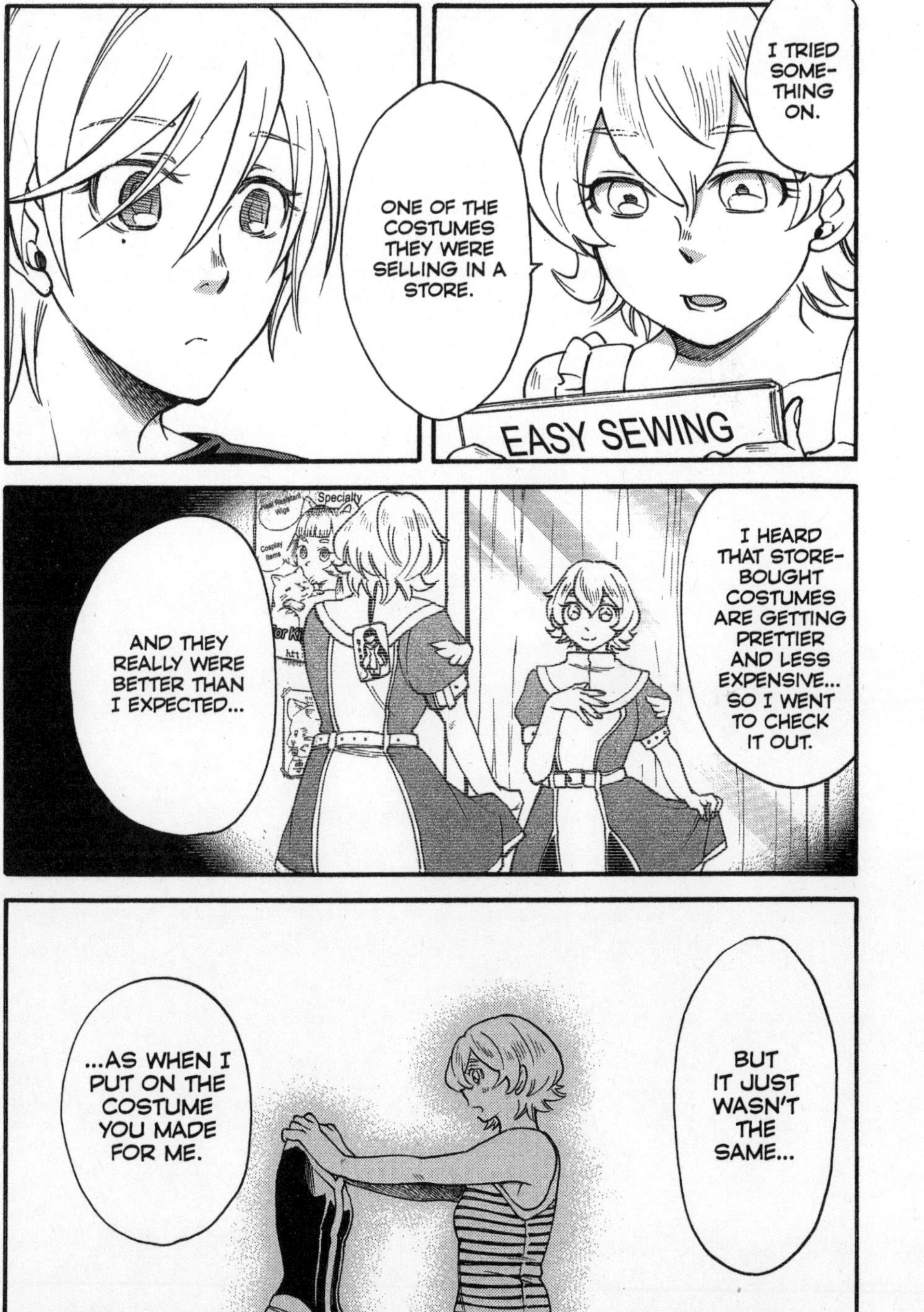
I TRIED SOME-THING ON.
ONE OF THE COSTUMES THEY WERE SELLING IN A STORE.
EASY SEWING
I HEARD THAT STORE-BOUGHT COSTUMES ARE GETTING PRETTIER AND LESS EXPENSIVE... SO I WENT TO CHECK IT OUT.
Specialty
AND THEY REALLY WERE BETTER THAN I EXPECTED...
BUT IT JUST WASN'T THE SAME...
...AS WHEN I PUT ON THE COSTUME YOU MADE FOR ME.

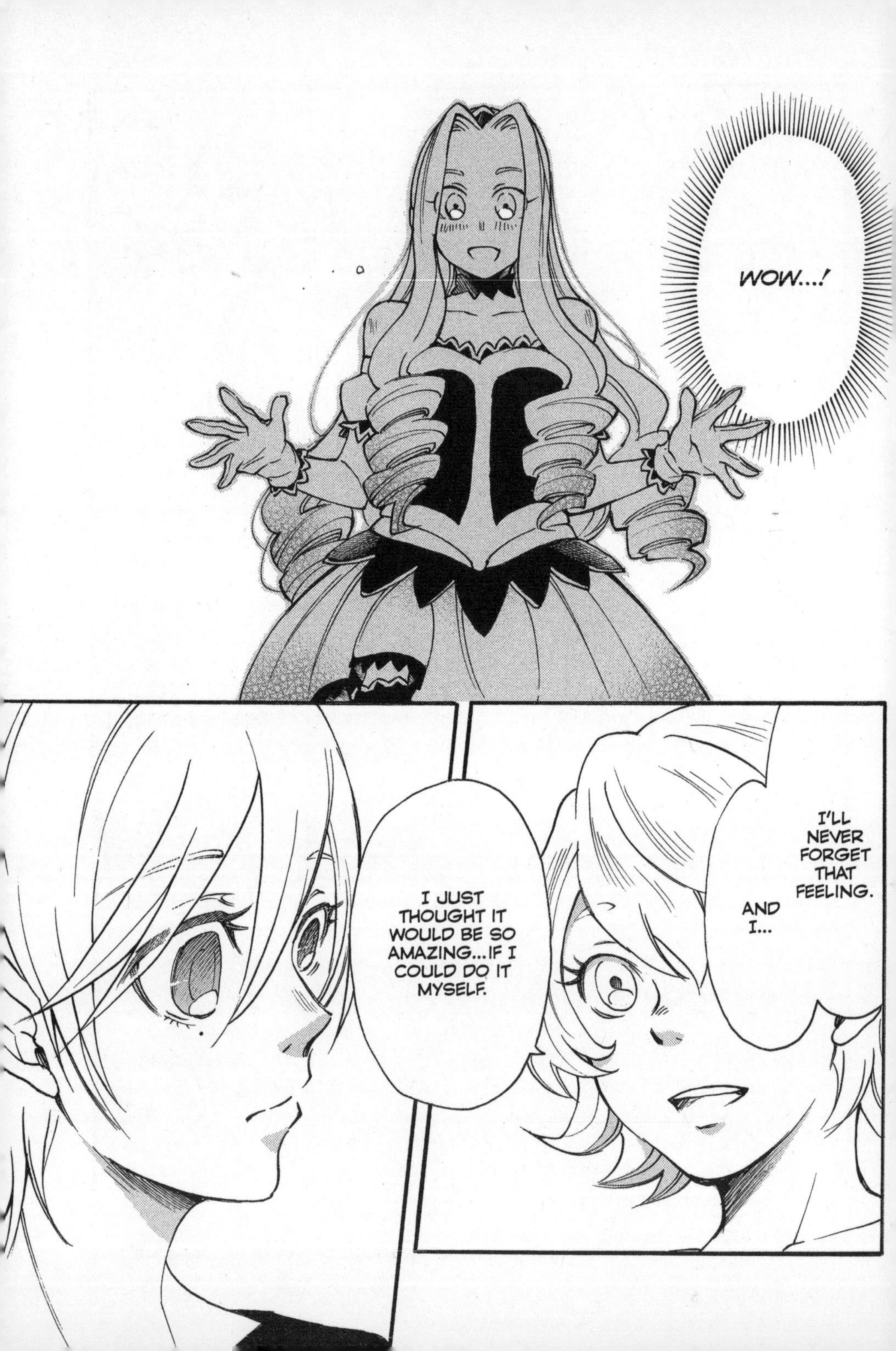
WOW...!
I'LL NEVER FORGET THAT FEELING.
AND I...
I JUST THOUGHT IT WOULD BE SO AMAZING...IF I COULD DO IT MYSELF.

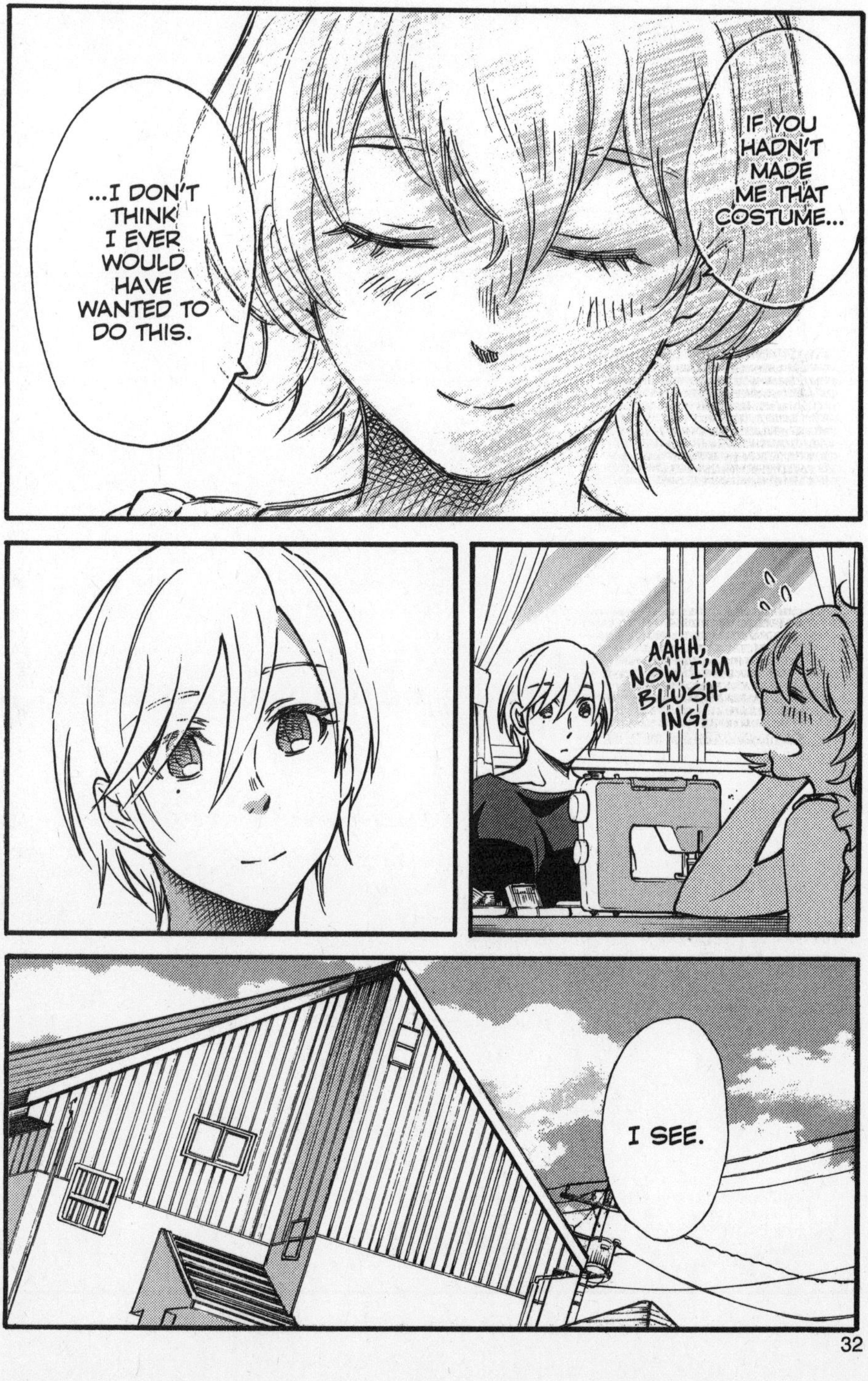
IF YOU HADN'T MADE ME THAT COSTUME...
...I DON'T THINK I EVER WOULD HAVE WANTED TO DO THIS.
AAHH, NOW I'M BLUSH-ING!
I SEE.

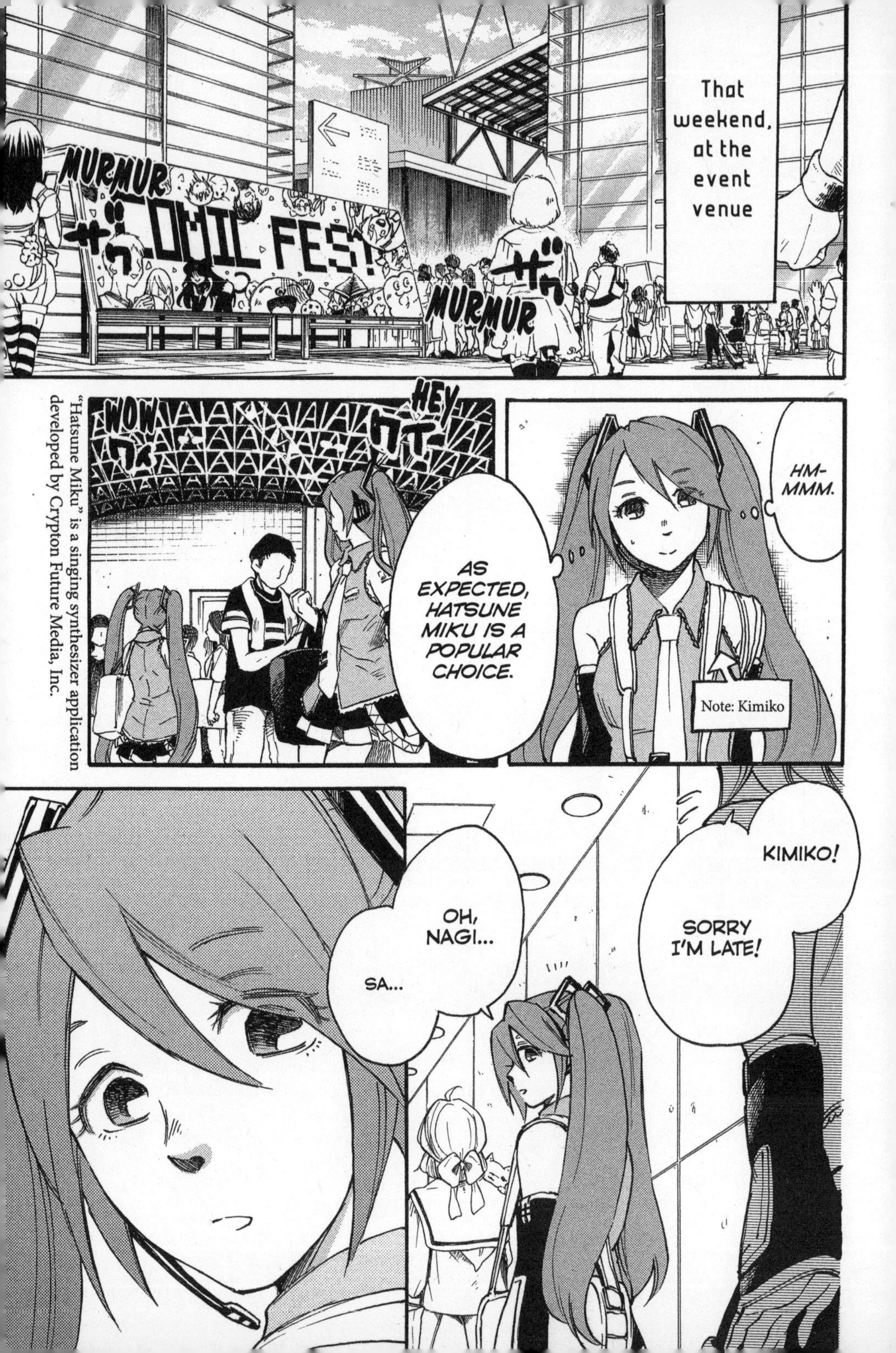
That weekend, at the event venue
MURMUR
COMIC FES!
MURMUR
HM-MMM.
AS EXPECTED, HATSUNE MIKU IS A POPULAR CHOICE.
Note: Kimiko
WOW
HEY
KIMIKO!
SORRY I'M LATE!
OH, NAGI...
SA...

"Hatsune Miku" is a singing synthesizer application developed by Crypton Future Media, Inc.

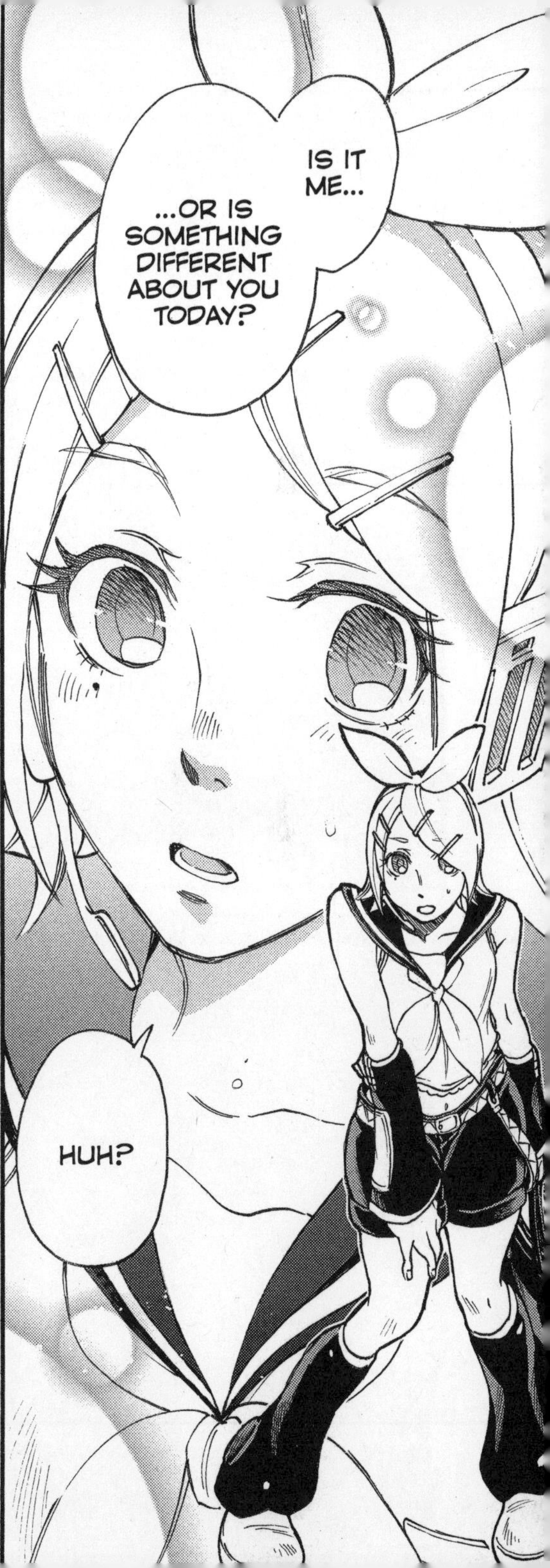
IS IT ME...
...OR IS SOMETHING DIFFERENT ABOUT YOU TODAY?
HUH?

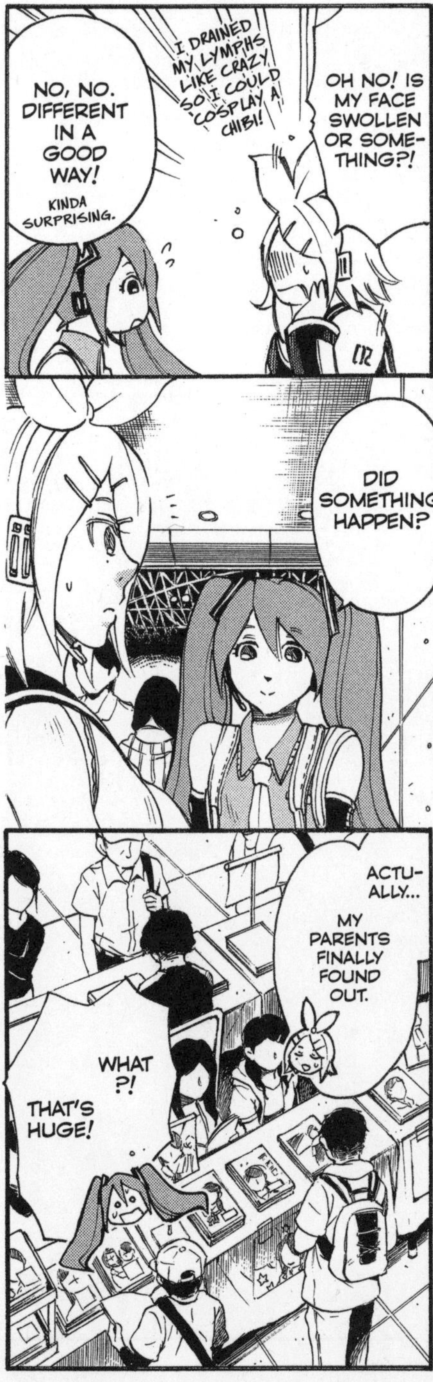
OH NO! IS MY FACE SWOLLEN OR SOME-THING?!
I DRAINED MY LYMPHS LIKE CRAZY SO I COULD COSPLAY A CHIBI!
NO, NO. DIFFERENT IN A GOOD WAY!
KINDA SURPRISING.
DID SOMETHING HAPPEN?
ACTU-ALLY...
MY PARENTS FINALLY FOUND OUT.
WHAT ?!
THAT'S HUGE!

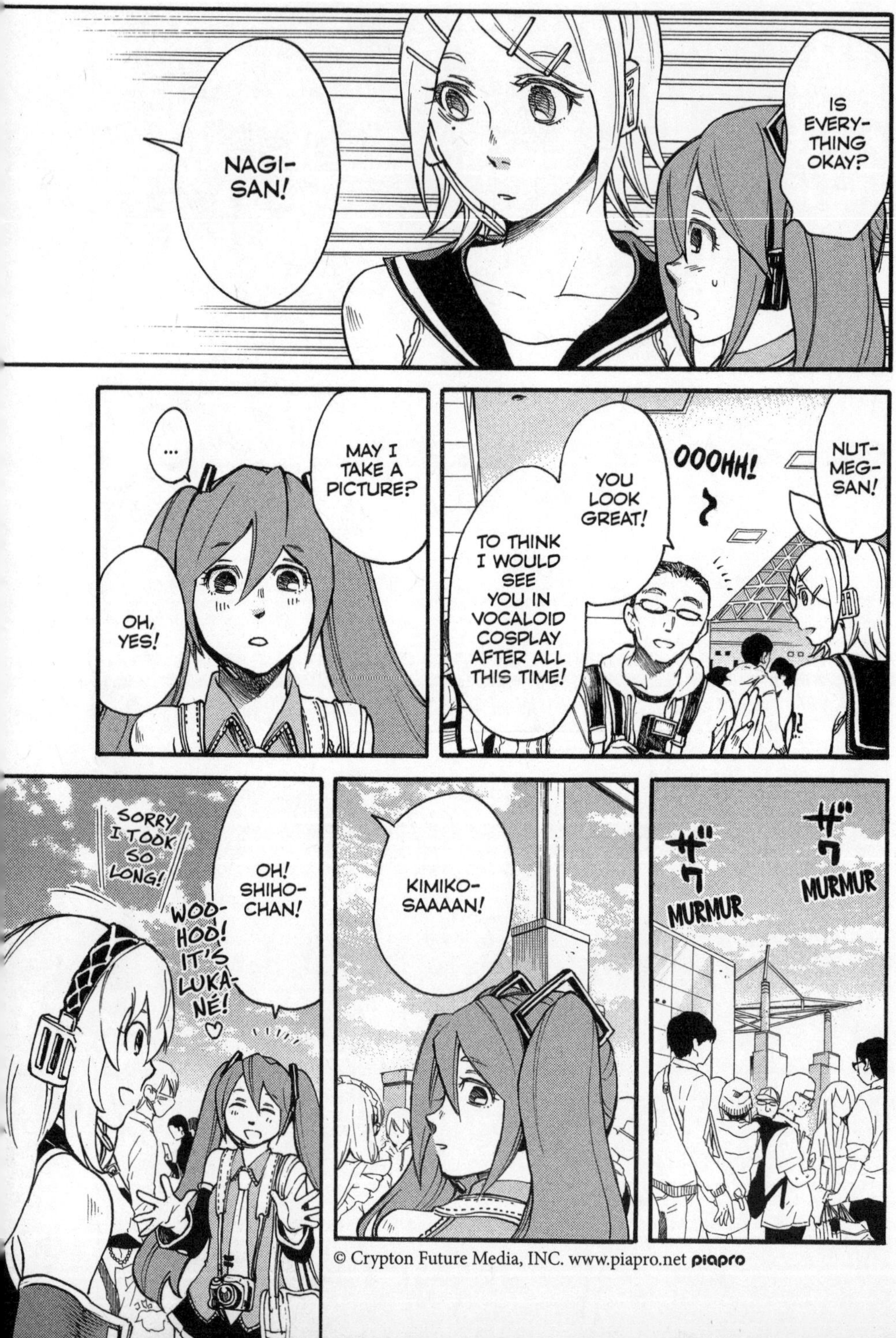
IS EVERYTHING OKAY?
NAGI-SAN!
NUT-MEG-SAN!
OOOHH!
YOU LOOK GREAT!
TO THINK I WOULD SEE YOU IN VOCALOID COSPLAY AFTER ALL THIS TIME!
MAY I TAKE A PICTURE?
...
OH, YES!
ザワ
MURMUR
ザワ
MURMUR
KIMIKO-SAAAAN!
OH! SHIHO-CHAN!
SORRY I TOOK SO LONG!
WOO-HOO! IT'S LUKA-NÉ! ♥

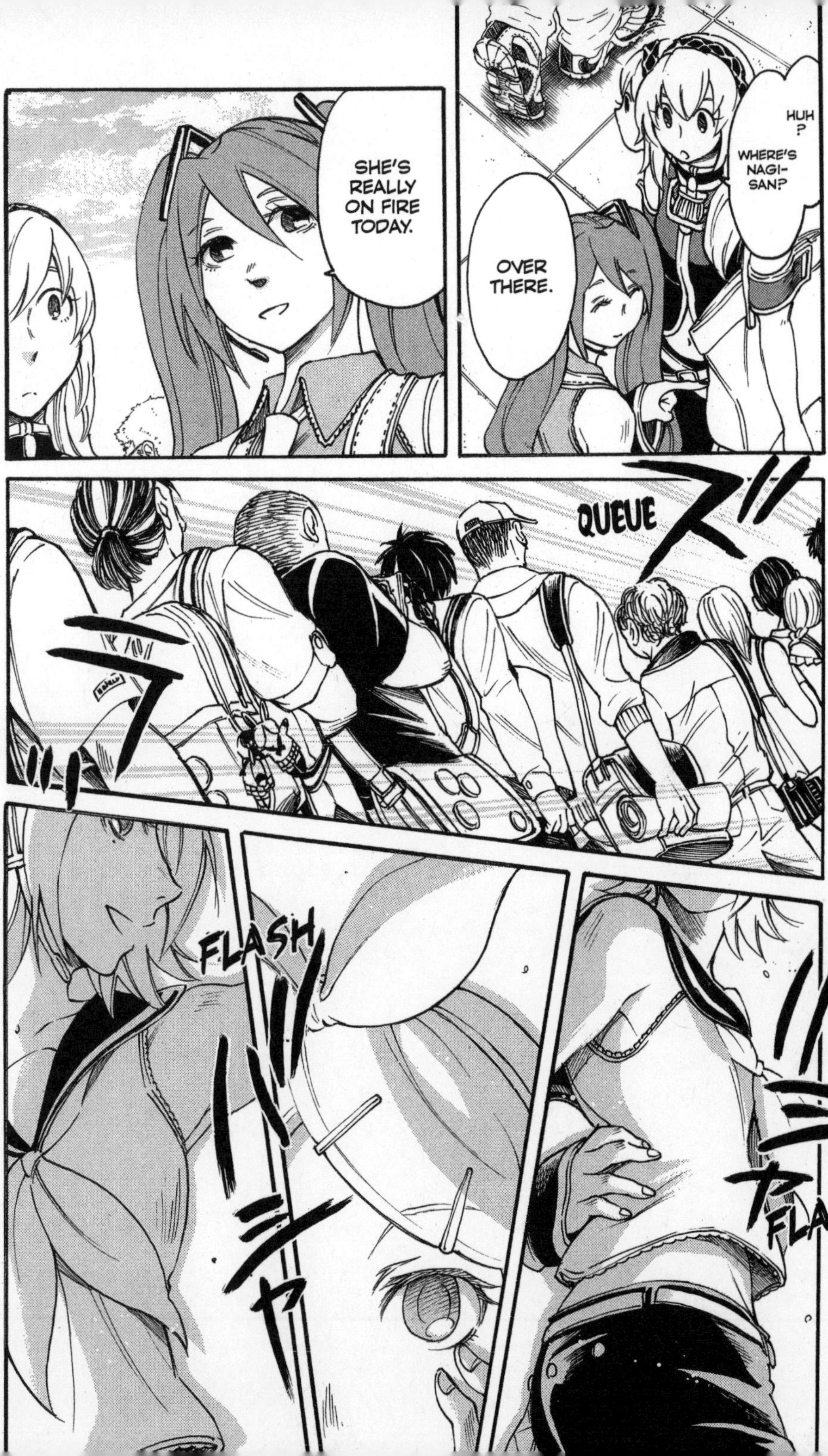
HUH? WHERE'S NAGI-SAN?
OVER THERE.
SHE'S REALLY ON FIRE TODAY.
QUEUE
FLASH
FLASH

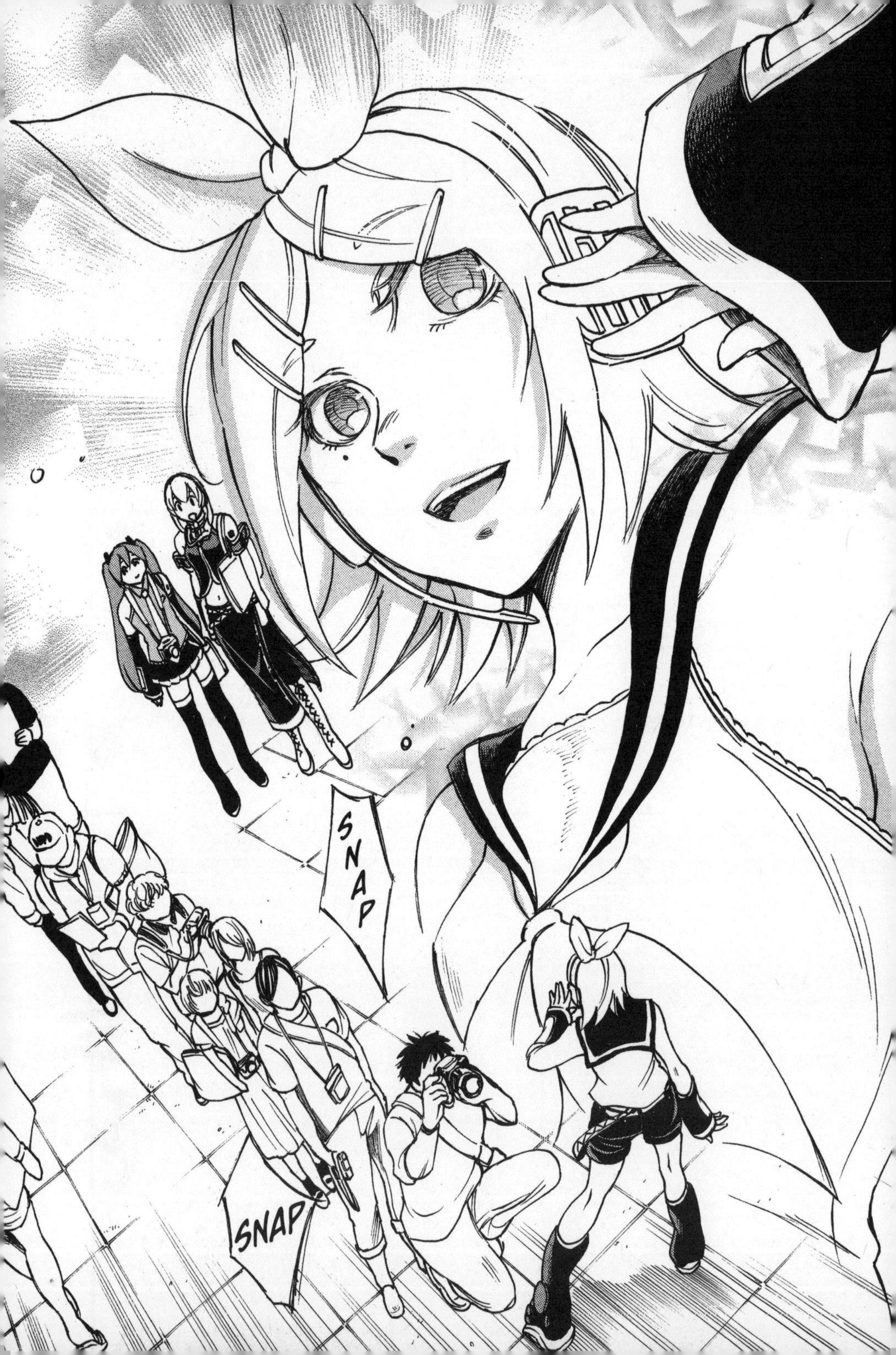
SNAP
SNAP

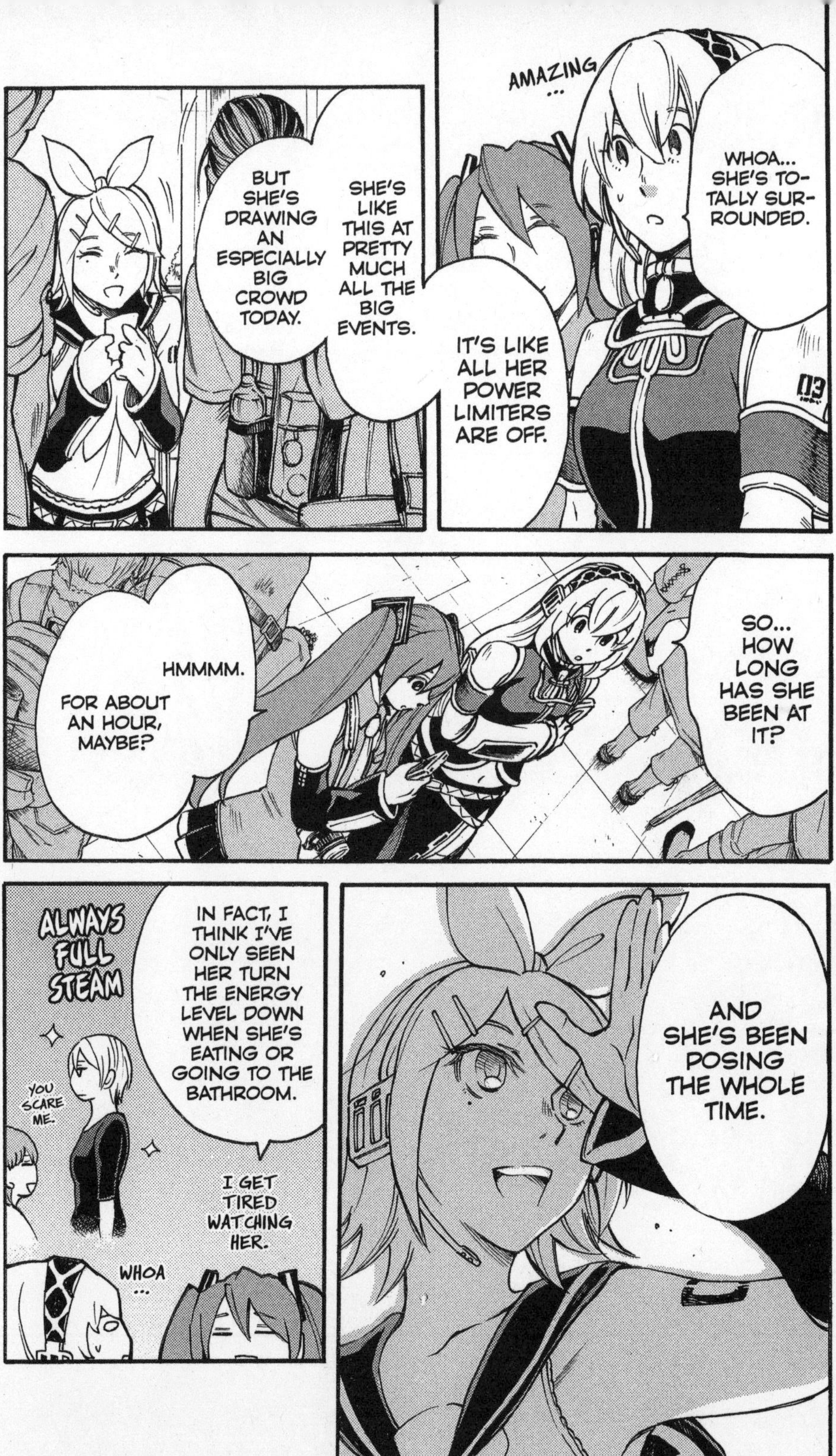
WHOA... SHE'S TO-TALLY SUR-ROUNDED.
AMAZING ...
IT'S LIKE ALL HER POWER LIMITERS ARE OFF.
SHE'S LIKE THIS AT PRETTY MUCH ALL THE BIG EVENTS.
BUT SHE'S DRAWING AN ESPECIALLY BIG CROWD TODAY.
SO... HOW LONG HAS SHE BEEN AT IT?
HMMMM.
FOR ABOUT AN HOUR, MAYBE?
AND SHE'S BEEN POSING THE WHOLE TIME.
IN FACT, I THINK I'VE ONLY SEEN HER TURN THE ENERGY LEVEL DOWN WHEN SHE'S EATING OR GOING TO THE BATHROOM.
ALWAYS FULL STEAM
YOU SCARE ME.
I GET TIRED WATCHING HER.
WHOA ...

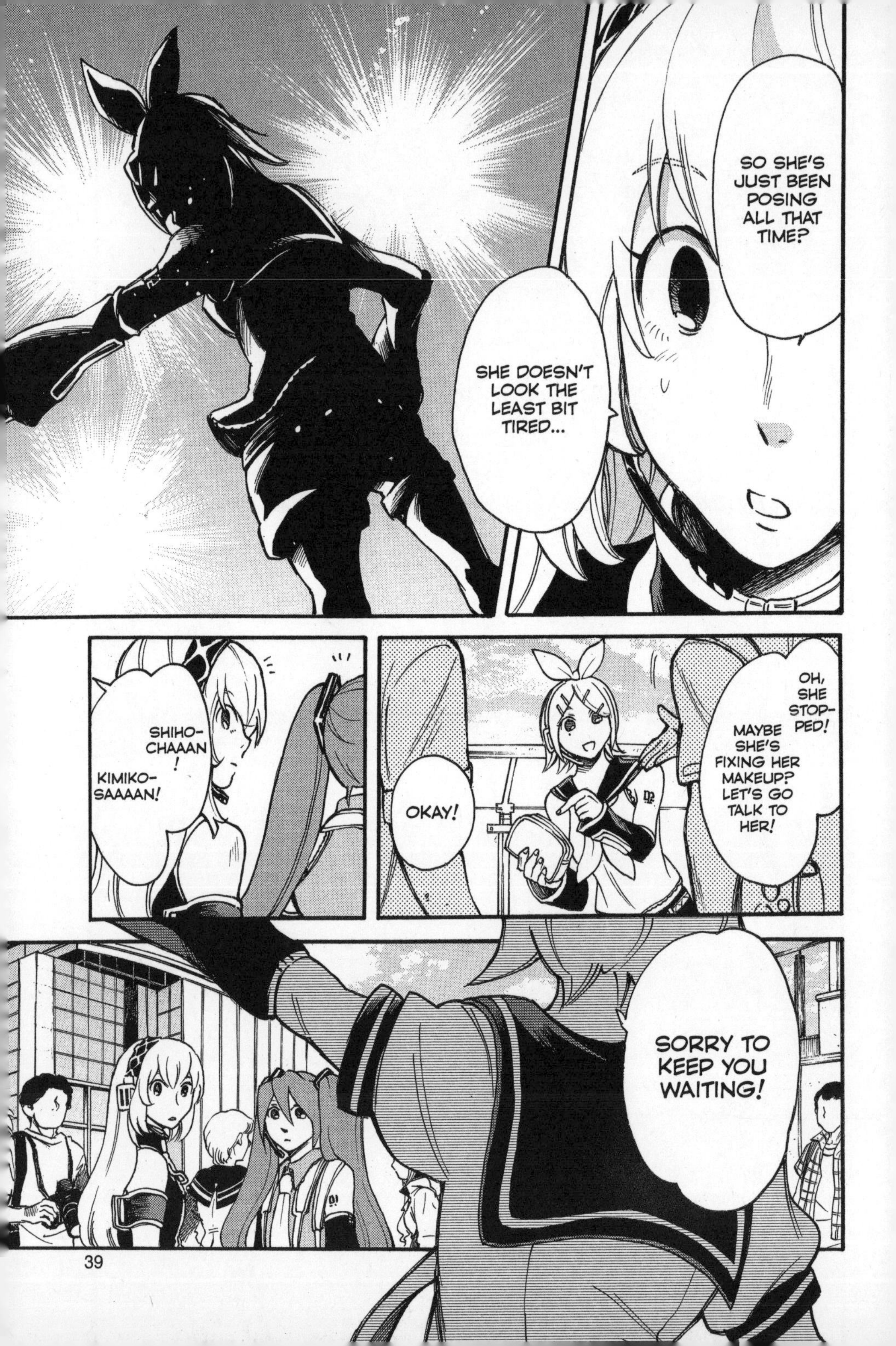
SO SHE'S JUST BEEN POSING ALL THAT TIME?
SHE DOESN'T LOOK THE LEAST BIT TIRED...
OH, SHE STOP-PED!
MAYBE SHE'S FIXING HER MAKEUP? LET'S GO TALK TO HER!
OKAY!
SHIHO-CHAAAN!
KIMIKO-SAAAAN!
SORRY TO KEEP YOU WAITING!

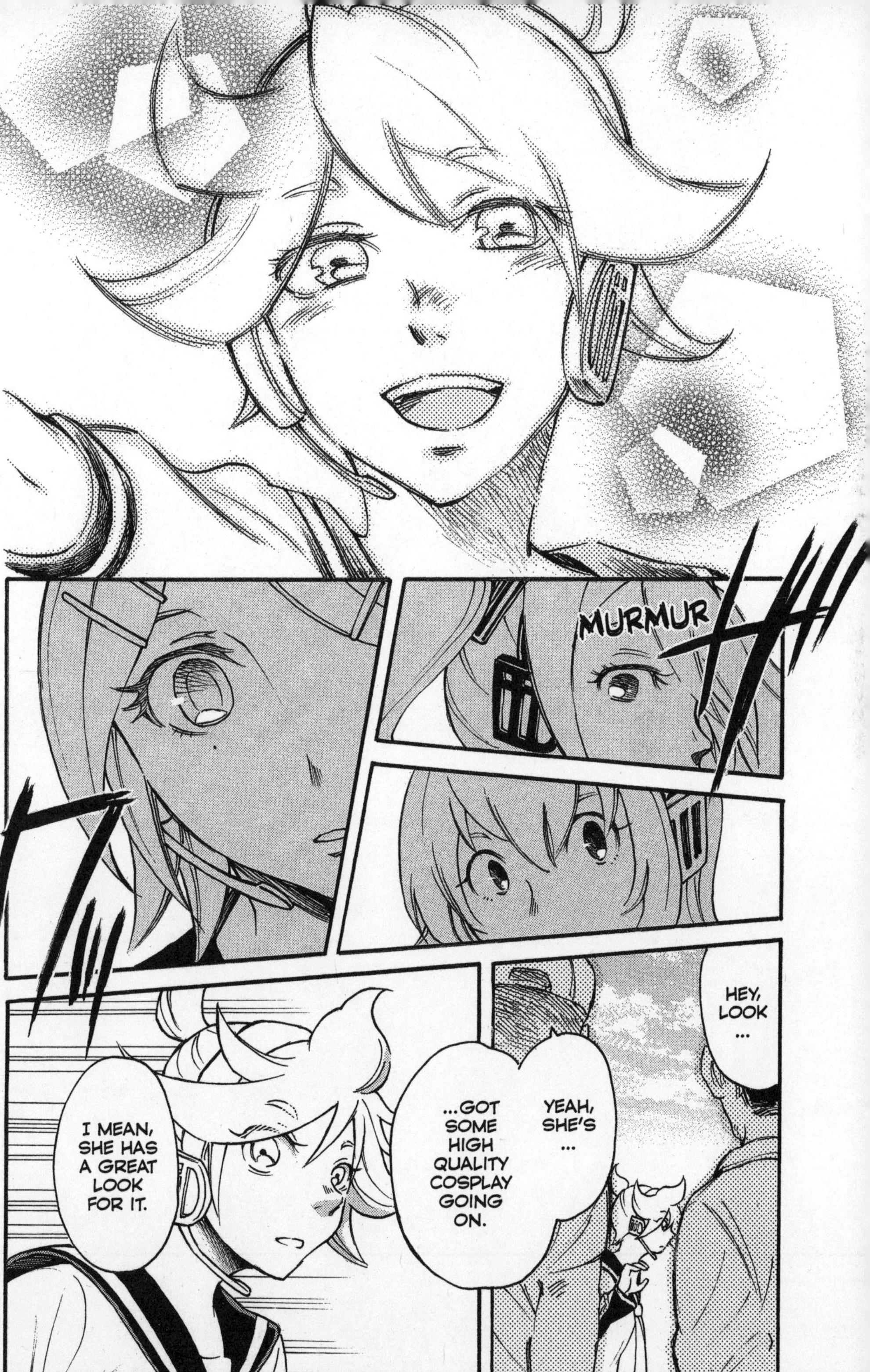
MURMUR
HEY, LOOK ...
YEAH, SHE'S ...
...GOT SOME HIGH QUALITY COSPLAY GOING ON.
I MEAN, SHE HAS A GREAT LOOK FOR IT.

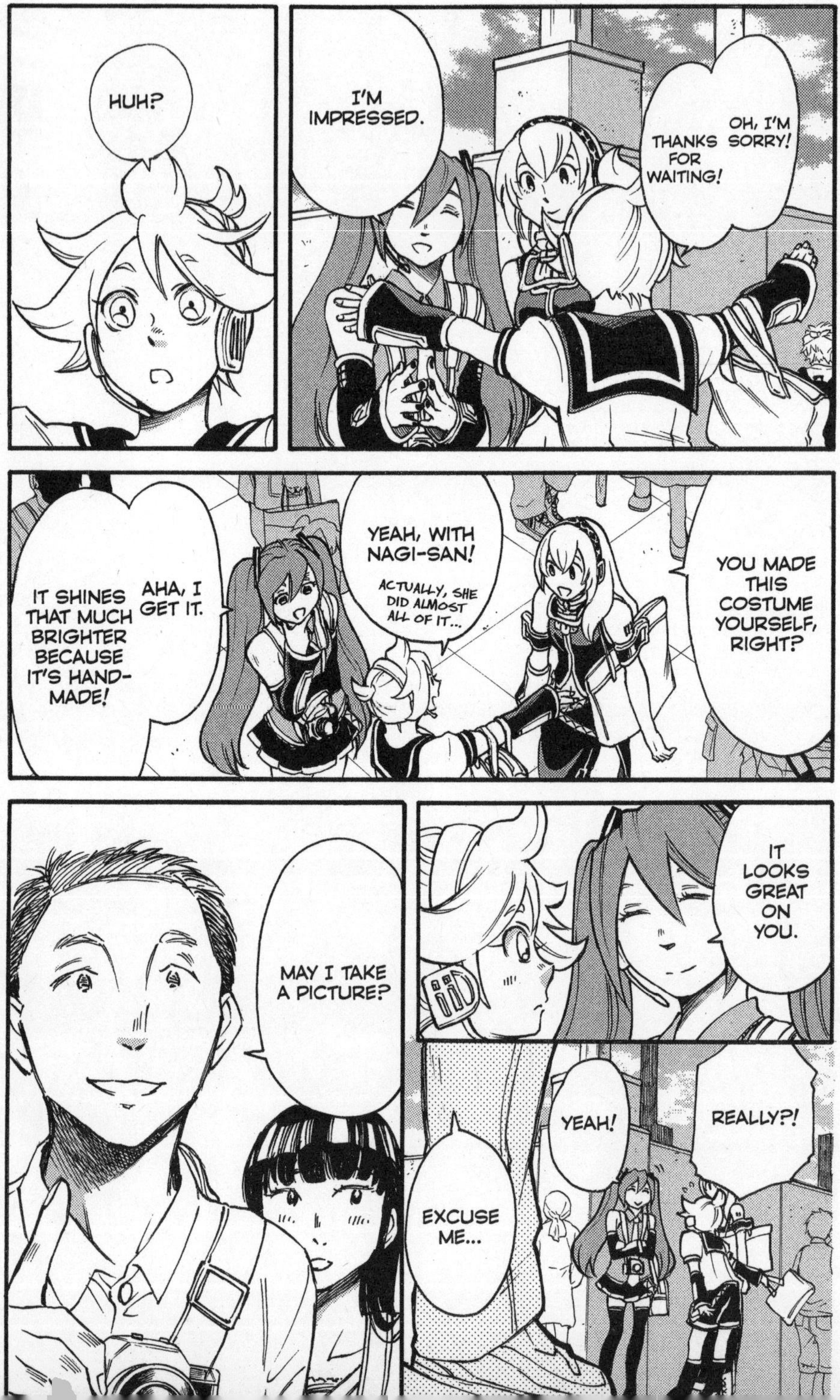
OH, I'M SORRY! THANKS FOR WAITING!
I'M IMPRESSED.
HUH?
YOU MADE THIS COSTUME YOURSELF, RIGHT?
YEAH, WITH NAGI-SAN!
ACTUALLY, SHE DID ALMOST ALL OF IT...
AHA, I GET IT.
IT SHINES THAT MUCH BRIGHTER BECAUSE IT'S HAND-MADE!
IT LOOKS GREAT ON YOU.
REALLY?!
YEAH!
EXCUSE ME...
MAY I TAKE A PICTURE?

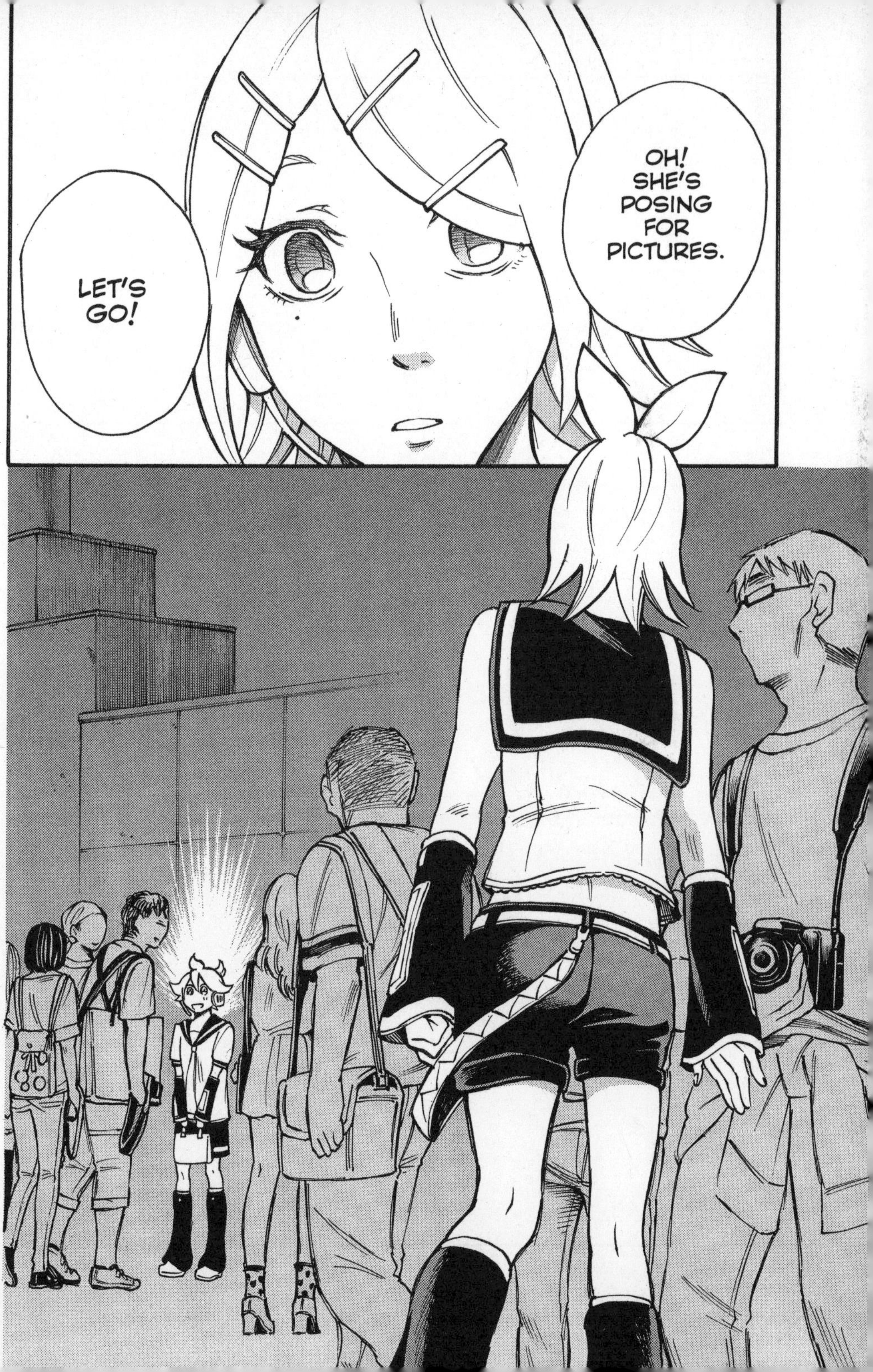
OH! SHE'S POSING FOR PICTURES.
LET'S GO!

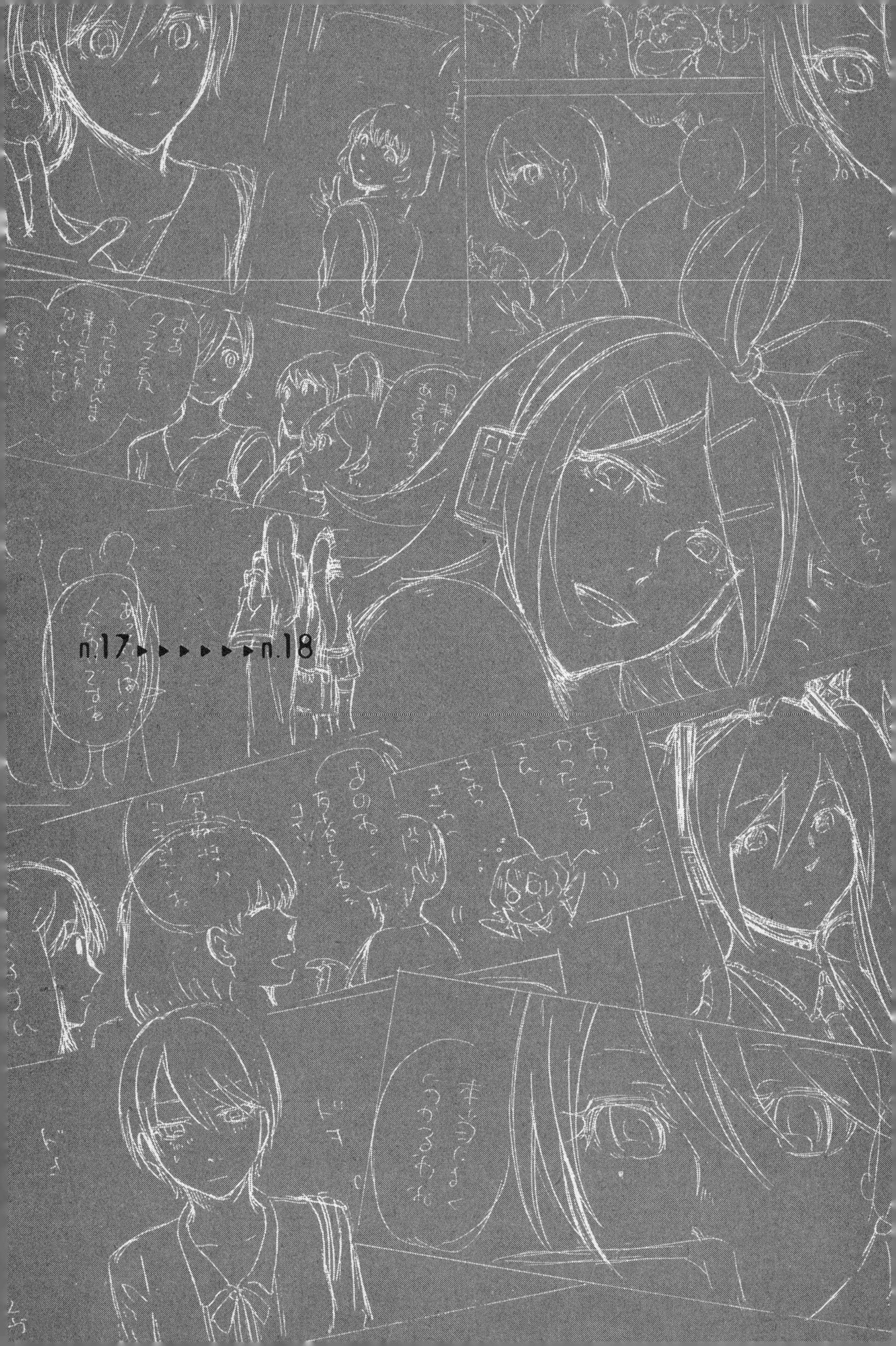
n.17▶▶▶▶▶▶▶n.18

MIKU & FRIENDS COLLABORATION 1

初音ミク

HATSUNE MIKU

×

KIMIKO BABA

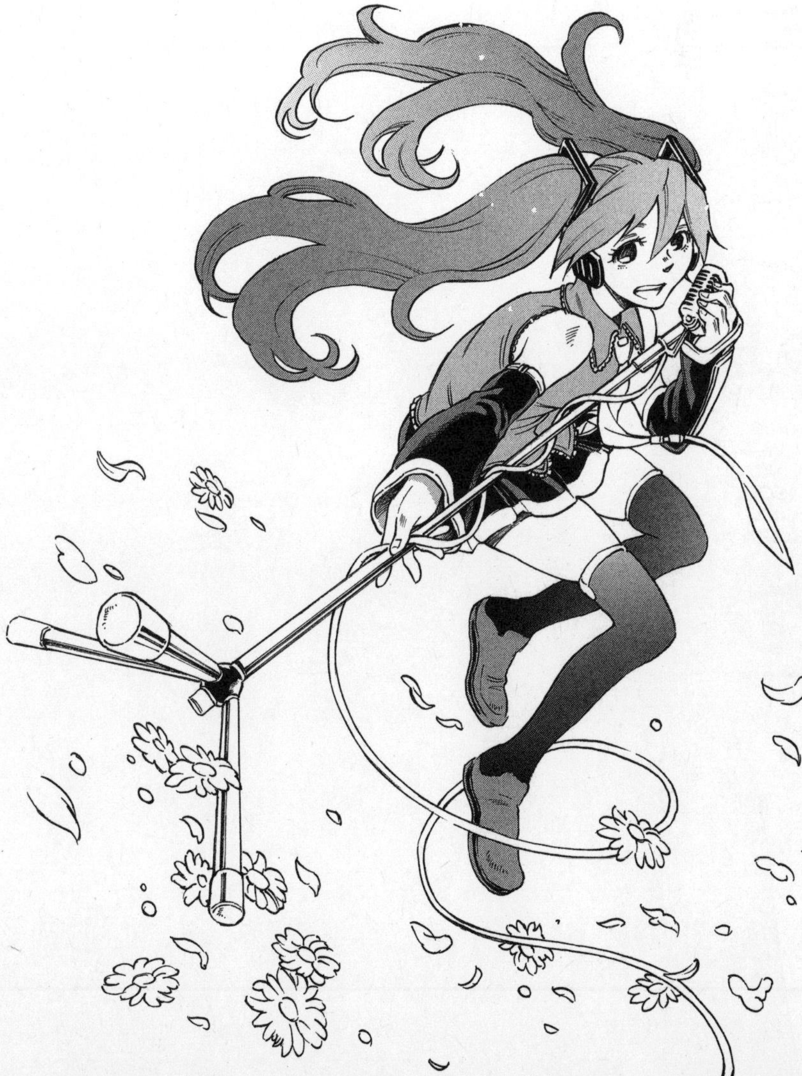

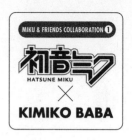

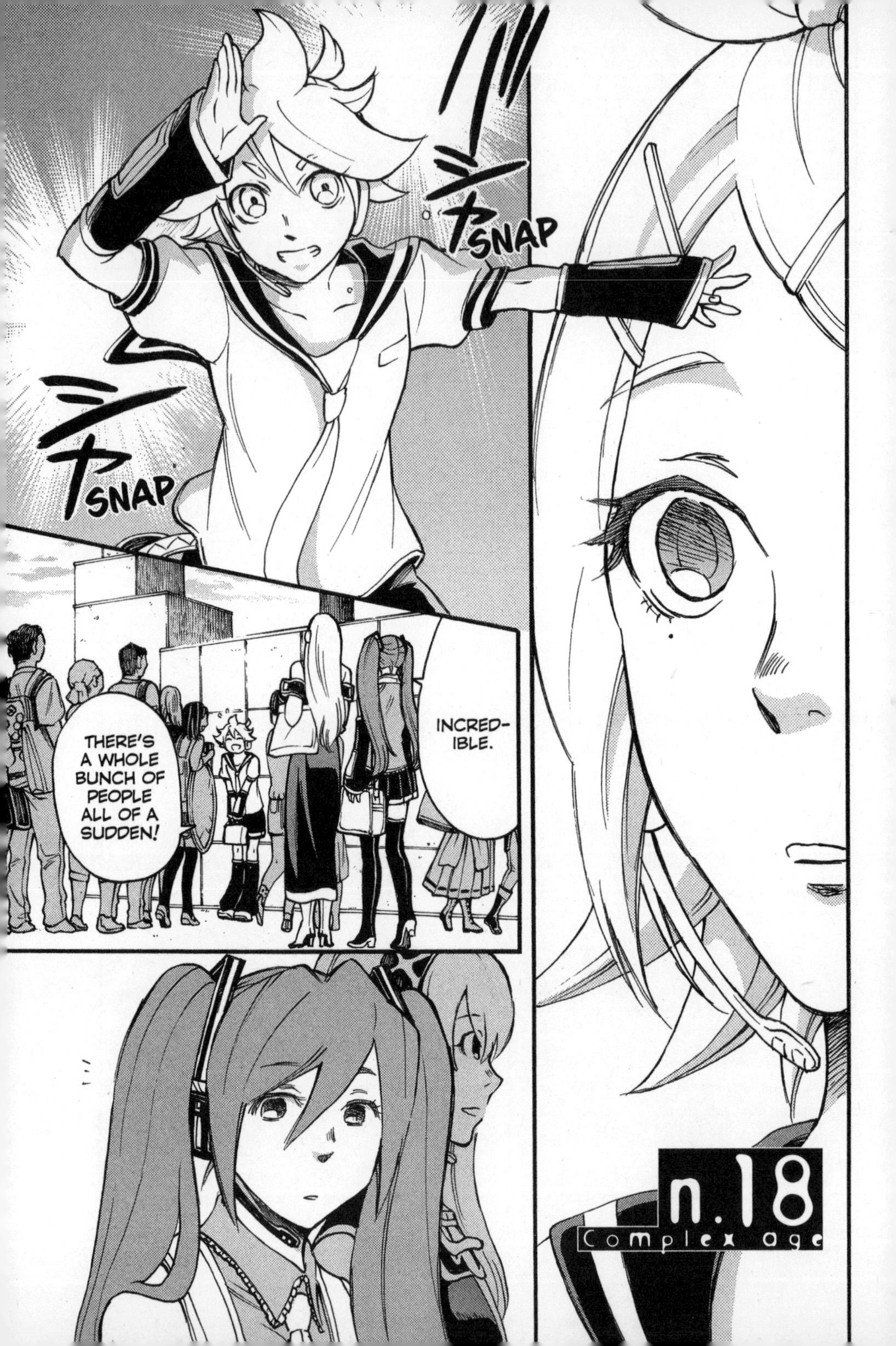
n.18
Complex age
SNAP
SNAP
INCREDIBLE.
THERE'S A WHOLE BUNCH OF PEOPLE ALL OF A SUDDEN!

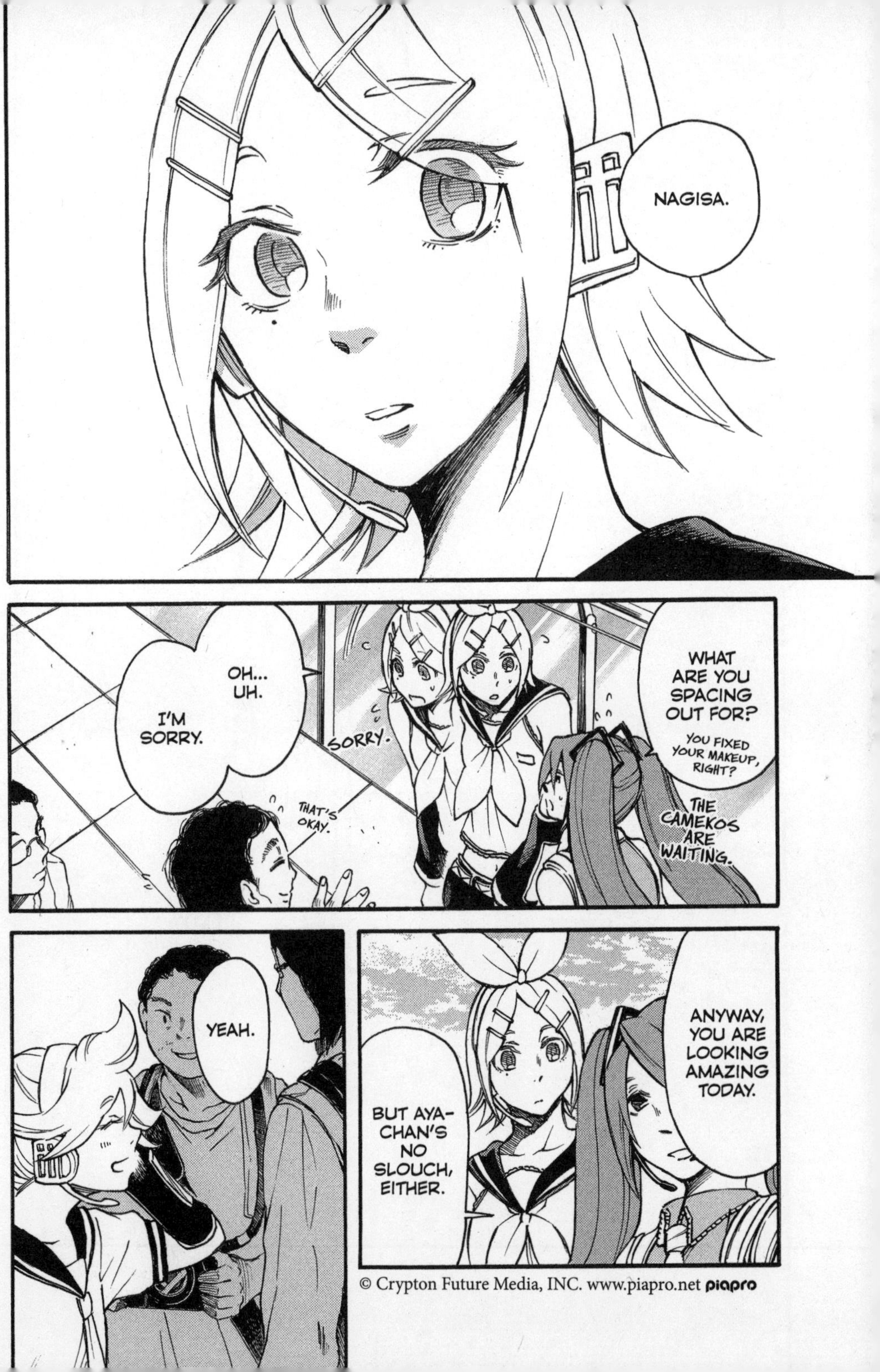
NAGISA.
WHAT ARE YOU SPACING OUT FOR?
YOU FIXED YOUR MAKEUP, RIGHT?
THE CAMEKOS ARE WAITING.
OH... UH.
I'M SORRY.
SORRY.
THAT'S OKAY.
ANYWAY, YOU ARE LOOKING AMAZING TODAY.
BUT AYA-CHAN'S NO SLOUCH, EITHER.
YEAH.

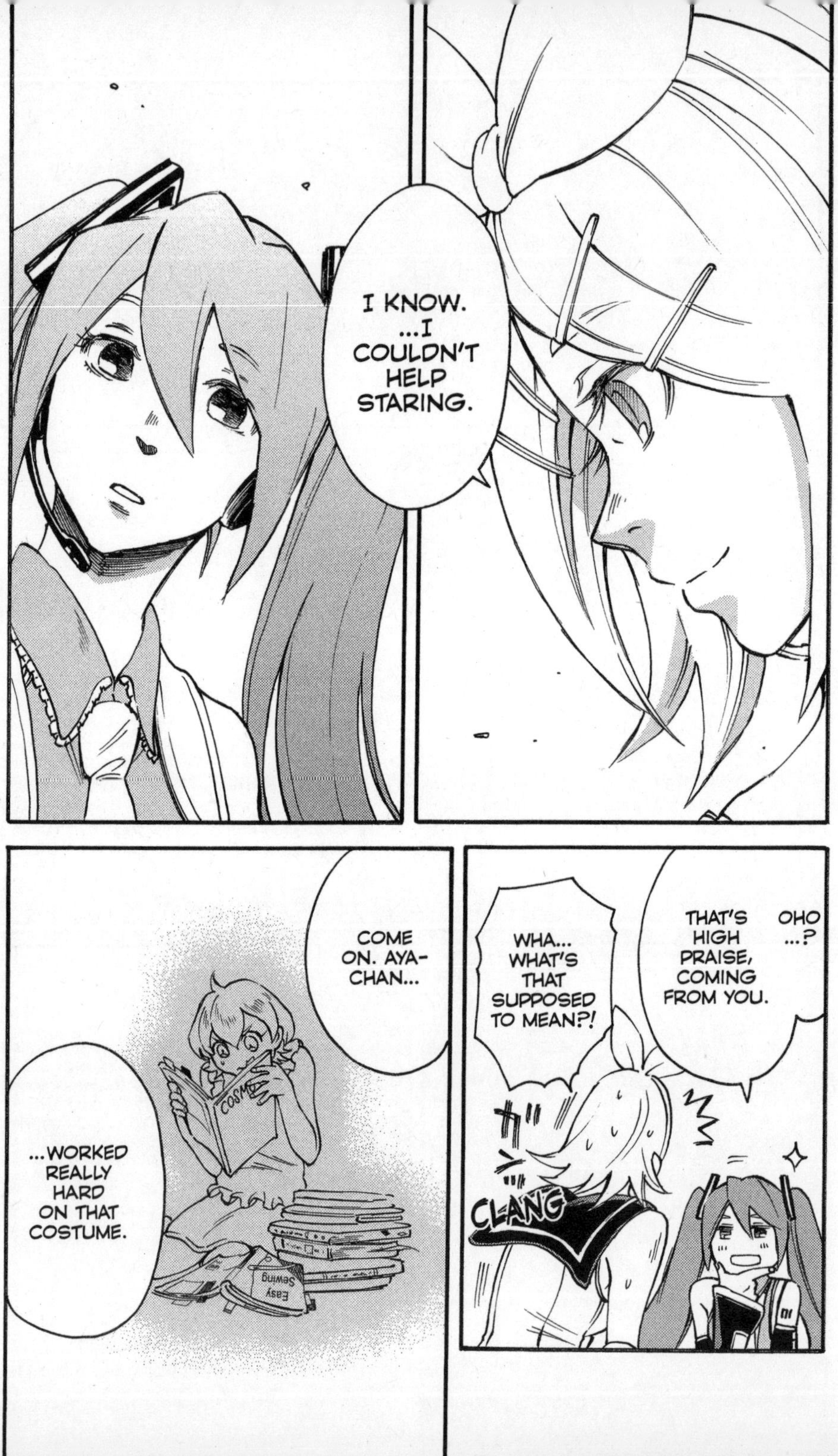
I KNOW. ...I COULDN'T HELP STARING.
OHO ...? THAT'S HIGH PRAISE, COMING FROM YOU.
WHA... WHAT'S THAT SUPPOSED TO MEAN?!
CLANG
COME ON. AYA-CHAN...
...WORKED REALLY HARD ON THAT COSTUME.
Easy Sewing

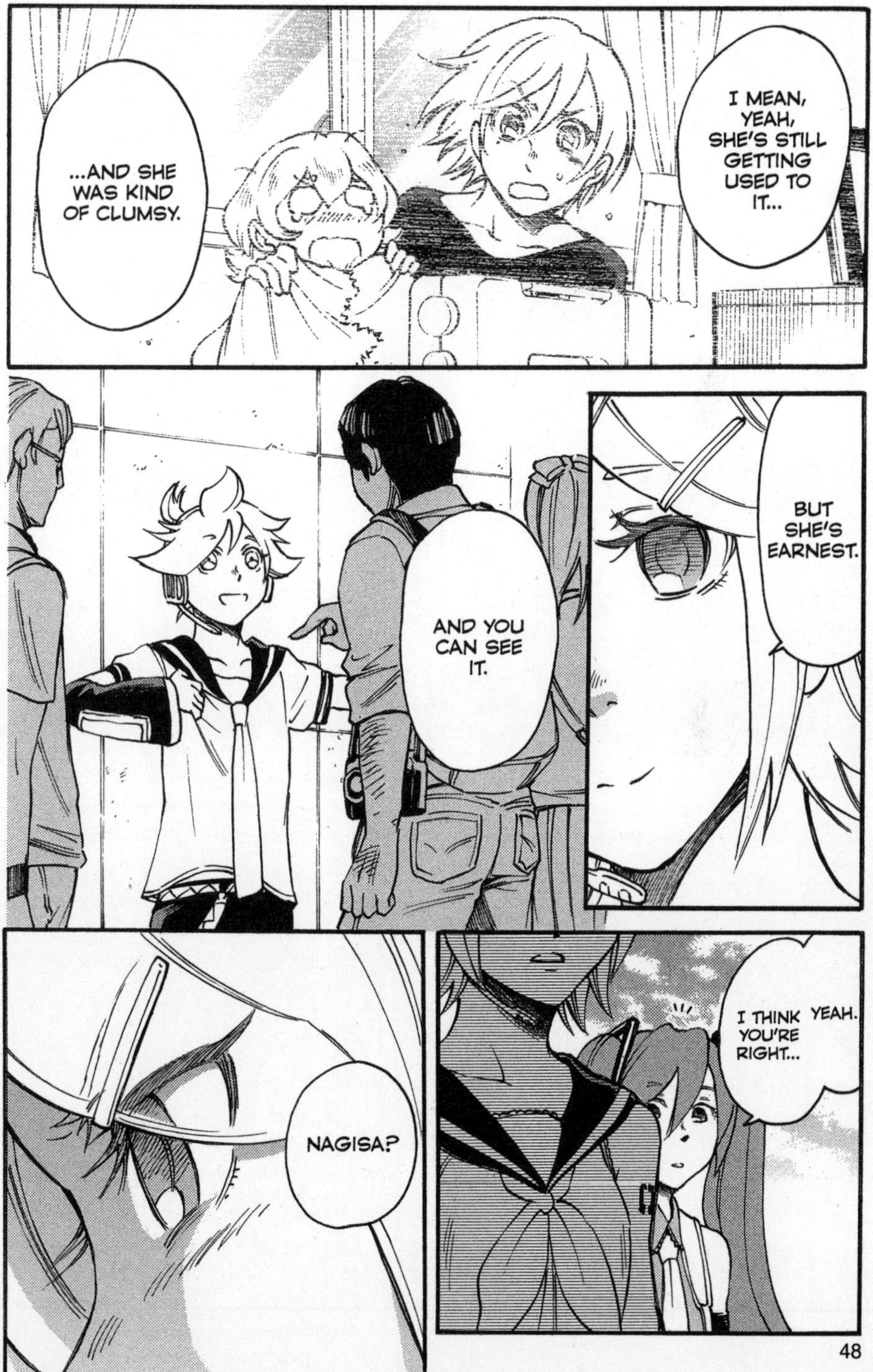
I MEAN, YEAH, SHE'S STILL GETTING USED TO IT...
...AND SHE WAS KIND OF CLUMSY.
BUT SHE'S EARNEST.
AND YOU CAN SEE IT.
YEAH.
I THINK YOU'RE RIGHT...
NAGISA?

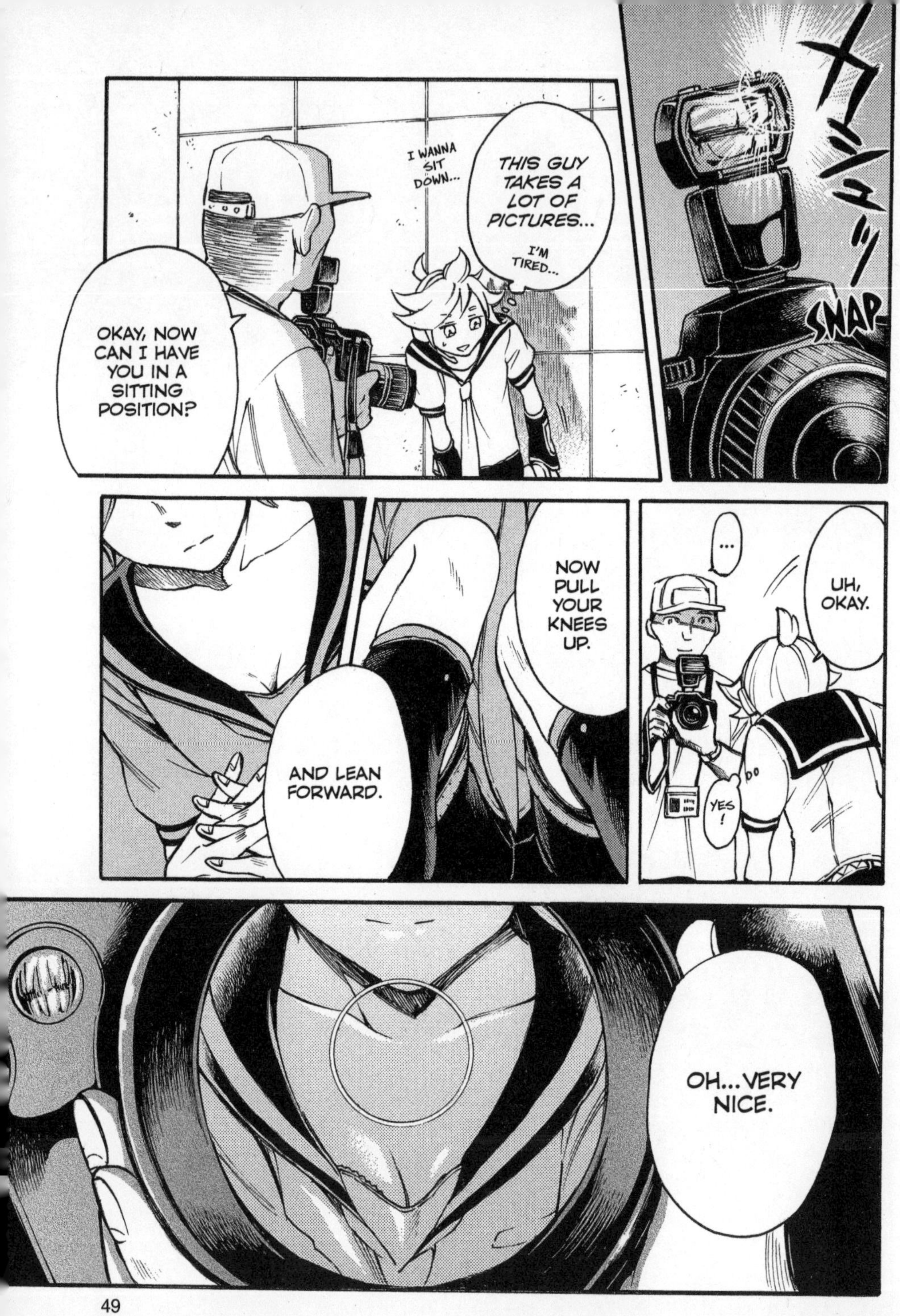
SNAP
THIS GUY TAKES A LOT OF PICTURES...
I'M TIRED...
I WANNA SIT DOWN...
OKAY, NOW CAN I HAVE YOU IN A SITTING POSITION?
UH, OKAY.
...
DO
YES!
NOW PULL YOUR KNEES UP.
AND LEAN FORWARD.
OH...VERY NICE.

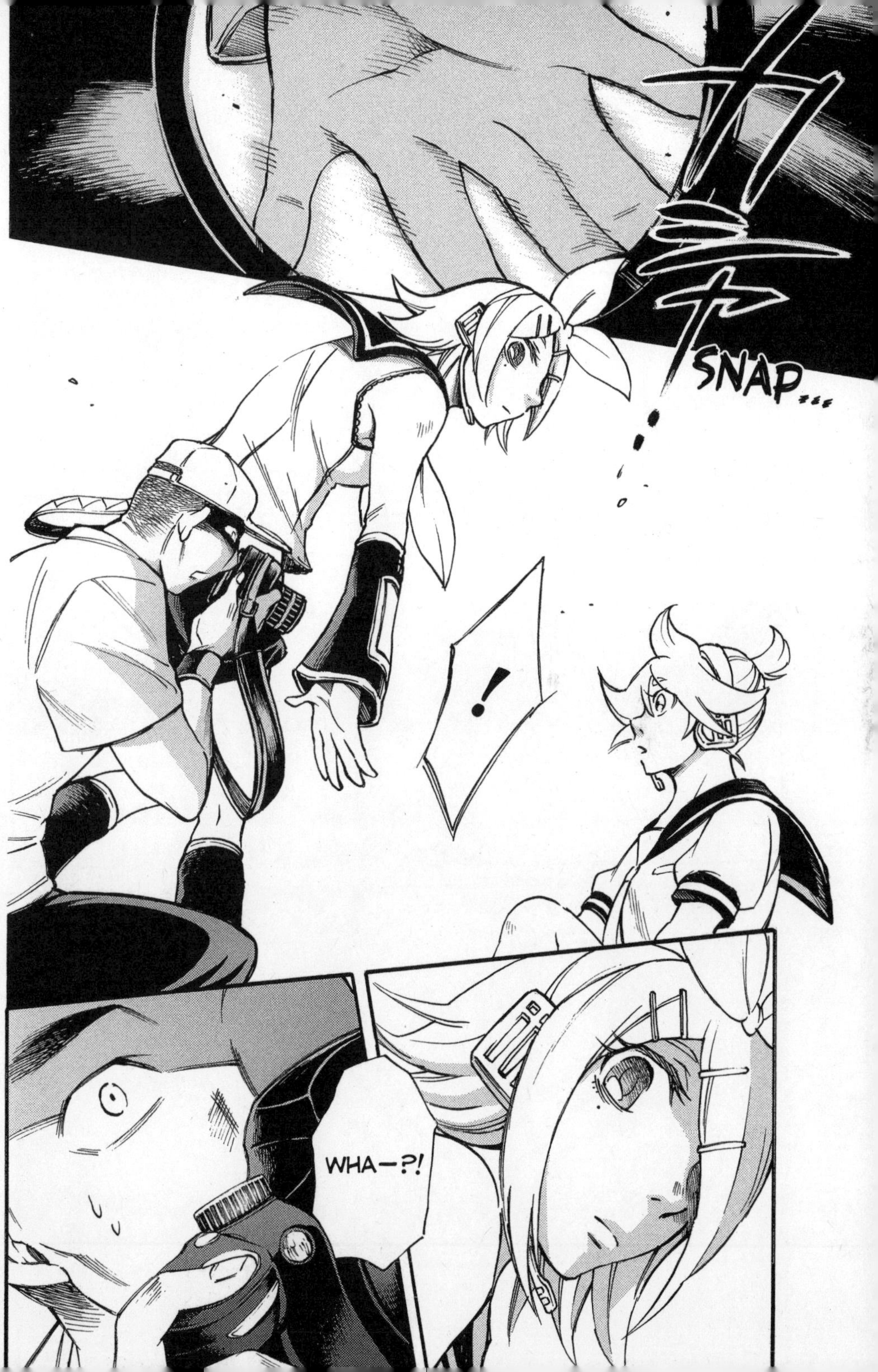
カシャ
SNAP...
!
WHA—?!

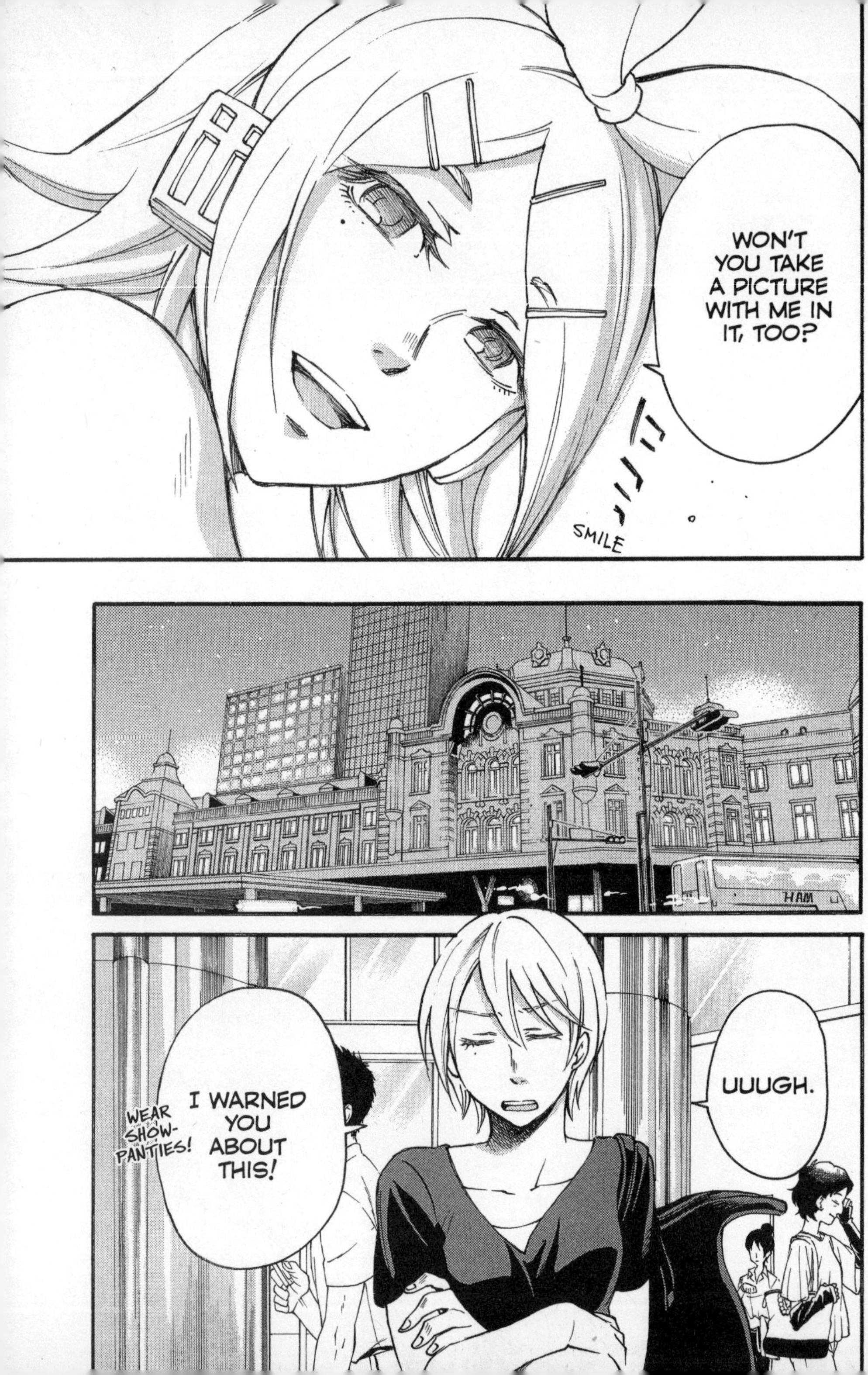
WON'T YOU TAKE A PICTURE WITH ME IN IT, TOO?
SMILE
HAM
UUUGH.
I WARNED YOU ABOUT THIS!
WEAR SHOW-PANTIES!

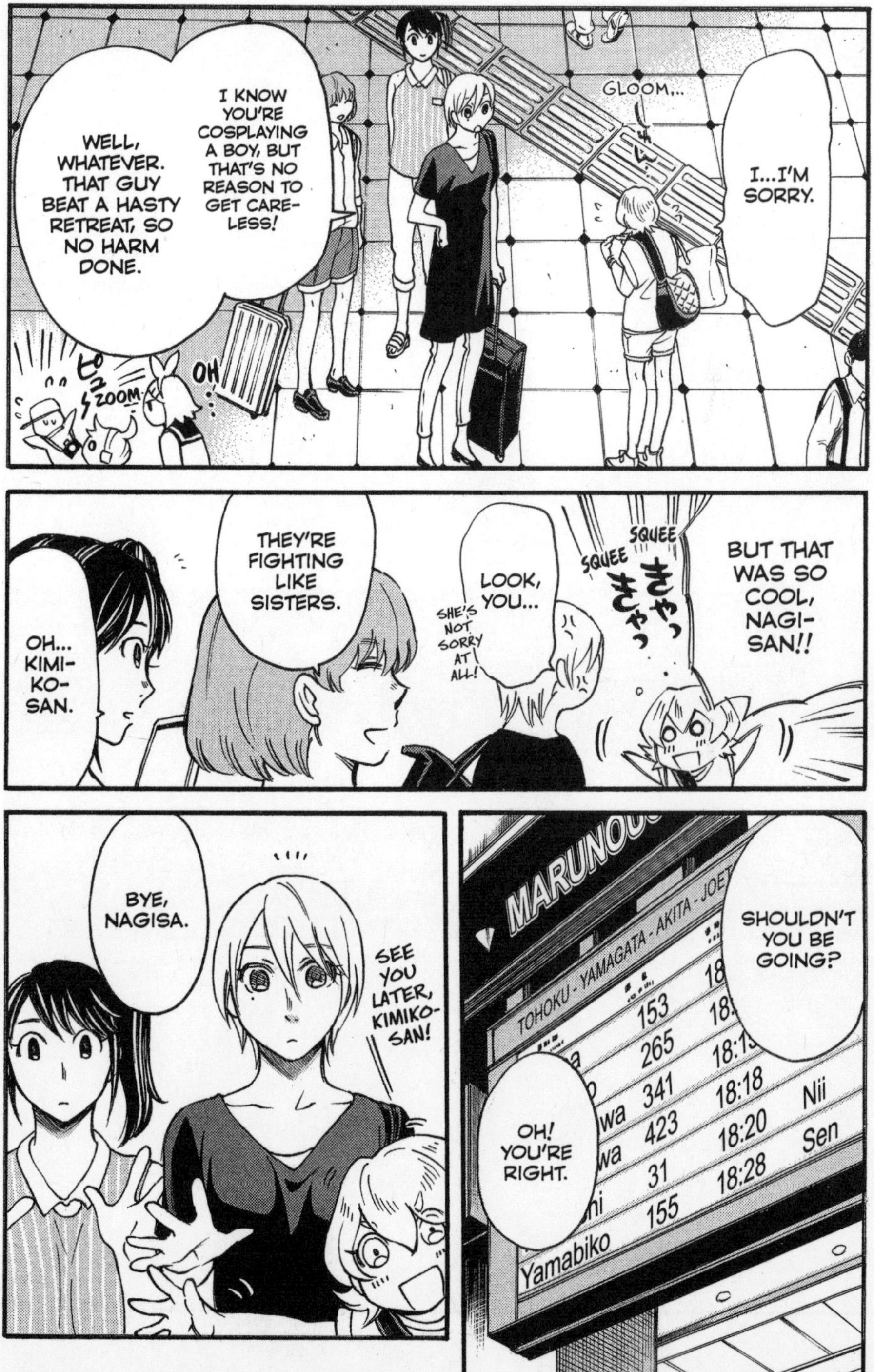

I...I'M SORRY.
GLOOM...
I KNOW YOU'RE COSPLAYING A BOY, BUT THAT'S NO REASON TO GET CARE-LESS!
WELL, WHATEVER. THAT GUY BEAT A HASTY RETREAT, SO NO HARM DONE.
OH
ZOOM
BUT THAT WAS SO COOL, NAGI-SAN!!
SQUEE
SQUEE
きゃっ きゃっ
LOOK, YOU...
SHE'S NOT SORRY AT ALL!
THEY'RE FIGHTING LIKE SISTERS.
OH... KIMIKO-SAN.
TOHOKU - YAMAGATA - AKITA
153
265
18:15
341
18:18
423
18:20
Nii
31
18:28
Sen
Yamabiko
155
SHOULDN'T YOU BE GOING?
OH! YOU'RE RIGHT.
SEE YOU LATER, KIMIKO-SAN!
BYE, NAGISA.

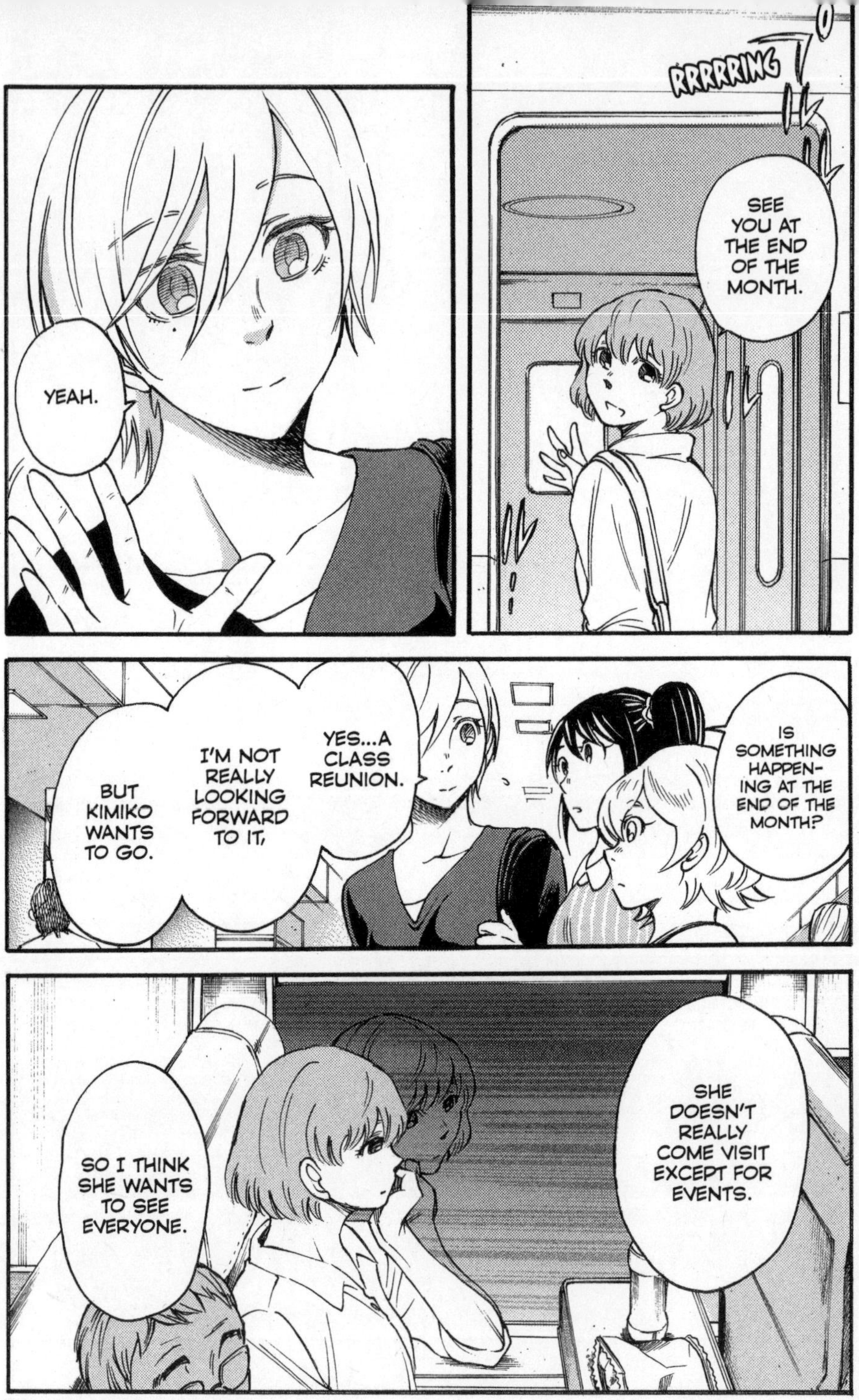
RRRRRING
SEE YOU AT THE END OF THE MONTH.
YEAH.
IS SOMETHING HAPPENING AT THE END OF THE MONTH?
YES...A CLASS REUNION.
I'M NOT REALLY LOOKING FORWARD TO IT,
BUT KIMIKO WANTS TO GO.
SHE DOESN'T REALLY COME VISIT EXCEPT FOR EVENTS.
SO I THINK SHE WANTS TO SEE EVERYONE.

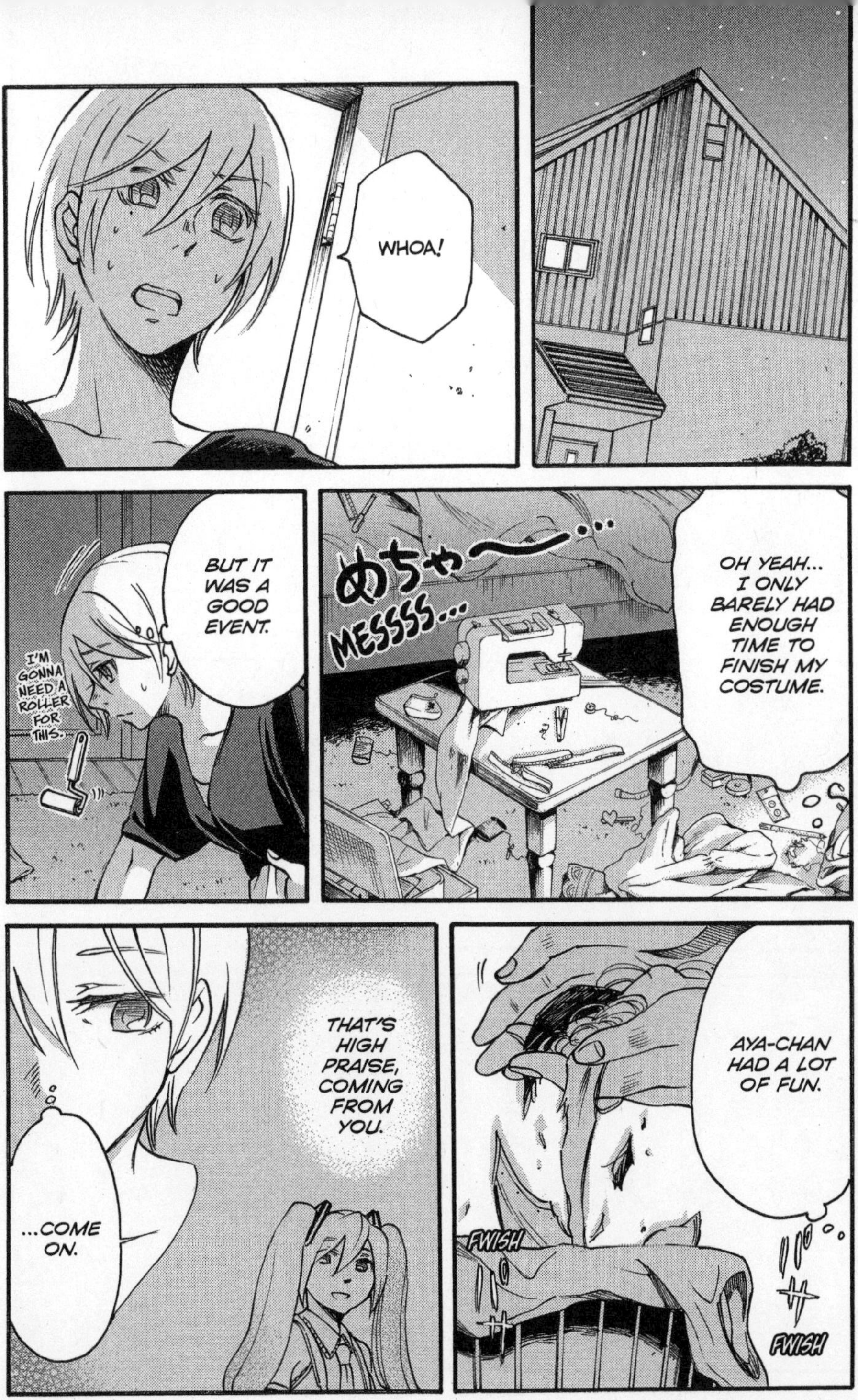
WHOA!
めちゃ〜…
MESSSS...
OH YEAH... I ONLY BARELY HAD ENOUGH TIME TO FINISH MY COSTUME.
BUT IT WAS A GOOD EVENT.
I'M GONNA NEED A ROLLER FOR THIS.
AYA-CHAN HAD A LOT OF FUN.
FWISH
FWISH
THAT'S HIGH PRAISE, COMING FROM YOU.
...COME ON.

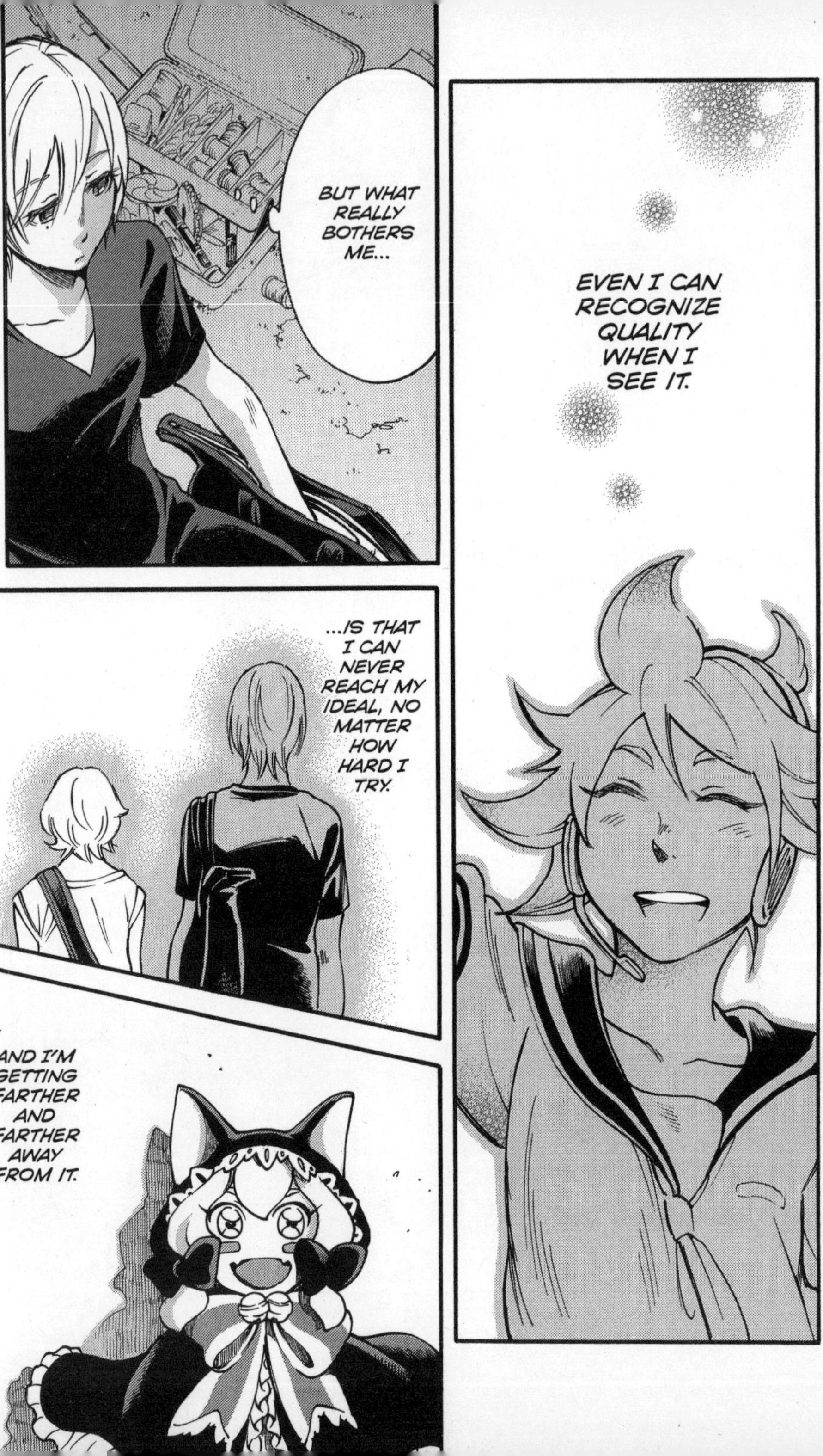
EVEN I CAN RECOGNIZE QUALITY WHEN I SEE IT.
BUT WHAT REALLY BOTHERS ME...
...IS THAT I CAN NEVER REACH MY IDEAL, NO MATTER HOW HARD I TRY.
AND I'M GETTING FARTHER AND FARTHER AWAY FROM IT.

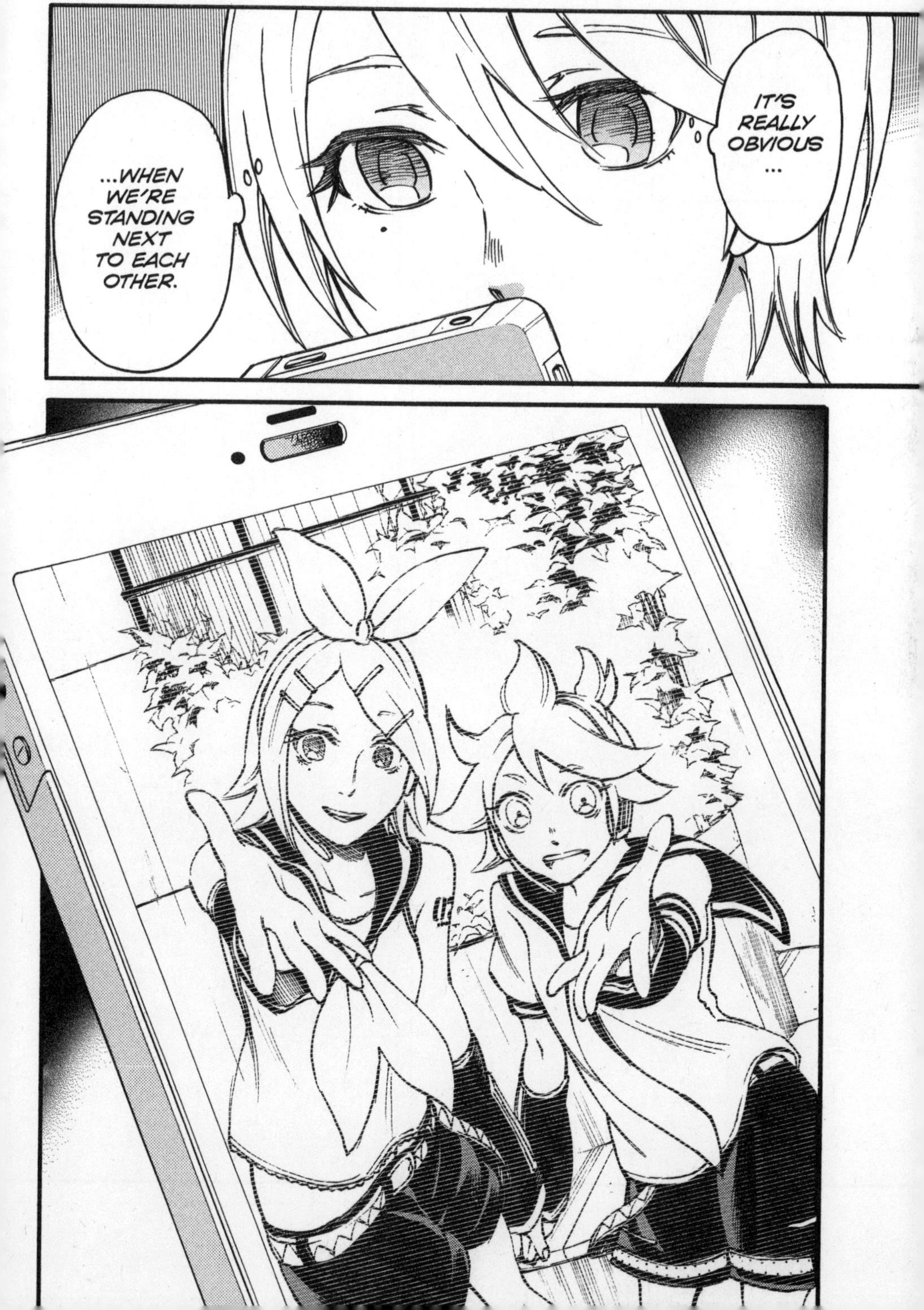
IT'S REALLY OBVIOUS ...
...WHEN WE'RE STANDING NEXT TO EACH OTHER.

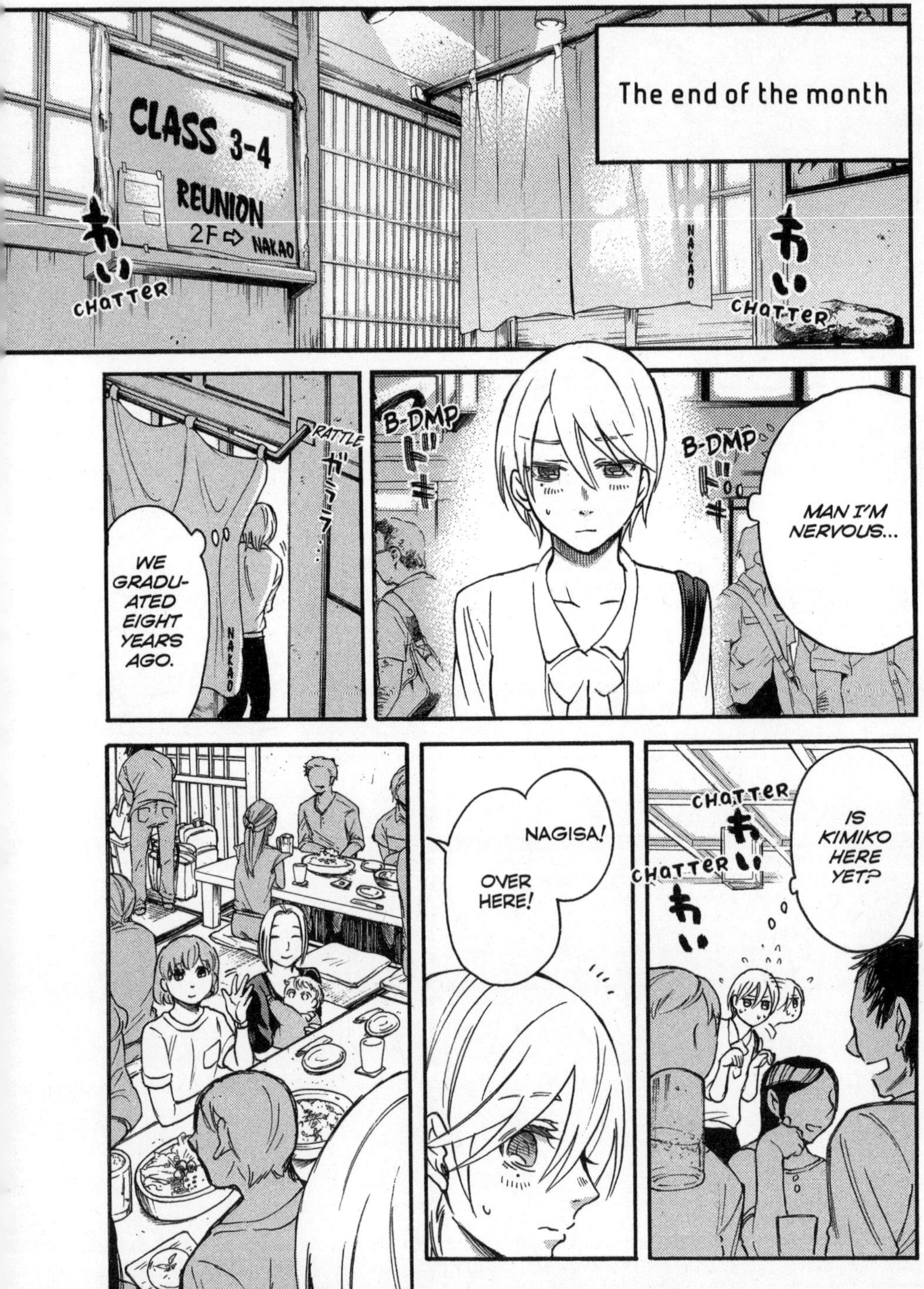

The end of the month
CLASS 3-4
REUNION
2F ⇨ NAKAO
NAKAO
わい
CHATTER
わい
CHATTER
B-DMP
ドキ
B-DMP
ドキ
MAN I'M NERVOUS...
RATTLE
ガララ…
WE GRADUATED EIGHT YEARS AGO.
NAKAO
IS KIMIKO HERE YET?
CHATTER
わい
CHATTER
わい
NAGISA!
OVER HERE!

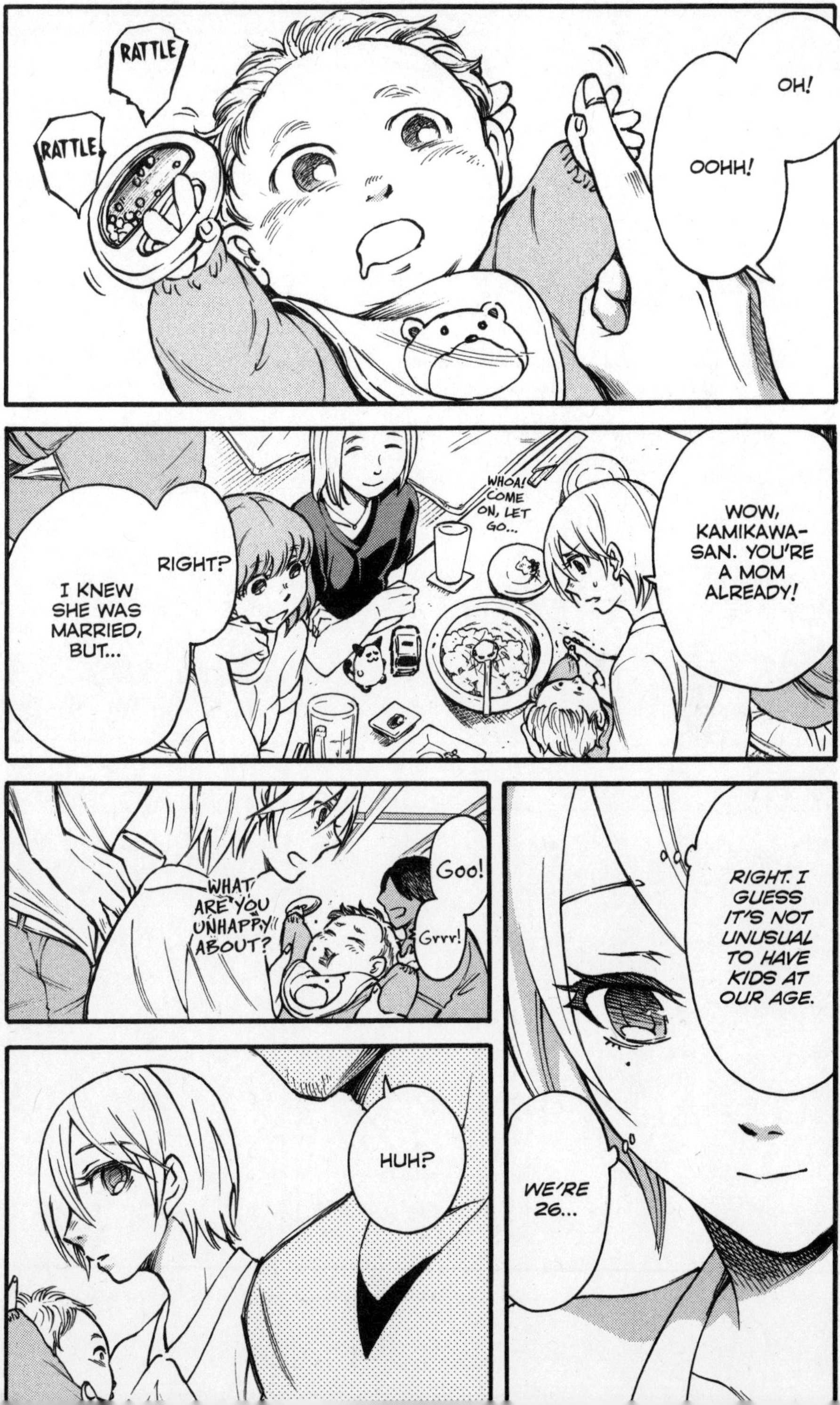
OH!
OOHH!
RATTLE
RATTLE
WOW, KAMIKAWA-SAN. YOU'RE A MOM ALREADY!
WHOA! COME ON, LET GO...
RIGHT?
I KNEW SHE WAS MARRIED, BUT...
RIGHT. I GUESS IT'S NOT UNUSUAL TO HAVE KIDS AT OUR AGE.
WE'RE 26...
Goo!
Grrr!
WHAT ARE YOU UNHAPPY ABOUT?
HUH?

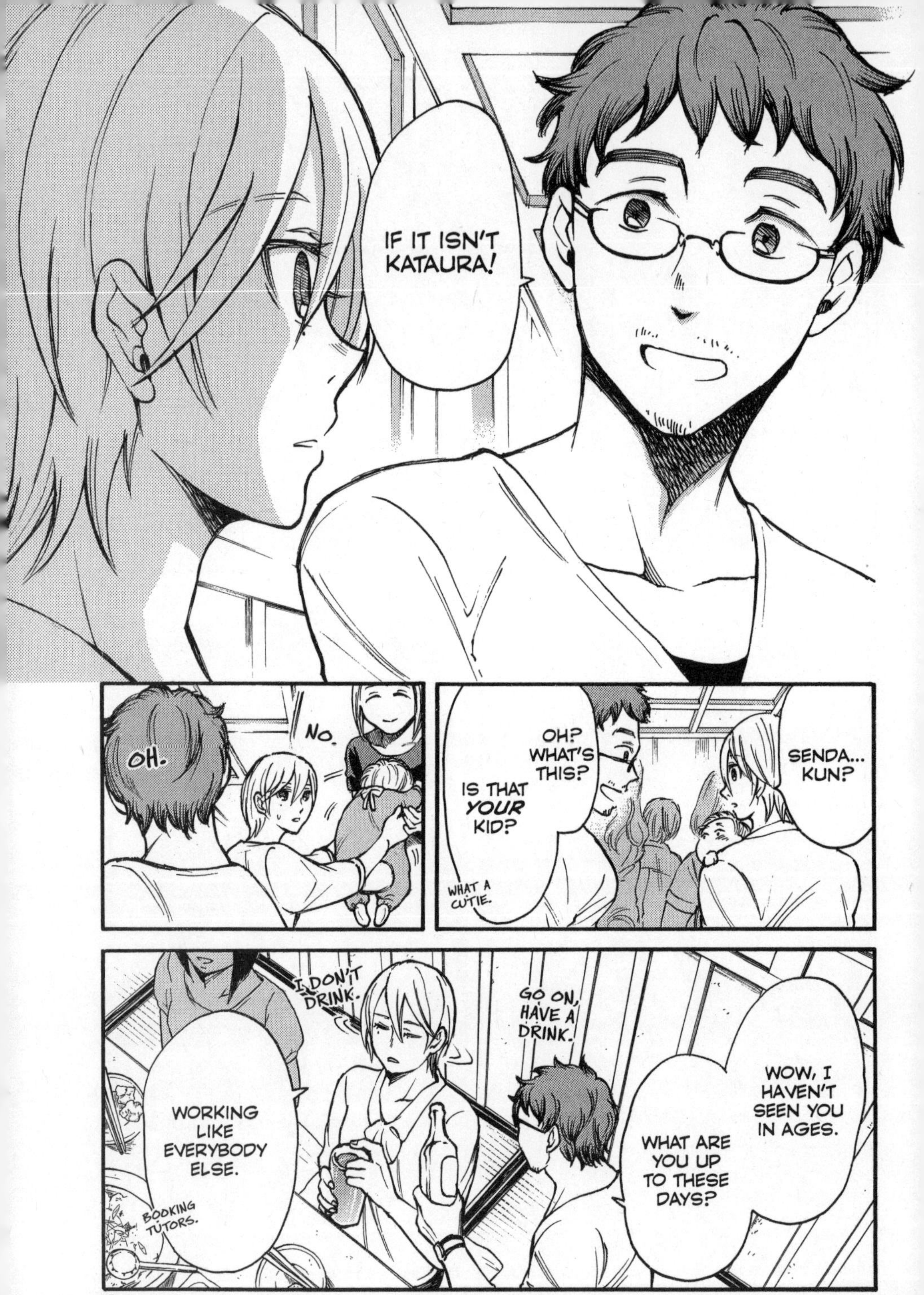
IF IT ISN'T KATAURA!
SENDA... KUN?
OH? WHAT'S THIS?
IS THAT *YOUR* KID?
WHAT A CUTIE.
NO.
OH.
WOW, I HAVEN'T SEEN YOU IN AGES.
WHAT ARE YOU UP TO THESE DAYS?
GO ON, HAVE A DRINK.
I DON'T DRINK.
WORKING LIKE EVERYBODY ELSE.
BOOKING TUTORS.

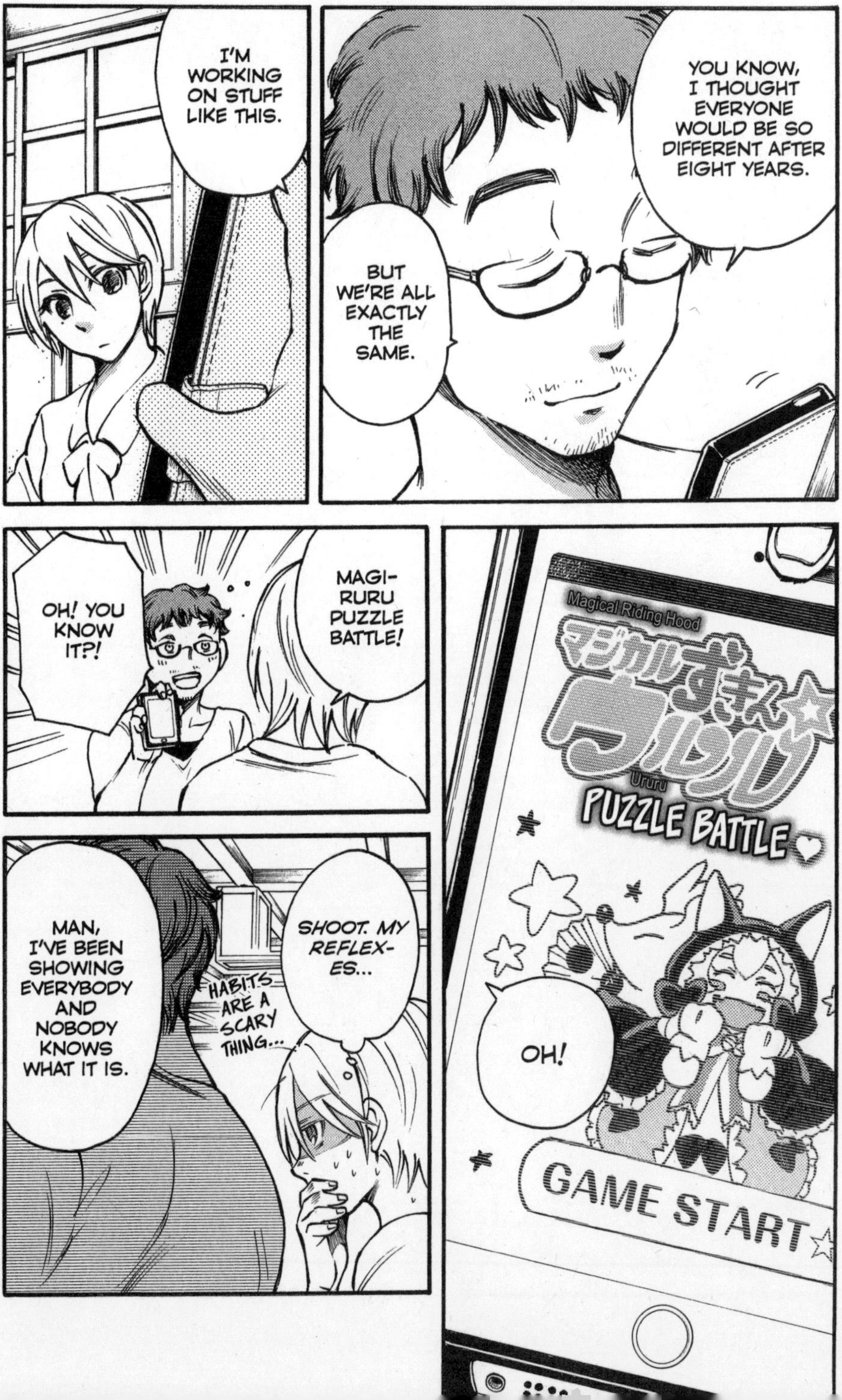
YOU KNOW, I THOUGHT EVERYONE WOULD BE SO DIFFERENT AFTER EIGHT YEARS.
BUT WE'RE ALL EXACTLY THE SAME.
I'M WORKING ON STUFF LIKE THIS.
Magical Riding Hood
マジカルずきん☆ウルル
Ururu
PUZZLE BATTLE
OH!
GAME START
MAGI-RURU PUZZLE BATTLE!
OH! YOU KNOW IT?!
SHOOT. MY REFLEX-ES...
HABITS ARE A SCARY THING...
MAN, I'VE BEEN SHOWING EVERYBODY AND NOBODY KNOWS WHAT IT IS.

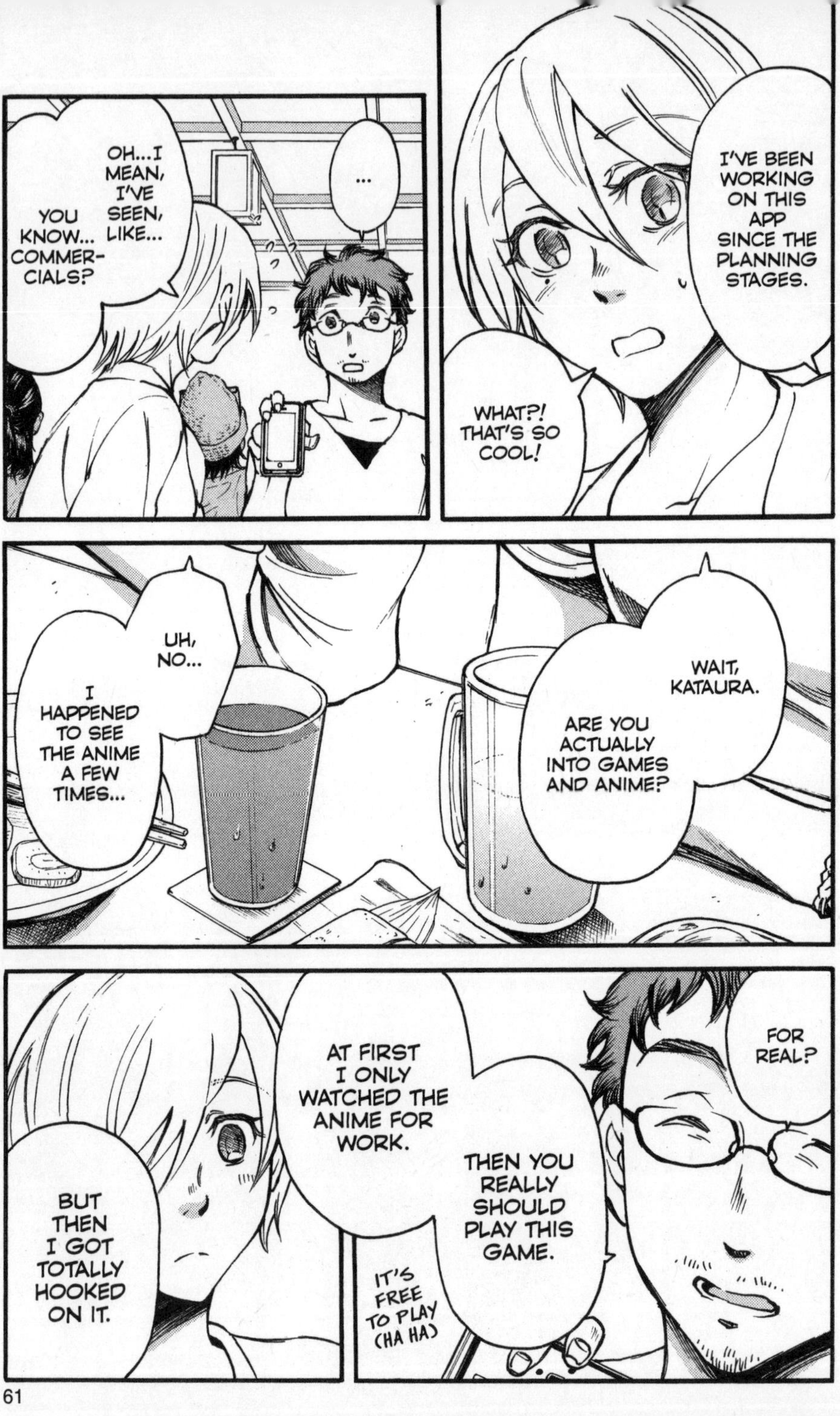
I'VE BEEN WORKING ON THIS APP SINCE THE PLANNING STAGES.
WHAT?! THAT'S SO COOL!
...
OH...I MEAN, I'VE SEEN, LIKE...
YOU KNOW... COMMERCIALS?
WAIT, KATAURA.
ARE YOU ACTUALLY INTO GAMES AND ANIME?
UH, NO...
I HAPPENED TO SEE THE ANIME A FEW TIMES...
FOR REAL?
THEN YOU REALLY SHOULD PLAY THIS GAME.
IT'S FREE TO PLAY (HA HA)
AT FIRST I ONLY WATCHED THE ANIME FOR WORK.
BUT THEN I GOT TOTALLY HOOKED ON IT.

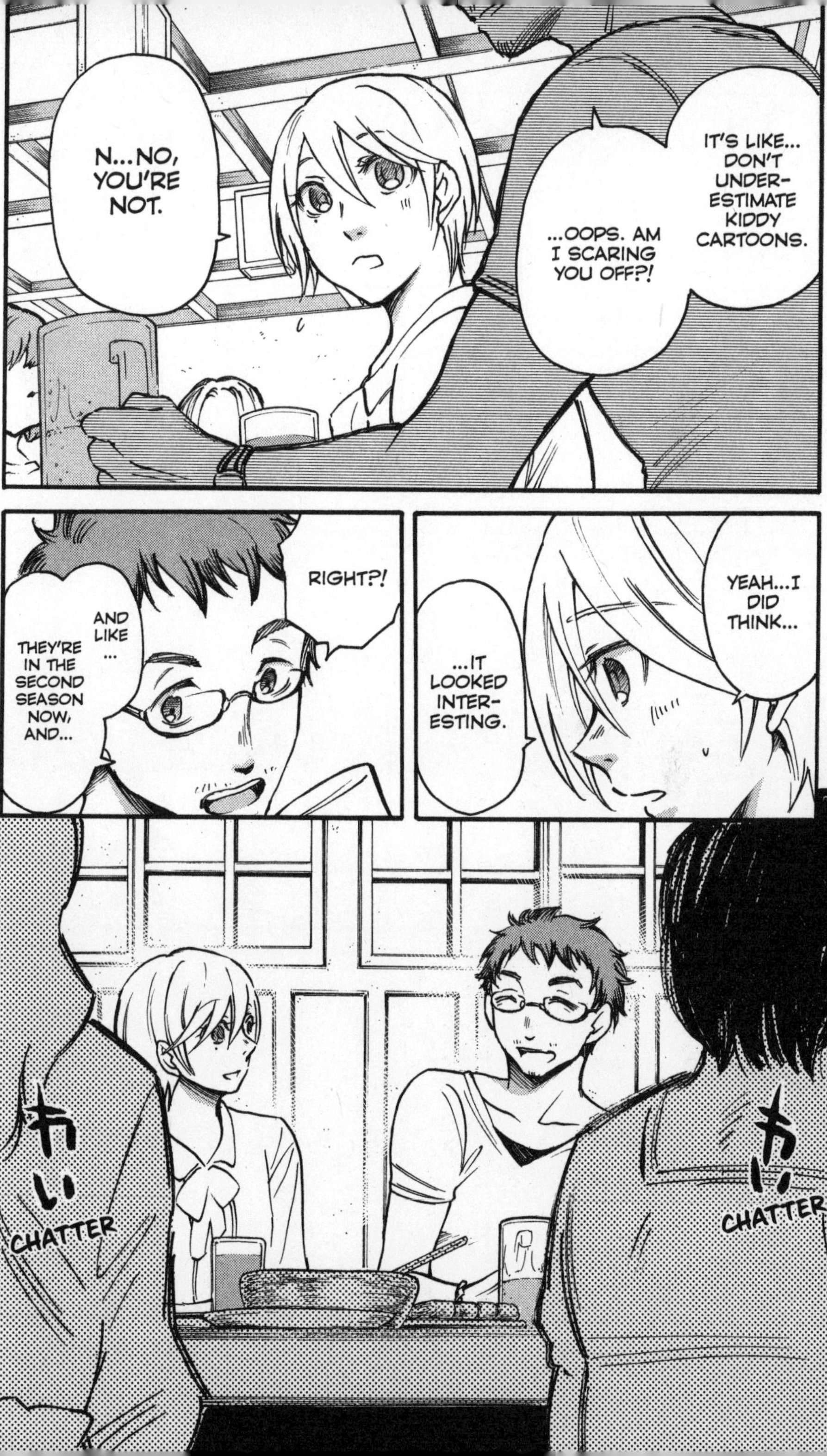
IT'S LIKE... DON'T UNDER-ESTIMATE KIDDY CARTOONS.
...OOPS. AM I SCARING YOU OFF?!
N...NO, YOU'RE NOT.
YEAH...I DID THINK...
...IT LOOKED INTER-ESTING.
RIGHT?!
AND LIKE ...
THEY'RE IN THE SECOND SEASON NOW, AND...
わい
CHATTER
わい
CHATTER

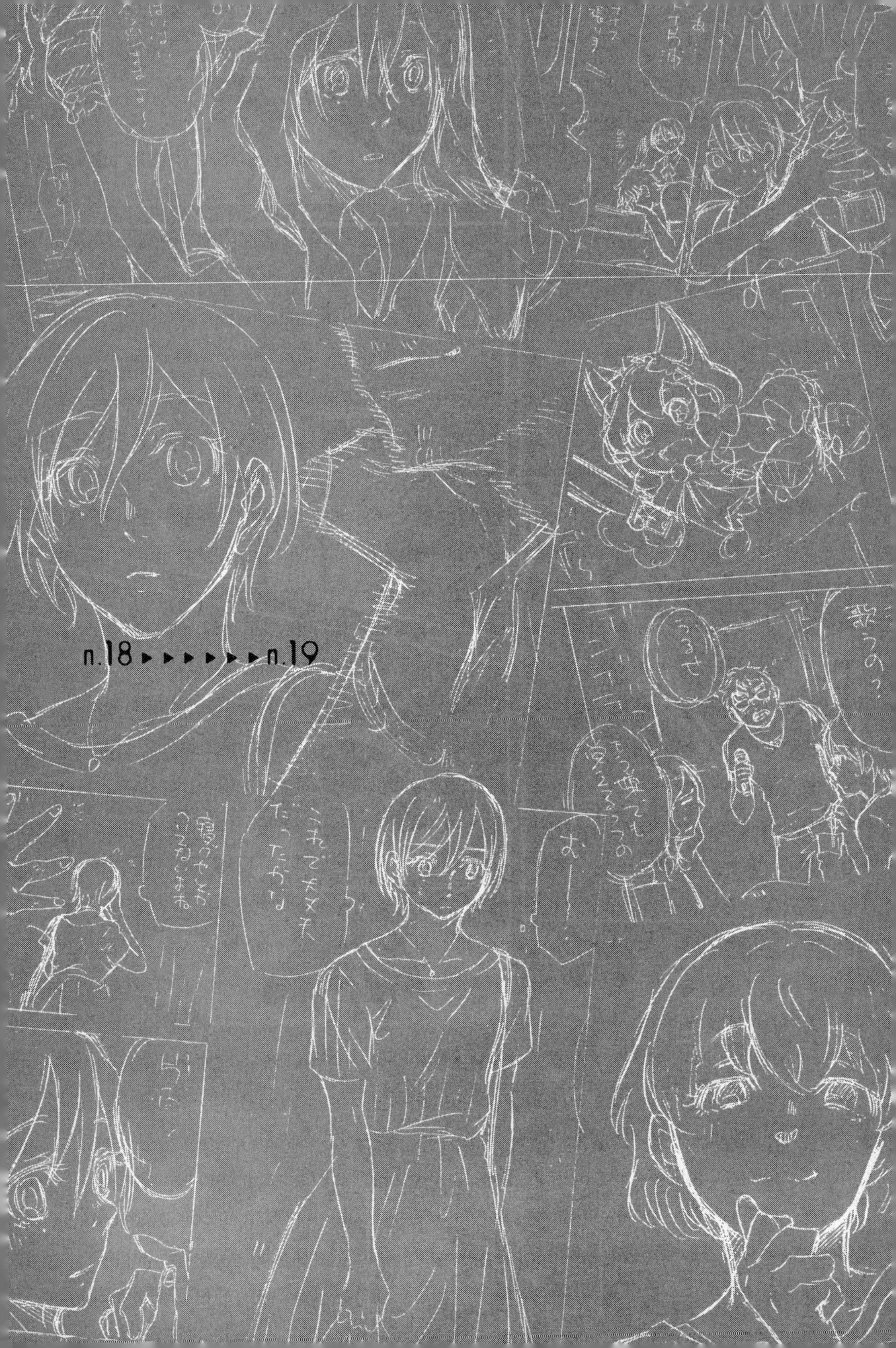

n.18 ▸▸▸▸▸▸▸▸ n.19

MIKU & FRIENDS COLLABORATION ②

鏡音リン・レン
KAGAMINE RIN / LEN

RIN × NAGISA KATAURA

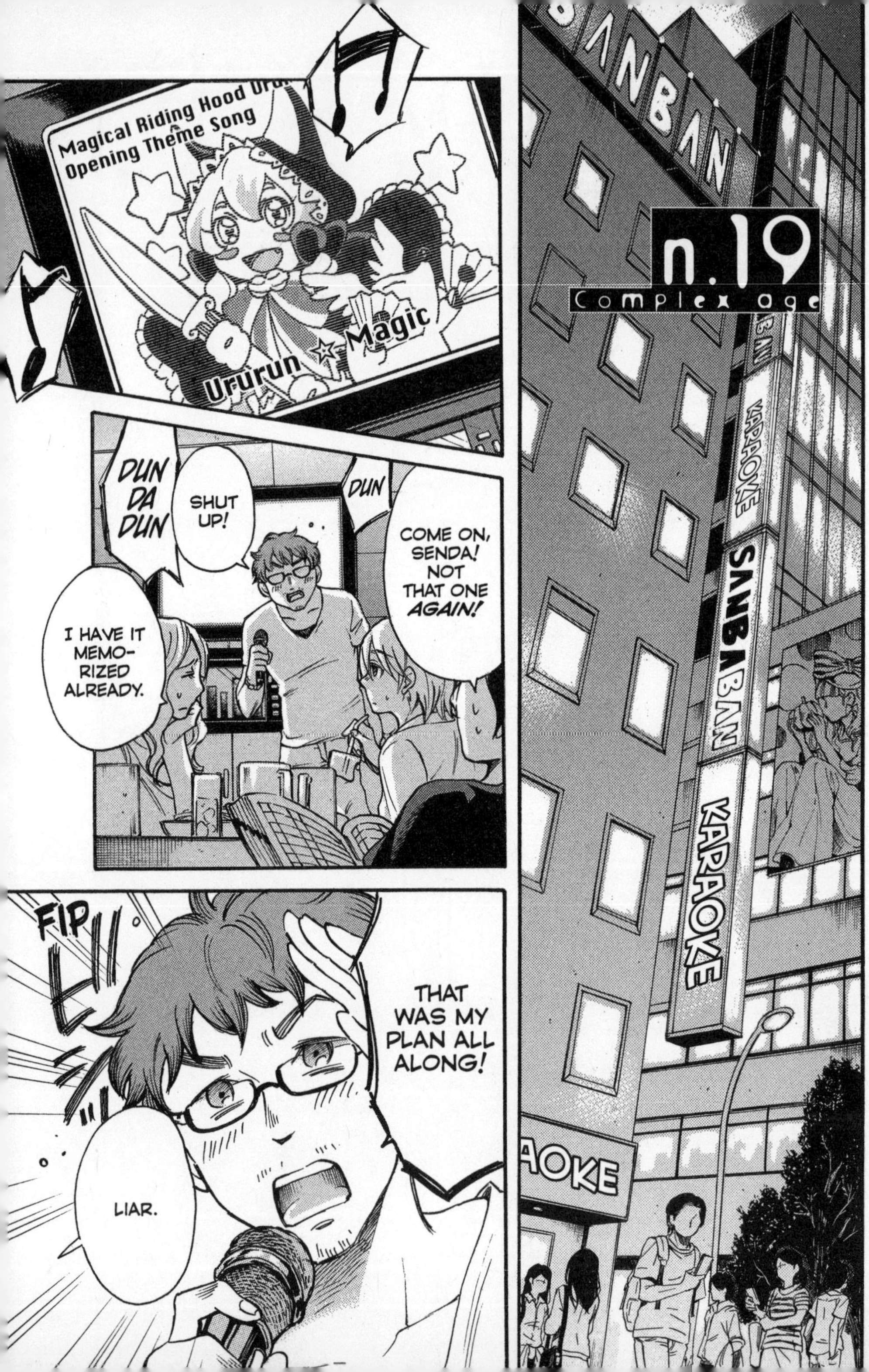
SANBAN
n.19
Complex age
KARAOKE
SANBABAN
KARAOKE
AOKE
Magical Riding Hood
Opening Theme Song
Ururun ☆ Magic
COME ON, SENDA! NOT THAT ONE *AGAIN!*
DUN
SHUT UP!
DUN DA DUN
I HAVE IT MEMO-RIZED ALREADY.
THAT WAS MY PLAN ALL ALONG!
FIP
LIAR.

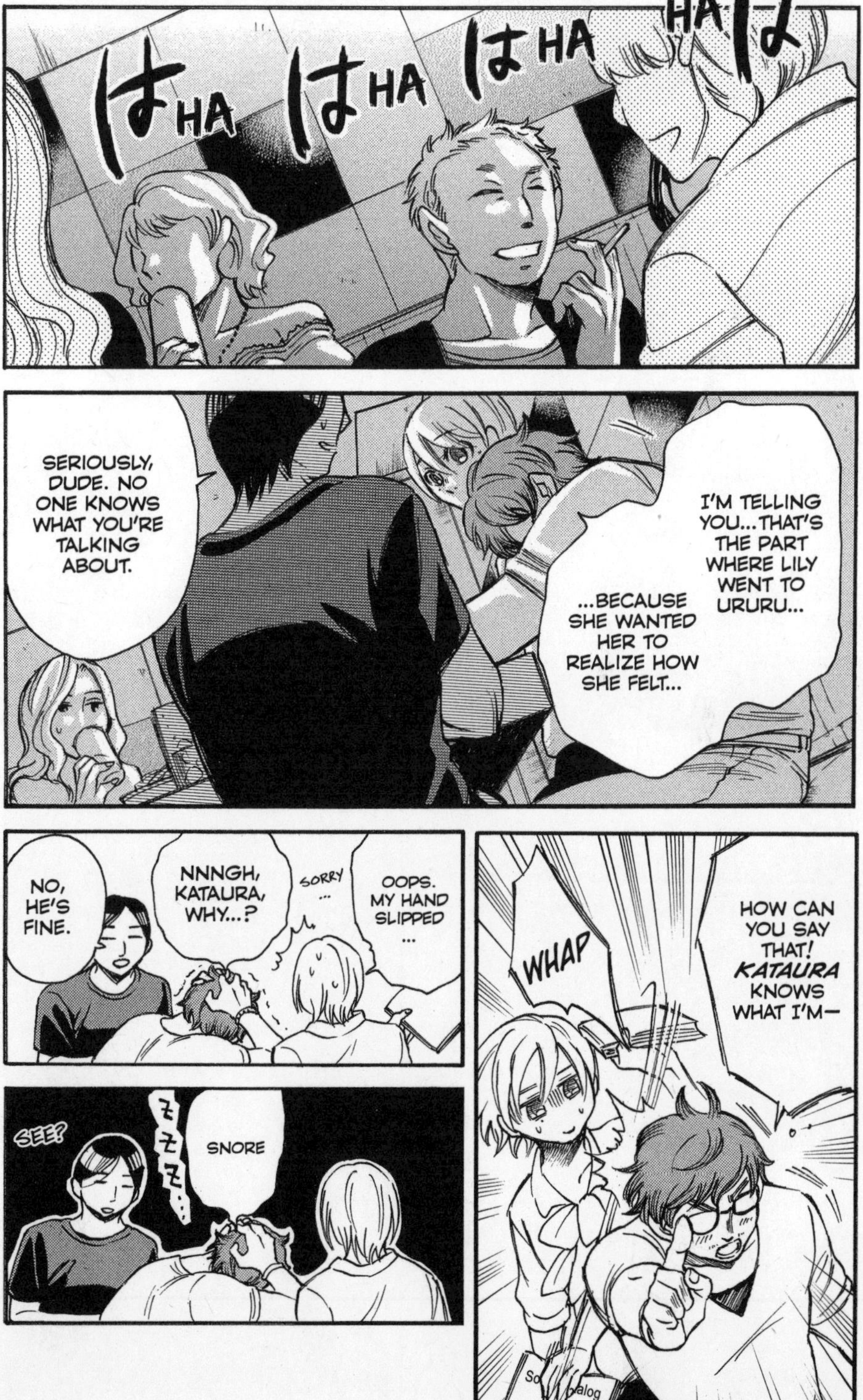
はHA はHA はHA HAは
I'M TELLING YOU...THAT'S THE PART WHERE LILY WENT TO URURU...
...BECAUSE SHE WANTED HER TO REALIZE HOW SHE FELT...
SERIOUSLY, DUDE. NO ONE KNOWS WHAT YOU'RE TALKING ABOUT.
HOW CAN YOU SAY THAT! *KATAURA* KNOWS WHAT I'M—
WHAP
OOPS. MY HAND SLIPPED ...
SORRY ...
NNNGH, KATAURA, WHY...?
NO, HE'S FINE.
SNORE
Z Z Z...
SEE?

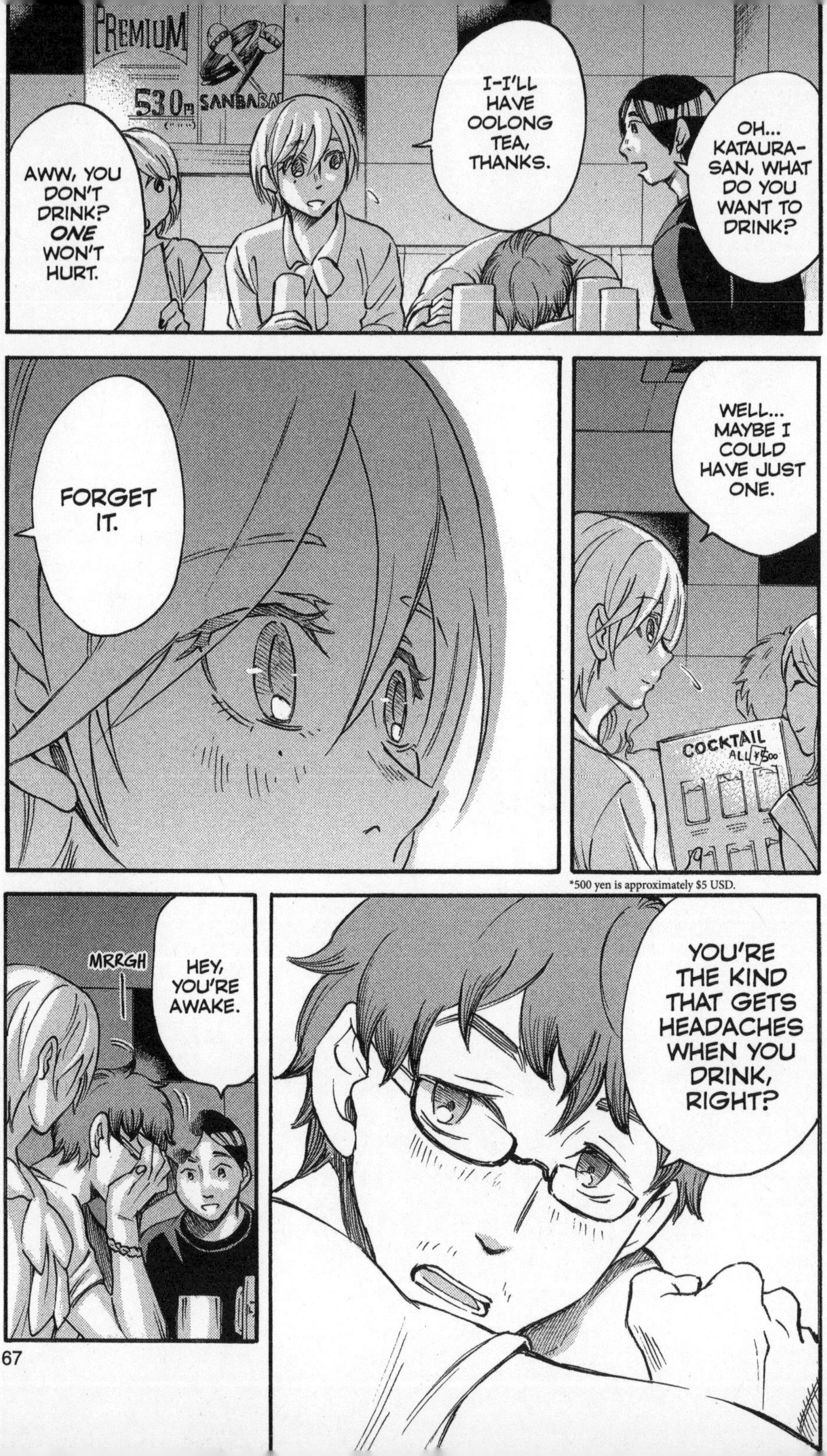
PREMIUM
530円
SANBABA
OH... KATAURA-SAN, WHAT DO YOU WANT TO DRINK?
I-I'LL HAVE OOLONG TEA, THANKS.
AWW, YOU DON'T DRINK? *ONE* WON'T HURT.
WELL... MAYBE I COULD HAVE JUST ONE.
COCKTAIL ALL ¥500
FORGET IT.
YOU'RE THE KIND THAT GETS HEADACHES WHEN YOU DRINK, RIGHT?
HEY, YOU'RE AWAKE.
MRRGH

*500 yen is approximately $5 USD.

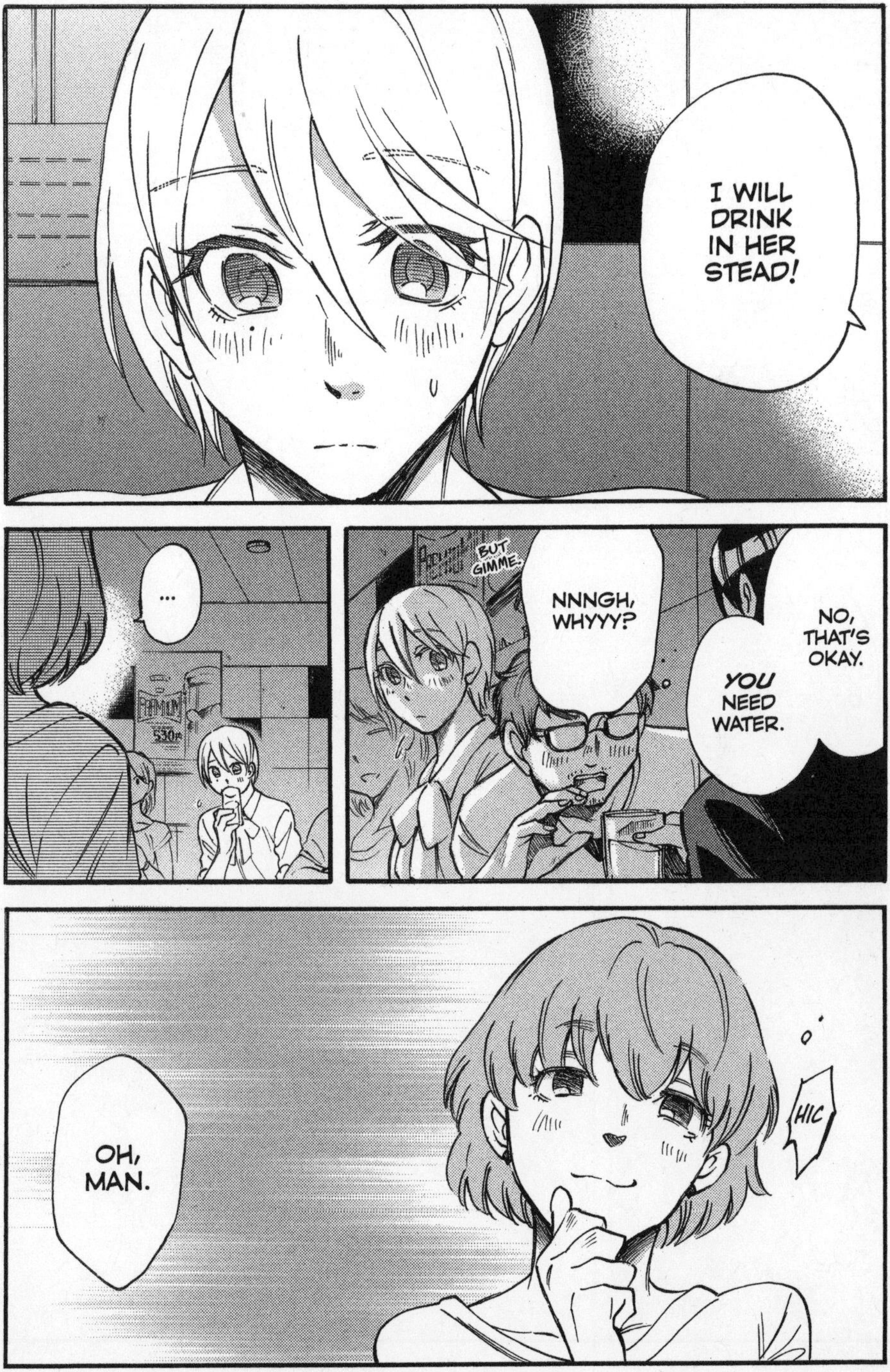
I WILL DRINK IN HER STEAD!
NNNGH, WHYYY?
BUT GIMME.
NO, THAT'S OKAY.
YOU NEED WATER.
...
HIC
OH, MAN.

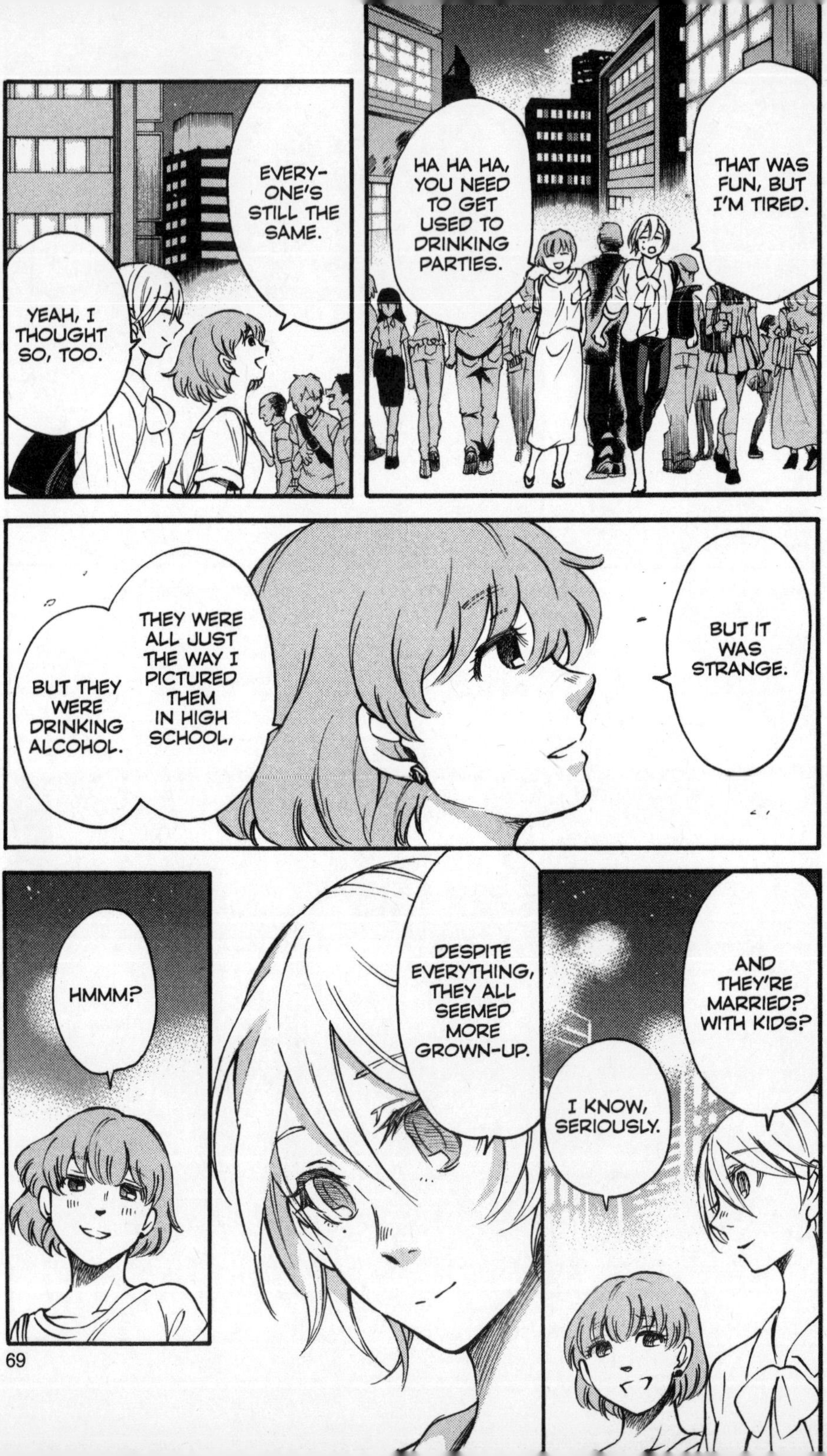
THAT WAS FUN, BUT I'M TIRED.
HA HA HA, YOU NEED TO GET USED TO DRINKING PARTIES.
EVERY-ONE'S STILL THE SAME.
YEAH, I THOUGHT SO, TOO.
BUT IT WAS STRANGE.
THEY WERE ALL JUST THE WAY I PICTURED THEM IN HIGH SCHOOL,
BUT THEY WERE DRINKING ALCOHOL.
AND THEY'RE MARRIED? WITH KIDS?
I KNOW, SERIOUSLY.
DESPITE EVERYTHING, THEY ALL SEEMED MORE GROWN-UP.
HMMM?

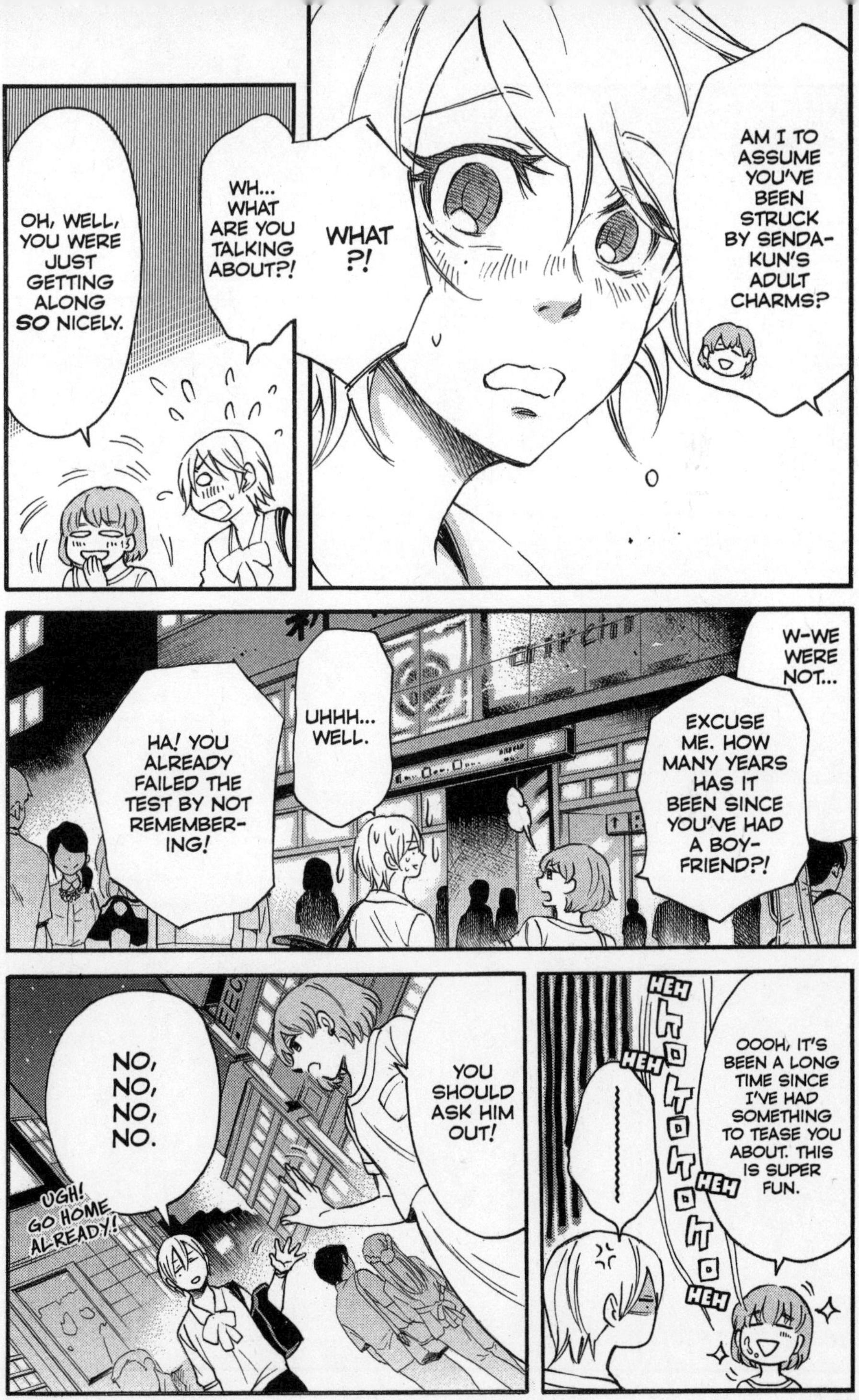
AM I TO ASSUME YOU'VE BEEN STRUCK BY SENDA-KUN'S ADULT CHARMS?
WHAT ?!
WH... WHAT ARE YOU TALKING ABOUT?!
OH, WELL, YOU WERE JUST GETTING ALONG SO NICELY.
W-WE WERE NOT...
EXCUSE ME. HOW MANY YEARS HAS IT BEEN SINCE YOU'VE HAD A BOY-FRIEND?!
UHHH... WELL.
HA! YOU ALREADY FAILED THE TEST BY NOT REMEMBER-ING!
OOOH, IT'S BEEN A LONG TIME SINCE I'VE HAD SOMETHING TO TEASE YOU ABOUT. THIS IS SUPER FUN.
HEH HEH HEH HEH
YOU SHOULD ASK HIM OUT!
NO, NO, NO, NO.
UGH! GO HOME ALREADY!

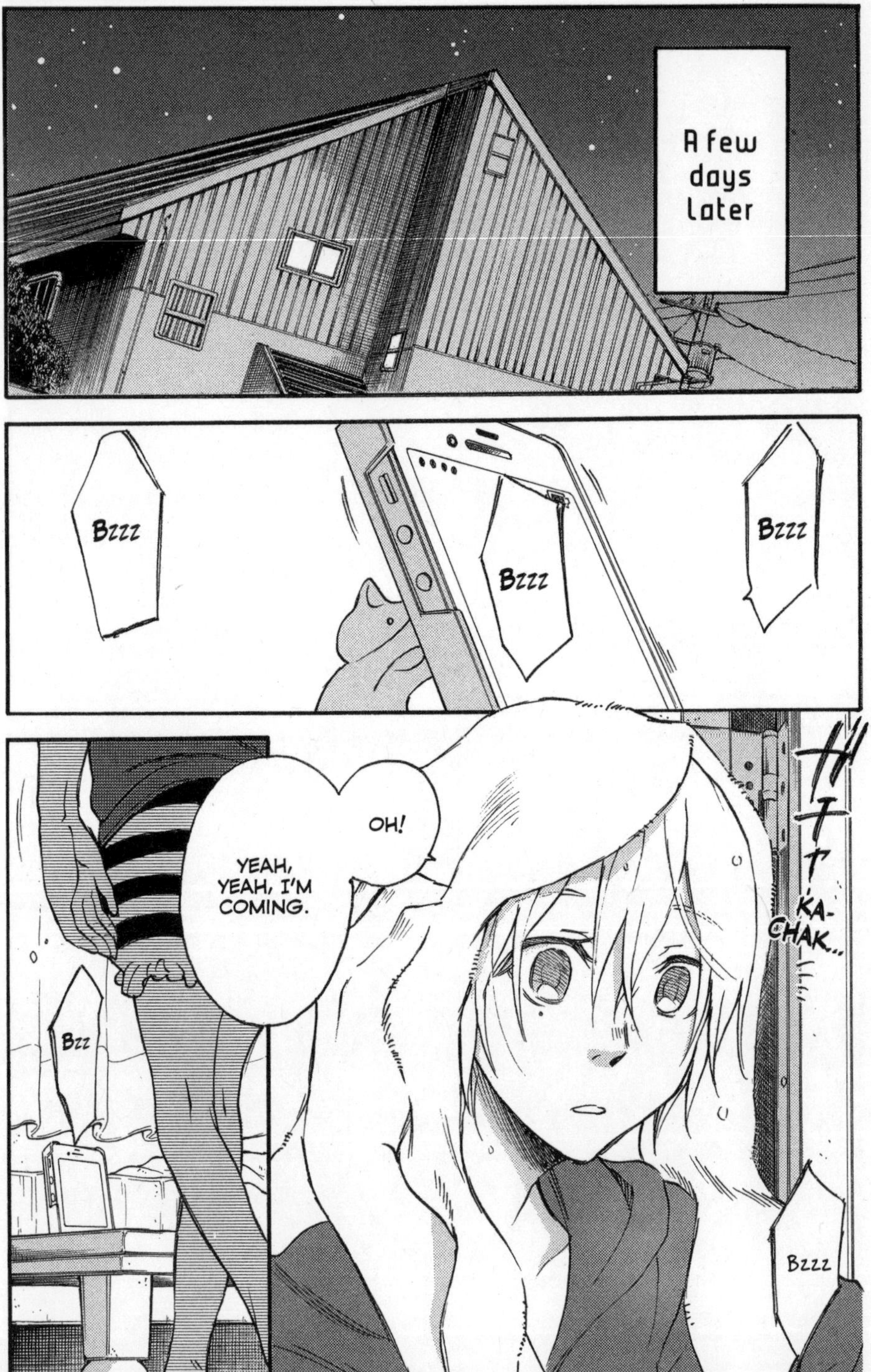
A few days later
Bzzz
Bzzz
Bzzz
KA-CHAK...
OH!
YEAH, YEAH, I'M COMING.
Bzzz
Bzz

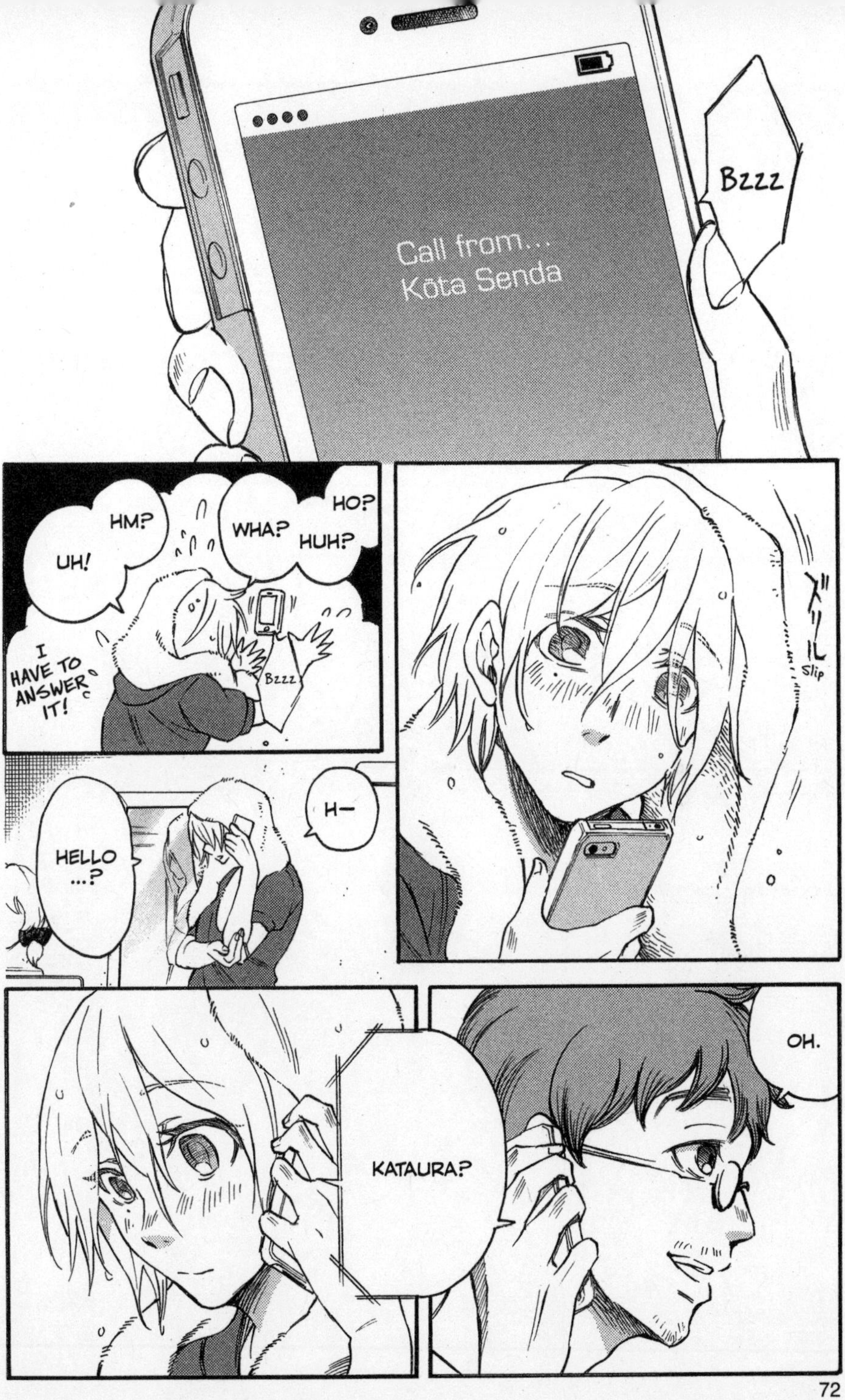
Bzzz
Call from...
Köta Senda
ズル
Slip
HO?
HUH?
WHA?
HM?
UH!
Bzzz
I HAVE TO ANSWER IT!
H—
HELLO ...?
OH.
KATAURA?

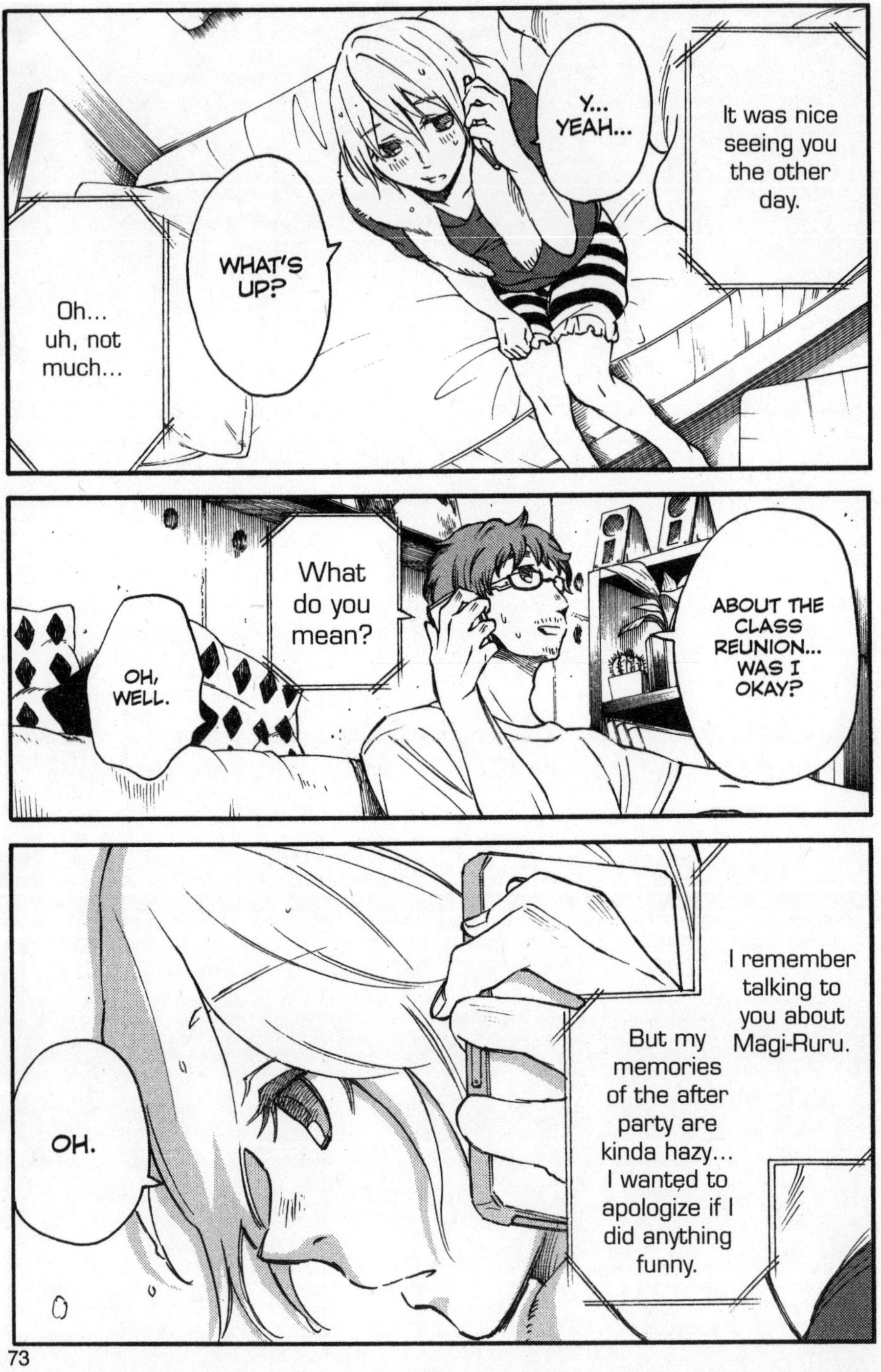
It was nice seeing you the other day.
Y... YEAH...
WHAT'S UP?
Oh... uh, not much...
ABOUT THE CLASS REUNION... WAS I OKAY?
What do you mean?
OH, WELL.
I remember talking to you about Magi-Ruru.
But my memories of the after party are kinda hazy... I wanted to apologize if I did anything funny.
OH.

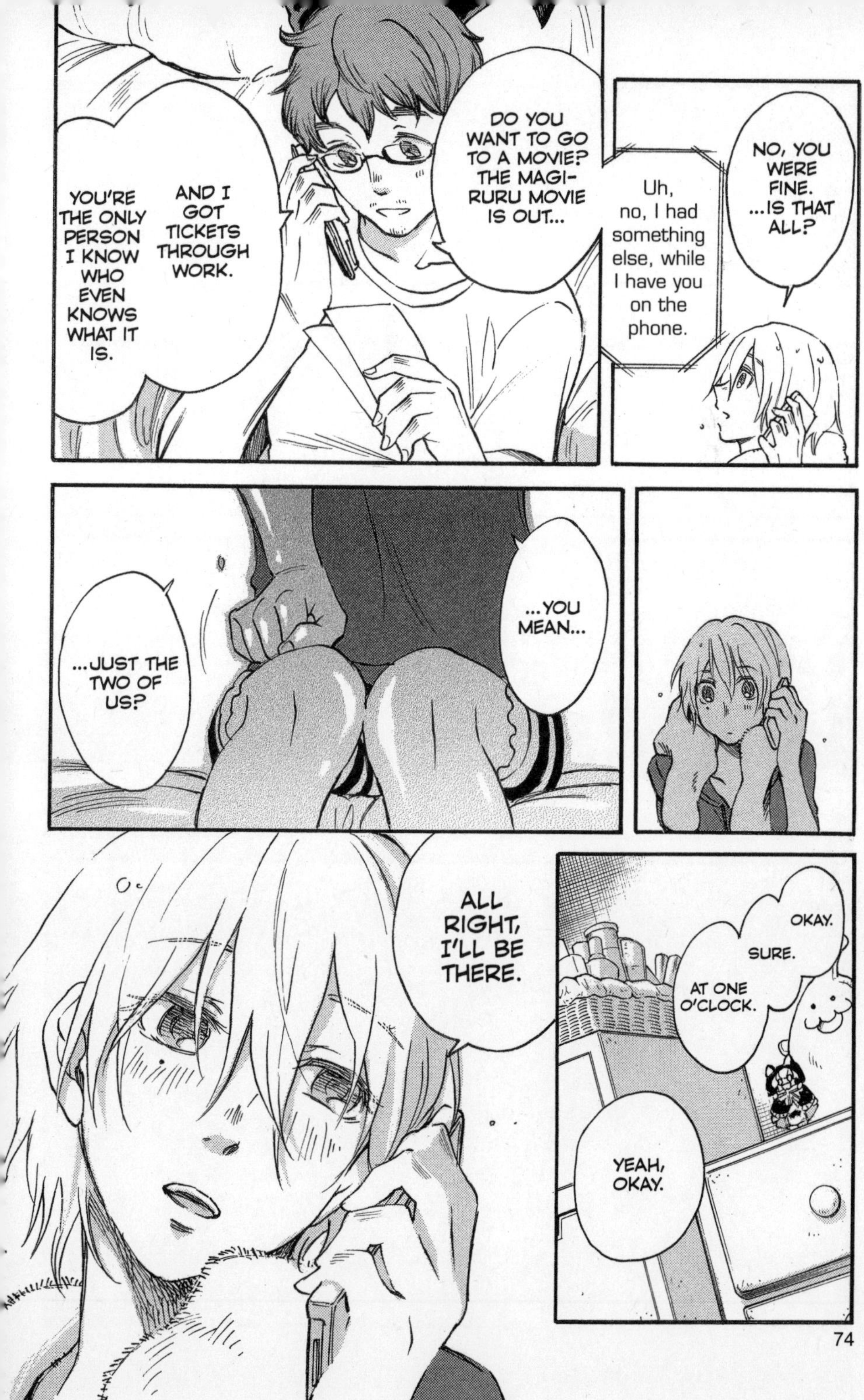
NO, YOU WERE FINE. ...IS THAT ALL?
Uh, no, I had something else, while I have you on the phone.
DO YOU WANT TO GO TO A MOVIE? THE MAGI-RURU MOVIE IS OUT...
AND I GOT TICKETS THROUGH WORK.
YOU'RE THE ONLY PERSON I KNOW WHO EVEN KNOWS WHAT IT IS.
...YOU MEAN...
...JUST THE TWO OF US?
OKAY.
SURE.
AT ONE O'CLOCK.
YEAH, OKAY.
ALL RIGHT, I'LL BE THERE.

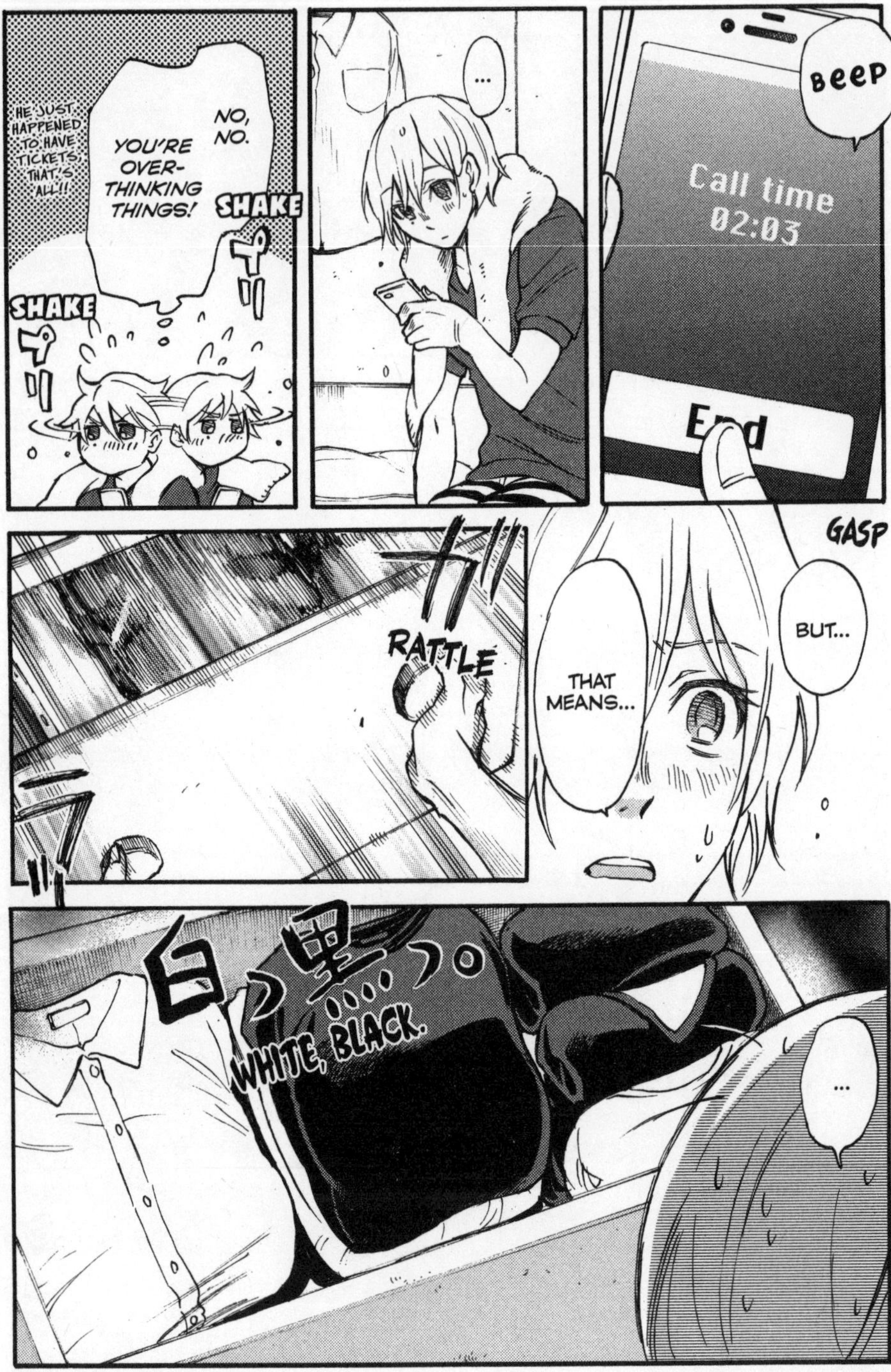
Beep
Call time
02:03
End
...
NO, NO.
YOU'RE OVER-THINKING THINGS!
HE JUST HAPPENED TO HAVE TICKETS, THAT'S ALL!!
SHAKE
SHAKE
GASP
BUT...
THAT MEANS...
RATTLE
白っ黒っ。
WHITE, BLACK.
...

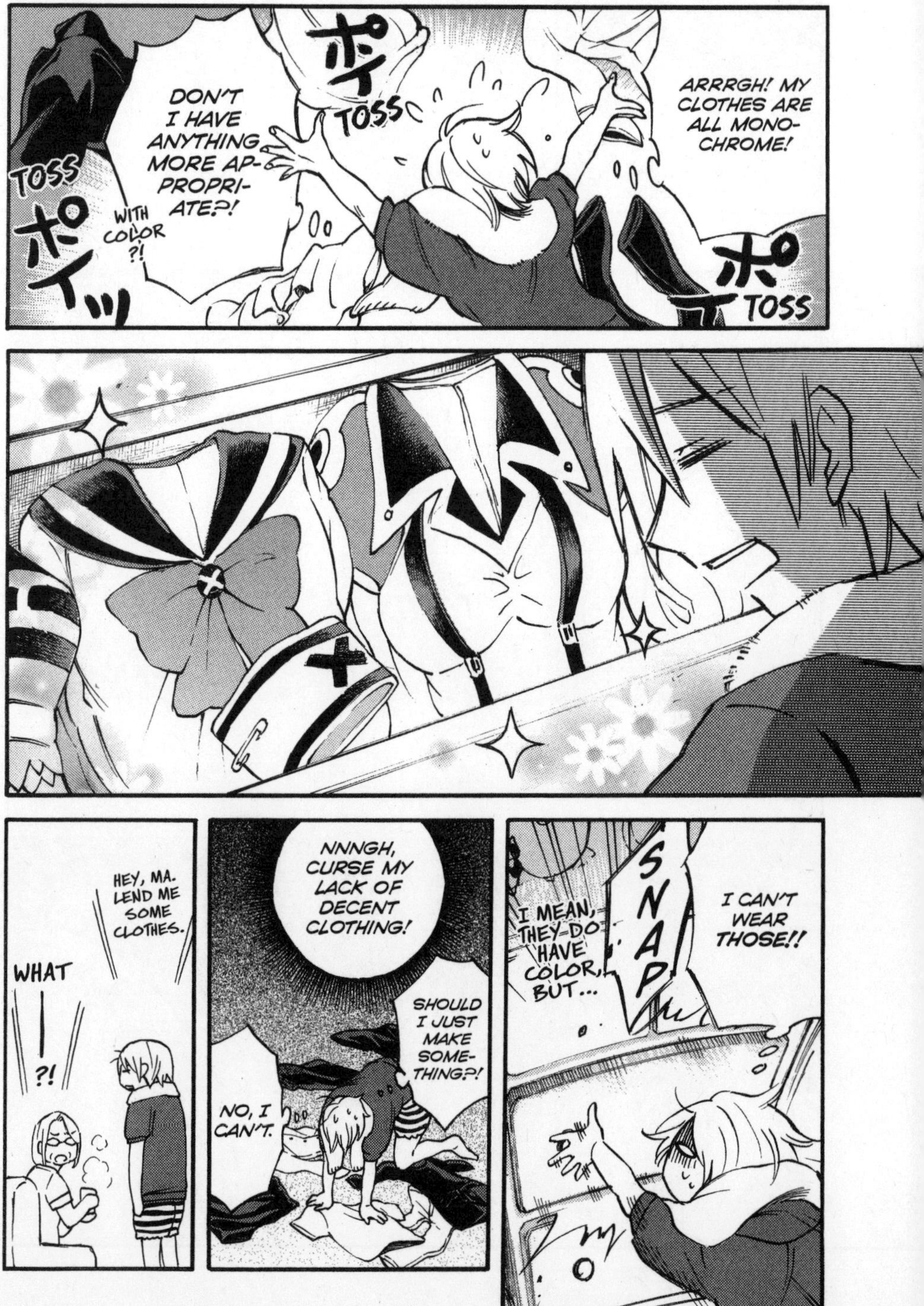
ARRRGH! MY CLOTHES ARE ALL MONO-CHROME!
ポイ
TOSS
DON'T I HAVE ANYTHING MORE AP-PROPRI-ATE?!
WITH COLOR ?!
TOSS
ポイッ
ポ
TOSS
I CAN'T WEAR THOSE!!
SNAP
I MEAN, THEY DO HAVE COLOR, BUT...
NNNGH, CURSE MY LACK OF DECENT CLOTHING!
SHOULD I JUST MAKE SOME-THING?!
NO, I CAN'T.
HEY, MA. LEND ME SOME CLOTHES.
WHAT —?!

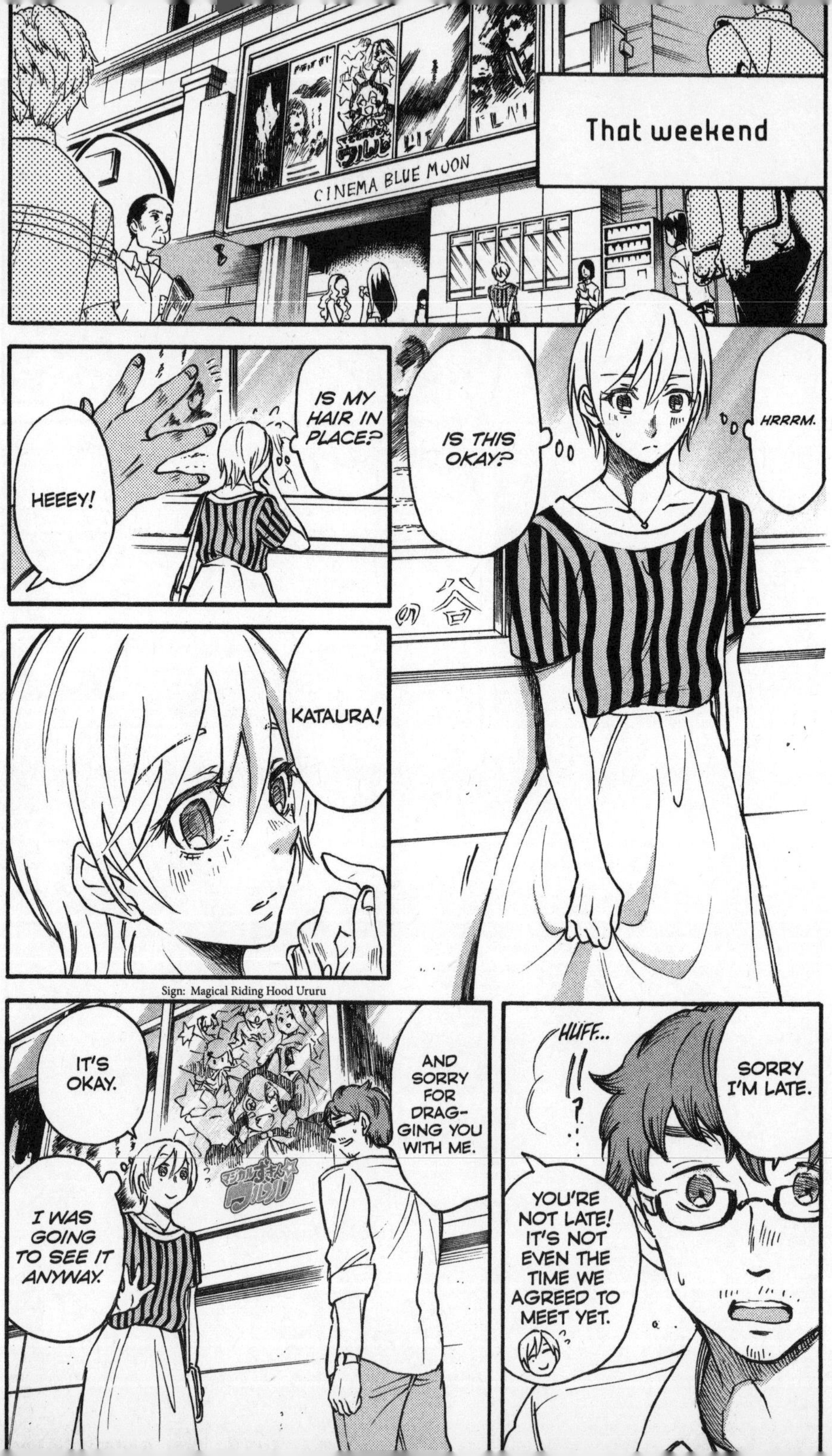
That weekend
CINEMA BLUE MOON
HRRRM.
IS THIS OKAY?
IS MY HAIR IN PLACE?
HEEEY!
KATAURA!
HUFF...
SORRY I'M LATE.
YOU'RE NOT LATE! IT'S NOT EVEN THE TIME WE AGREED TO MEET YET.
AND SORRY FOR DRAG-GING YOU WITH ME.
IT'S OKAY.
I WAS GOING TO SEE IT ANYWAY.
Sign: Magical Riding Hood Ururu

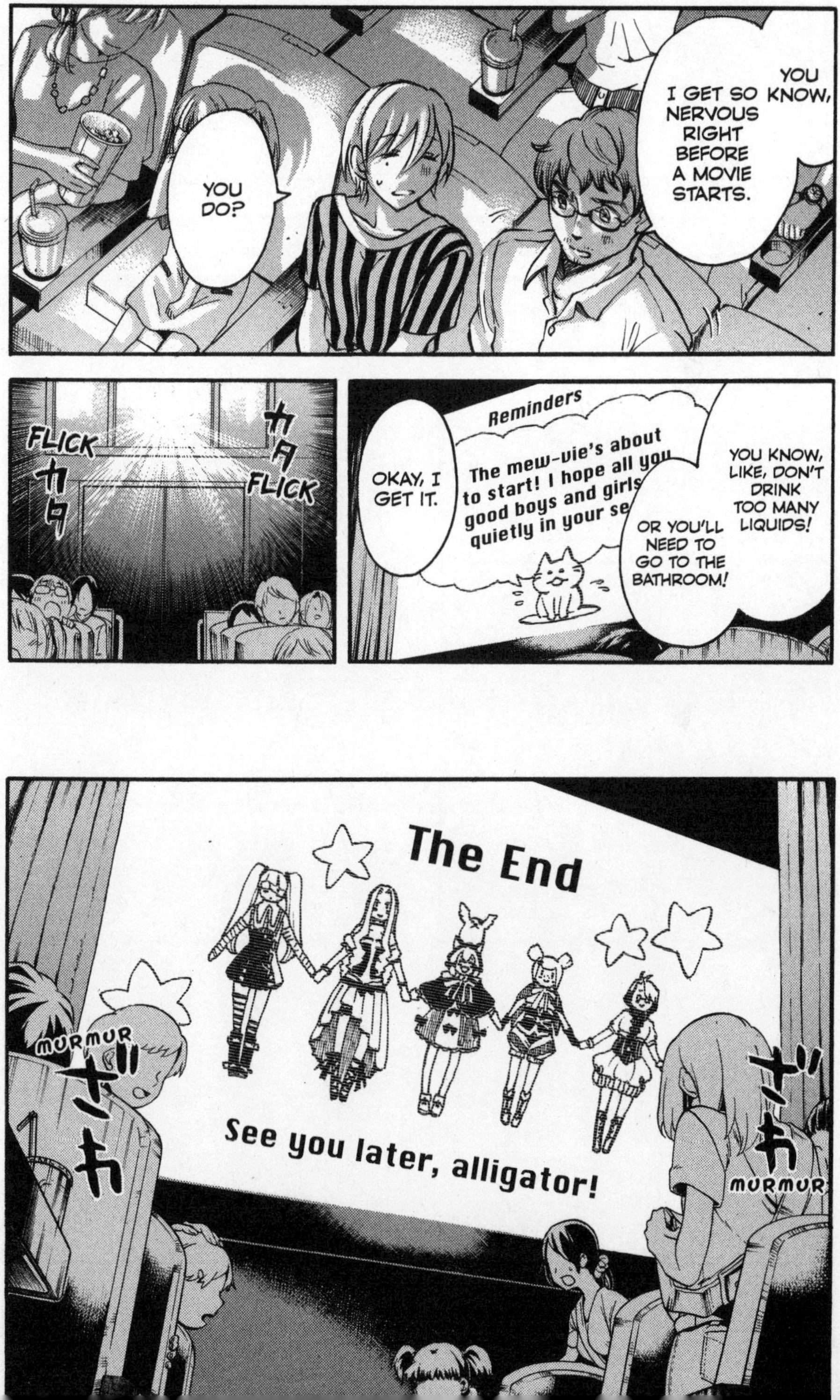
YOU KNOW, I GET SO NERVOUS RIGHT BEFORE A MOVIE STARTS.
YOU DO?
YOU KNOW, LIKE, DON'T DRINK TOO MANY LIQUIDS!
OR YOU'LL NEED TO GO TO THE BATHROOM!
Reminders
The mew-vie's about to start! I hope all you good boys and girls quietly in your se
OKAY, I GET IT.
カタ
FLICK
カタ
FLICK
The End
See you later, alligator!
ざわ
MURMUR
ざわ
MURMUR

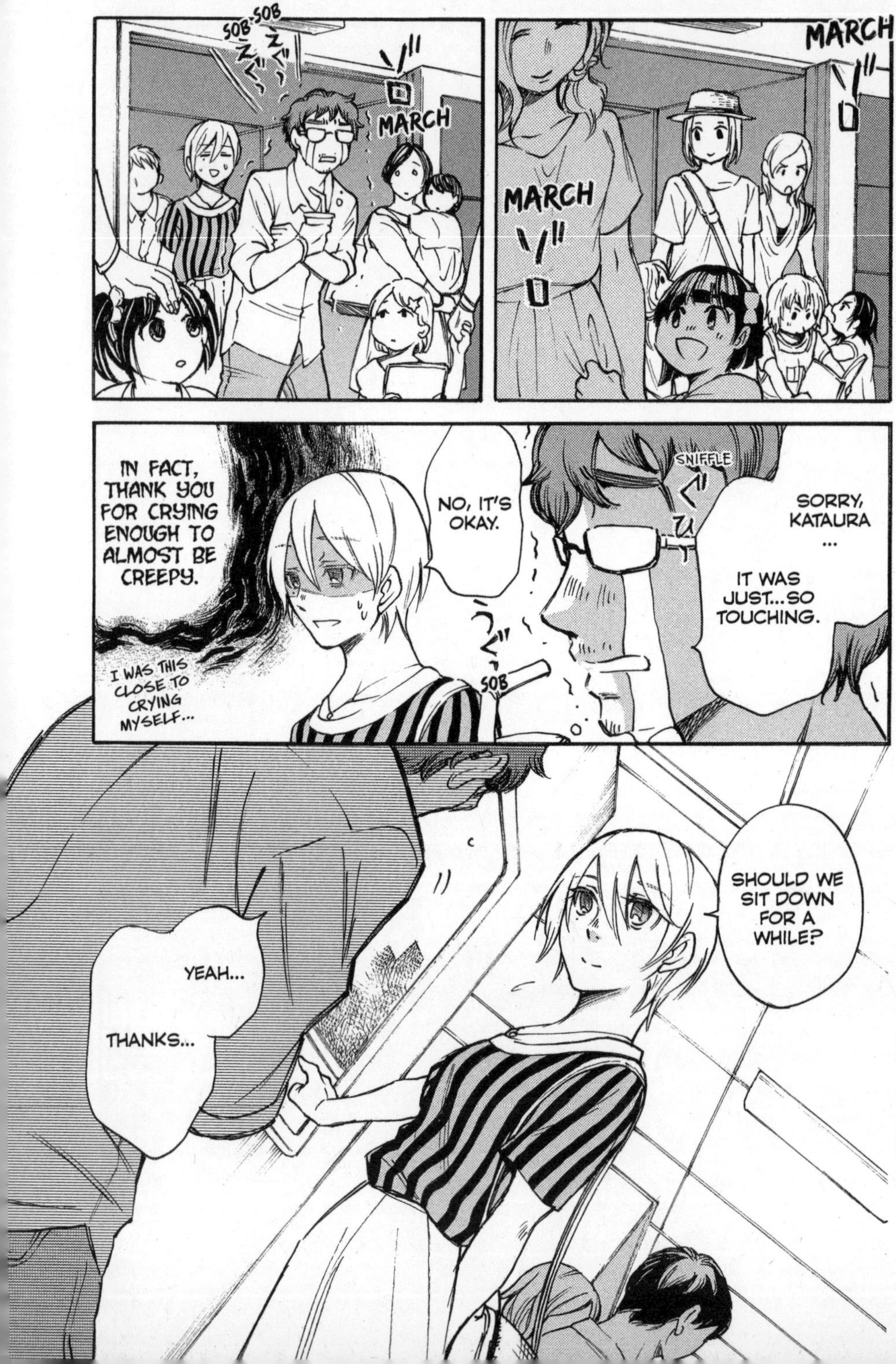
MARCH
MARCH
SOB SOB
MARCH
SNIFFLE
SORRY, KATAURA...
IT WAS JUST...SO TOUCHING.
NO, IT'S OKAY.
SOB
IN FACT, THANK YOU FOR CRYING ENOUGH TO ALMOST BE CREEPY.
I WAS THIS CLOSE TO CRYING MYSELF...
SHOULD WE SIT DOWN FOR A WHILE?
YEAH...
THANKS...

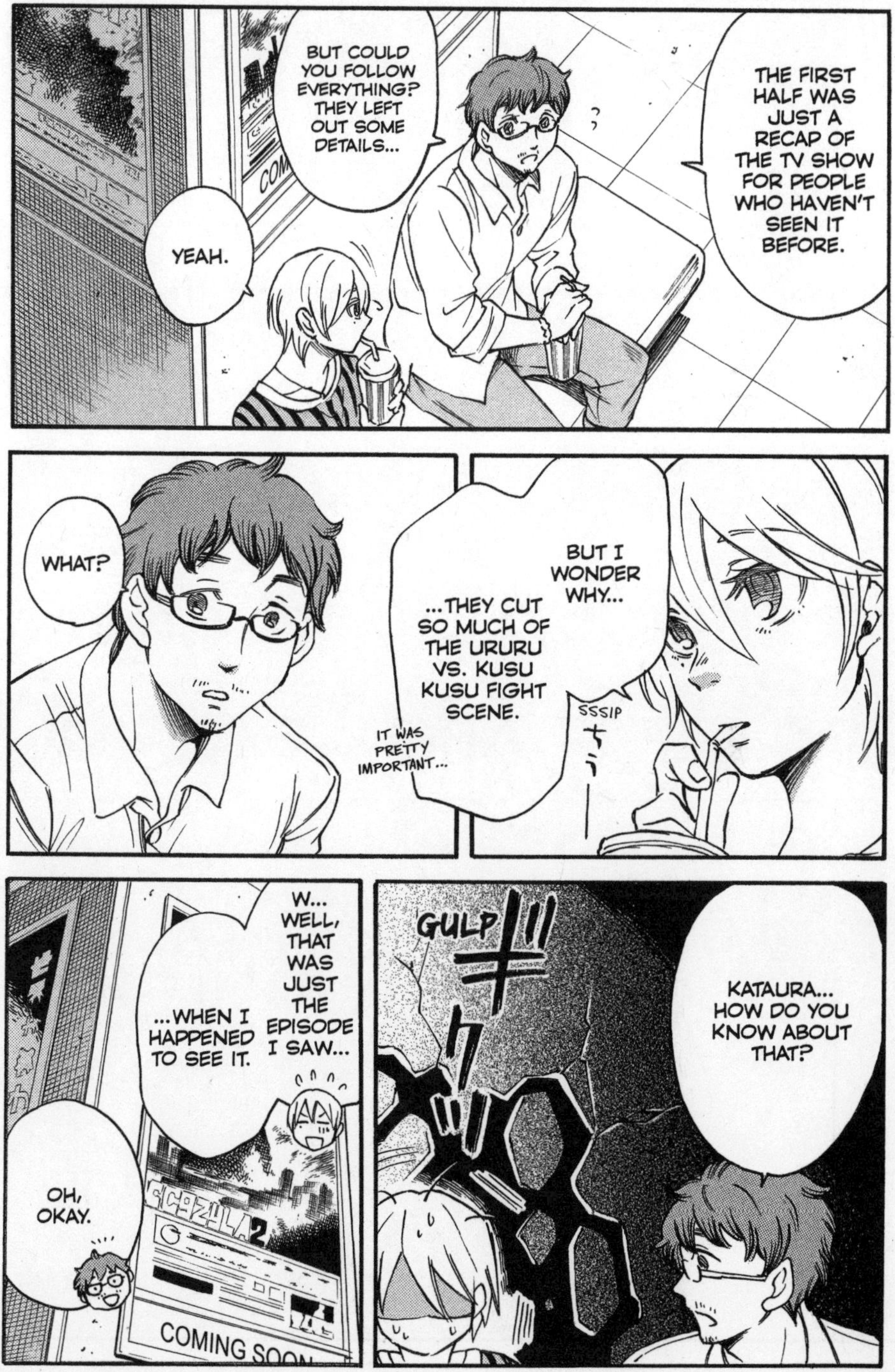
THE FIRST HALF WAS JUST A RECAP OF THE TV SHOW FOR PEOPLE WHO HAVEN'T SEEN IT BEFORE.
BUT COULD YOU FOLLOW EVERYTHING? THEY LEFT OUT SOME DETAILS...
YEAH.
BUT I WONDER WHY...
...THEY CUT SO MUCH OF THE URURU VS. KUSU KUSU FIGHT SCENE.
SSSIP
IT WAS PRETTY IMPORTANT...
WHAT?
KATAURA... HOW DO YOU KNOW ABOUT THAT?
GULP
W... WELL, THAT WAS JUST THE EPISODE I SAW...
...WHEN I HAPPENED TO SEE IT.
OH, OKAY.
COMING SOON

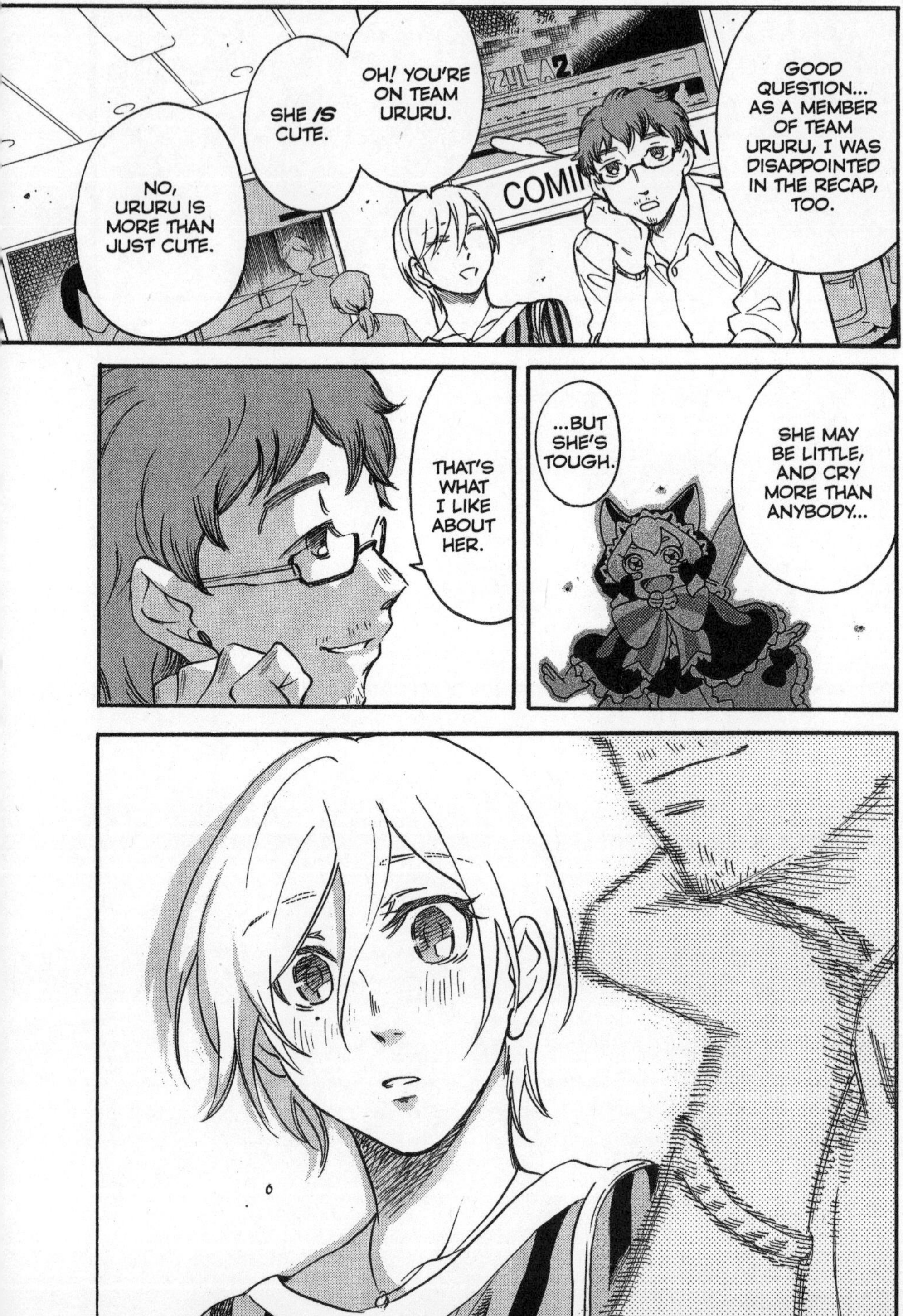
GOOD QUESTION... AS A MEMBER OF TEAM URURU, I WAS DISAPPOINTED IN THE RECAP, TOO.
OH! YOU'RE ON TEAM URURU.
SHE *IS* CUTE.
NO, URURU IS MORE THAN JUST CUTE.
SHE MAY BE LITTLE, AND CRY MORE THAN ANYBODY...
...BUT SHE'S TOUGH.
THAT'S WHAT I LIKE ABOUT HER.

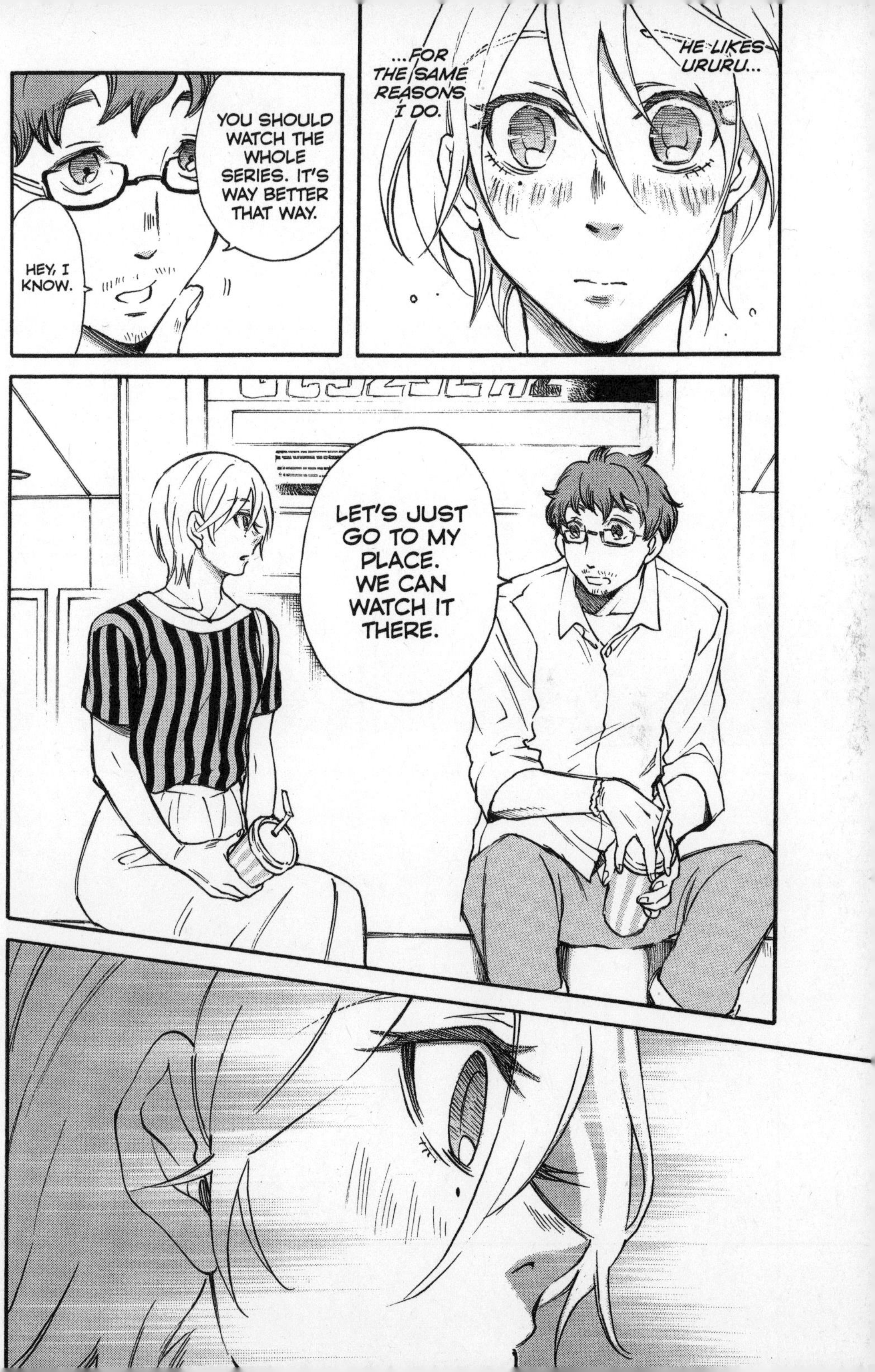
HE LIKES URURU...
...FOR THE SAME REASONS I DO.
YOU SHOULD WATCH THE WHOLE SERIES. IT'S WAY BETTER THAT WAY.
HEY, I KNOW.
LET'S JUST GO TO MY PLACE. WE CAN WATCH IT THERE.

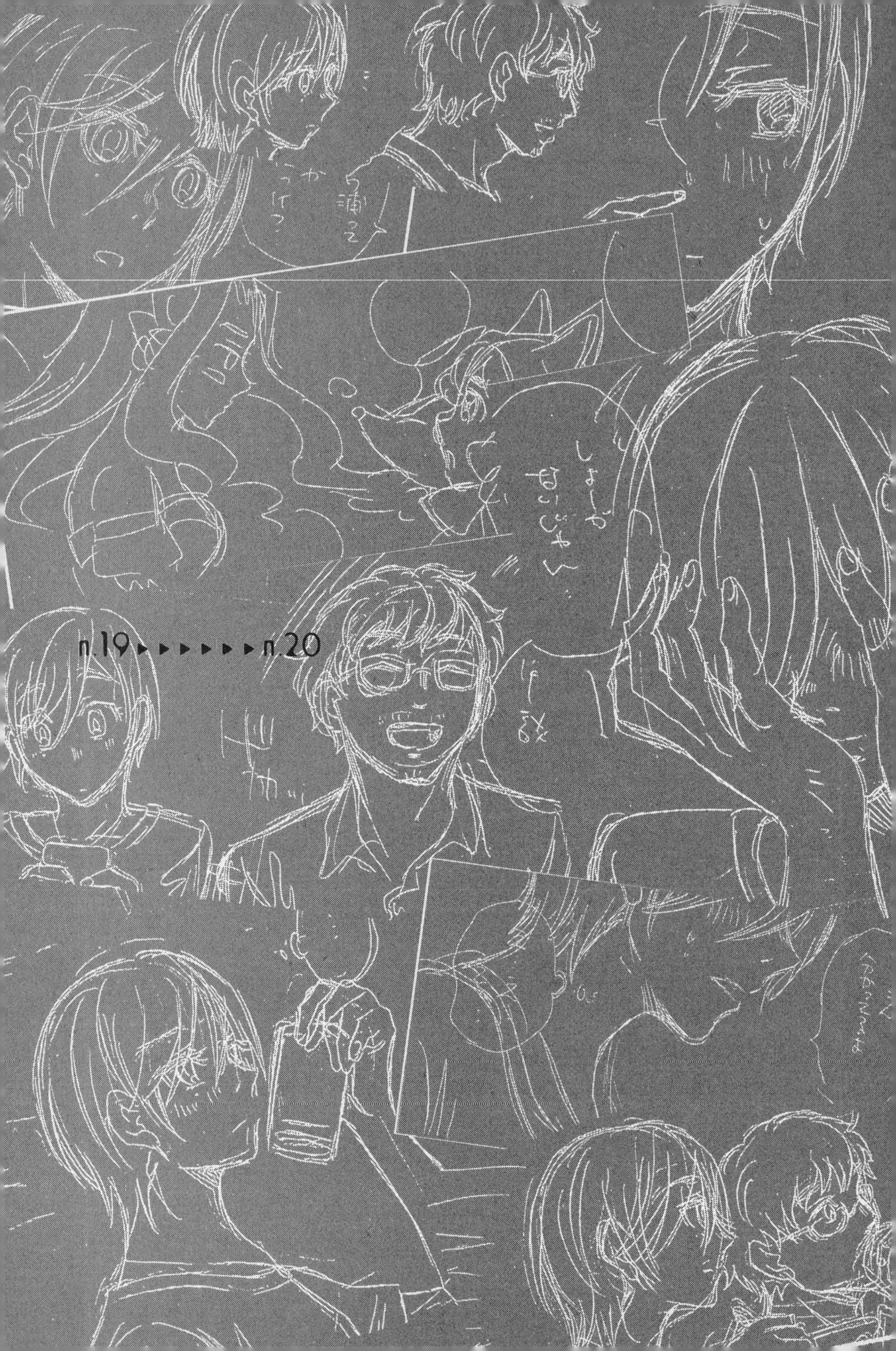
n.19 ▸▸▸▸▸▸▸ n.20

MIKU & FRIENDS COLLABORATION ❸

鏡音リン・レン
KAGAMINE RIN / LEN

LEN × AYA KURIHARA

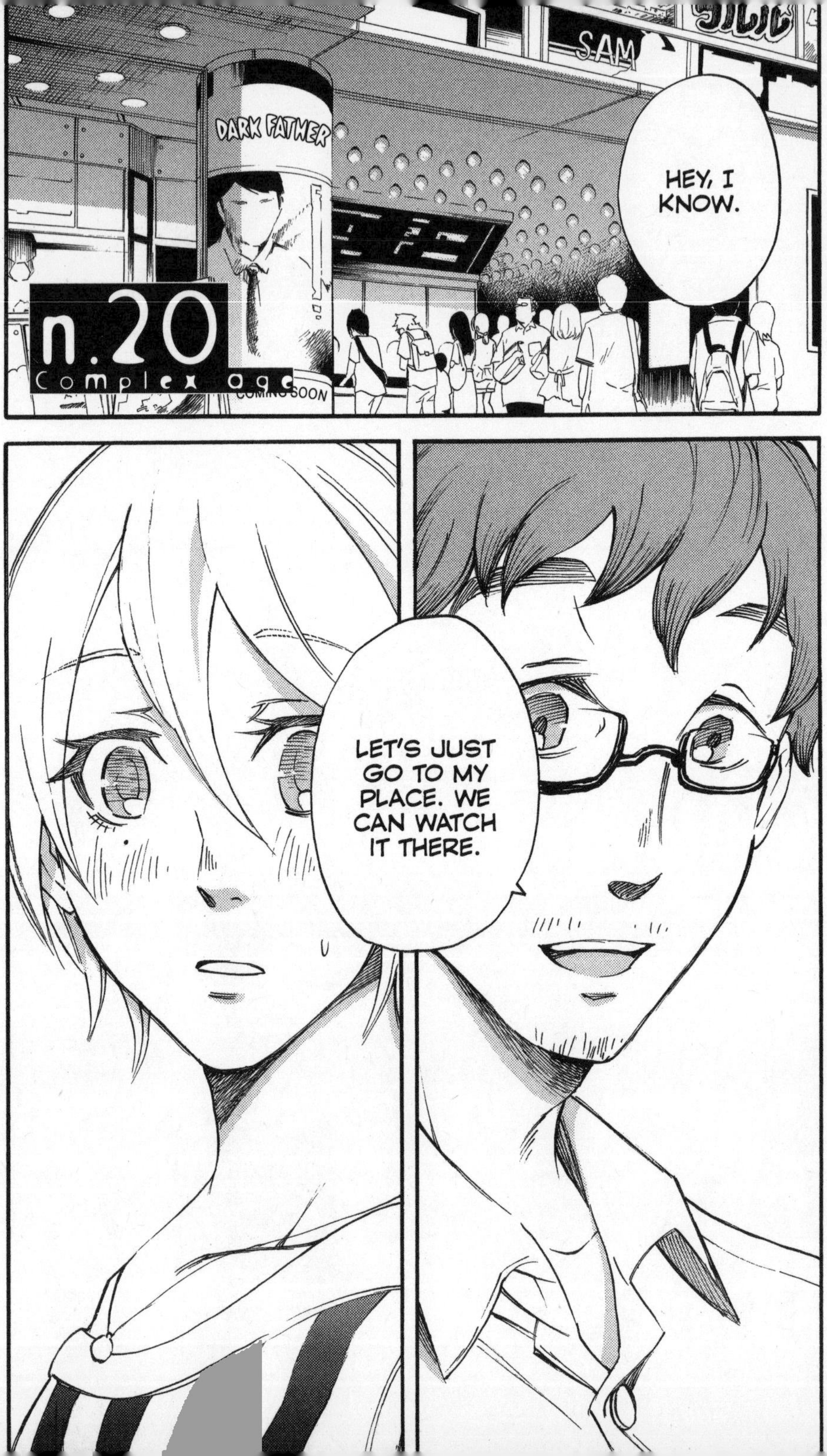
SAM
DARK FATHER
HEY, I KNOW.
n.20
Complex age
COMING SOON
LET'S JUST GO TO MY PLACE. WE CAN WATCH IT THERE.

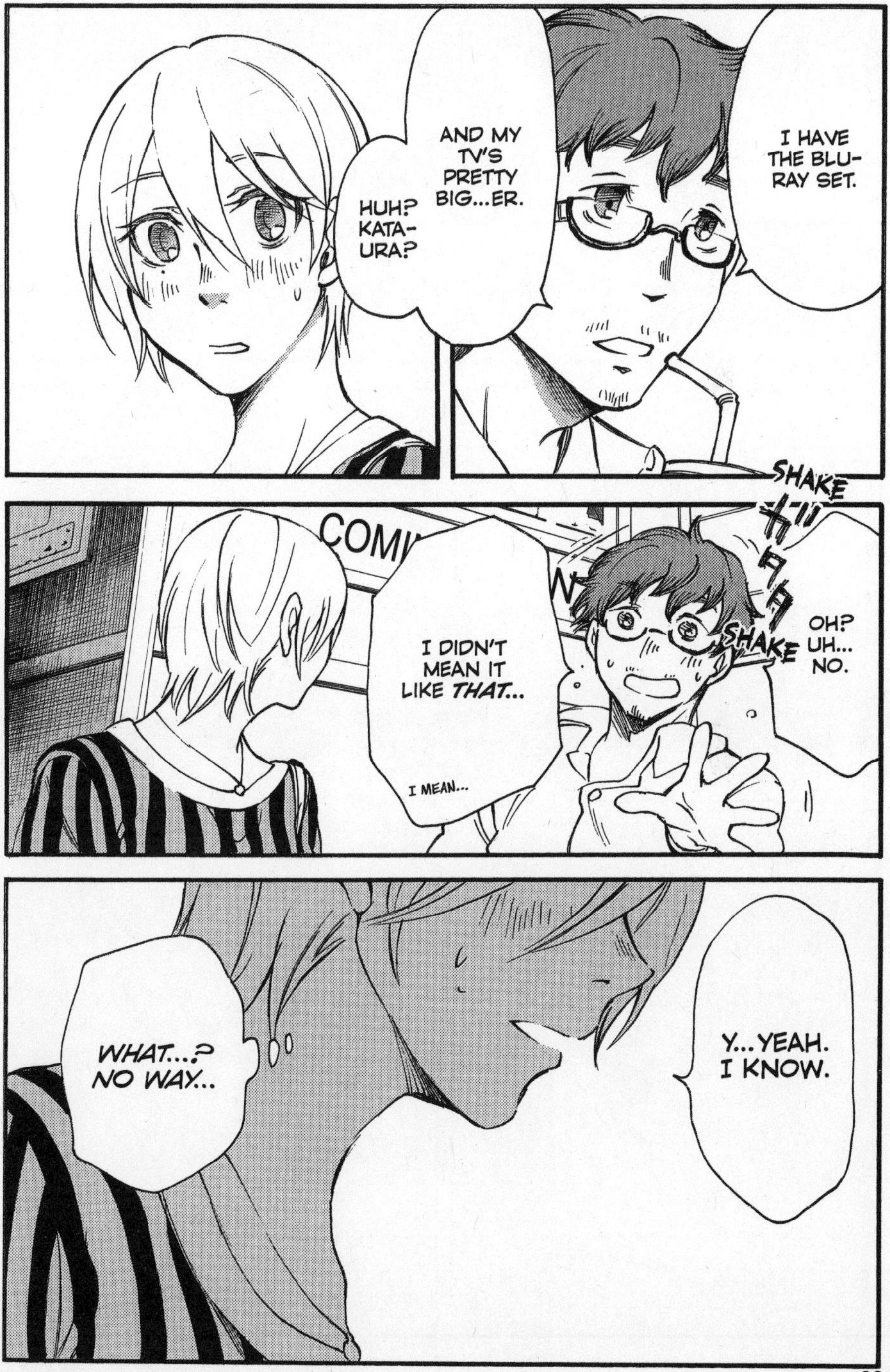
I HAVE THE BLU-RAY SET.
AND MY TV'S PRETTY BIG...ER.
HUH? KATA-URA?
SHAKE
SHAKE
OH? UH... NO.
I DIDN'T MEAN IT LIKE *THAT*...
I MEAN...
Y...YEAH. I KNOW.
WHAT...? NO WAY...

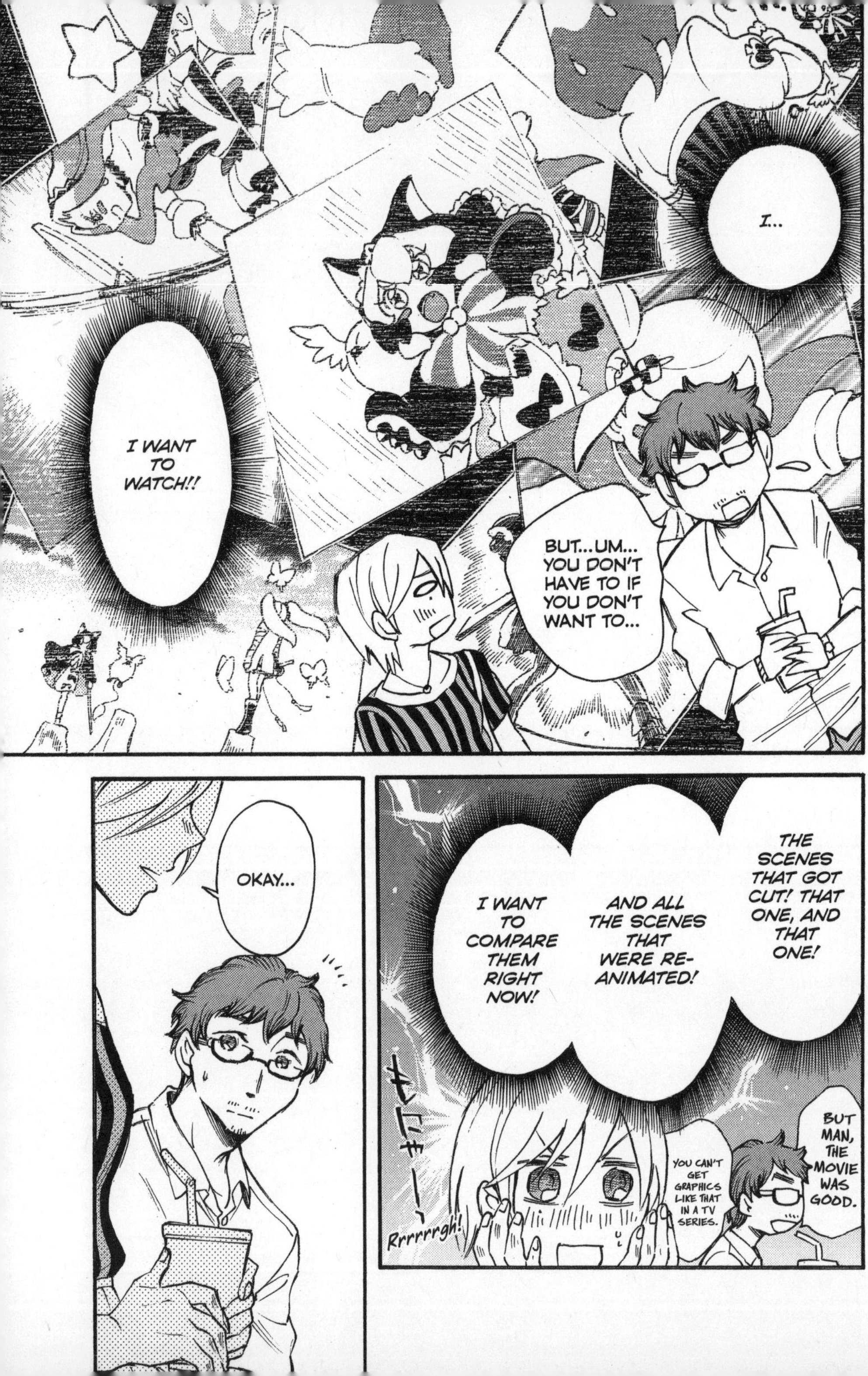
I...
I WANT TO WATCH!!
BUT...UM... YOU DON'T HAVE TO IF YOU DON'T WANT TO...
THE SCENES THAT GOT CUT! THAT ONE, AND THAT ONE!
AND ALL THE SCENES THAT WERE RE-ANIMATED!
I WANT TO COMPARE THEM RIGHT NOW!
BUT MAN, THE MOVIE WAS GOOD.
YOU CAN'T GET GRAPHICS LIKE THAT IN A TV SERIES.
Rrrrrrgh!
OKAY...

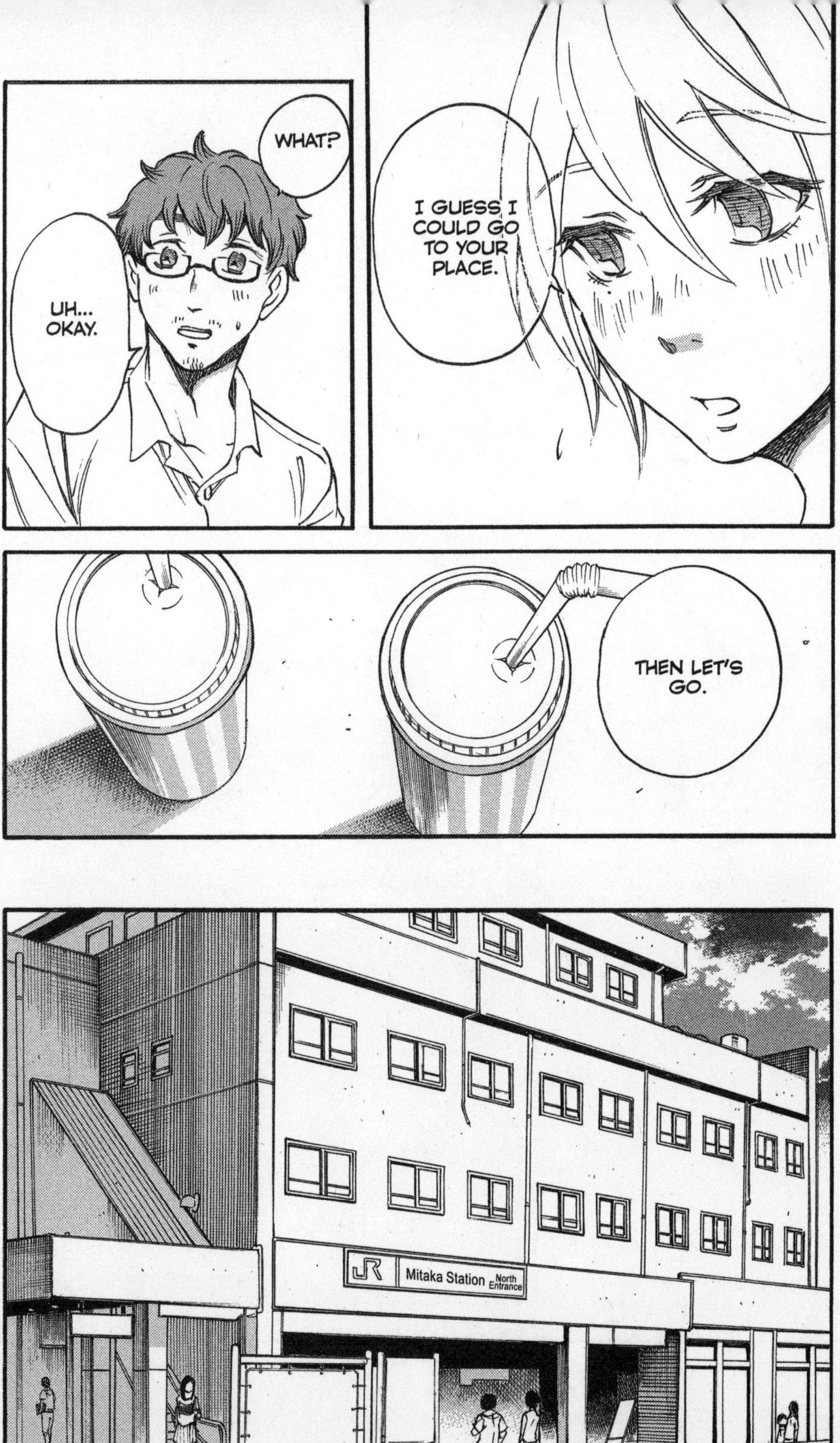
I GUESS I COULD GO TO YOUR PLACE.
WHAT?
UH... OKAY.
THEN LET'S GO.
JR
Mitaka Station North Entrance

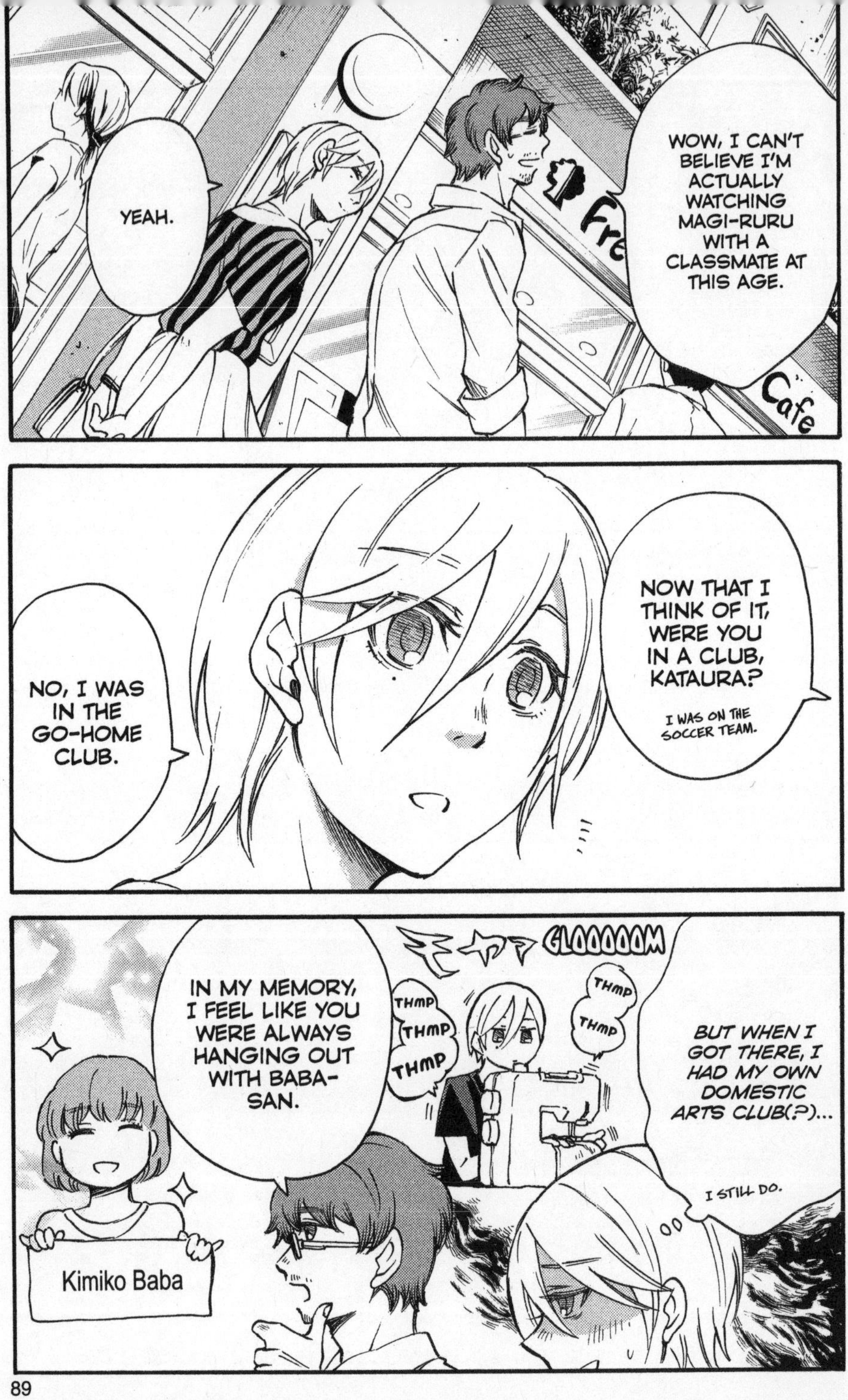
WOW, I CAN'T BELIEVE I'M ACTUALLY WATCHING MAGI-RURU WITH A CLASSMATE AT THIS AGE.
Fre
Cafe
YEAH.
NOW THAT I THINK OF IT, WERE YOU IN A CLUB, KATAURA?
I WAS ON THE SOCCER TEAM.
NO, I WAS IN THE GO-HOME CLUB.
BUT WHEN I GOT THERE, I HAD MY OWN DOMESTIC ARTS CLUB(?)...
I STILL DO.
GLOOOOOM
THMP
THMP
THMP
THMP
THMP
IN MY MEMORY, I FEEL LIKE YOU WERE ALWAYS HANGING OUT WITH BABA-SAN.
Kimiko Baba

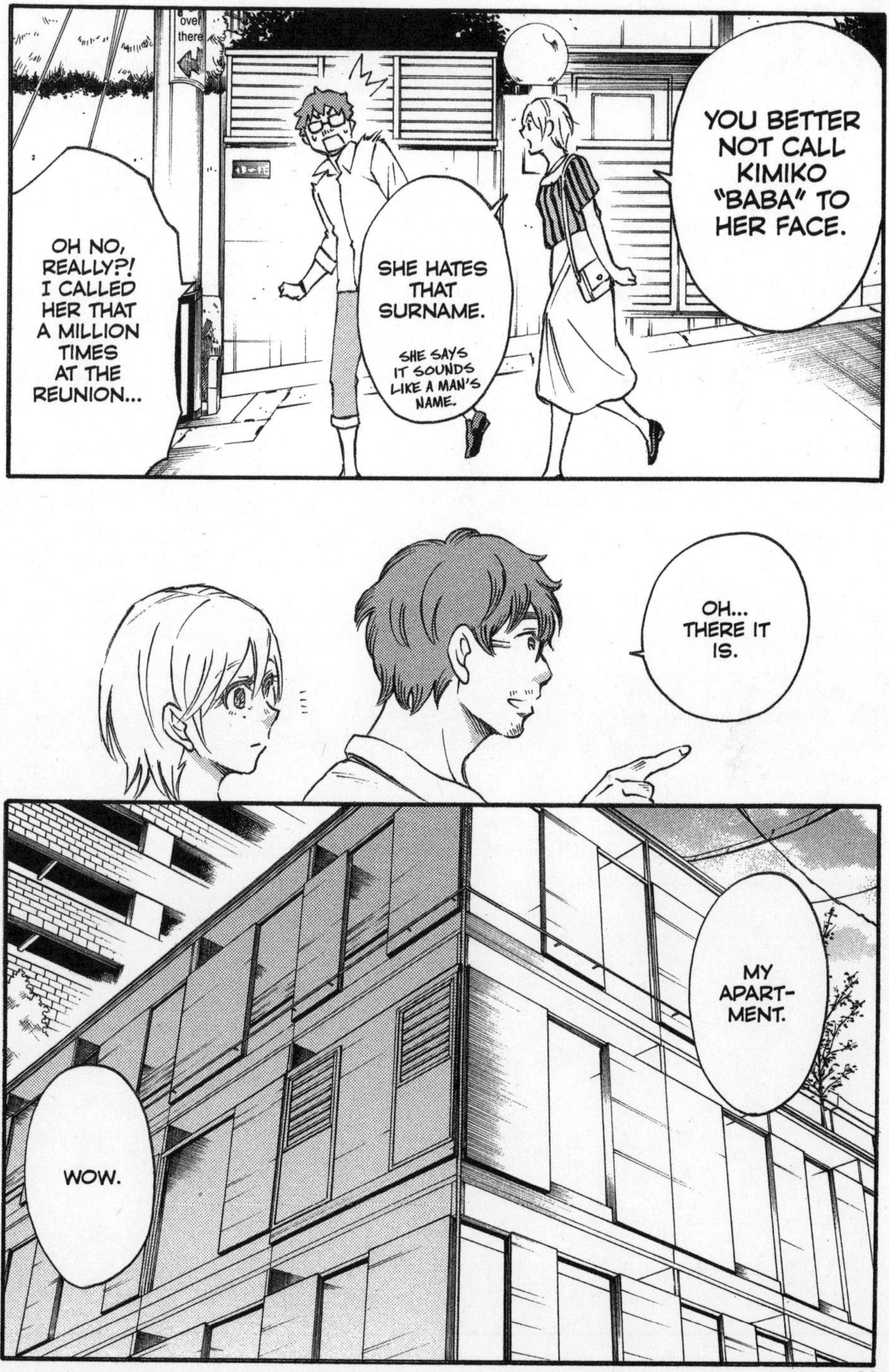
over there
YOU BETTER NOT CALL KIMIKO "BABA" TO HER FACE.
SHE HATES THAT SURNAME.
SHE SAYS IT SOUNDS LIKE A MAN'S NAME.
OH NO, REALLY?! I CALLED HER THAT A MILLION TIMES AT THE REUNION...
OH... THERE IT IS.
MY APARTMENT.
WOW.

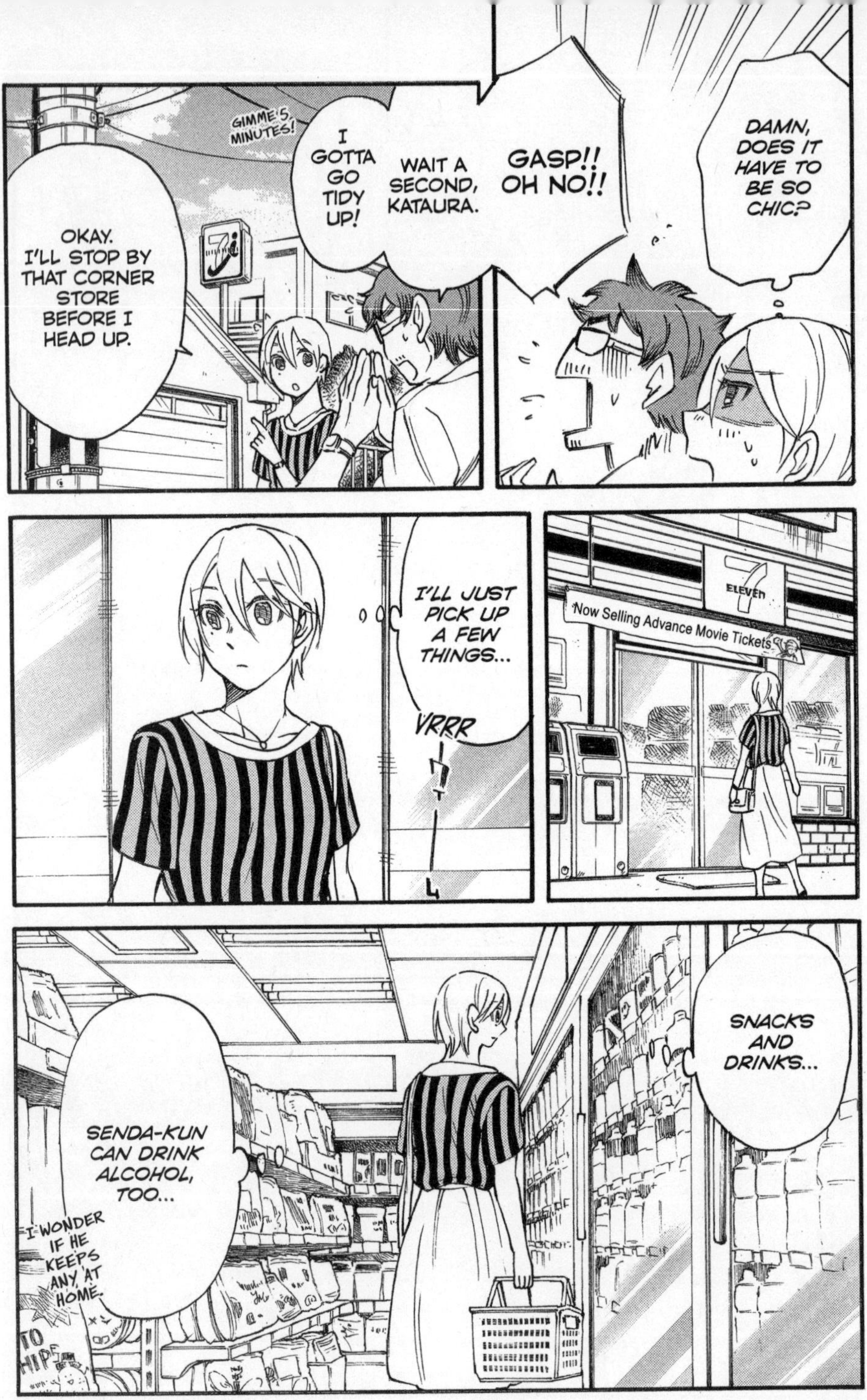
GASP!! OH NO!!
DAMN, DOES IT HAVE TO BE SO CHIC?
WAIT A SECOND, KATAURA.
I GOTTA GO TIDY UP!
GIMME 5 MINUTES!
OKAY. I'LL STOP BY THAT CORNER STORE BEFORE I HEAD UP.
7 ELEVEn
Now Selling Advance Movie Tickets
I'LL JUST PICK UP A FEW THINGS...
VRRR
SNACKS AND DRINKS...
SENDA-KUN CAN DRINK ALCOHOL, TOO...
I WONDER IF HE KEEPS ANY AT HOME.

...

SORRY TO KEEP YOU WAITING.

OH...YOU BOUGHT SOME STUFF?

YEAH, THIS AND THAT.

THANKS. I'LL TAKE THAT.

DING- DONG

WELL, IT'S NOT A BIG PLACE, BUT COME ON IN.

THANKS FOR HAVING ME.

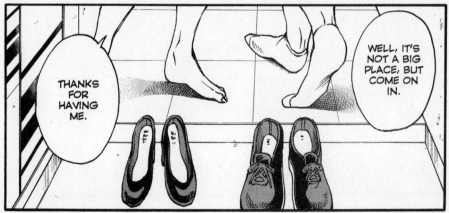

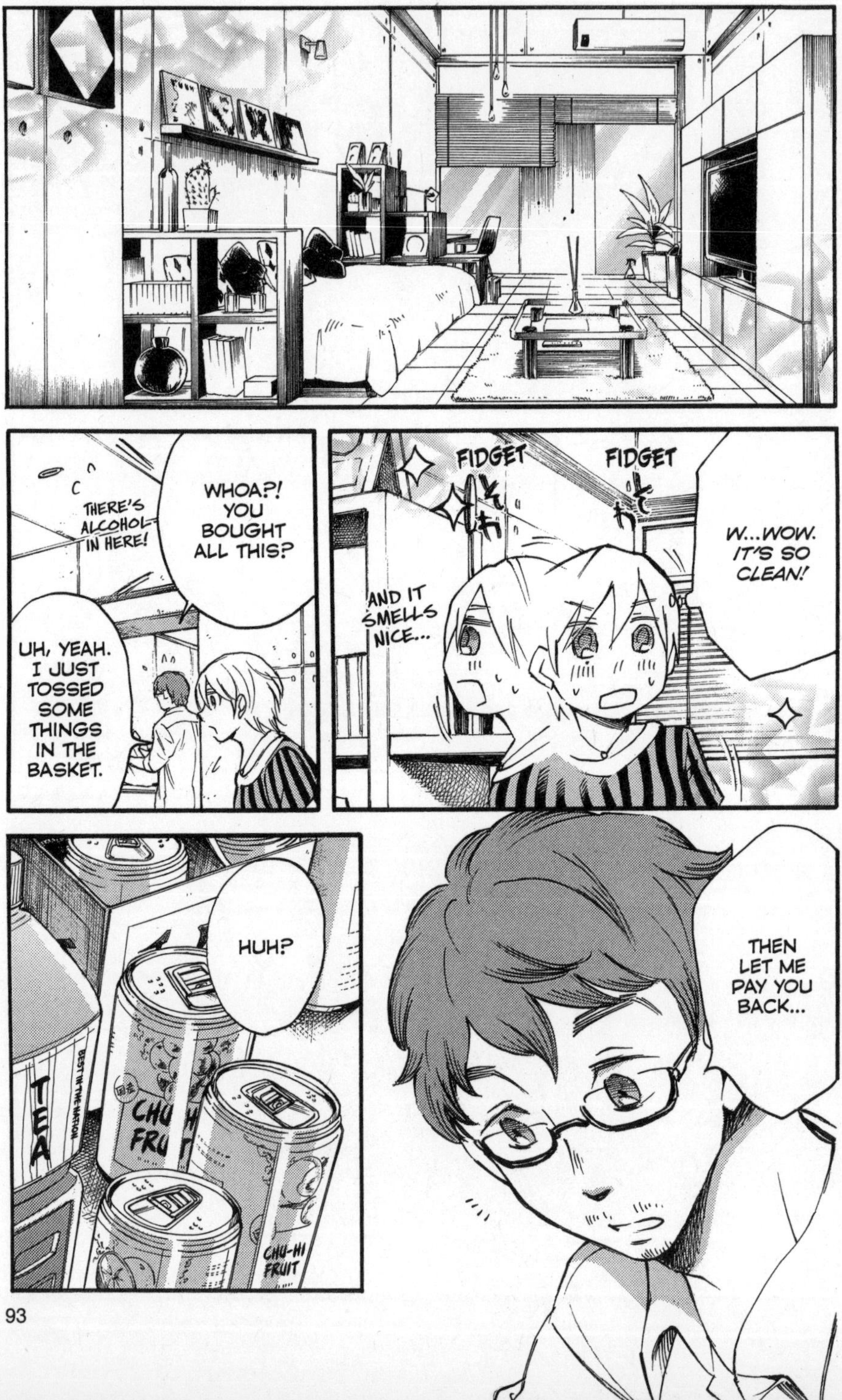
FIDGET
FIDGET
W...WOW. IT'S SO CLEAN!
AND IT SMELLS NICE...
WHOA?! YOU BOUGHT ALL THIS?
THERE'S ALCOHOL IN HERE!
UH, YEAH. I JUST TOSSED SOME THINGS IN THE BASKET.
THEN LET ME PAY YOU BACK...
HUH?
BEST IN THE NATION
TEA
CHU-HI FRUIT
CHU-HI FRUIT

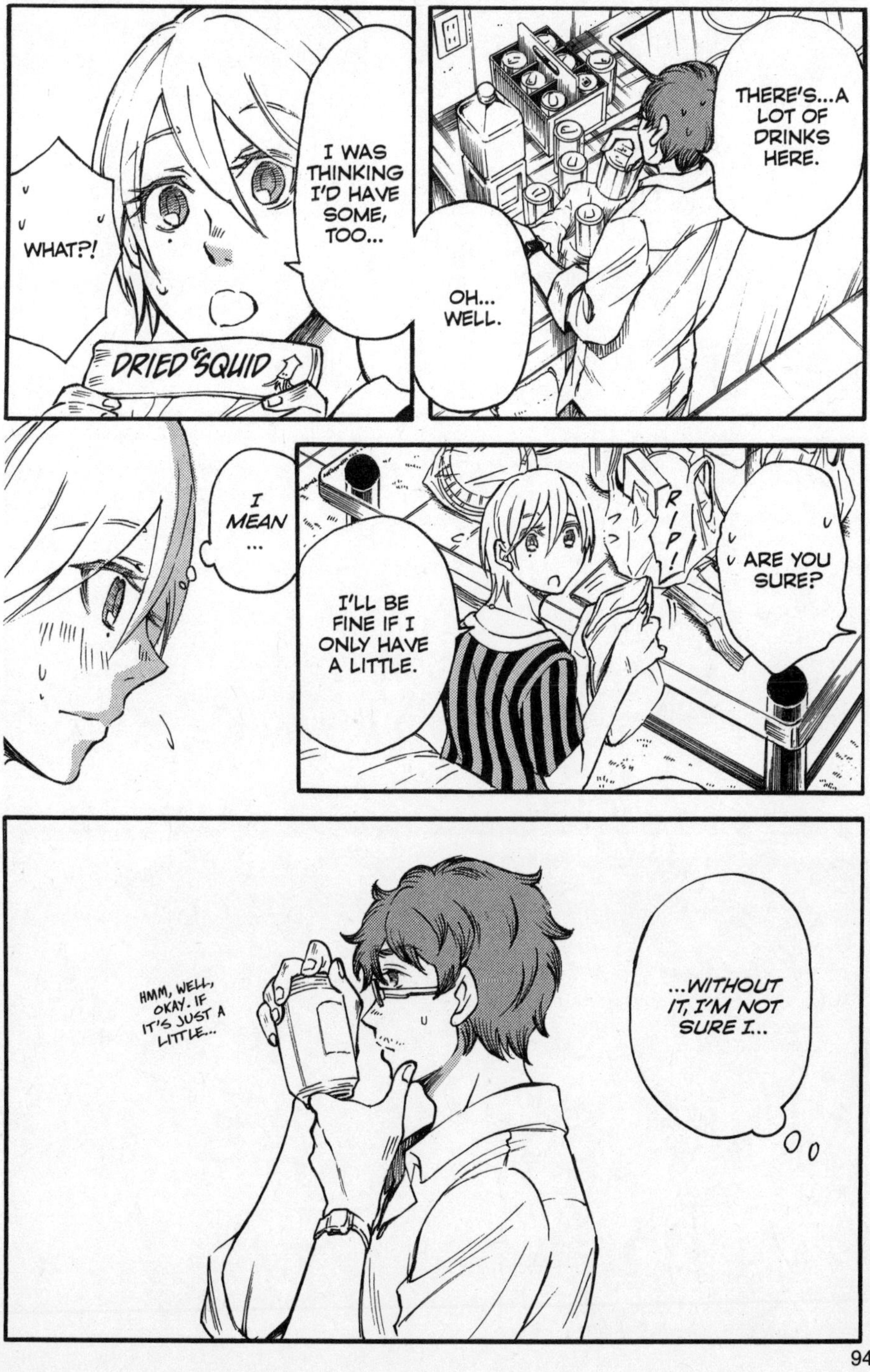
THERE'S...A LOT OF DRINKS HERE.
I WAS THINKING I'D HAVE SOME, TOO...
OH... WELL.
WHAT?!
DRIED SQUID
ARE YOU SURE?
RIP!
I MEAN ...
I'LL BE FINE IF I ONLY HAVE A LITTLE.
...WITHOUT IT, I'M NOT SURE I...
HMM, WELL, OKAY. IF IT'S JUST A LITTLE...

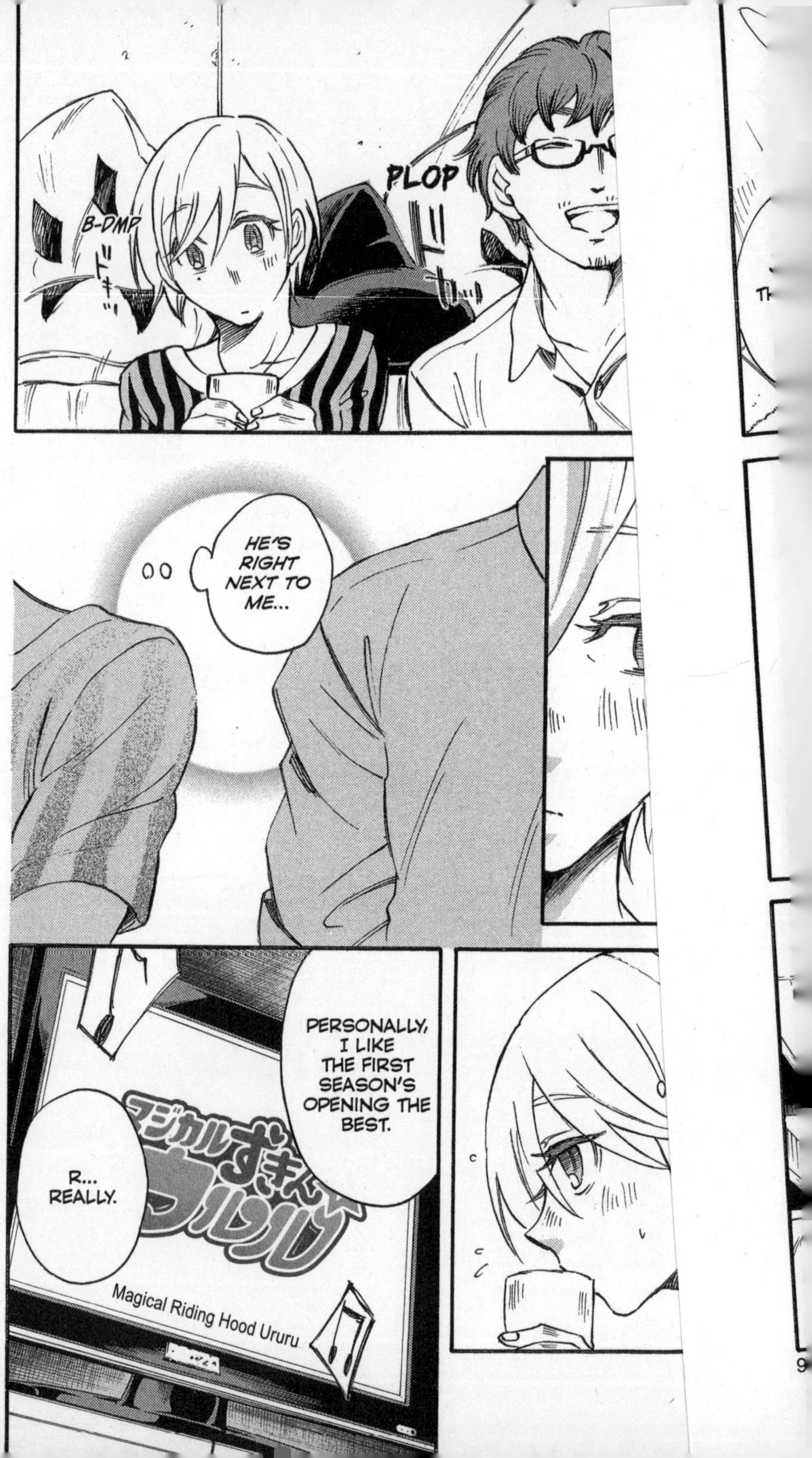
PLOP
B-DMP
HE'S RIGHT NEXT TO ME...
PERSONALLY, I LIKE THE FIRST SEASON'S OPENING THE BEST.
R... REALLY.
Magical Riding Hood Ururu

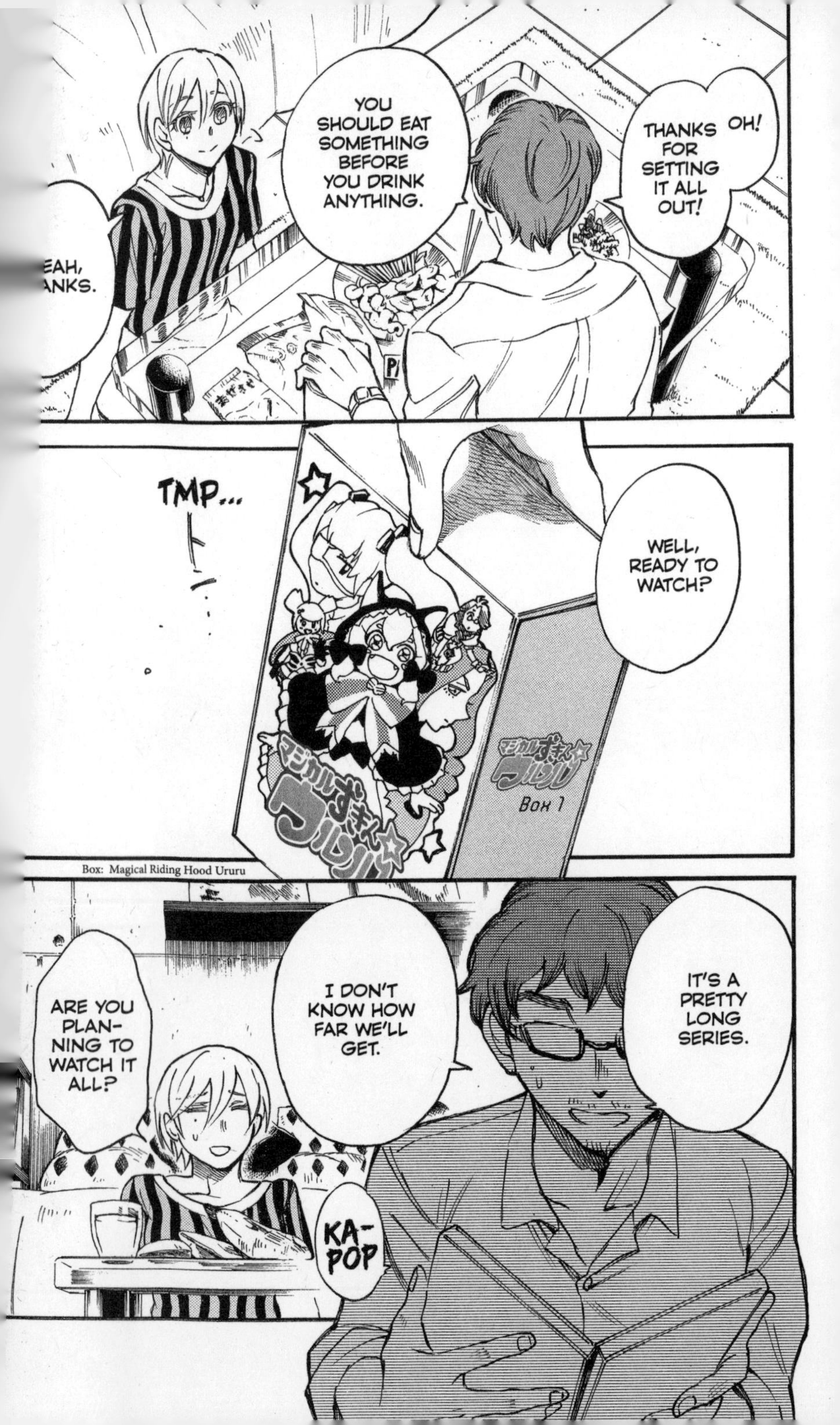
OH! THANKS FOR SETTING IT ALL OUT!
YOU SHOULD EAT SOMETHING BEFORE YOU DRINK ANYTHING.
EAH, ANKS.
WELL, READY TO WATCH?
TMP...
マジカルずきん☆ウルル
Box 1
IT'S A PRETTY LONG SERIES.
I DON'T KNOW HOW FAR WE'LL GET.
KA-POP
ARE YOU PLAN-NING TO WATCH IT ALL?

Box: Magical Riding Hood Ururu

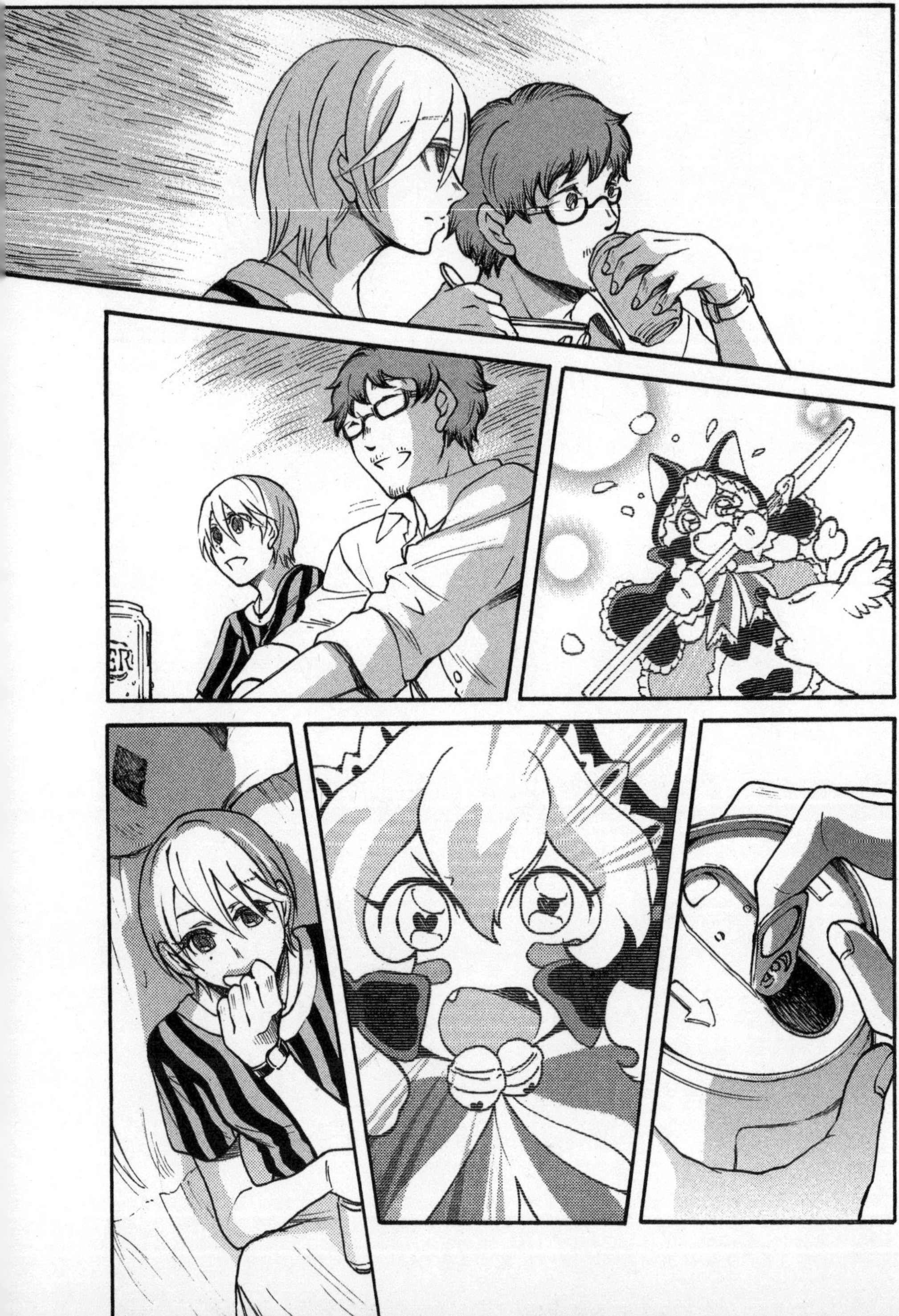

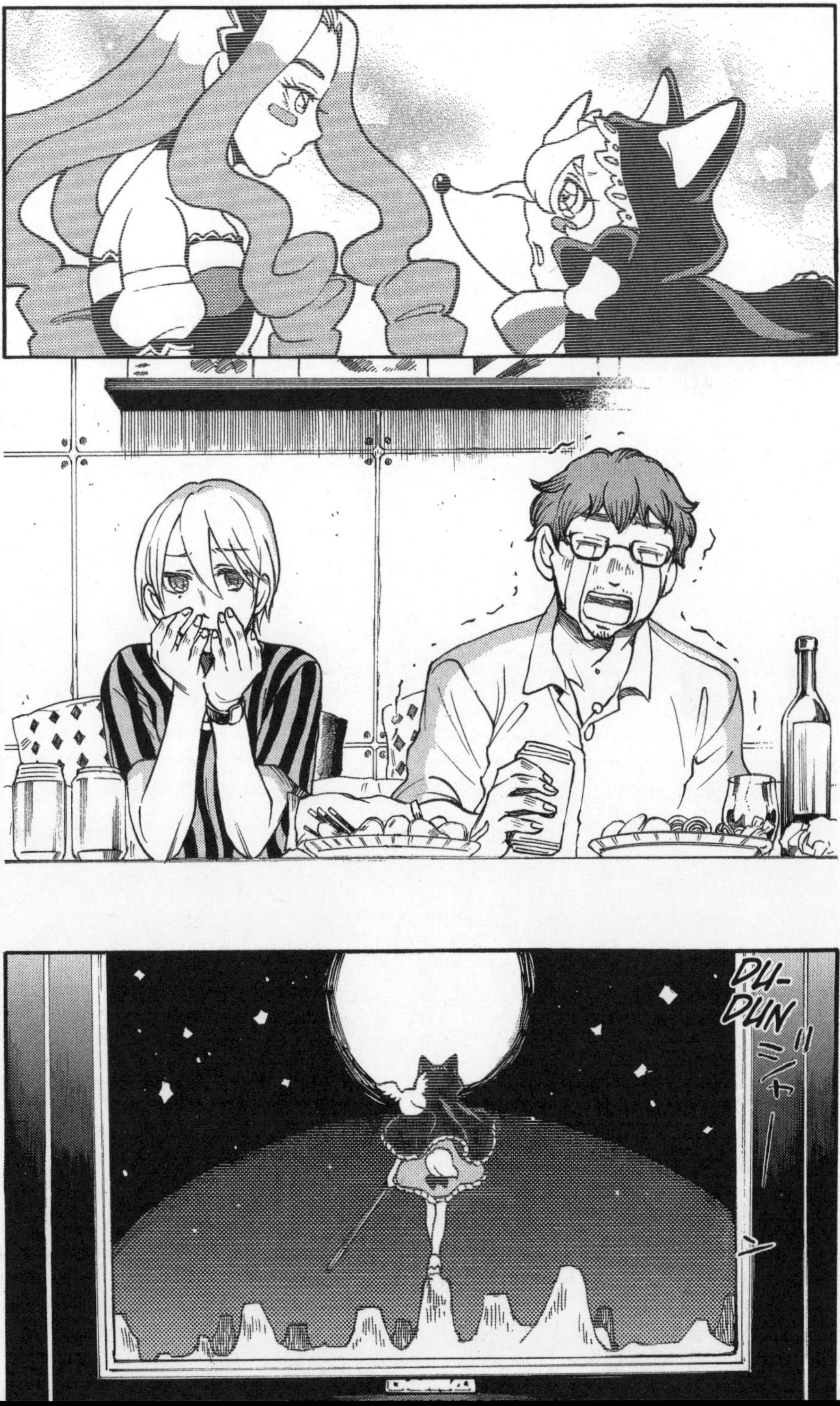
DU-DUN

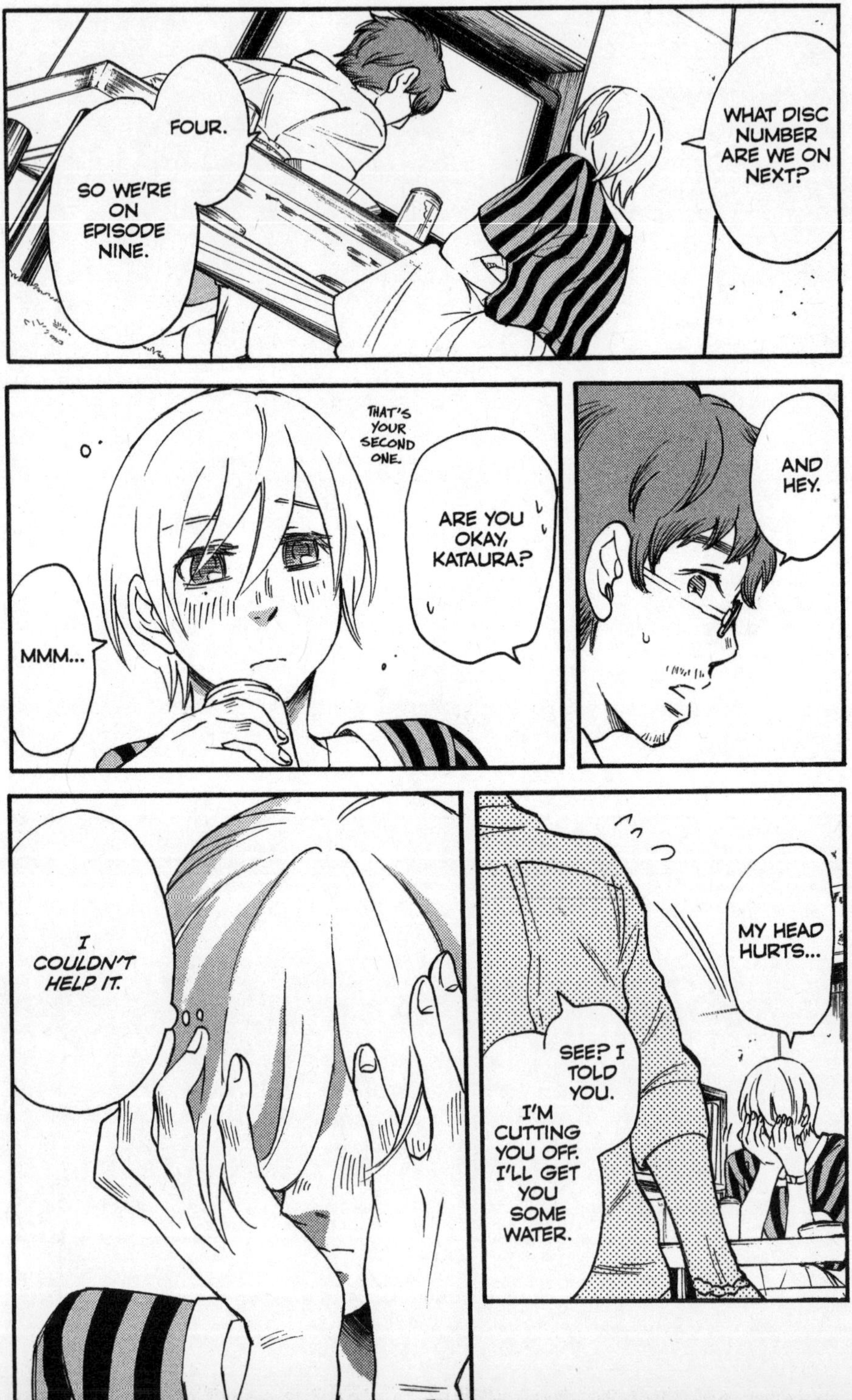
WHAT DISC NUMBER ARE WE ON NEXT?
FOUR.
SO WE'RE ON EPISODE NINE.
AND HEY.
THAT'S YOUR SECOND ONE.
ARE YOU OKAY, KATAURA?
MMM...
MY HEAD HURTS...
SEE? I TOLD YOU.
I'M CUTTING YOU OFF. I'LL GET YOU SOME WATER.
I COULDN'T HELP IT.

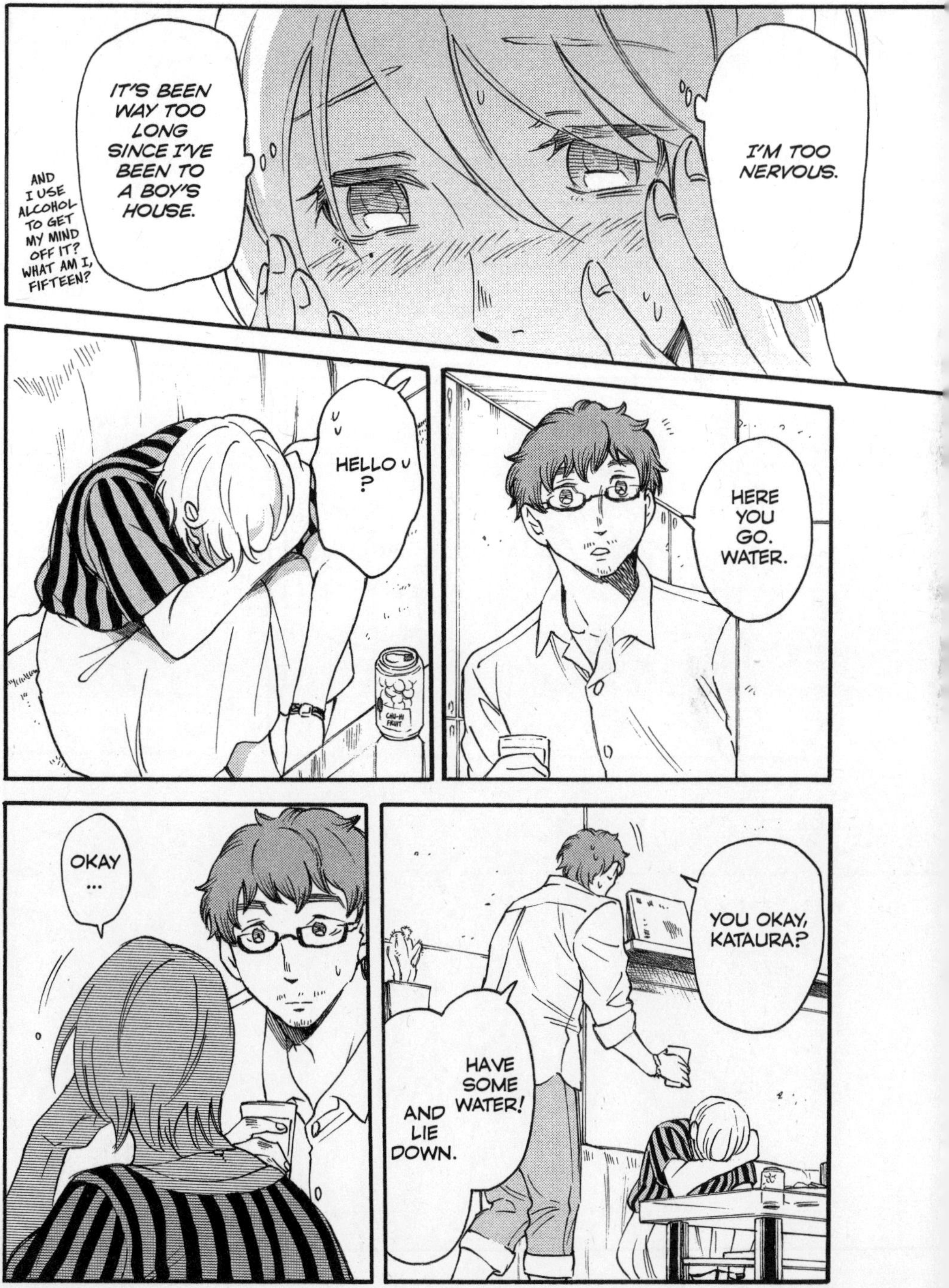
I'M TOO NERVOUS.
IT'S BEEN WAY TOO LONG SINCE I'VE BEEN TO A BOY'S HOUSE.
AND I USE ALCOHOL TO GET MY MIND OFF IT? WHAT AM I, FIFTEEN?
HERE YOU GO. WATER.
HELLO ?
YOU OKAY, KATAURA?
HAVE SOME WATER!
AND LIE DOWN.
OKAY ...

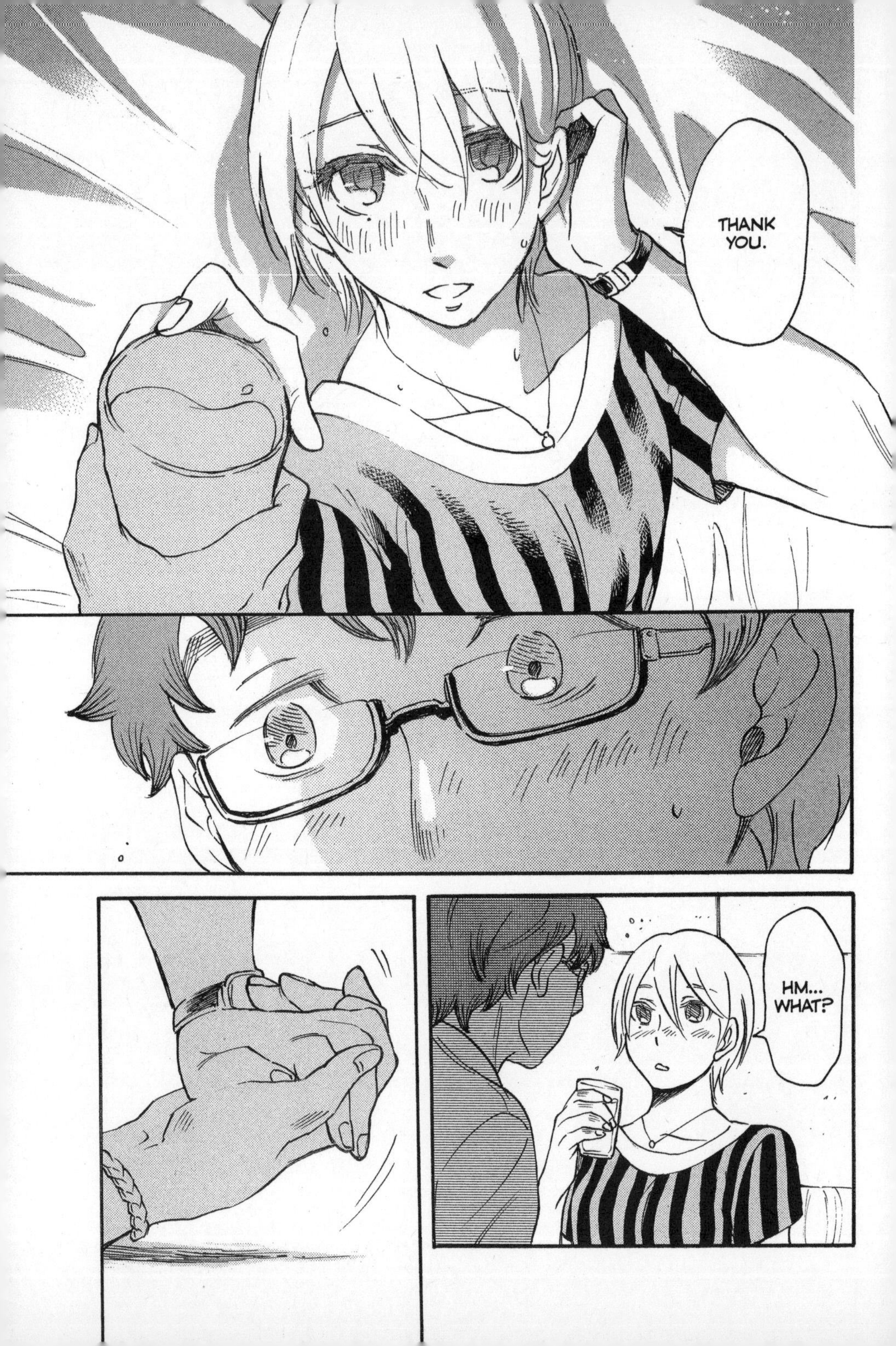
THANK YOU.
HM... WHAT?

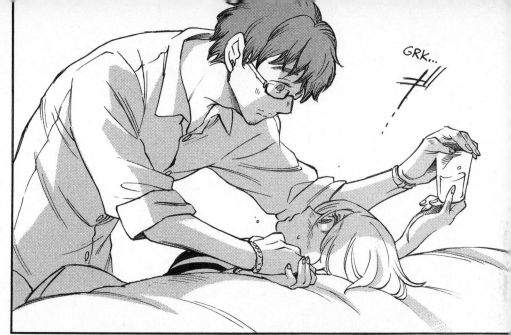

GRK...

OH...

NOW THAT I THINK OF IT...

...IT'S BEEN A LONG TIME SINCE I'VE HAD TO LOOK UP AT SOMEONE, TOO.

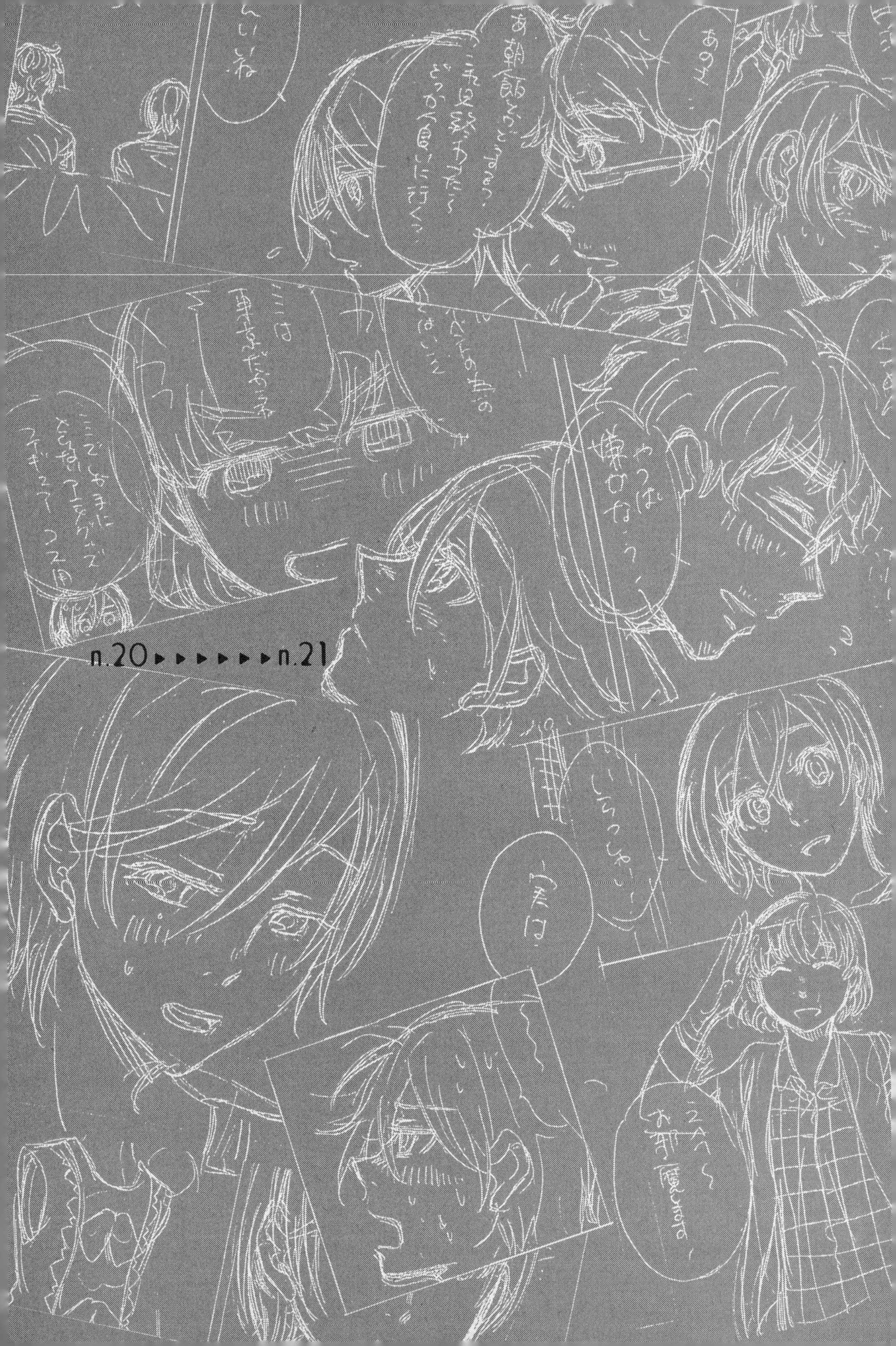
あのさ…
やっぱ嫌かなっ
n.20▸▸▸▸▸▸▸n.21

MIKU & FRIENDS COLLABORATION 4

巡音ルカ

MEGURINE LUKA

×

SHIHO

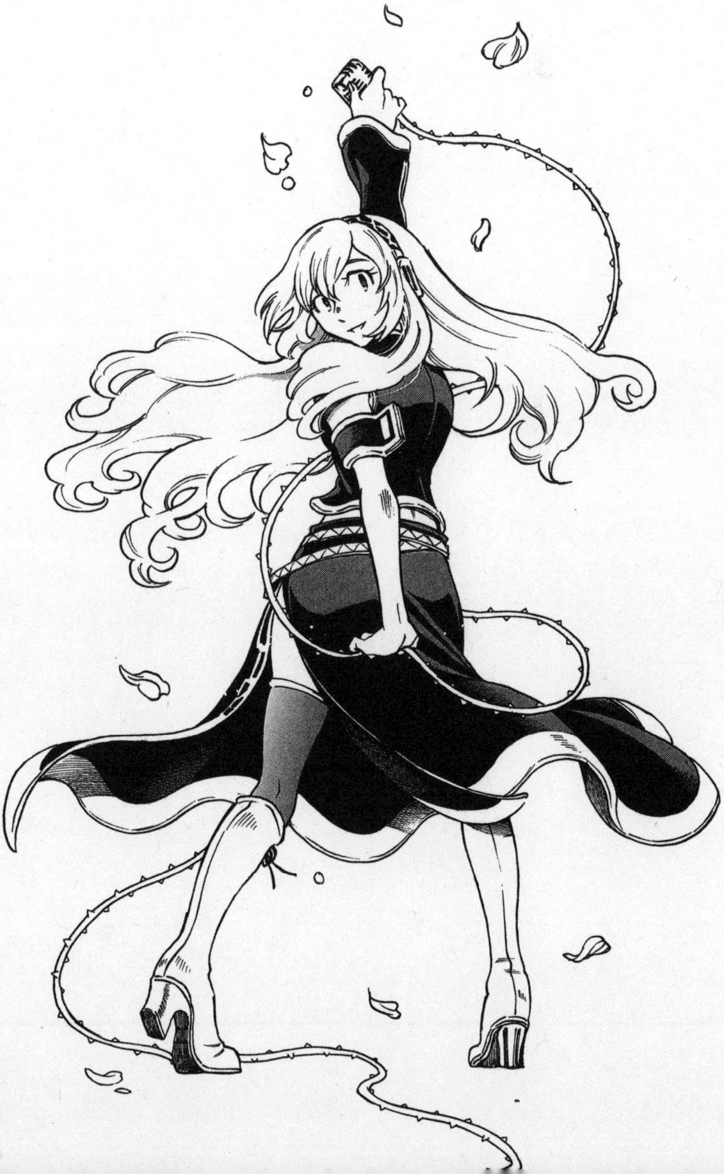

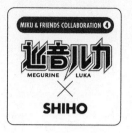

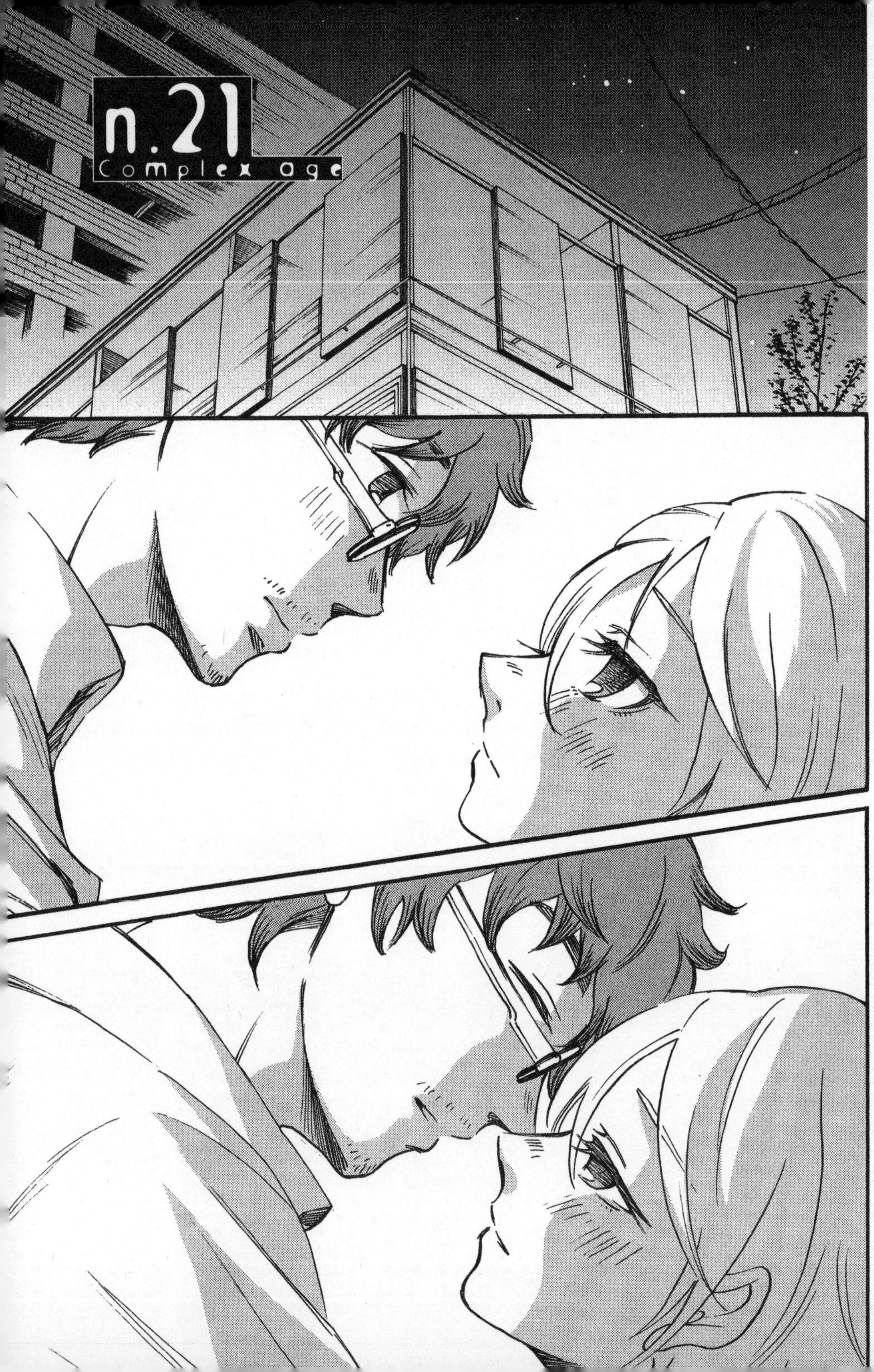
n.21
Complex age

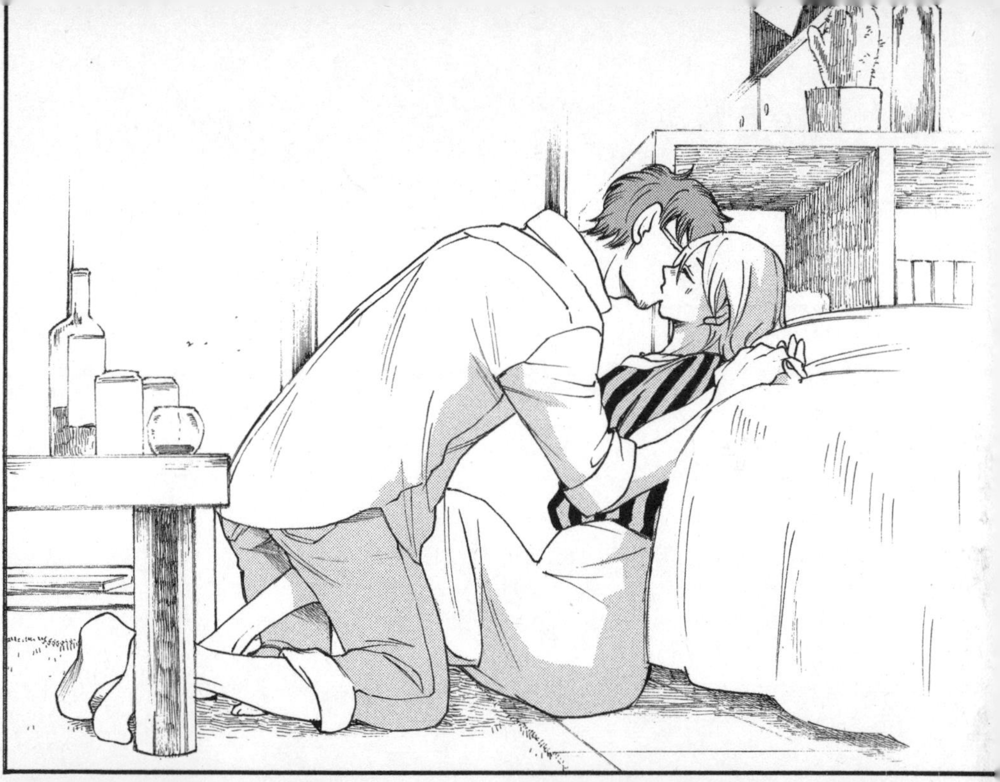

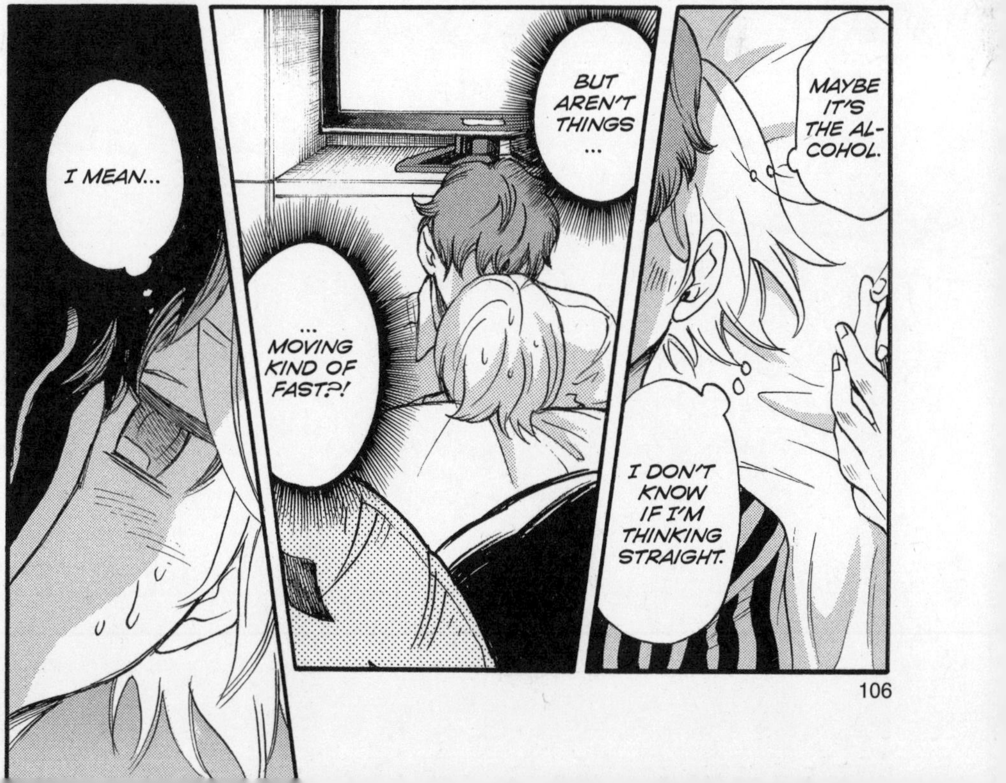
MAYBE IT'S THE AL-COHOL.
I DON'T KNOW IF I'M THINKING STRAIGHT.
BUT AREN'T THINGS ...
... MOVING KIND OF FAST?!
I MEAN...

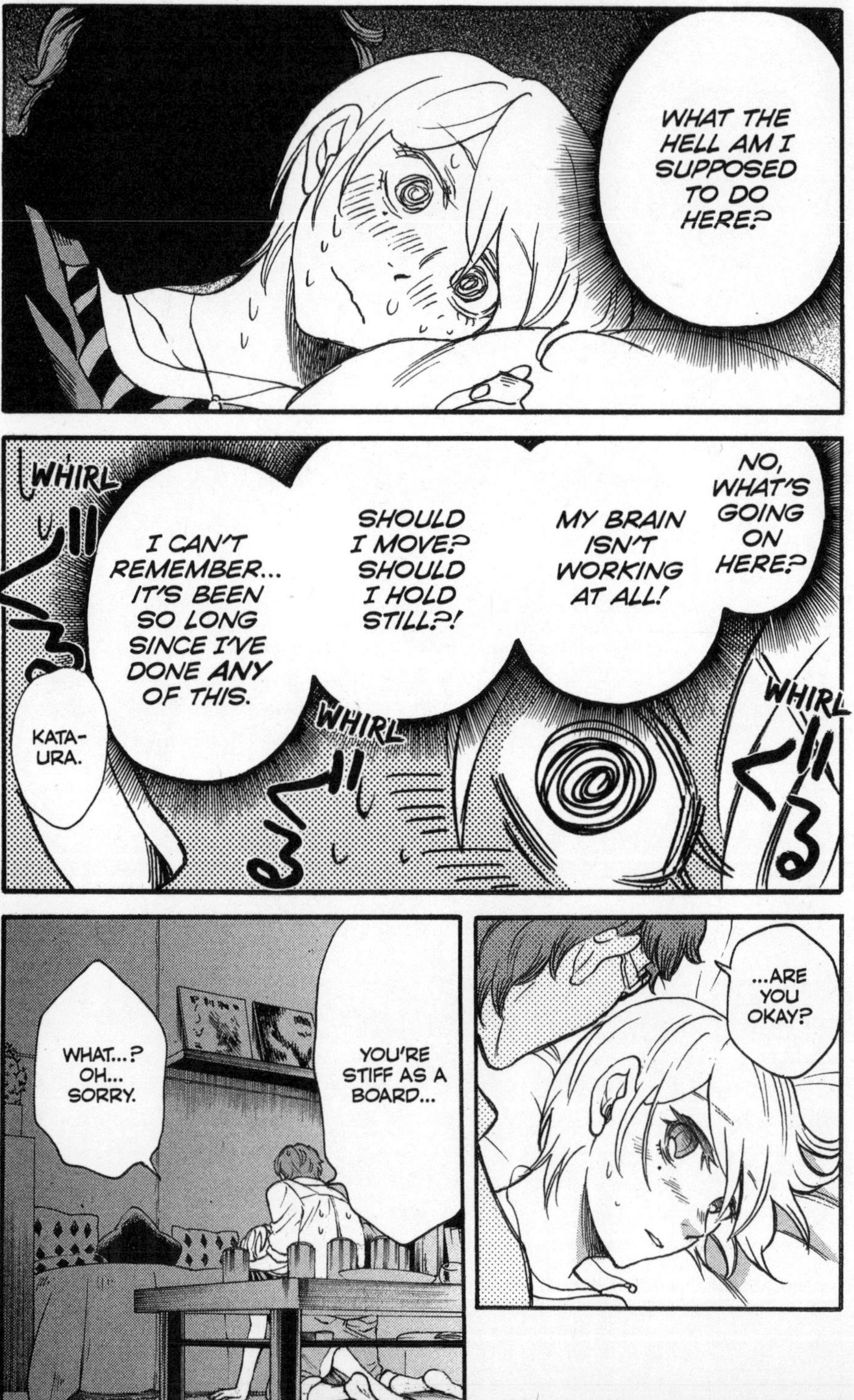
WHAT THE HELL AM I SUPPOSED TO DO HERE?
NO, WHAT'S GOING ON HERE?
MY BRAIN ISN'T WORKING AT ALL!
SHOULD I MOVE? SHOULD I HOLD STILL?!
I CAN'T REMEMBER... IT'S BEEN SO LONG SINCE I'VE DONE ANY OF THIS.
WHIRL
WHIRL
WHIRL
KATA-URA.
...ARE YOU OKAY?
YOU'RE STIFF AS A BOARD...
WHAT...? OH... SORRY.

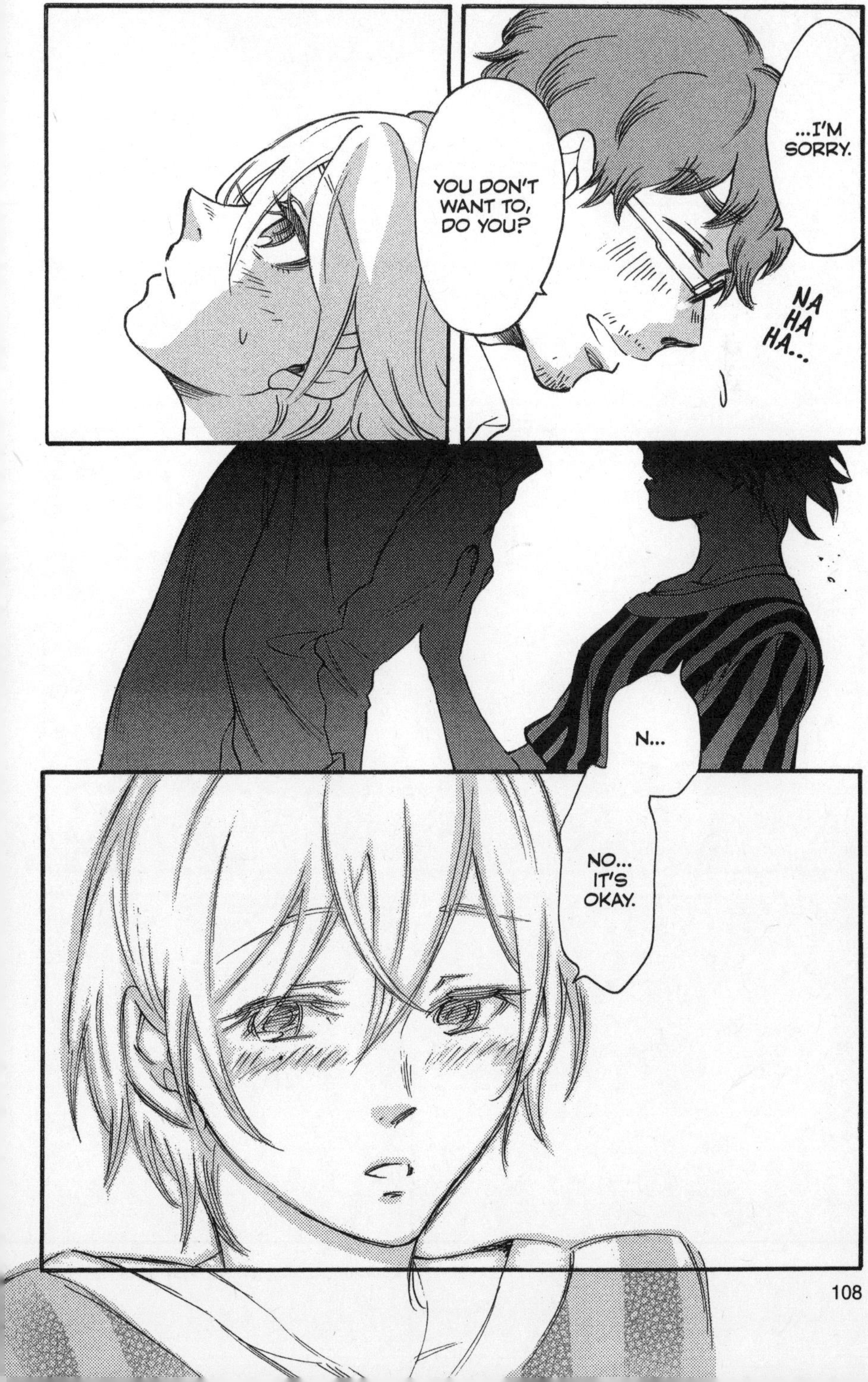
...I'M SORRY.
NA HA HA...
YOU DON'T WANT TO, DO YOU?
N...
NO... IT'S OKAY.

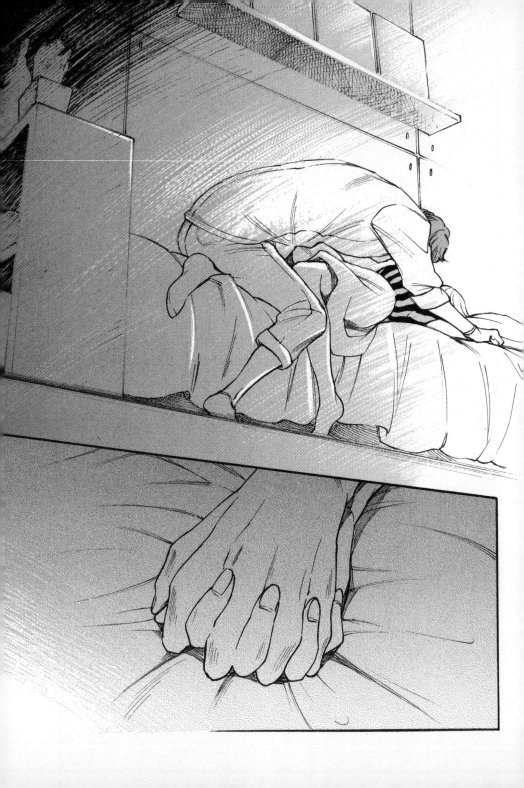

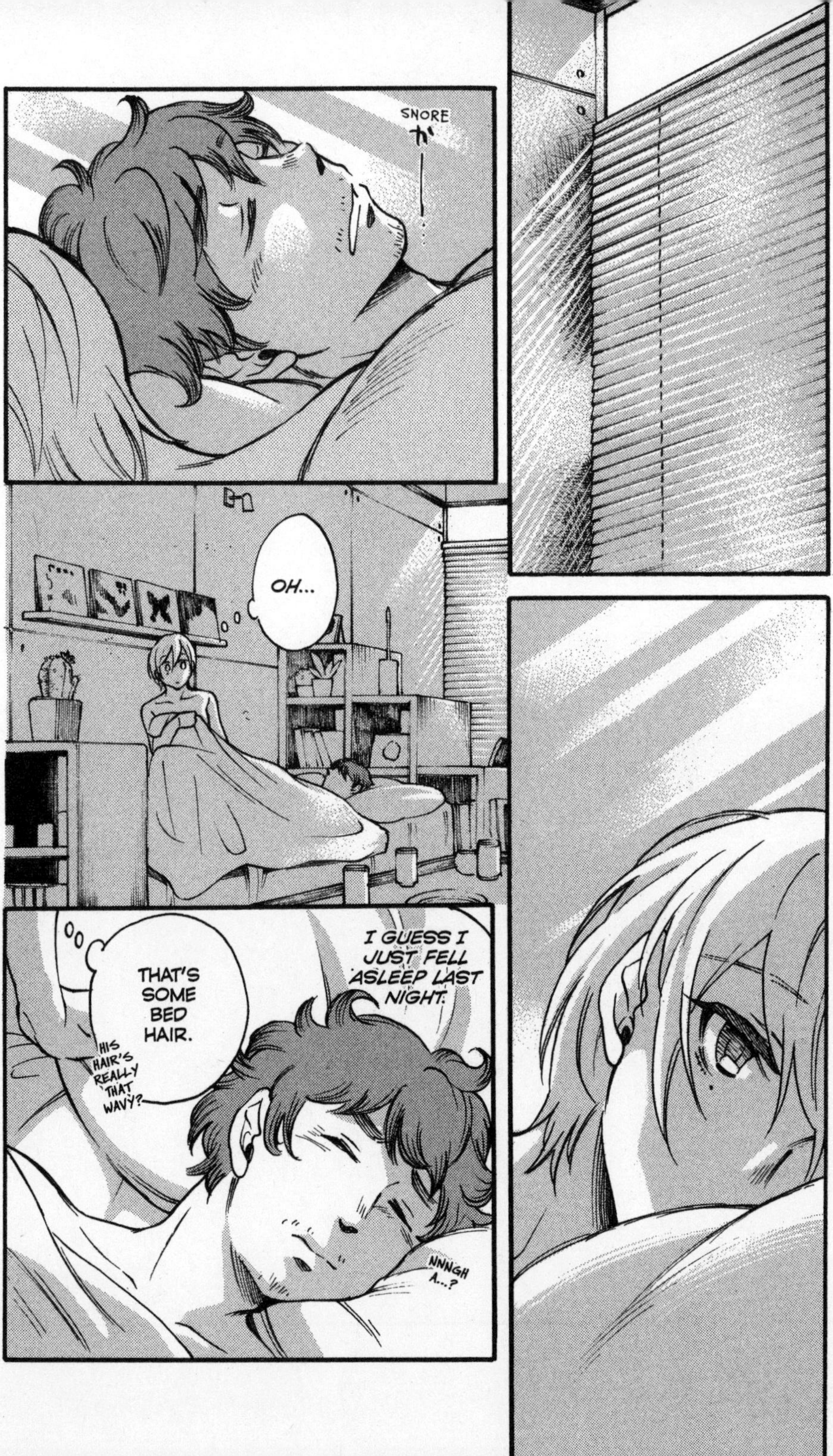
SNORE
ガー
OH...
I GUESS I JUST FELL ASLEEP LAST NIGHT.
THAT'S SOME BED HAIR.
HIS HAIR'S REALLY THAT WAVY?
NNNGH A...?

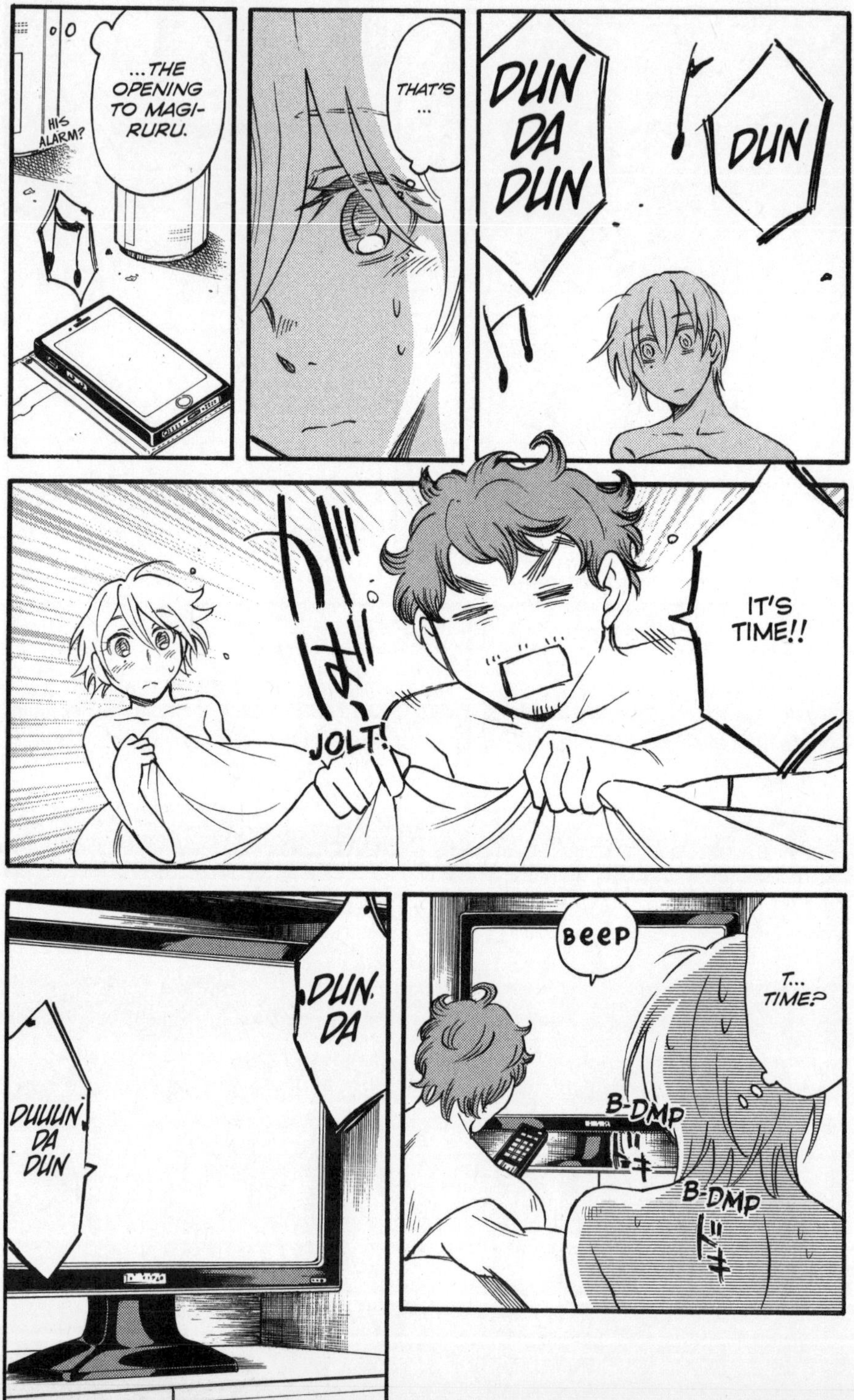
DUN DA DUN
DUN
THAT'S ...
...THE OPENING TO MAGI-RURU.
HIS ALARM?
IT'S TIME!!
JOLT!
T... TIME?
Beep
B-DMP
ドキ
B-DMP
ドキ
DUN. DA
DUUUN DA DUN

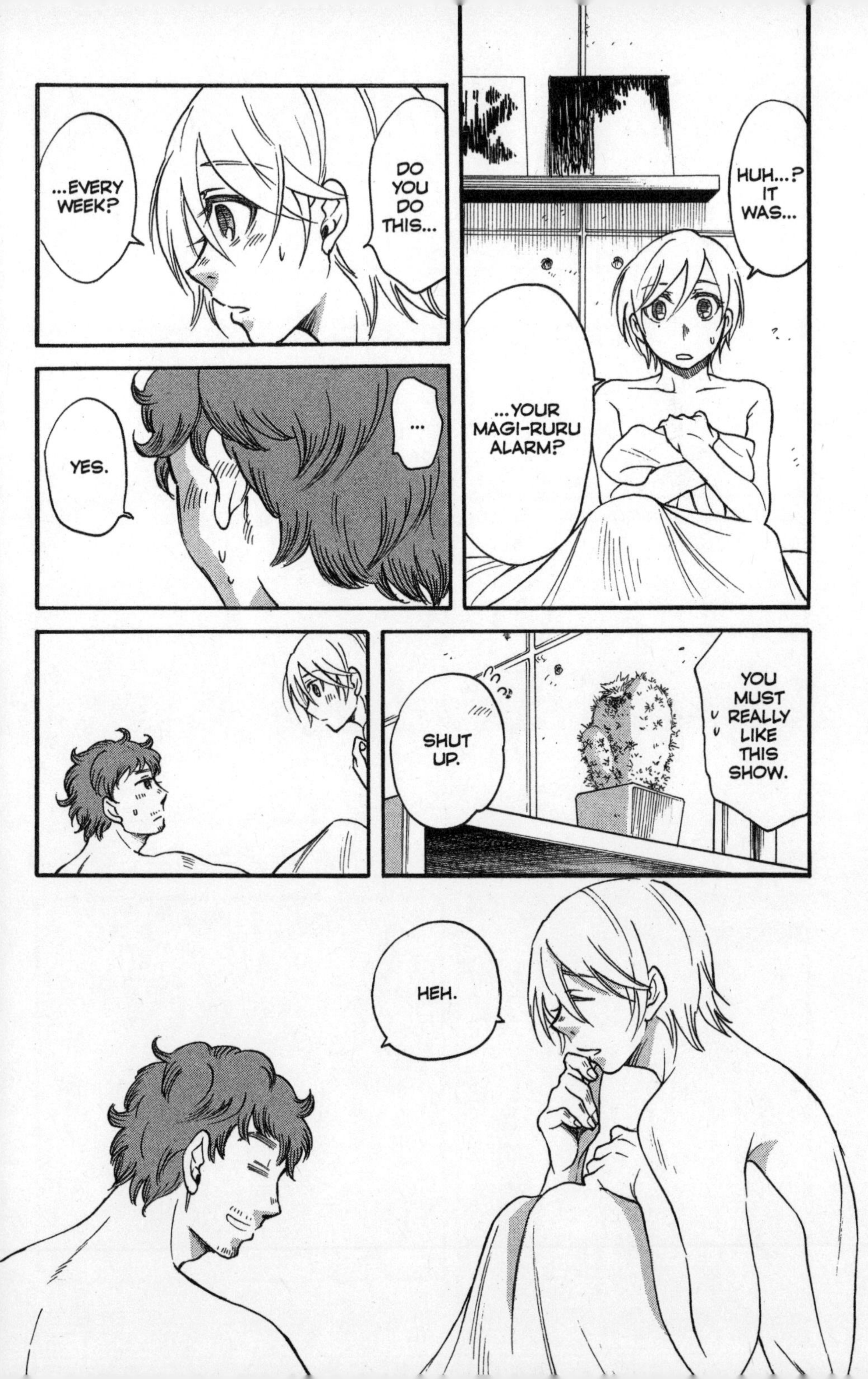
HUH...? IT WAS...
...YOUR MAGI-RURU ALARM?
DO YOU DO THIS...
...EVERY WEEK?
...
YES.
YOU MUST REALLY LIKE THIS SHOW.
SHUT UP.
HEH.

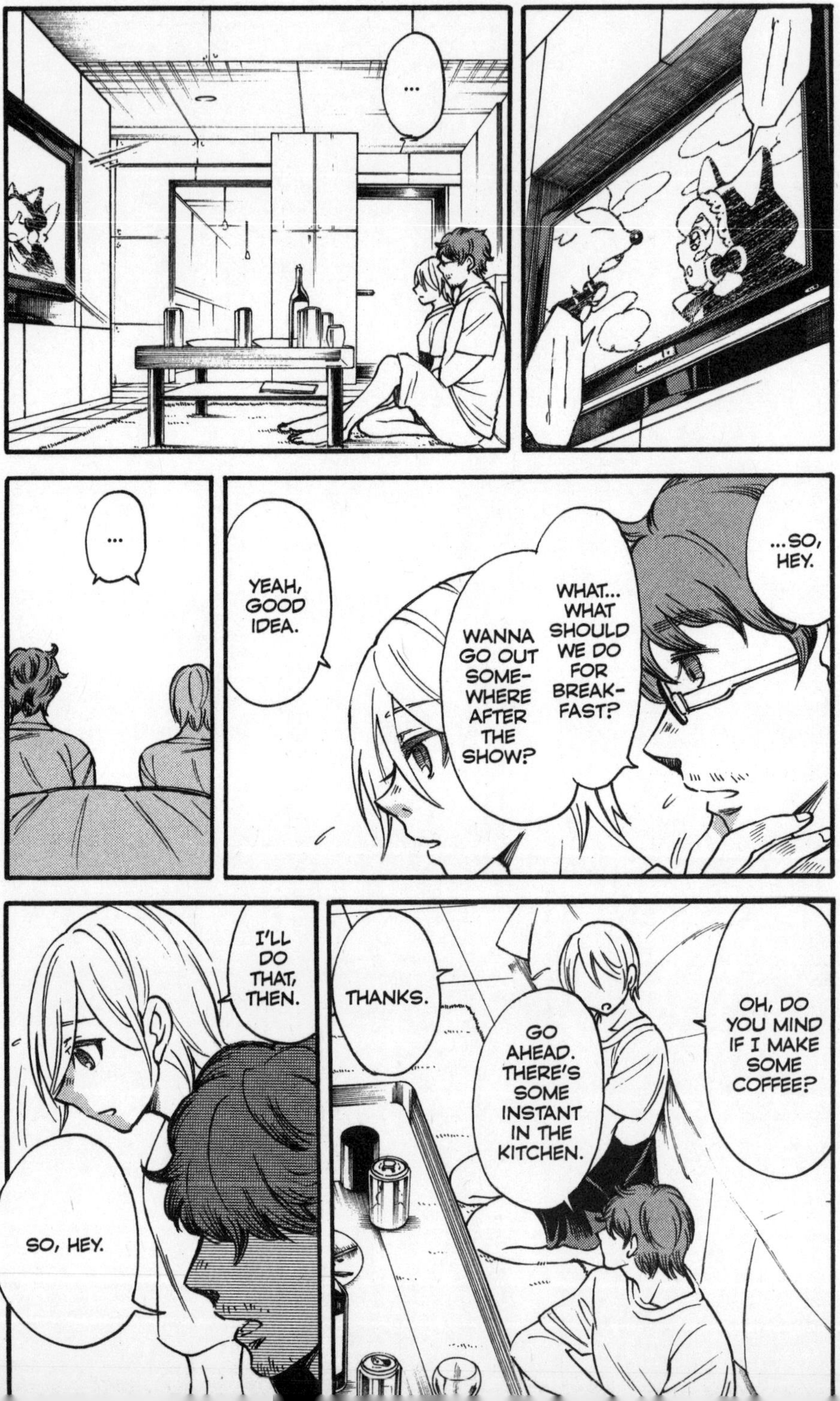
...
...SO, HEY.
WHAT... WHAT SHOULD WE DO FOR BREAKFAST?
WANNA GO OUT SOMEWHERE AFTER THE SHOW?
YEAH, GOOD IDEA.
...
OH, DO YOU MIND IF I MAKE SOME COFFEE?
GO AHEAD. THERE'S SOME INSTANT IN THE KITCHEN.
THANKS.
I'LL DO THAT, THEN.
SO, HEY.

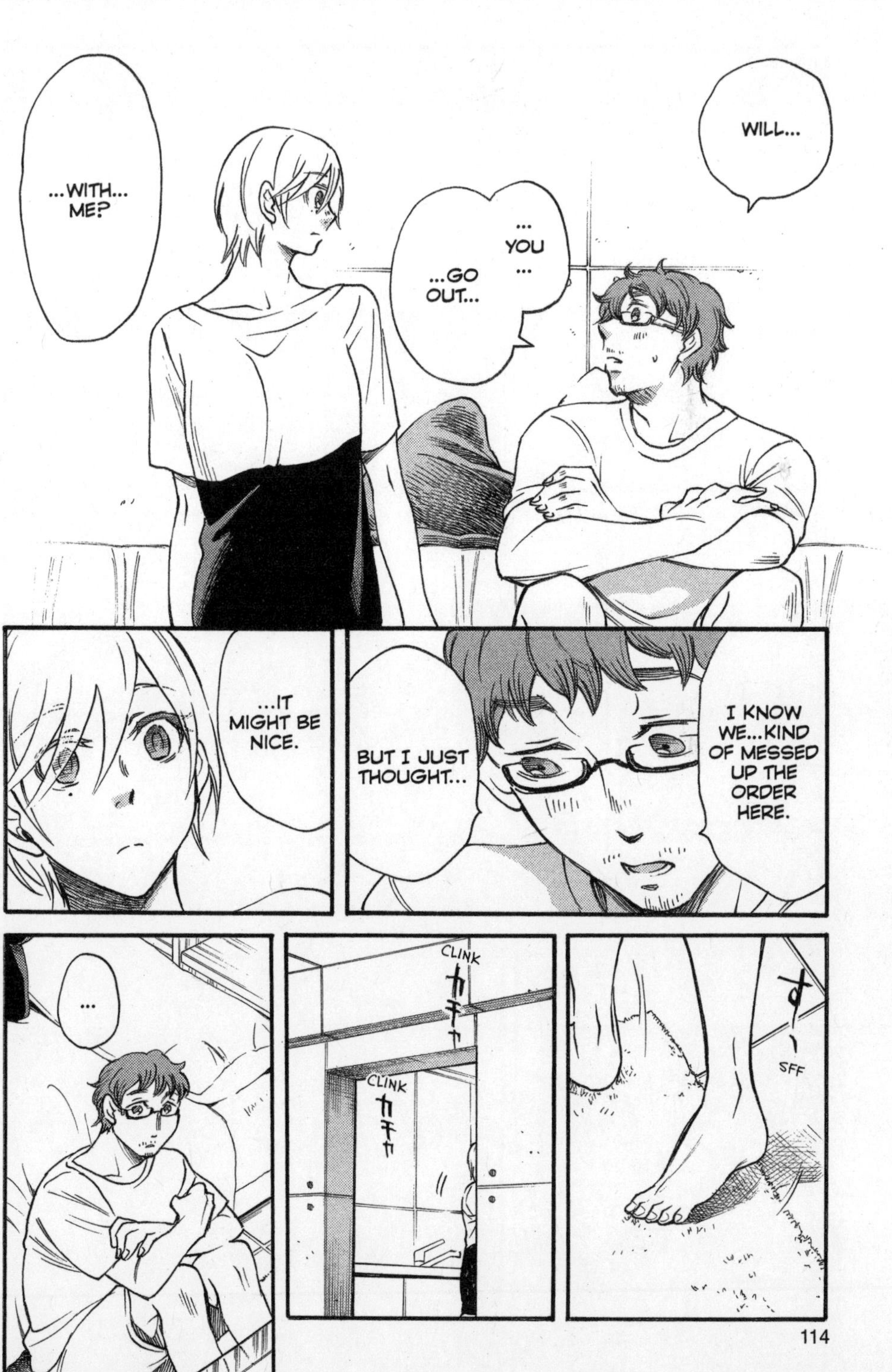
WILL...
... YOU ...
...GO OUT...
...WITH... ME?
I KNOW WE...KIND OF MESSED UP THE ORDER HERE.
BUT I JUST THOUGHT...
...IT MIGHT BE NICE.
SFF
CLINK
カチャ
CLINK
カチャ
...

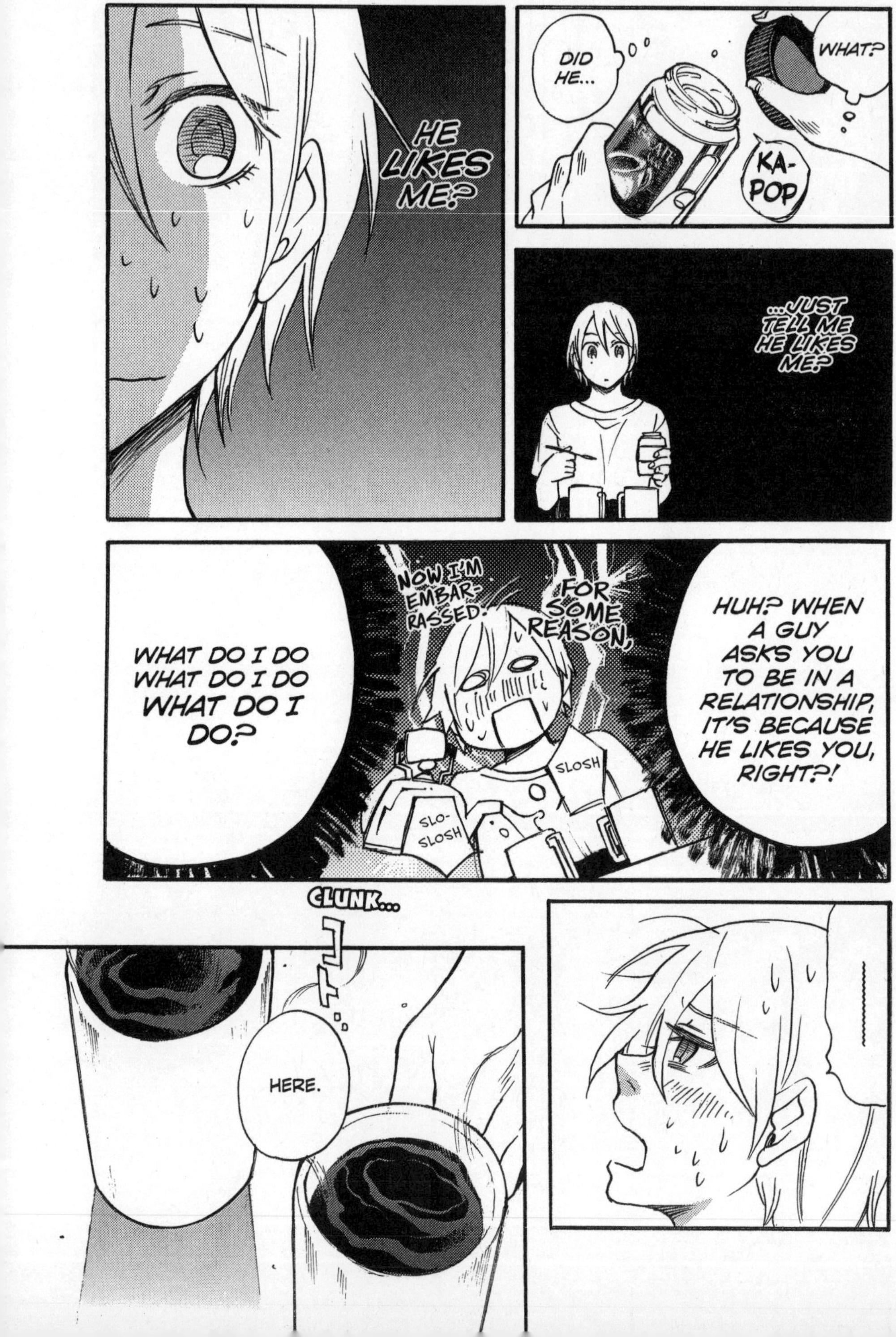
WHAT?
DID HE...
KA-POP
...JUST TELL ME HE LIKES ME?
HE LIKES ME?
HUH? WHEN A GUY ASKS YOU TO BE IN A RELATIONSHIP, IT'S BECAUSE HE LIKES YOU, RIGHT?!
FOR SOME REASON,
NOW I'M EMBARRASSED.
SLOSH
SLO-SLOSH
WHAT DO I DO WHAT DO I DO WHAT DO I DO?
......
CLUNK...
HERE.

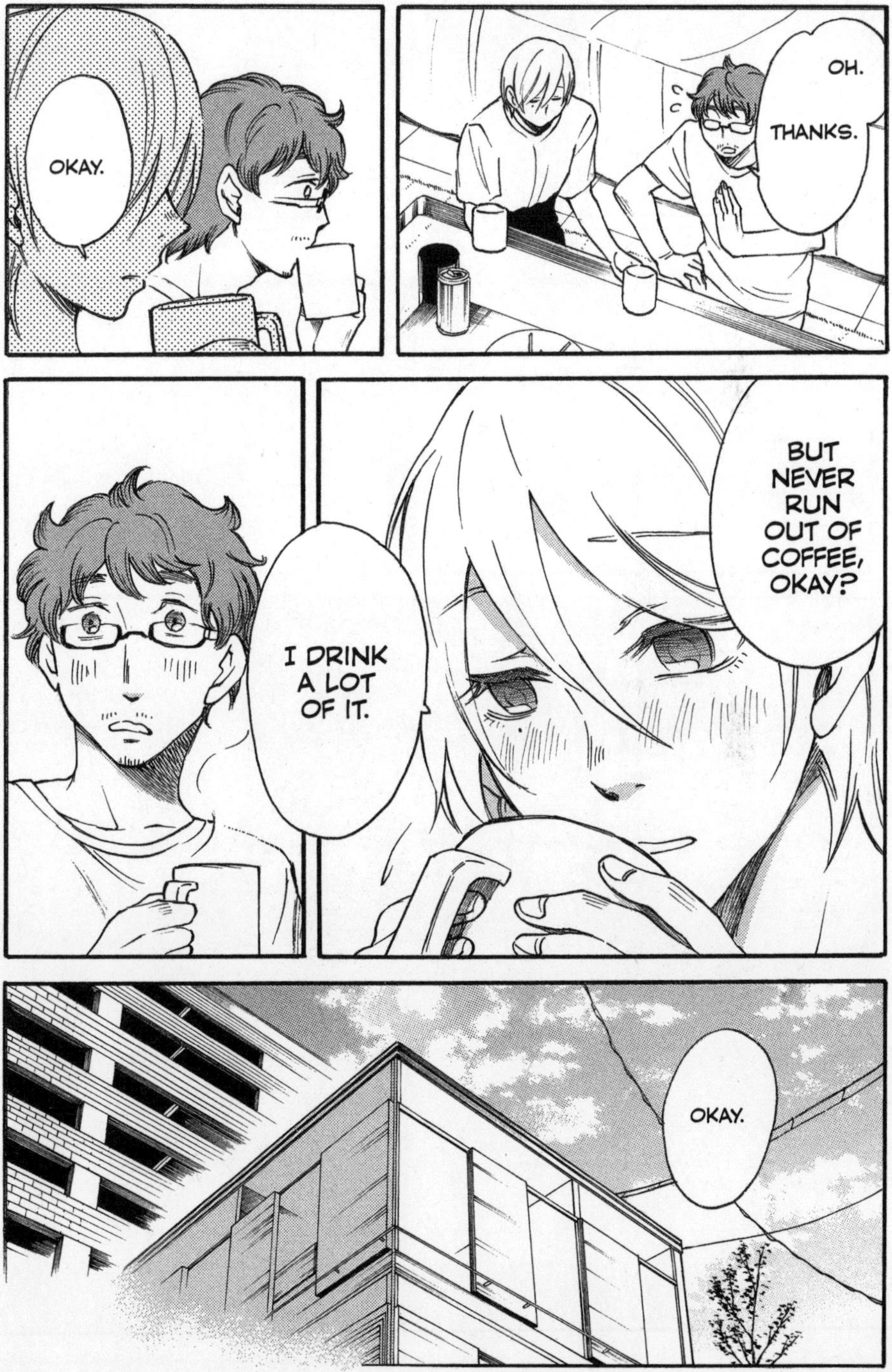
OH.
THANKS.
OKAY.
BUT NEVER RUN OUT OF COFFEE, OKAY?
I DRINK A LOT OF IT.
OKAY.

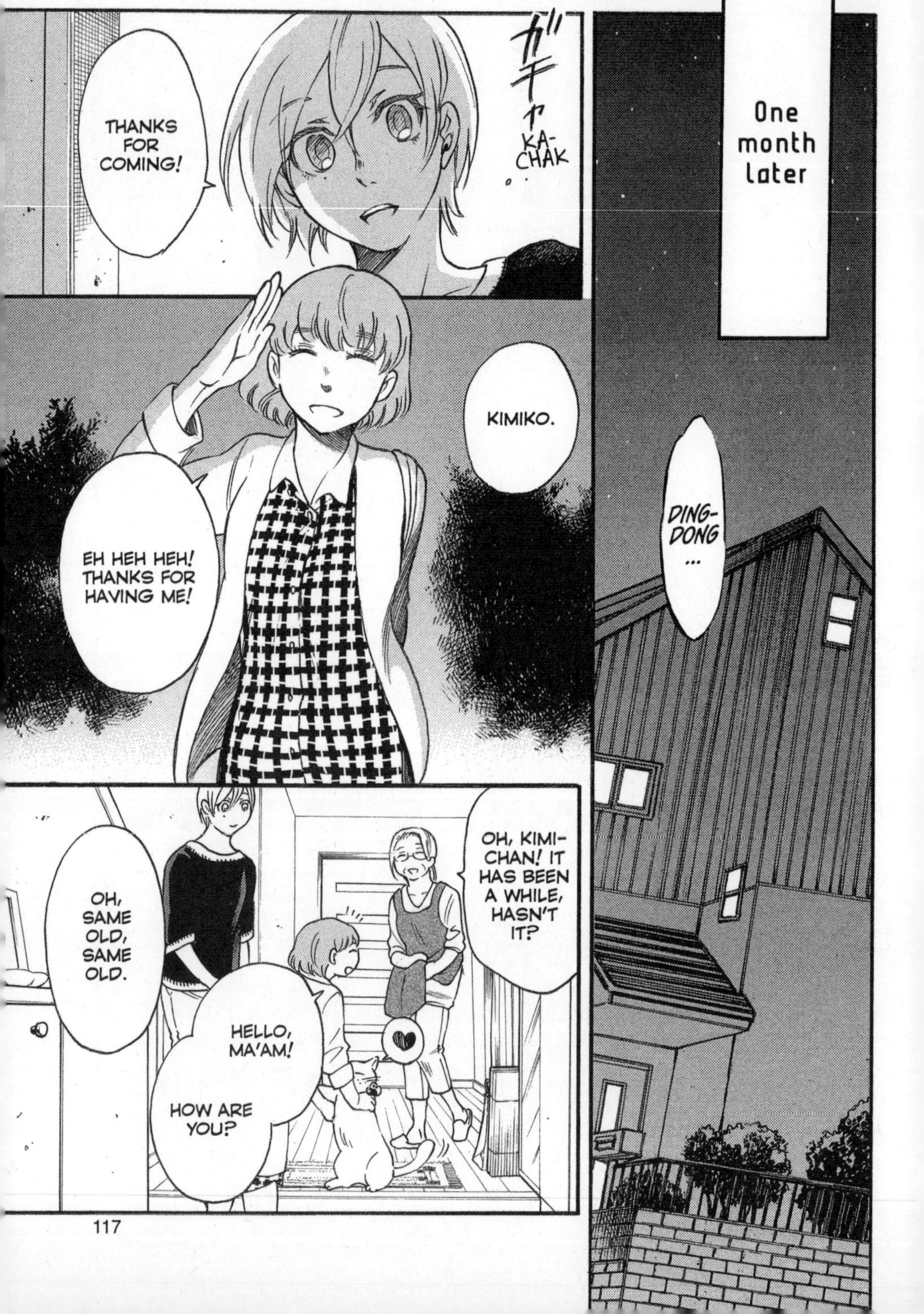
One month later
DING-DONG...
KA-CHAK
THANKS FOR COMING!
KIMIKO.
EH HEH HEH! THANKS FOR HAVING ME!
OH, KIMI-CHAN! IT HAS BEEN A WHILE, HASN'T IT?
HELLO, MA'AM!
HOW ARE YOU?
OH, SAME OLD, SAME OLD.

VOICE ACTOR EVENT: An event where the voice actors from an anime or game appear on stage and do talk shows and concerts.

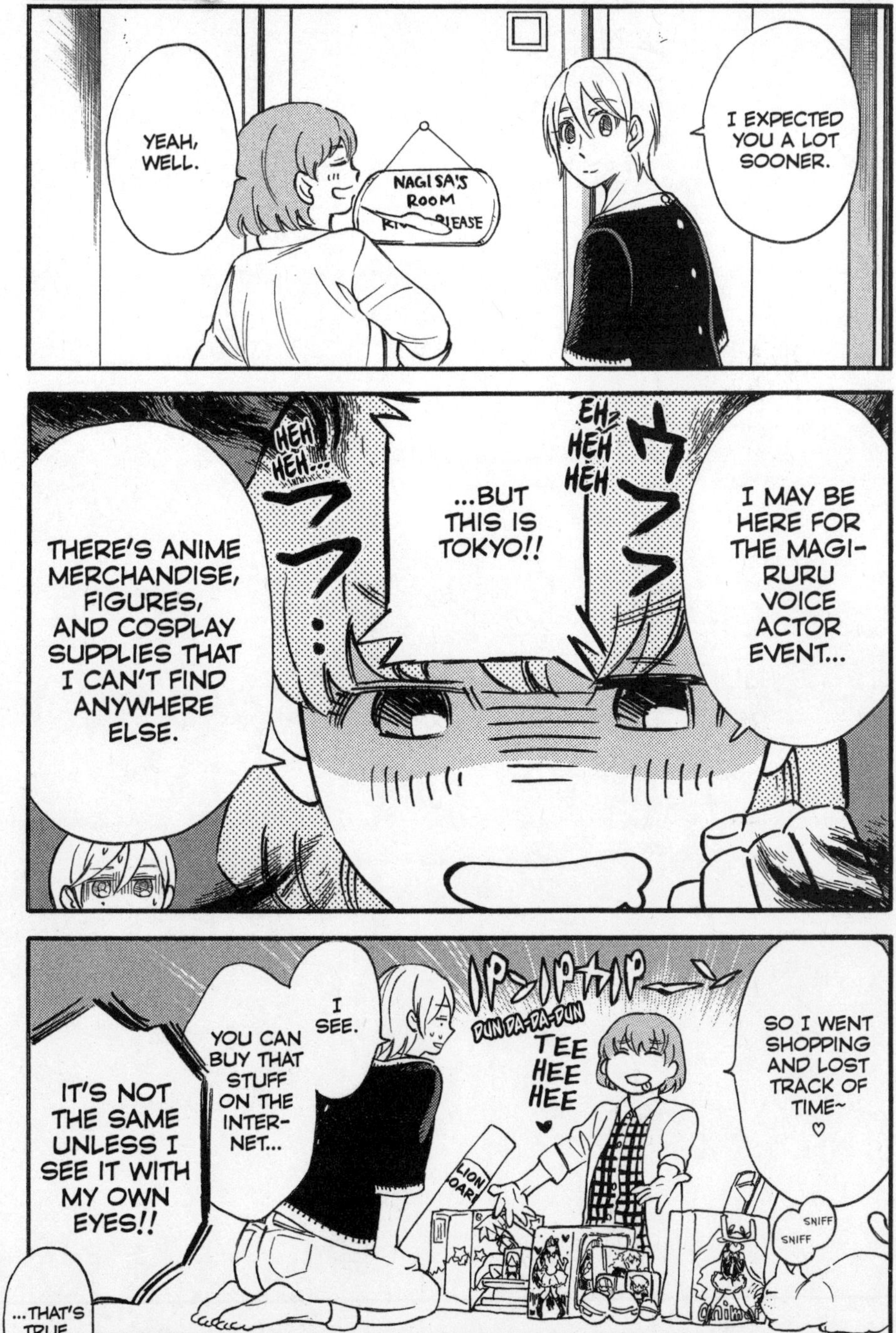
I EXPECTED YOU A LOT SOONER.
YEAH, WELL.
I MAY BE HERE FOR THE MAGI-RURU VOICE ACTOR EVENT...
EH-HEH HEH HEH
...BUT THIS IS TOKYO!!
HEH HEH...
THERE'S ANIME MERCHANDISE, FIGURES, AND COSPLAY SUPPLIES THAT I CAN'T FIND ANYWHERE ELSE.
SO I WENT SHOPPING AND LOST TRACK OF TIME~ ♡
SNIFF SNIFF
DUN DA-DA-DUN
TEE HEE HEE ♥
I SEE.
YOU CAN BUY THAT STUFF ON THE INTERNET...
IT'S NOT THE SAME UNLESS I SEE IT WITH MY OWN EYES!!
...THAT'S TRUE.

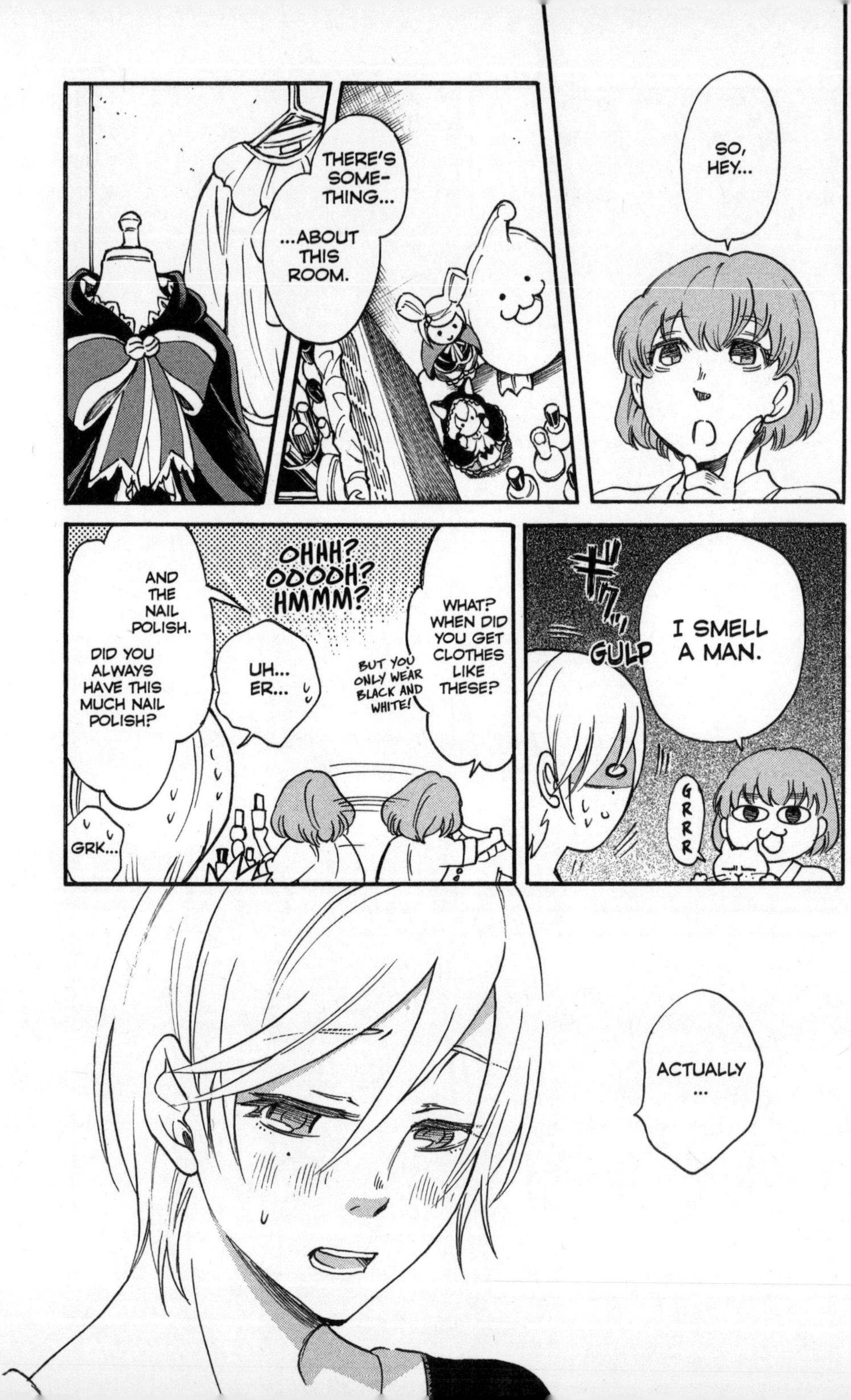
SO, HEY...
THERE'S SOME-THING...
...ABOUT THIS ROOM.
I SMELL A MAN.
GULP
GRRR
WHAT? WHEN DID YOU GET CLOTHES LIKE THESE?
BUT YOU ONLY WEAR BLACK AND WHITE!
OHHH? OOOOH? HMMM?
UH... ER...
AND THE NAIL POLISH.
DID YOU ALWAYS HAVE THIS MUCH NAIL POLISH?
GRK...
ACTUALLY...

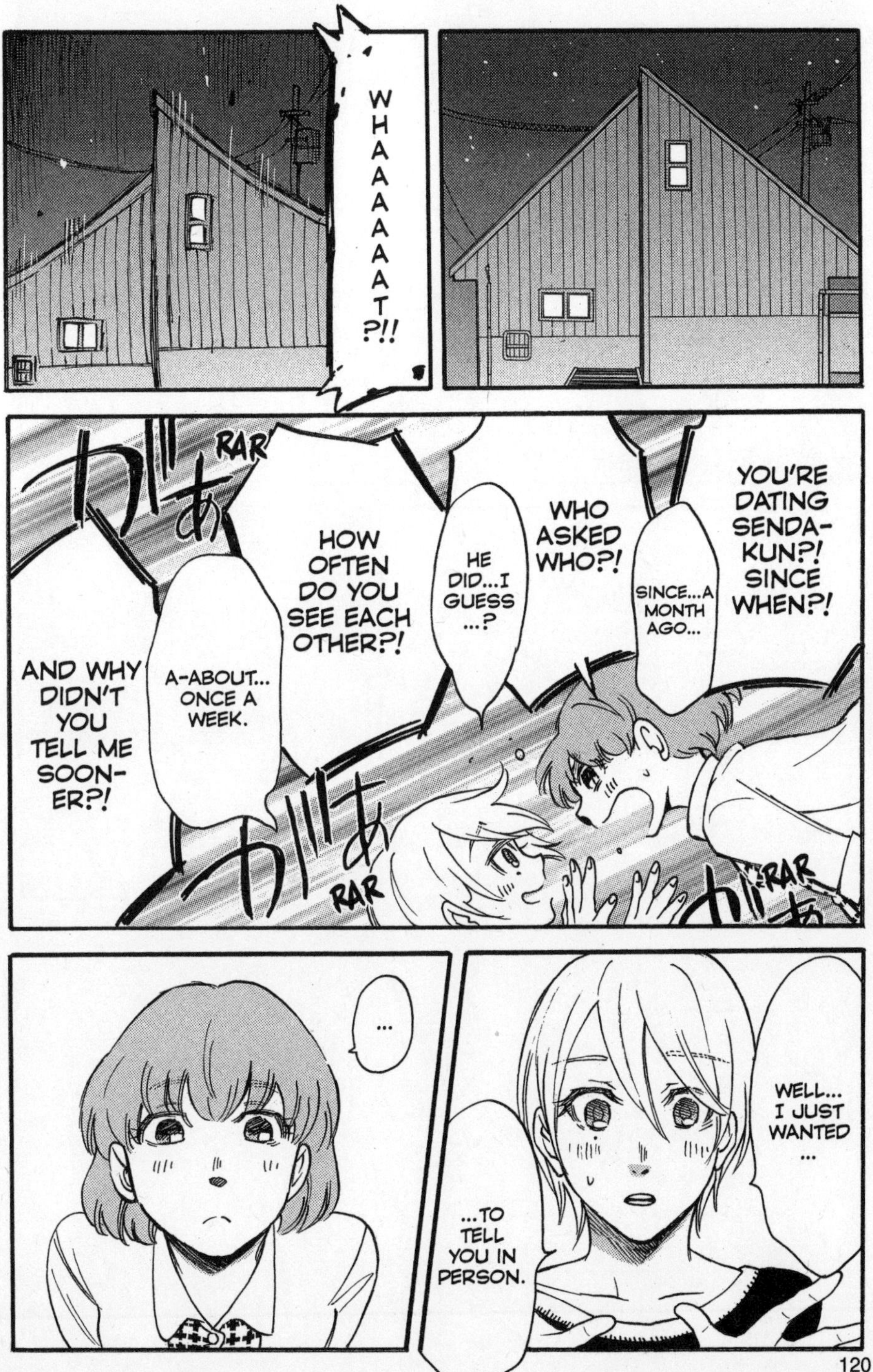
WHAAAAAAAT?!!
YOU'RE DATING SENDA-KUN?! SINCE WHEN?!
SINCE...A MONTH AGO...
WHO ASKED WHO?!
HE DID...I GUESS ...?
HOW OFTEN DO YOU SEE EACH OTHER?!
A-ABOUT... ONCE A WEEK.
AND WHY DIDN'T YOU TELL ME SOONER?!
RAR
RAR
RAR
WELL... I JUST WANTED ...
...TO TELL YOU IN PERSON.
...

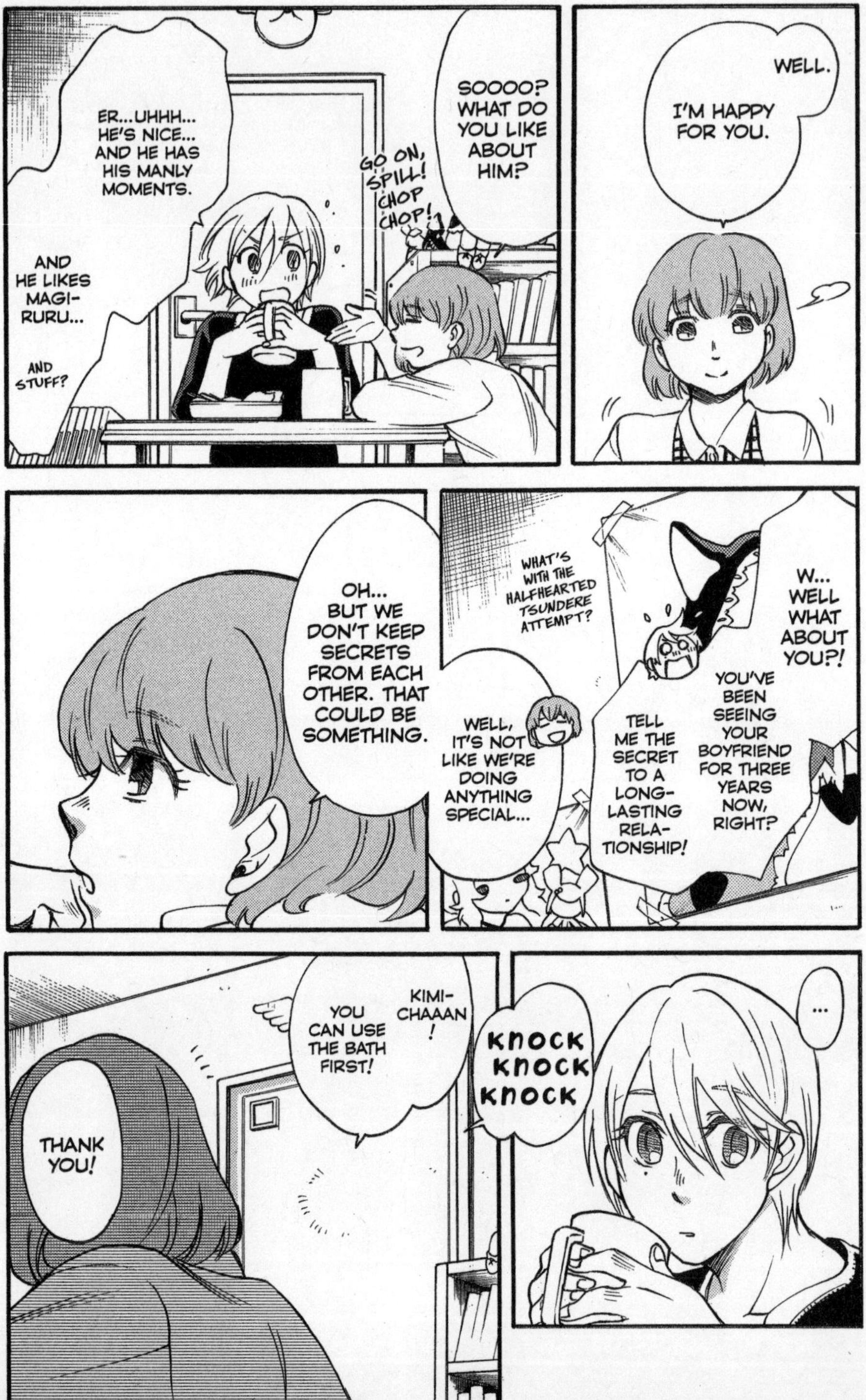
WELL.
I'M HAPPY FOR YOU.
SOOOO? WHAT DO YOU LIKE ABOUT HIM?
GO ON, SPILL! CHOP CHOP!
ER...UHHH... HE'S NICE... AND HE HAS HIS MANLY MOMENTS.
AND HE LIKES MAGI-RURU...
AND STUFF?
W... WELL WHAT ABOUT YOU?!
YOU'VE BEEN SEEING YOUR BOYFRIEND FOR THREE YEARS NOW, RIGHT?
TELL ME THE SECRET TO A LONG-LASTING RELA-TIONSHIP!
WHAT'S WITH THE HALFHEARTED TSUNDERE ATTEMPT?
WELL, IT'S NOT LIKE WE'RE DOING ANYTHING SPECIAL...
OH... BUT WE DON'T KEEP SECRETS FROM EACH OTHER. THAT COULD BE SOMETHING.
...
KNOCK KNOCK KNOCK
KIMI-CHAAAN!
YOU CAN USE THE BATH FIRST!
THANK YOU!

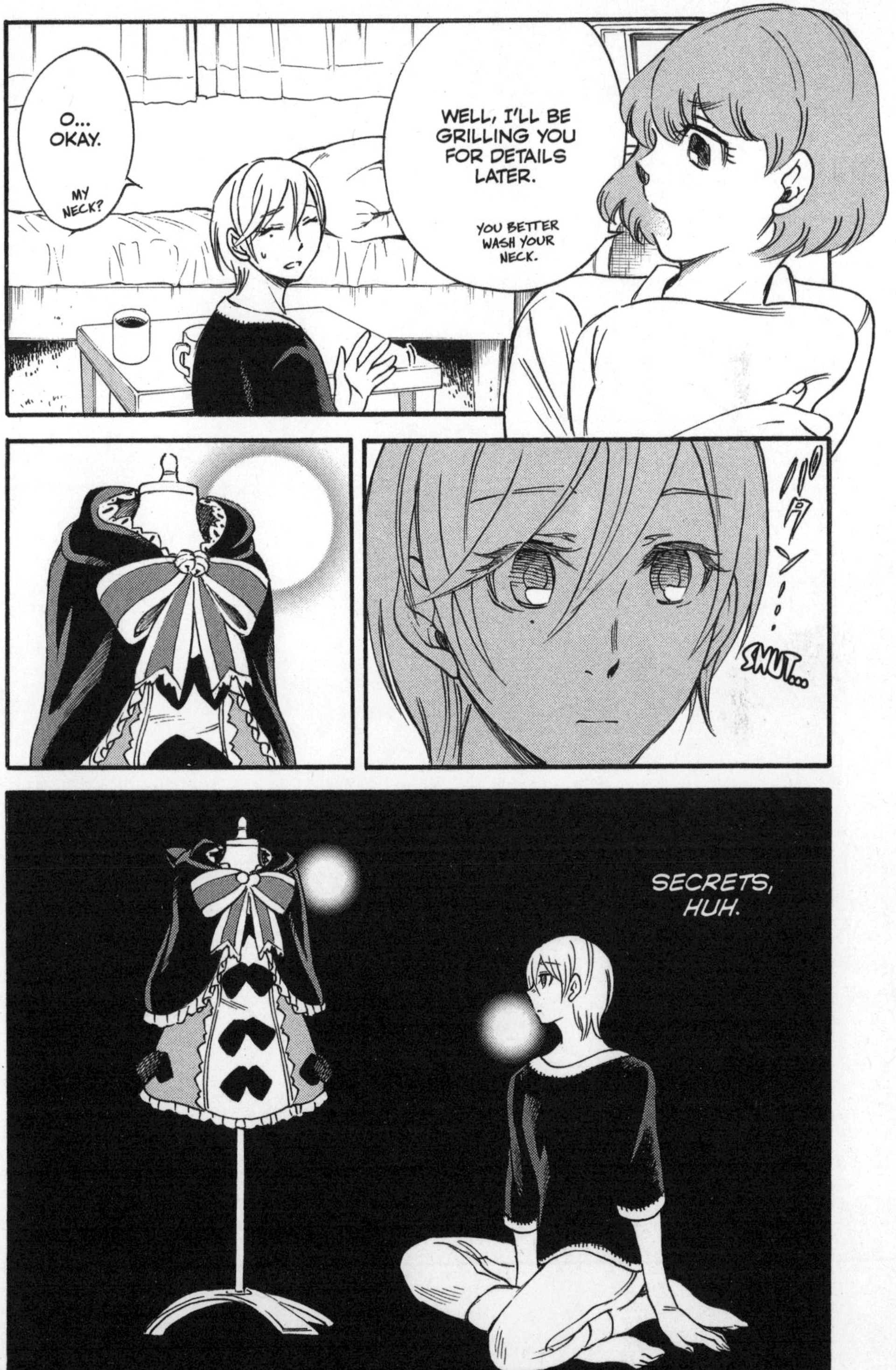
WELL, I'LL BE GRILLING YOU FOR DETAILS LATER.
YOU BETTER WASH YOUR NECK.
O... OKAY.
MY NECK?
SHUT...
SECRETS, HUH.

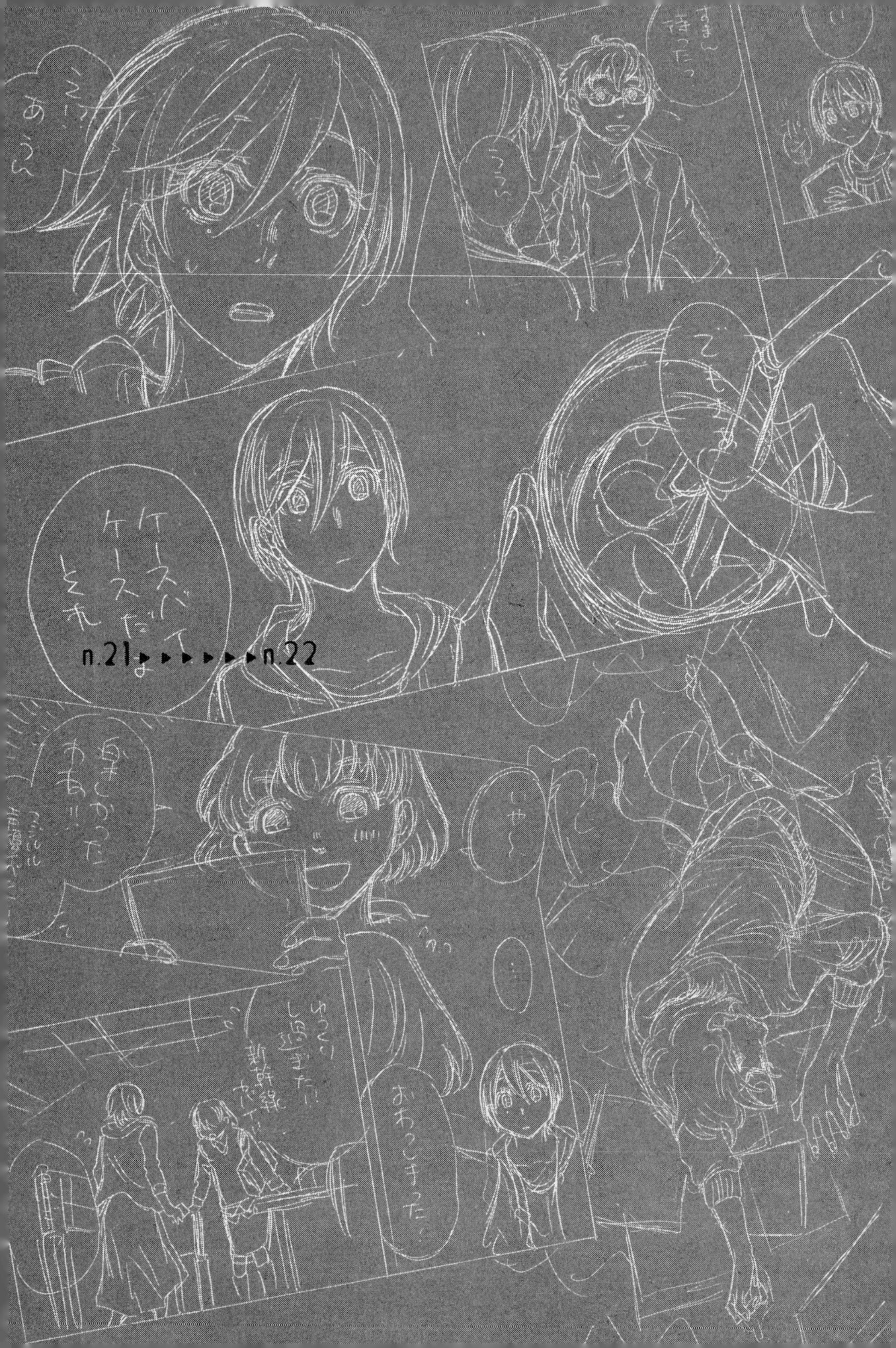
すまん〜 待ったっ
ケースバイケースだな
おわっちまった
ゆっくりし過ぎた!! 新幹線やバイ!!

n.21▶▶▶▶▶▶▶n.22

MIKU & FRIENDS COLLABORATION 5

MEIKO × HAYAMA

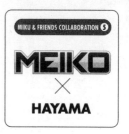

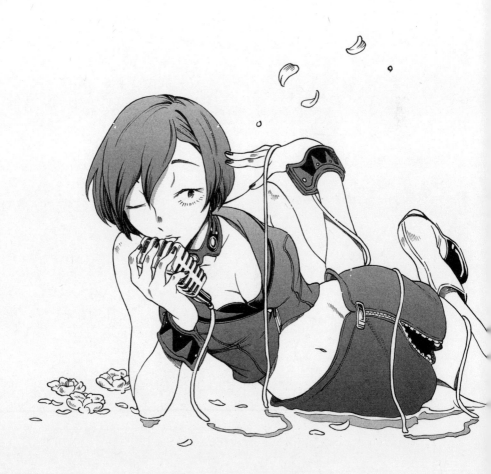

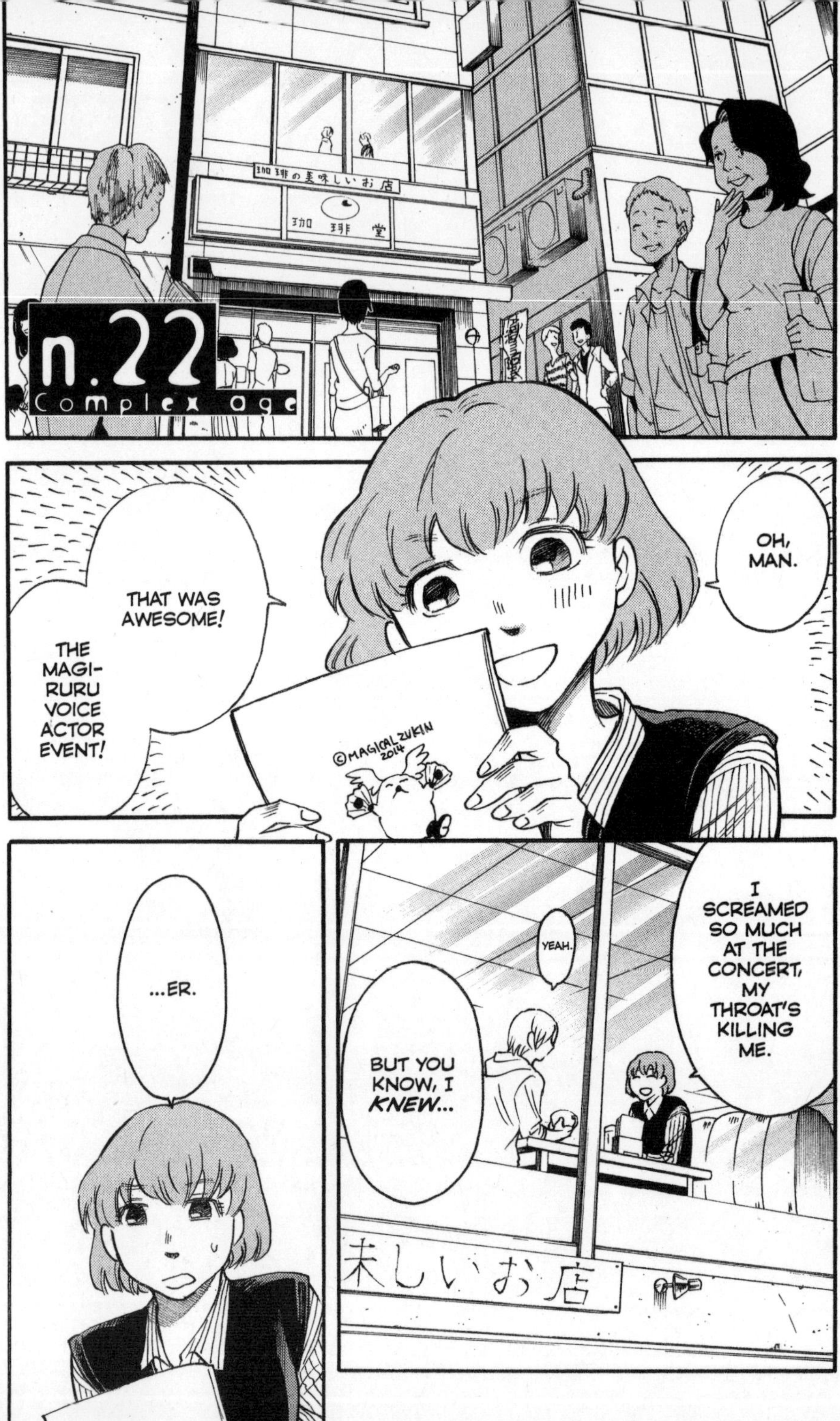
n.22
Complex age
珈琲の美味しいお店
珈琲堂
OH, MAN.
THAT WAS AWESOME!
THE MAGI-RURU VOICE ACTOR EVENT!
©MAGICALZUKIN 2014
I SCREAMED SO MUCH AT THE CONCERT, MY THROAT'S KILLING ME.
YEAH.
BUT YOU KNOW, I *KNEW*...
...ER.

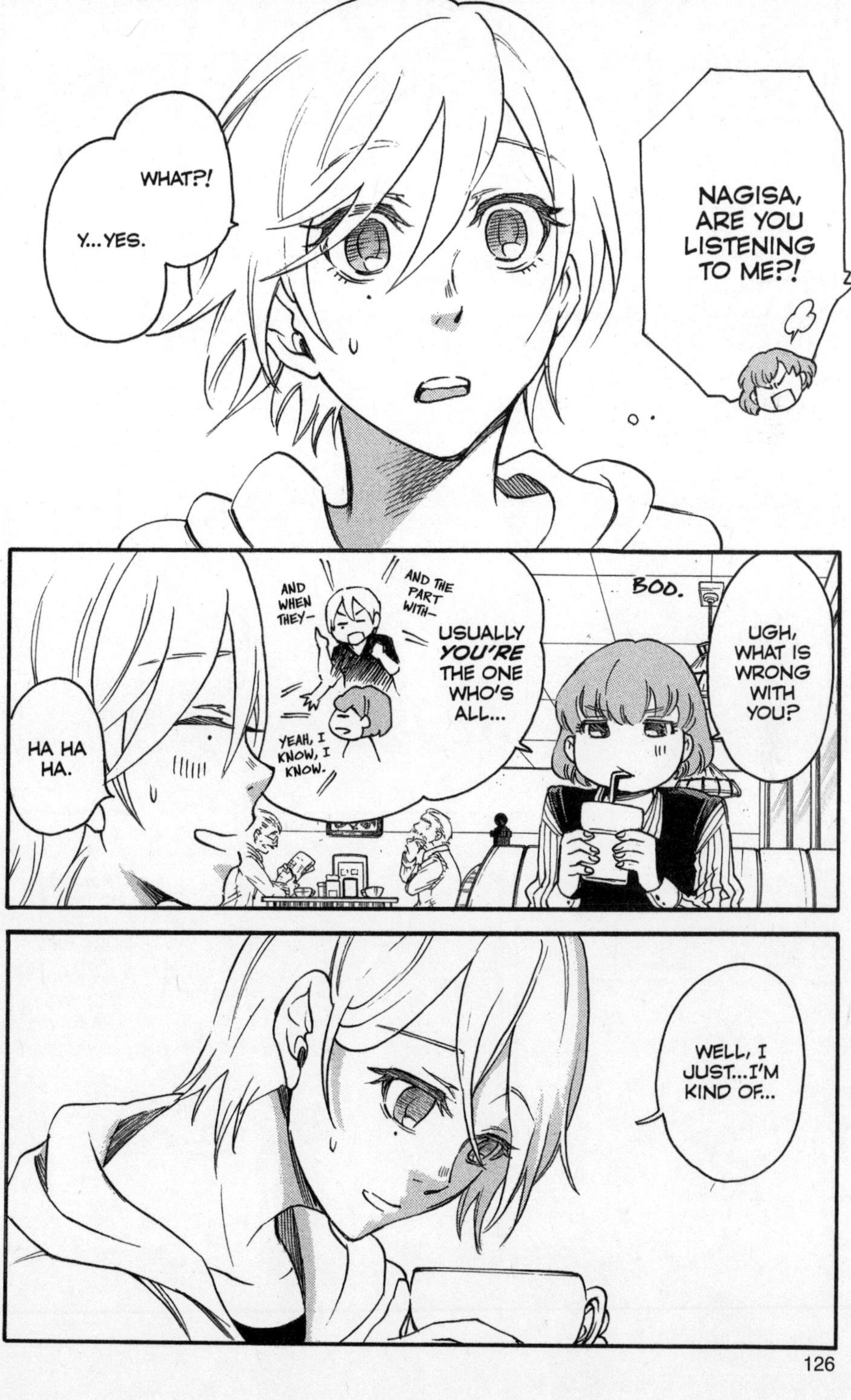
NAGISA, ARE YOU LISTENING TO ME?!
WHAT?!
Y...YES.
UGH, WHAT IS WRONG WITH YOU?
BOO.
USUALLY *YOU'RE* THE ONE WHO'S ALL...
AND THE PART WITH—
AND WHEN THEY—
YEAH, I KNOW, I KNOW.
HA HA HA.
WELL, I JUST...I'M KIND OF...

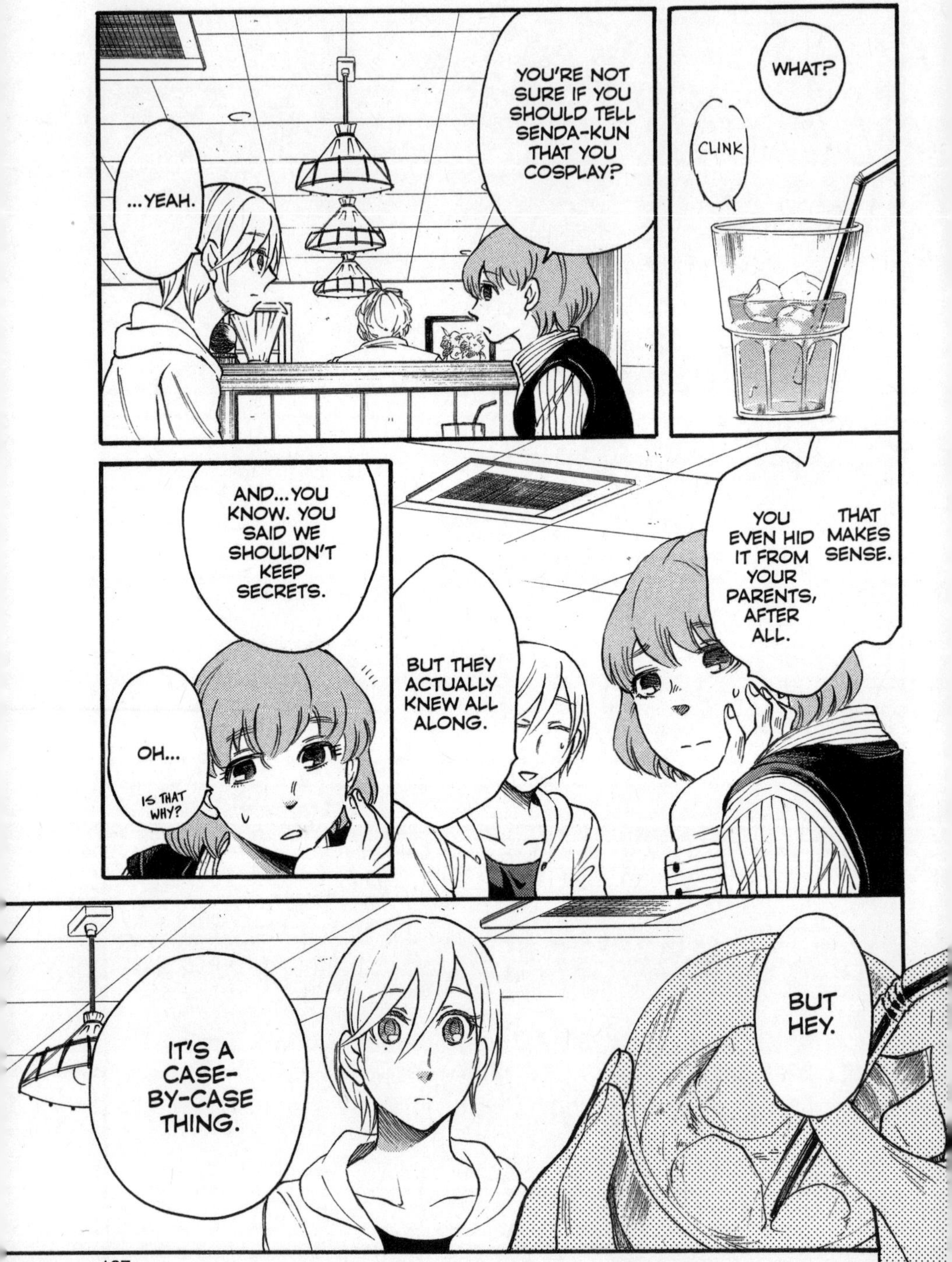
WHAT?
CLINK
YOU'RE NOT SURE IF YOU SHOULD TELL SENDA-KUN THAT YOU COSPLAY?
...YEAH.
THAT MAKES SENSE.
YOU EVEN HID IT FROM YOUR PARENTS, AFTER ALL.
AND...YOU KNOW. YOU SAID WE SHOULDN'T KEEP SECRETS.
BUT THEY ACTUALLY KNEW ALL ALONG.
OH...
IS THAT WHY?
BUT HEY.
IT'S A CASE-BY-CASE THING.

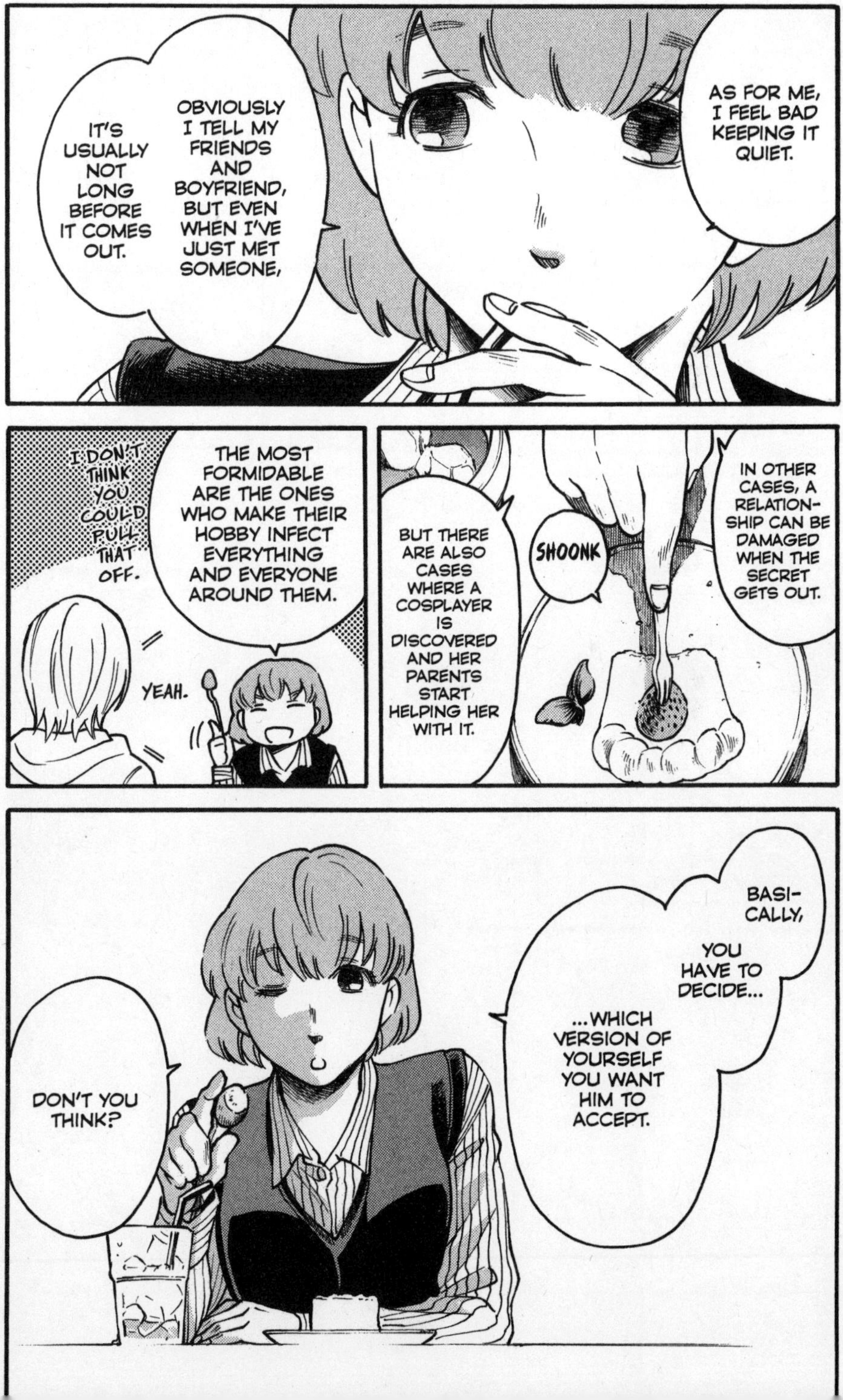
AS FOR ME, I FEEL BAD KEEPING IT QUIET.
OBVIOUSLY I TELL MY FRIENDS AND BOYFRIEND, BUT EVEN WHEN I'VE JUST MET SOMEONE,
IT'S USUALLY NOT LONG BEFORE IT COMES OUT.
IN OTHER CASES, A RELATION-SHIP CAN BE DAMAGED WHEN THE SECRET GETS OUT.
SHOONK
BUT THERE ARE ALSO CASES WHERE A COSPLAYER IS DISCOVERED AND HER PARENTS START HELPING HER WITH IT.
THE MOST FORMIDABLE ARE THE ONES WHO MAKE THEIR HOBBY INFECT EVERYTHING AND EVERYONE AROUND THEM.
I DON'T THINK YOU COULD PULL THAT OFF.
YEAH.
BASI-CALLY,
YOU HAVE TO DECIDE...
...WHICH VERSION OF YOURSELF YOU WANT HIM TO ACCEPT.
DON'T YOU THINK?

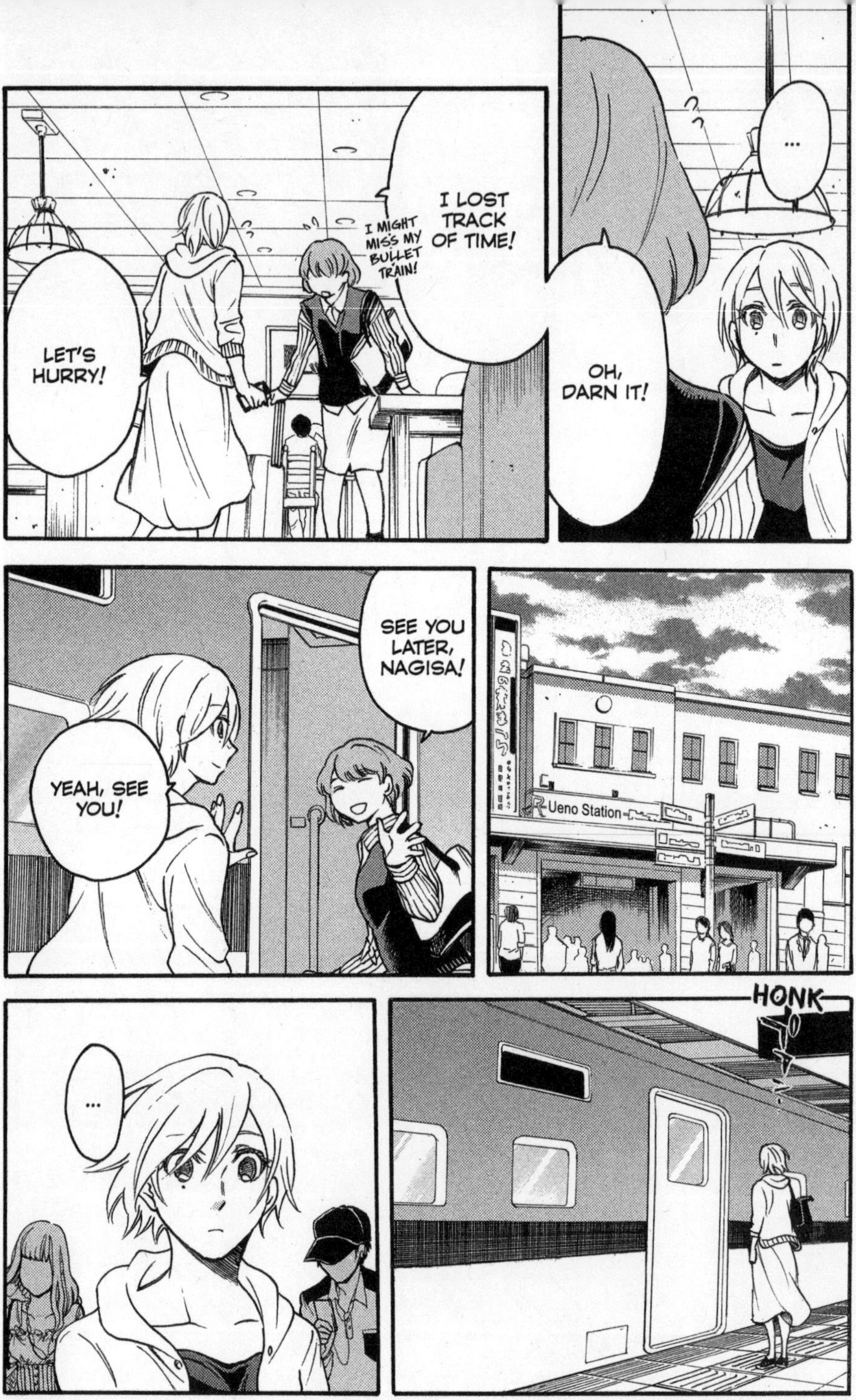
...
OH, DARN IT!
I LOST TRACK OF TIME!
I MIGHT MISS MY BULLET TRAIN!
LET'S HURRY!
Ueno Station
SEE YOU LATER, NAGISA!
YEAH, SEE YOU!
HONK
...

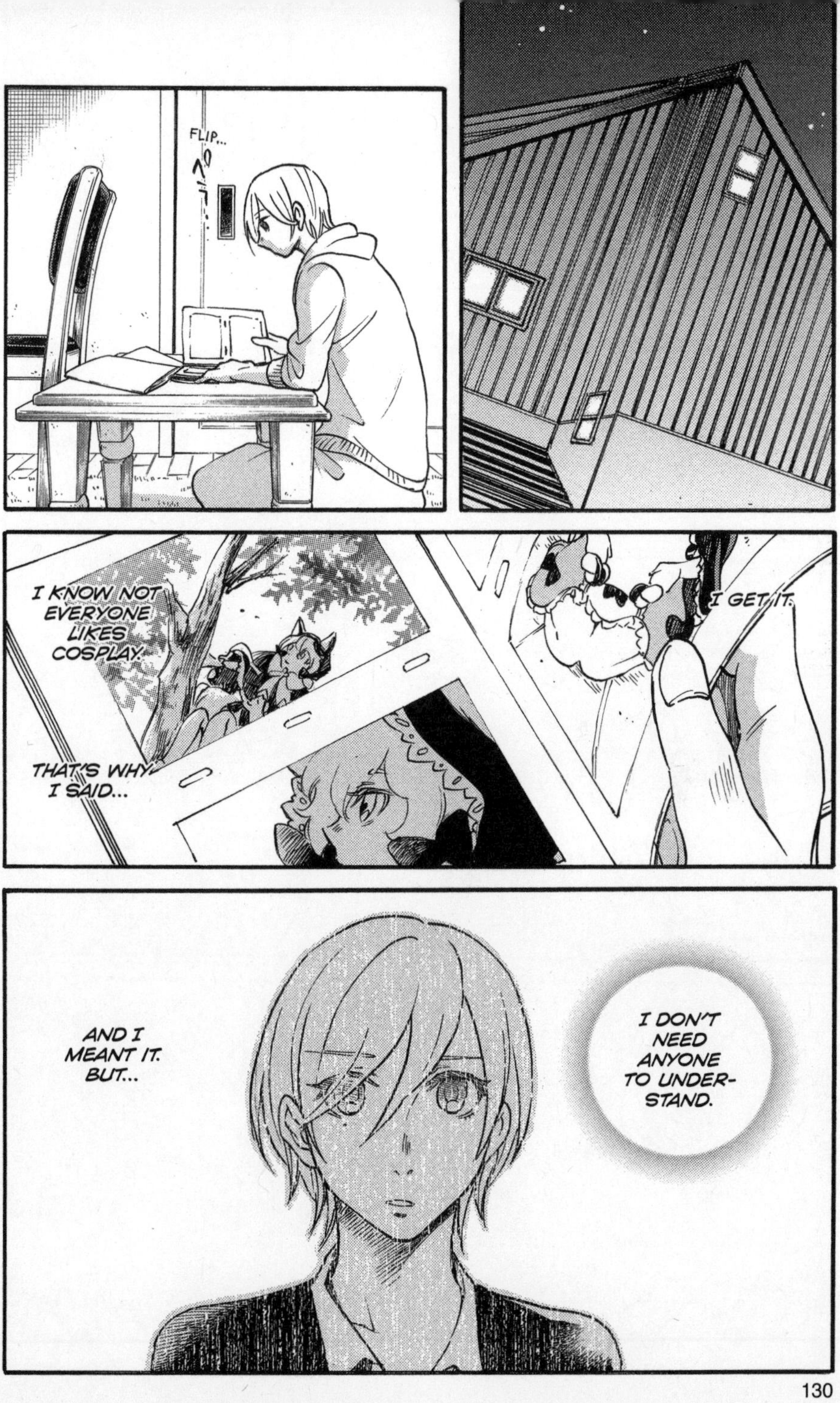
FLIP...
I GET IT.
I KNOW NOT EVERYONE LIKES COSPLAY.
THAT'S WHY I SAID...
I DON'T NEED ANYONE TO UNDER-STAND.
AND I MEANT IT. BUT...

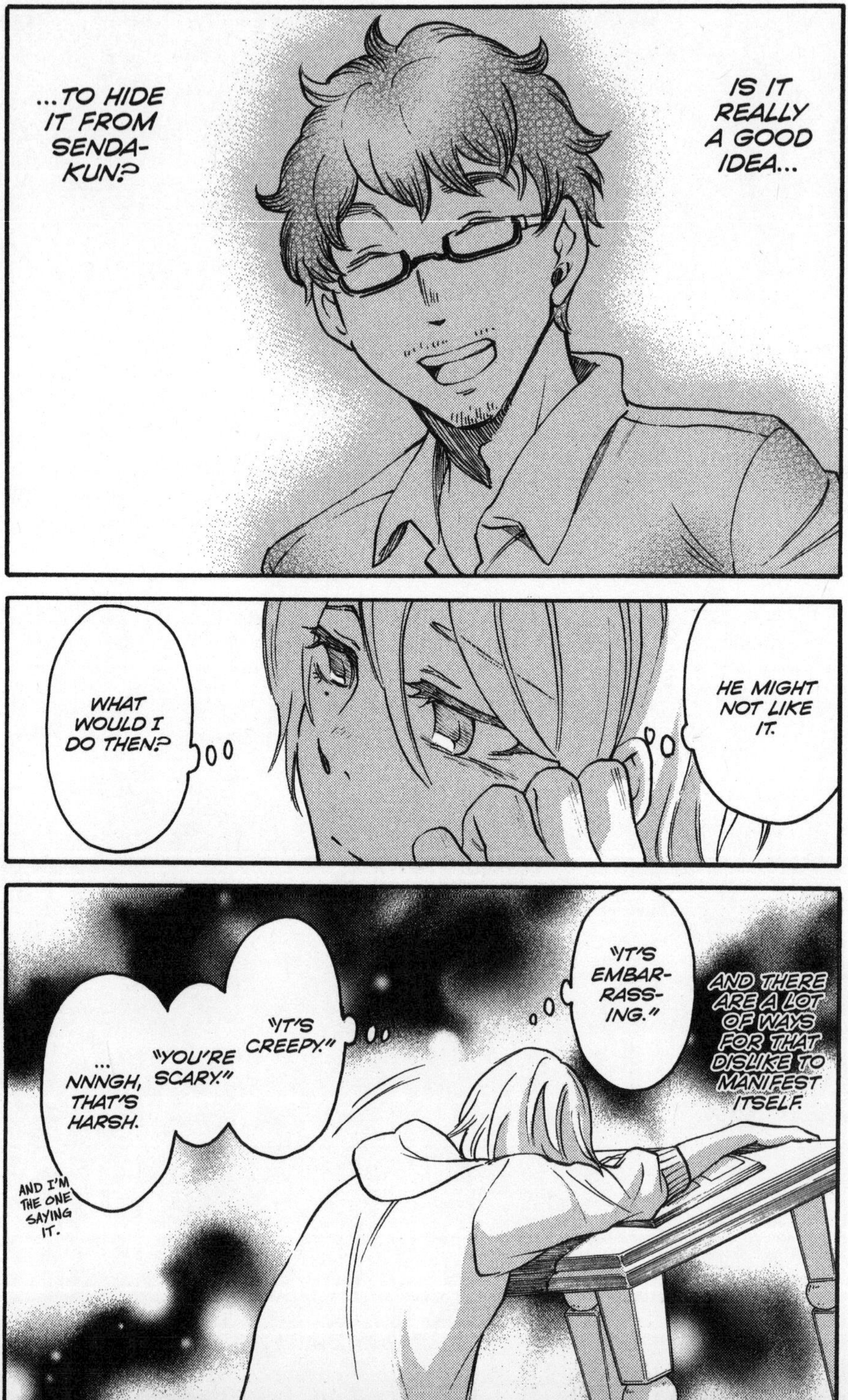
IS IT REALLY A GOOD IDEA...
...TO HIDE IT FROM SENDA-KUN?
HE MIGHT NOT LIKE IT.
WHAT WOULD I DO THEN?
AND THERE ARE A LOT OF WAYS FOR THAT DISLIKE TO MANIFEST ITSELF.
"IT'S EMBARRASSING."
"IT'S CREEPY."
"YOU'RE SCARY."
...NNNGH, THAT'S HARSH.
AND I'M THE ONE SAYING IT.

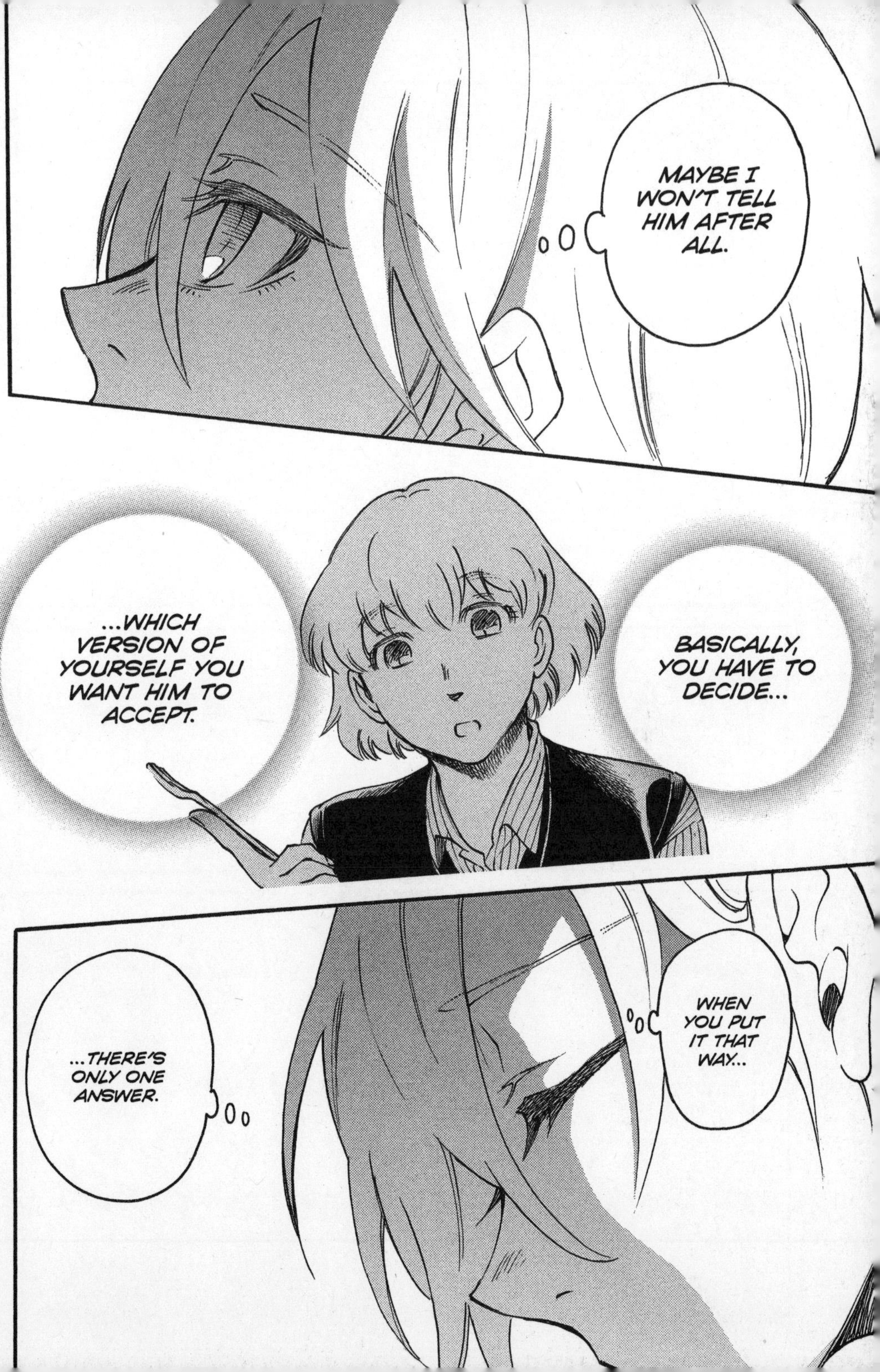
MAYBE I WON'T TELL HIM AFTER ALL.
BASICALLY, YOU HAVE TO DECIDE...
...WHICH VERSION OF YOURSELF YOU WANT HIM TO ACCEPT.
WHEN YOU PUT IT THAT WAY...
...THERE'S ONLY ONE ANSWER.

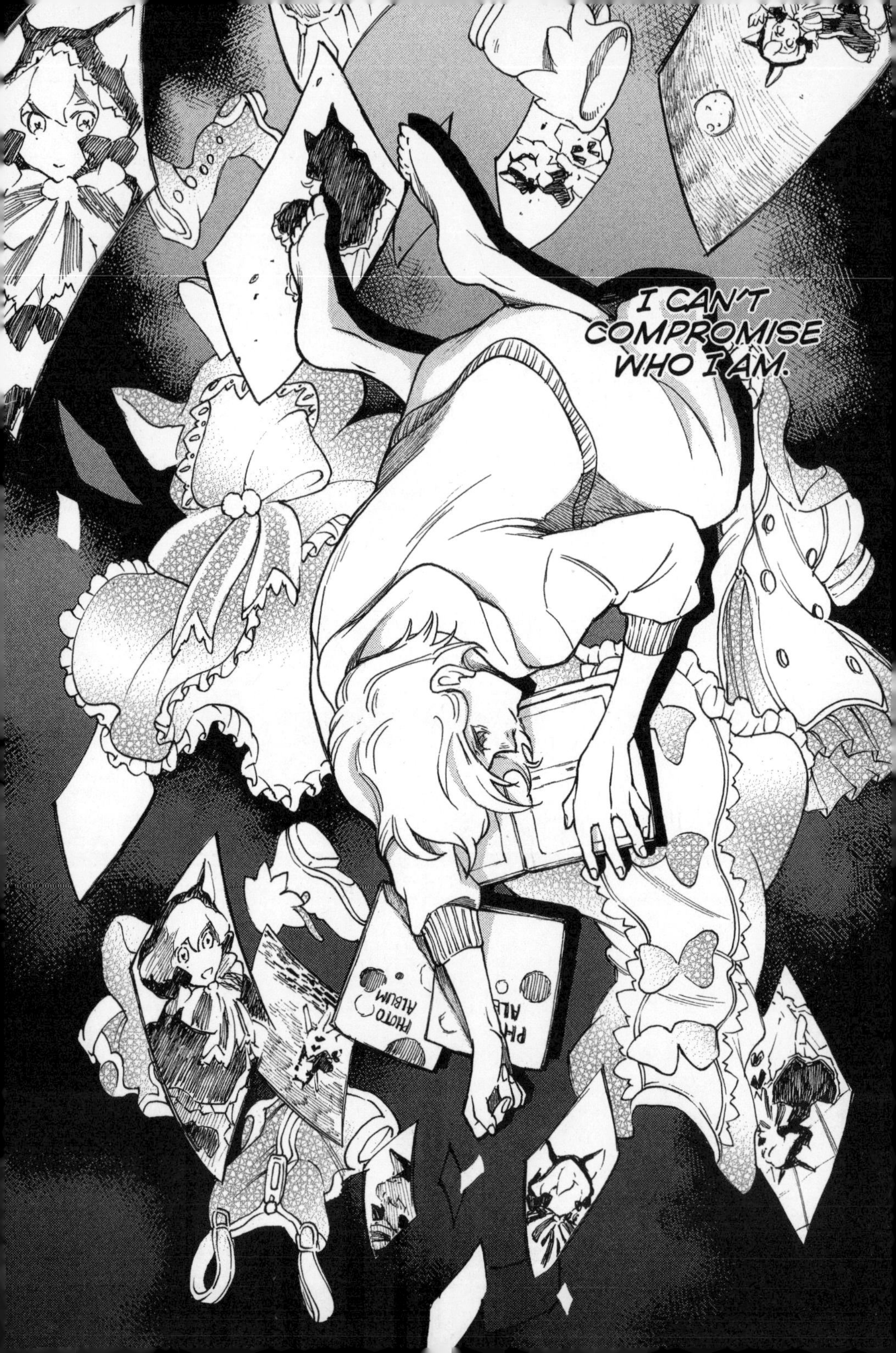
I CAN'T COMPROMISE WHO I AM.
PHOTO ALBUM

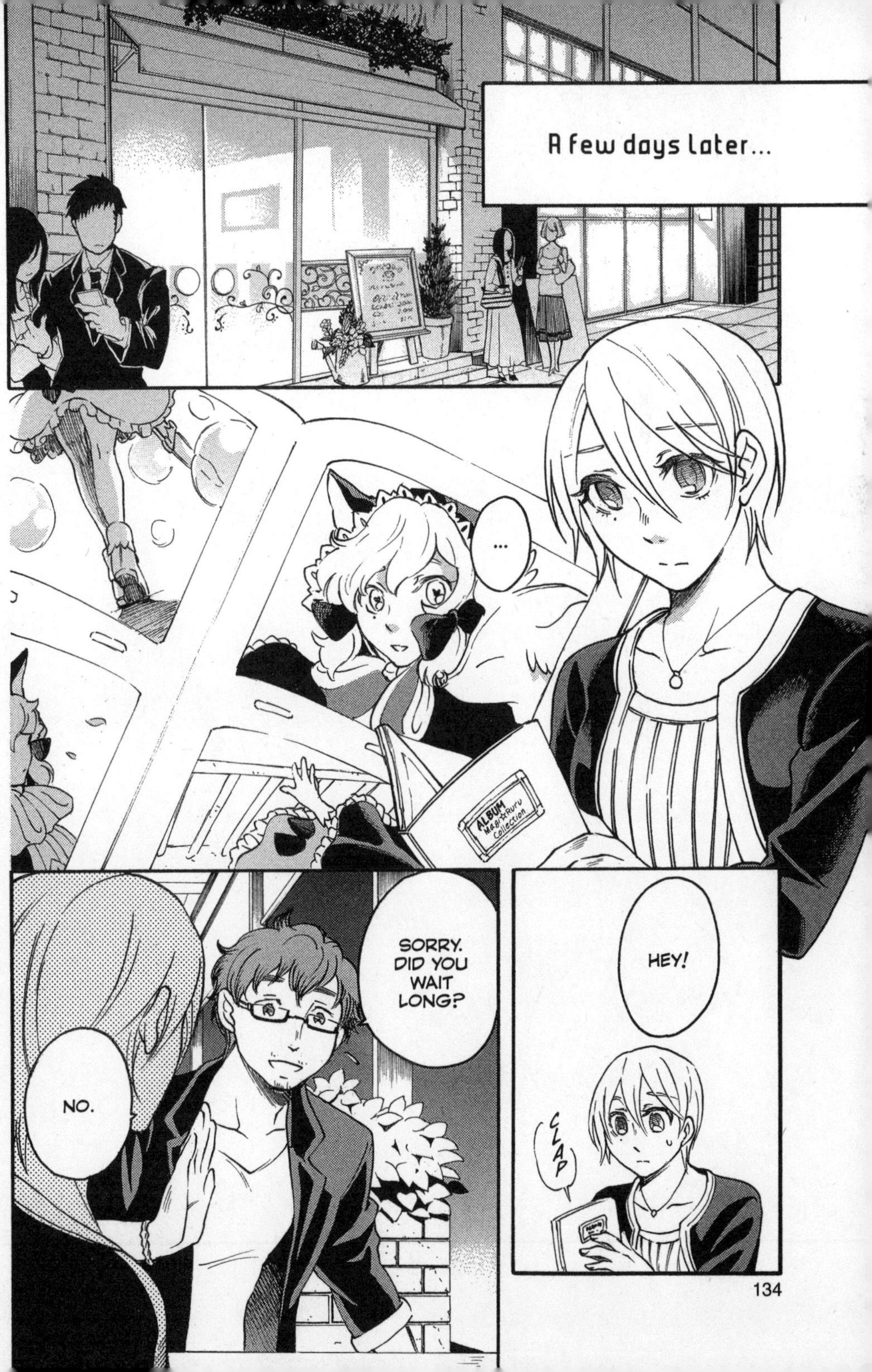
A few days later...
...
ALBUM Magi☆Ruru Collection
HEY!
CLAP
SORRY. DID YOU WAIT LONG?
NO.

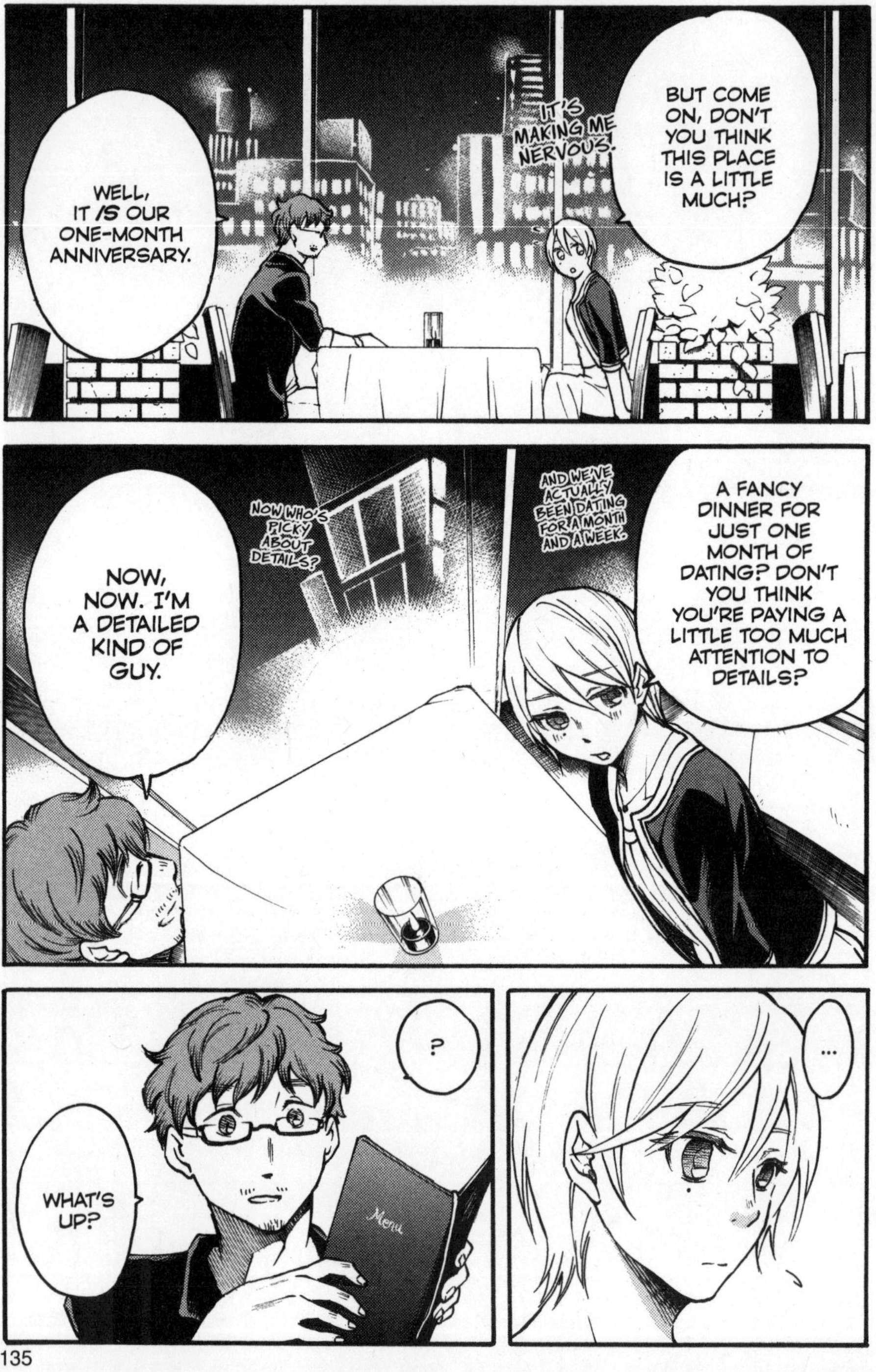
BUT COME ON, DON'T YOU THINK THIS PLACE IS A LITTLE MUCH?
IT'S MAKING ME NERVOUS!
WELL, IT *IS* OUR ONE-MONTH ANNIVERSARY.
A FANCY DINNER FOR JUST ONE MONTH OF DATING? DON'T YOU THINK YOU'RE PAYING A LITTLE TOO MUCH ATTENTION TO DETAILS?
AND WE'VE ACTUALLY BEEN DATING FOR A MONTH AND A WEEK.
NOW WHO'S PICKY ABOUT DETAILS?
NOW, NOW. I'M A DETAILED KIND OF GUY.
...
?
WHAT'S UP?
Menu

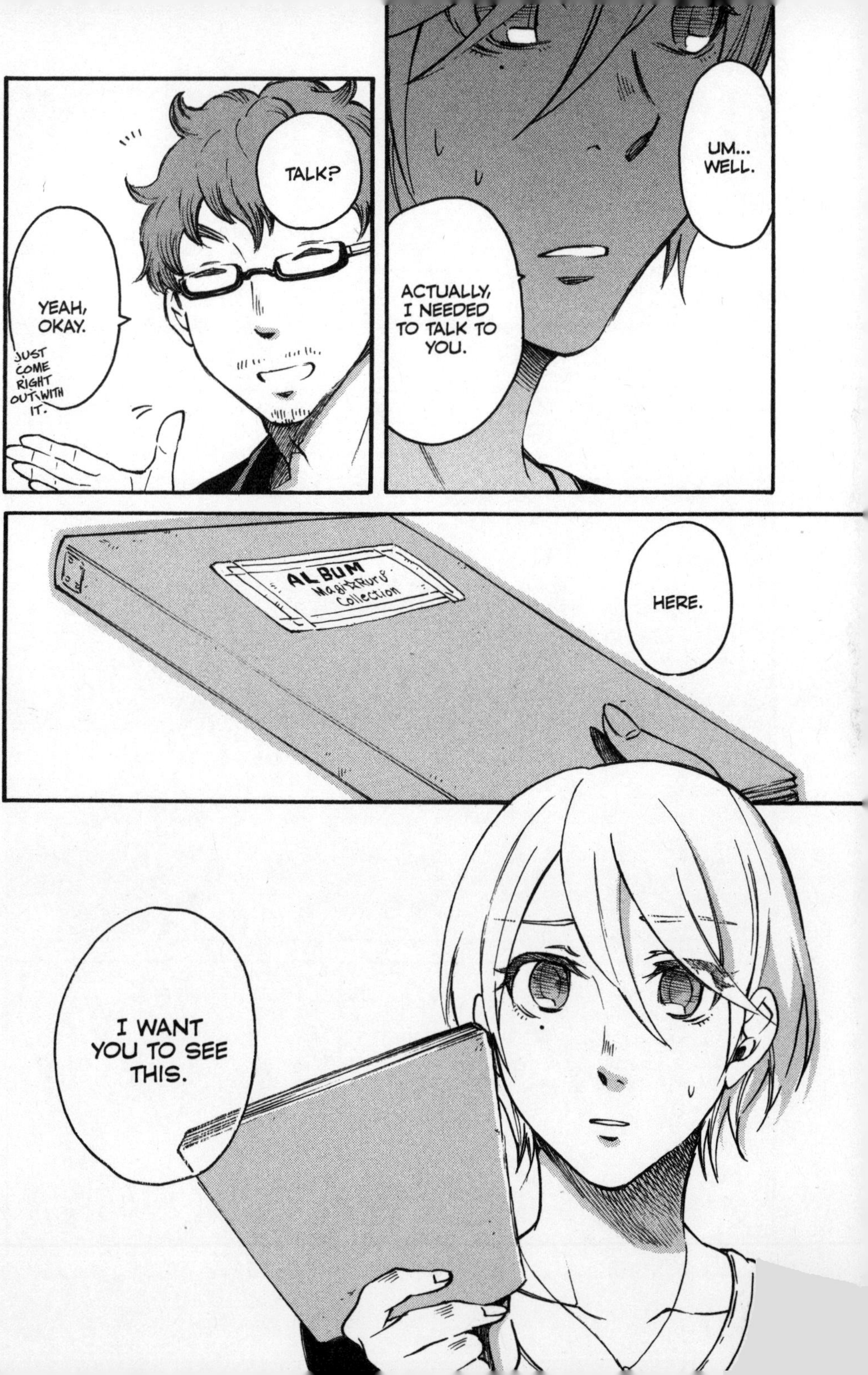
UM... WELL.
ACTUALLY, I NEEDED TO TALK TO YOU.
TALK?
YEAH, OKAY.
JUST COME RIGHT OUT WITH IT.
HERE.
ALBUM
I WANT YOU TO SEE THIS.

COMIKET: Comic Market, the world's largest *dōjinshi* fair, attended by many cosplayers. The December 2014 Comiket recorded an attendance of 560,000.

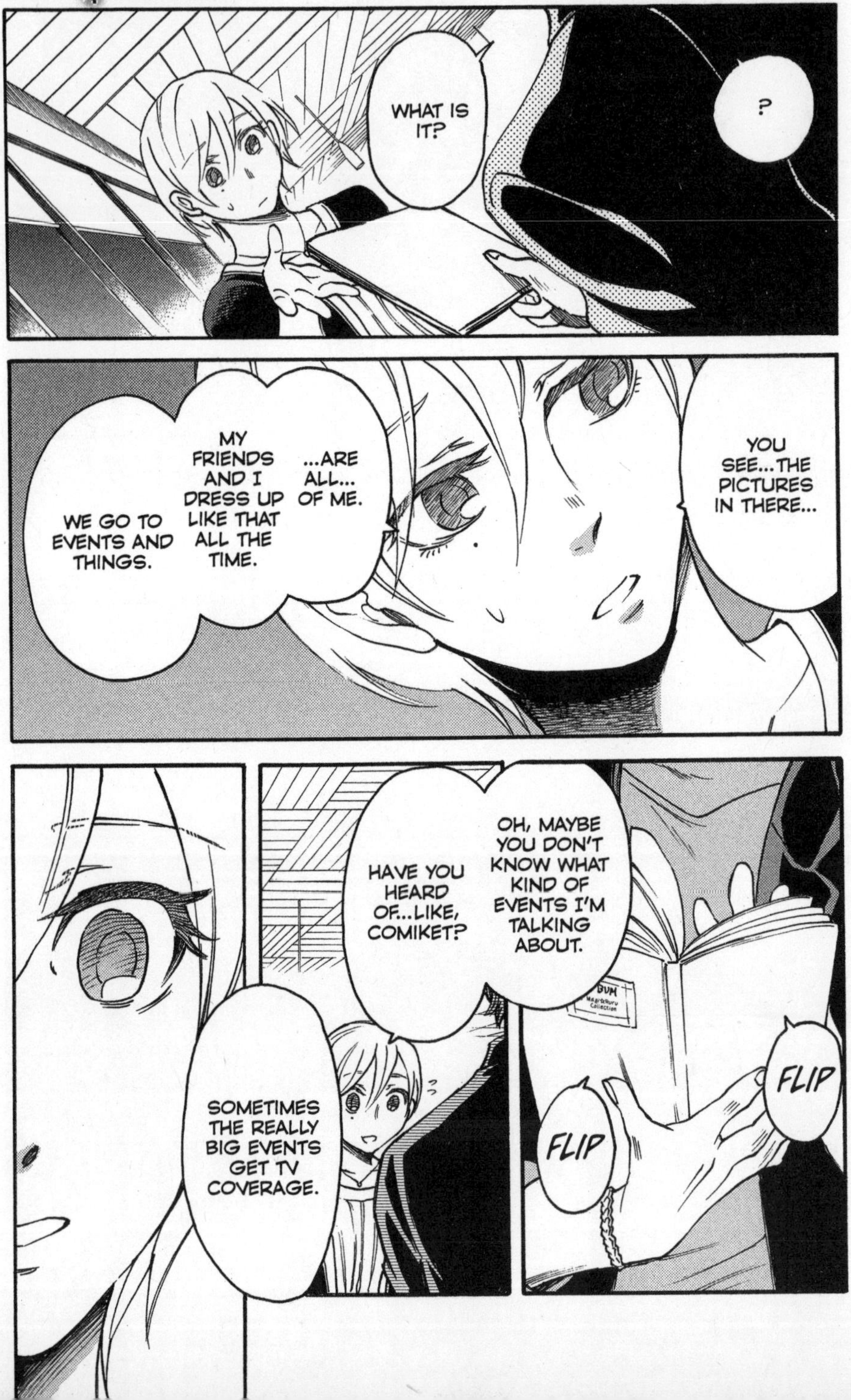
?
WHAT IS IT?
YOU SEE...THE PICTURES IN THERE...
...ARE ALL... OF ME.
MY FRIENDS AND I DRESS UP LIKE THAT ALL THE TIME.
WE GO TO EVENTS AND THINGS.
FLIP
FLIP
OH, MAYBE YOU DON'T KNOW WHAT KIND OF EVENTS I'M TALKING ABOUT.
HAVE YOU HEARD OF...LIKE, COMIKET?
SOMETIMES THE REALLY BIG EVENTS GET TV COVERAGE.

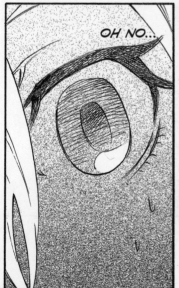

OH NO...

UH...

WOW...
I DIDN'T
EXPECT
THAT.

...ARE
ALL...
YOU?

THESE...

UM...

ER...

WELL,
YEAH.
BUT...

NO...

I...I'M
SORRY.
YOU MUST
BE IN
SHOCK.

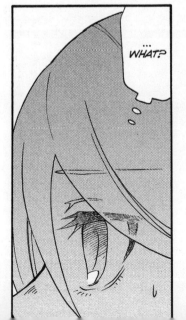

...
WHAT?

...I
THINK...
IT'S
FINE.

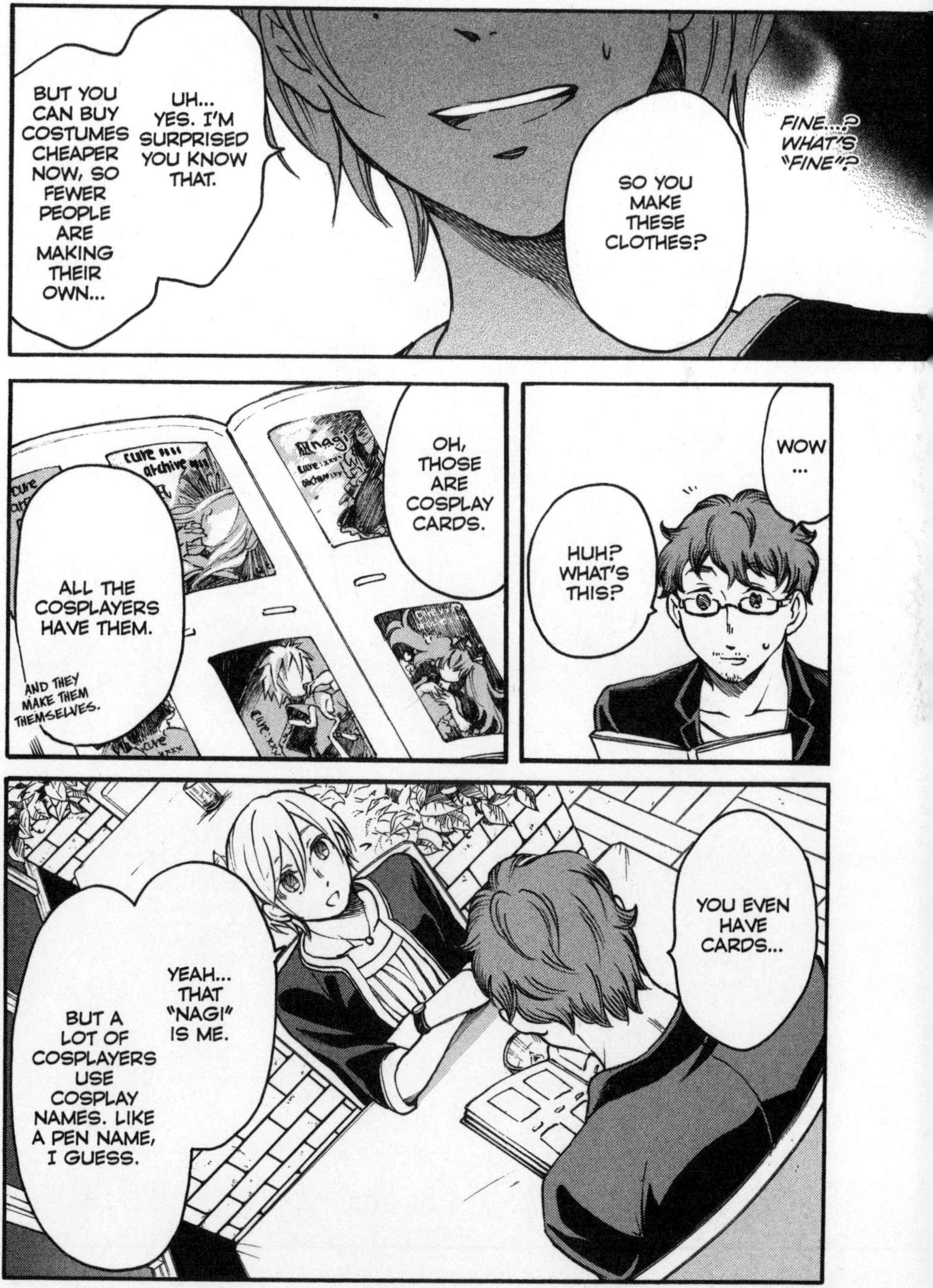
FINE...? WHAT'S "FINE"?
SO YOU MAKE THESE CLOTHES?
UH... YES. I'M SURPRISED YOU KNOW THAT.
BUT YOU CAN BUY COSTUMES CHEAPER NOW, SO FEWER PEOPLE ARE MAKING THEIR OWN...
WOW ...
HUH? WHAT'S THIS?
OH, THOSE ARE COSPLAY CARDS.
ALL THE COSPLAYERS HAVE THEM.
AND THEY MAKE THEM THEMSELVES.
YOU EVEN HAVE CARDS...
YEAH... THAT "NAGI" IS ME.
BUT A LOT OF COSPLAYERS USE COSPLAY NAMES. LIKE A PEN NAME, I GUESS.

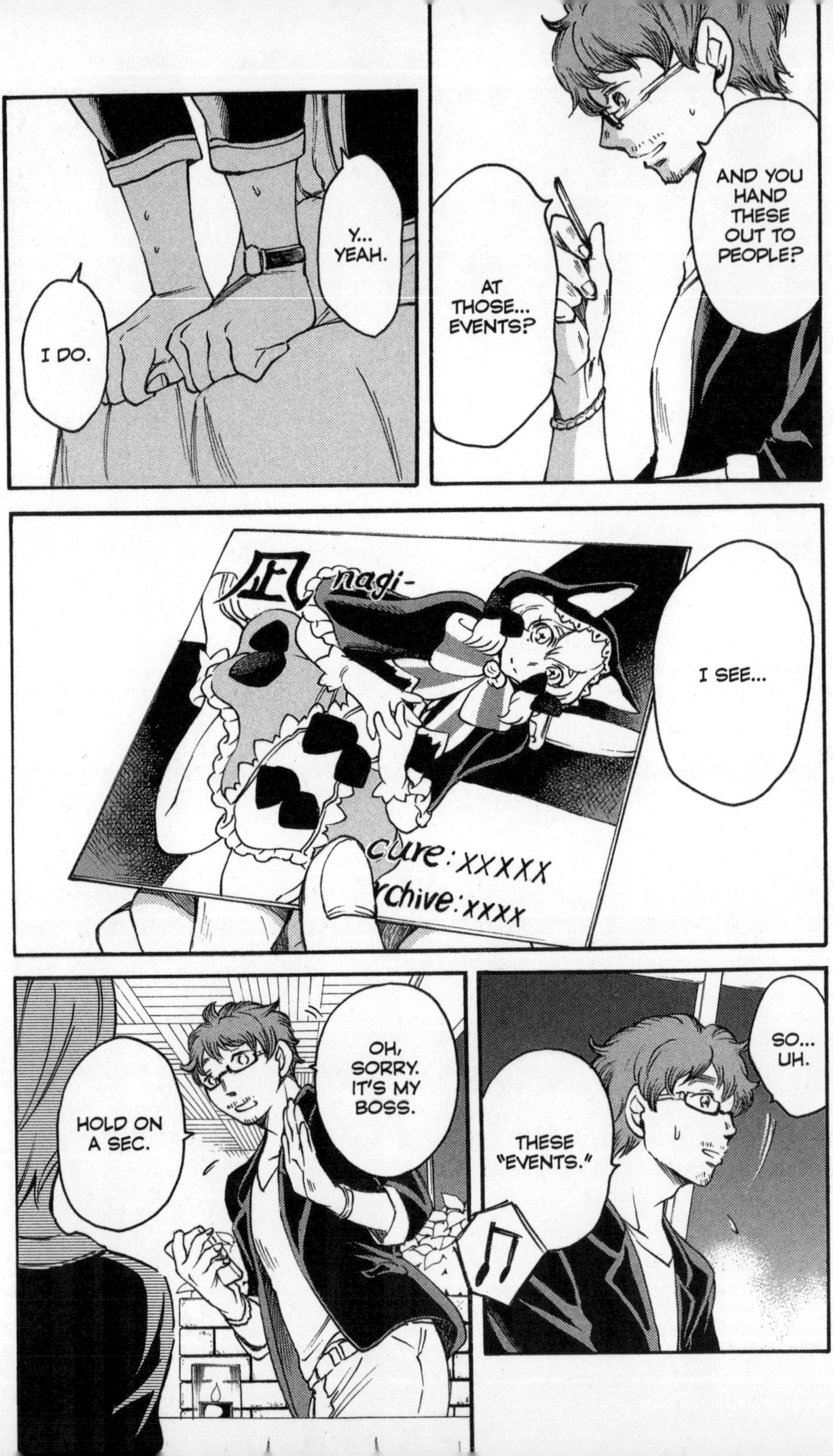
AND YOU HAND THESE OUT TO PEOPLE?
AT THOSE... EVENTS?
Y... YEAH.
I DO.
I SEE...
凪-nagi-
cure:XXXXX
rchive:XXXX
SO... UH.
THESE "EVENTS."
OH, SORRY. IT'S MY BOSS.
HOLD ON A SEC.

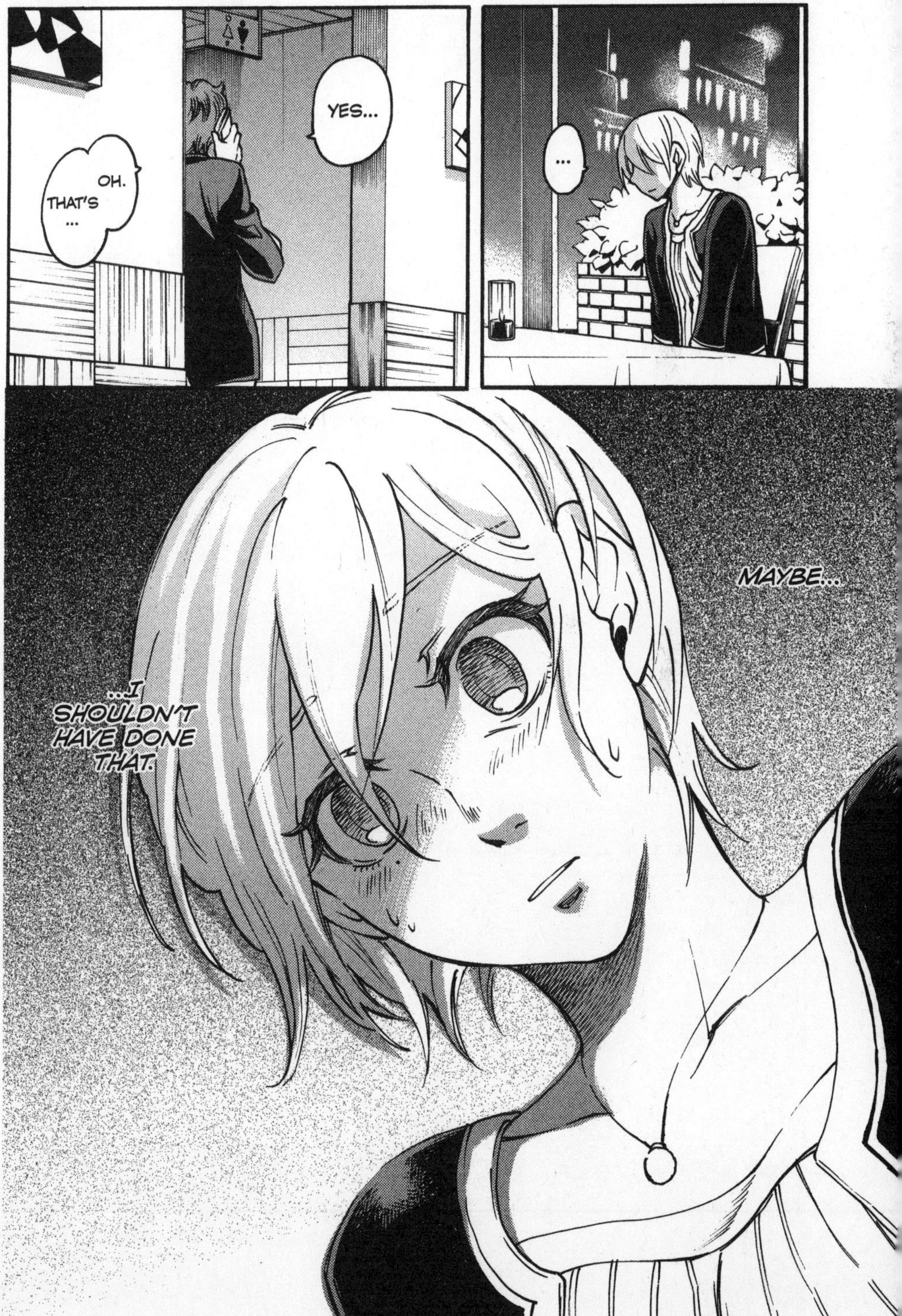
...
YES...
OH. THAT'S ...
MAYBE...
...I SHOULDN'T HAVE DONE THAT.

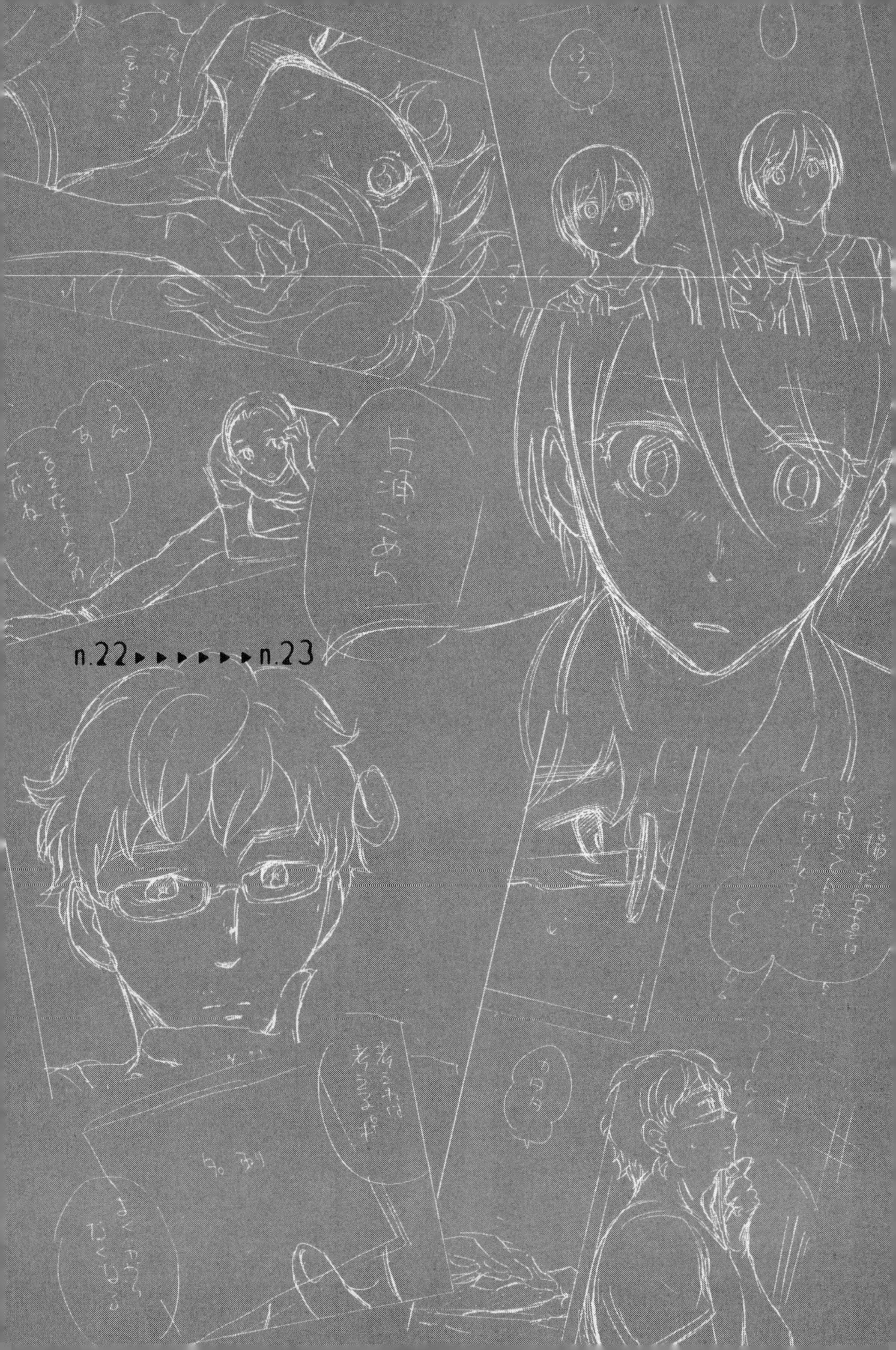

n.22▶▶▶▶▶▶▶n.23

LAST ONE.

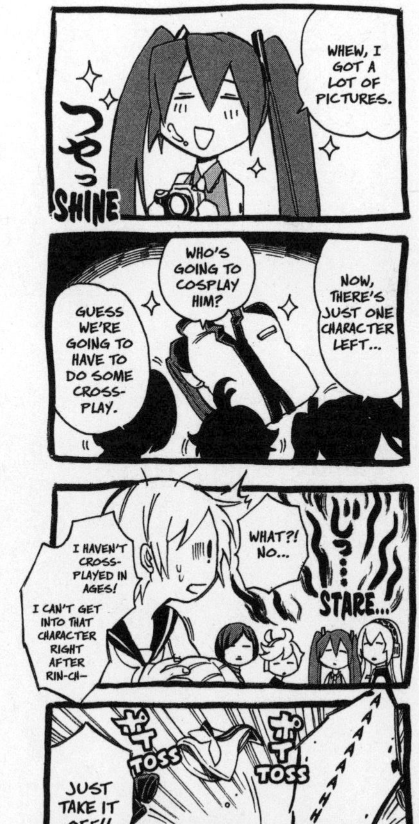
WHEW, I GOT A LOT OF PICTURES.
つやっ
SHINE
NOW, THERE'S JUST ONE CHARACTER LEFT...
WHO'S GOING TO COSPLAY HIM?
GUESS WE'RE GOING TO HAVE TO DO SOME CROSS-PLAY.
じーっ...
STARE...
WHAT?! NO...
I HAVEN'T CROSS-PLAYED IN AGES!
I CAN'T GET INTO THAT CHARACTER RIGHT AFTER RIN-CH–
ポイ
TOSS
ポイ
TOSS
JUST TAKE IT OFF!!

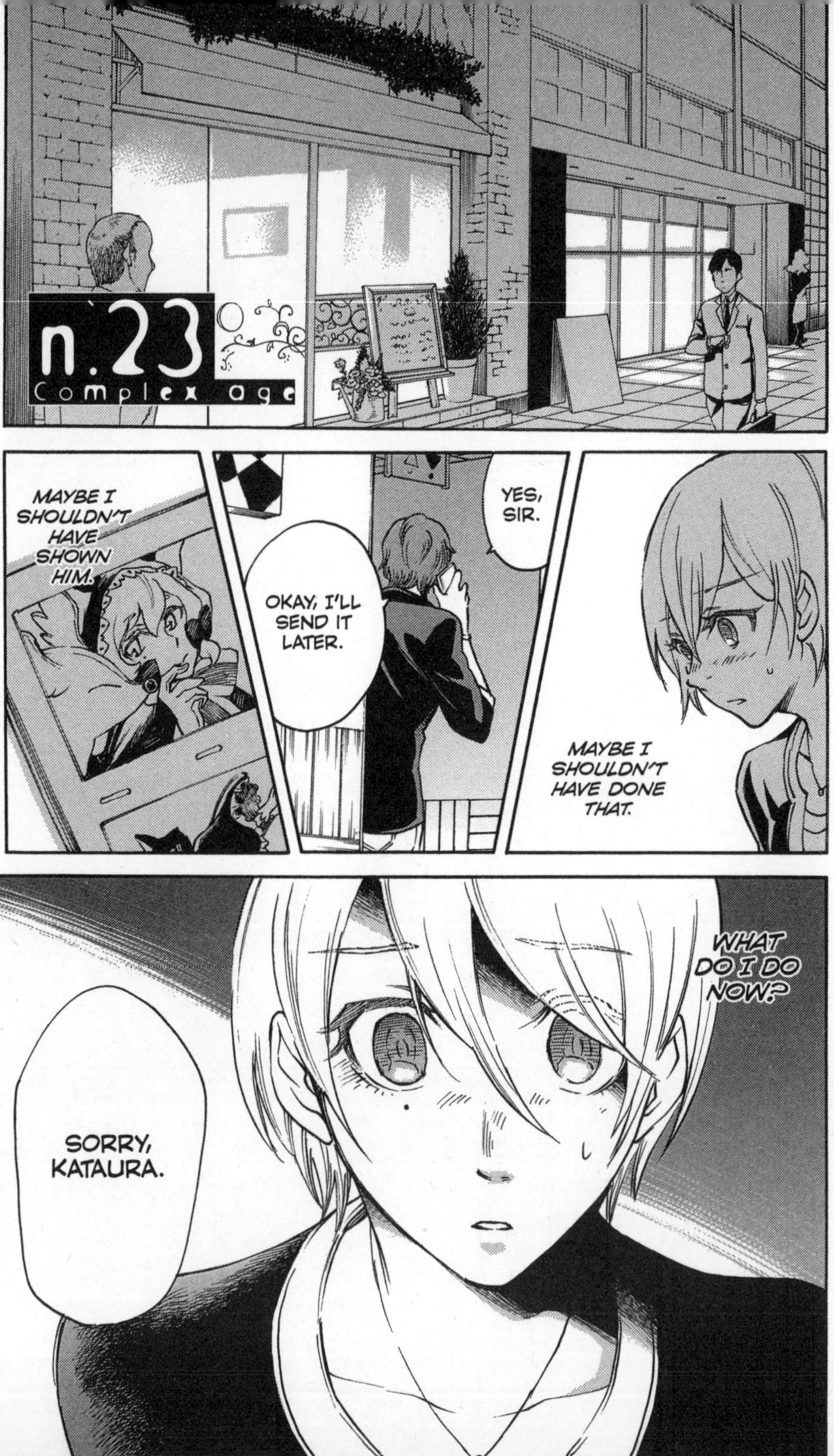
n.23
Complex age
MAYBE I SHOULDN'T HAVE DONE THAT.
YES, SIR.
OKAY, I'LL SEND IT LATER.
MAYBE I SHOULDN'T HAVE SHOWN HIM.
WHAT DO I DO NOW?
SORRY, KATAURA.

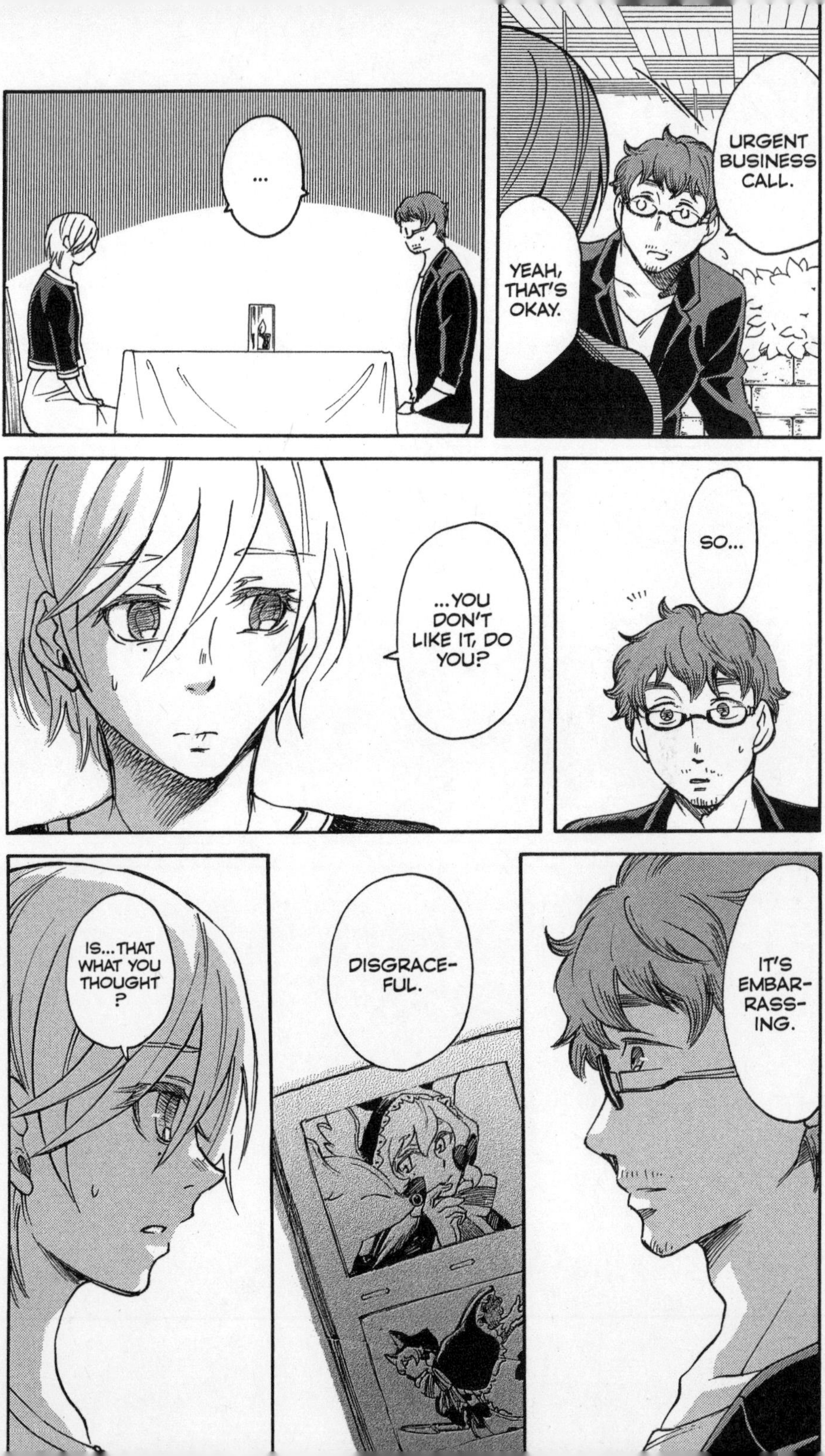
URGENT BUSINESS CALL.
YEAH, THAT'S OKAY.
...
SO...
...YOU DON'T LIKE IT, DO YOU?
IT'S EMBAR-RASS-ING.
DISGRACE-FUL.
IS...THAT WHAT YOU THOUGHT?

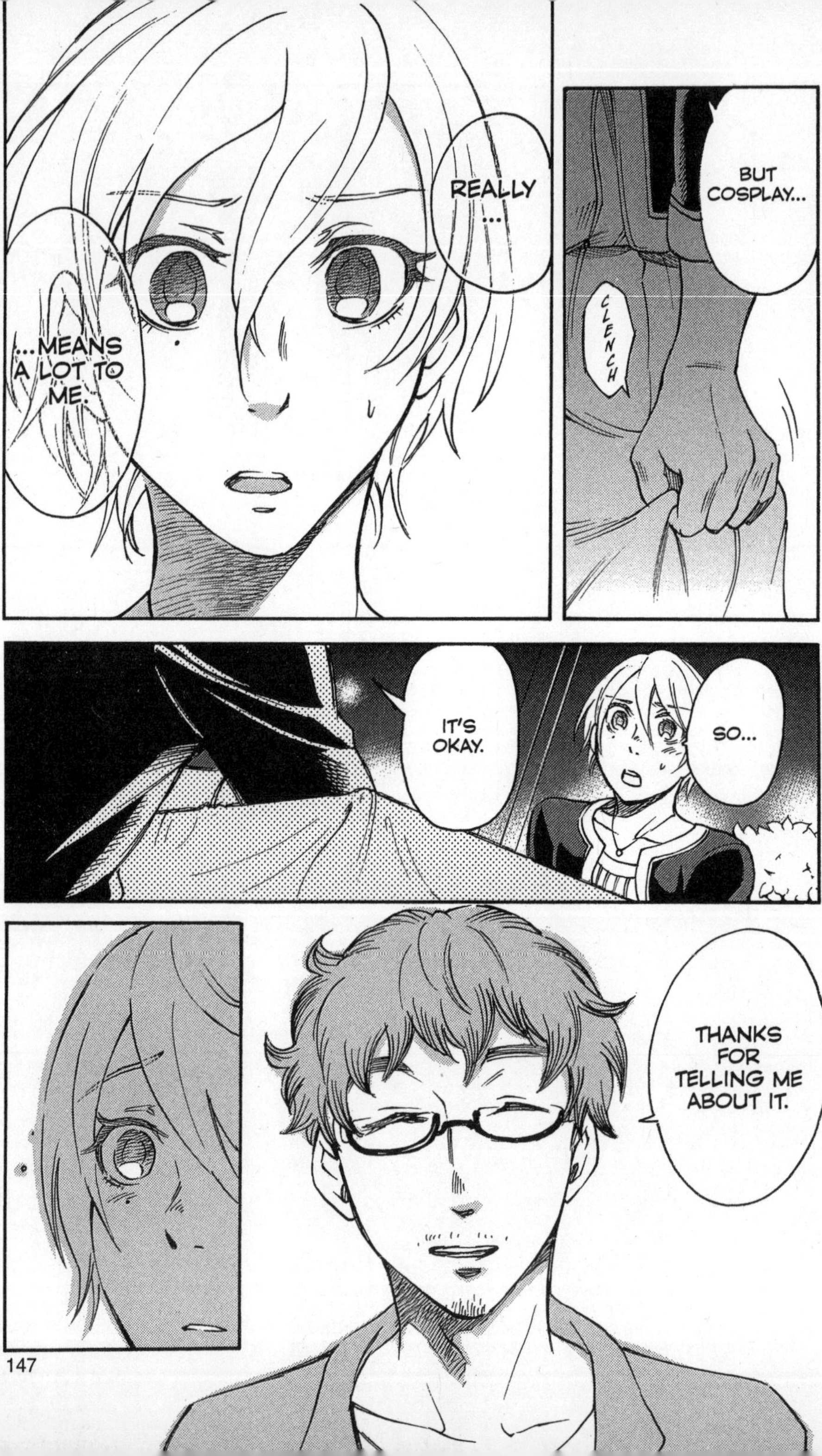
BUT COSPLAY...
CLENCH
REALLY...
...MEANS A LOT TO ME.
SO...
IT'S OKAY.
THANKS FOR TELLING ME ABOUT IT.

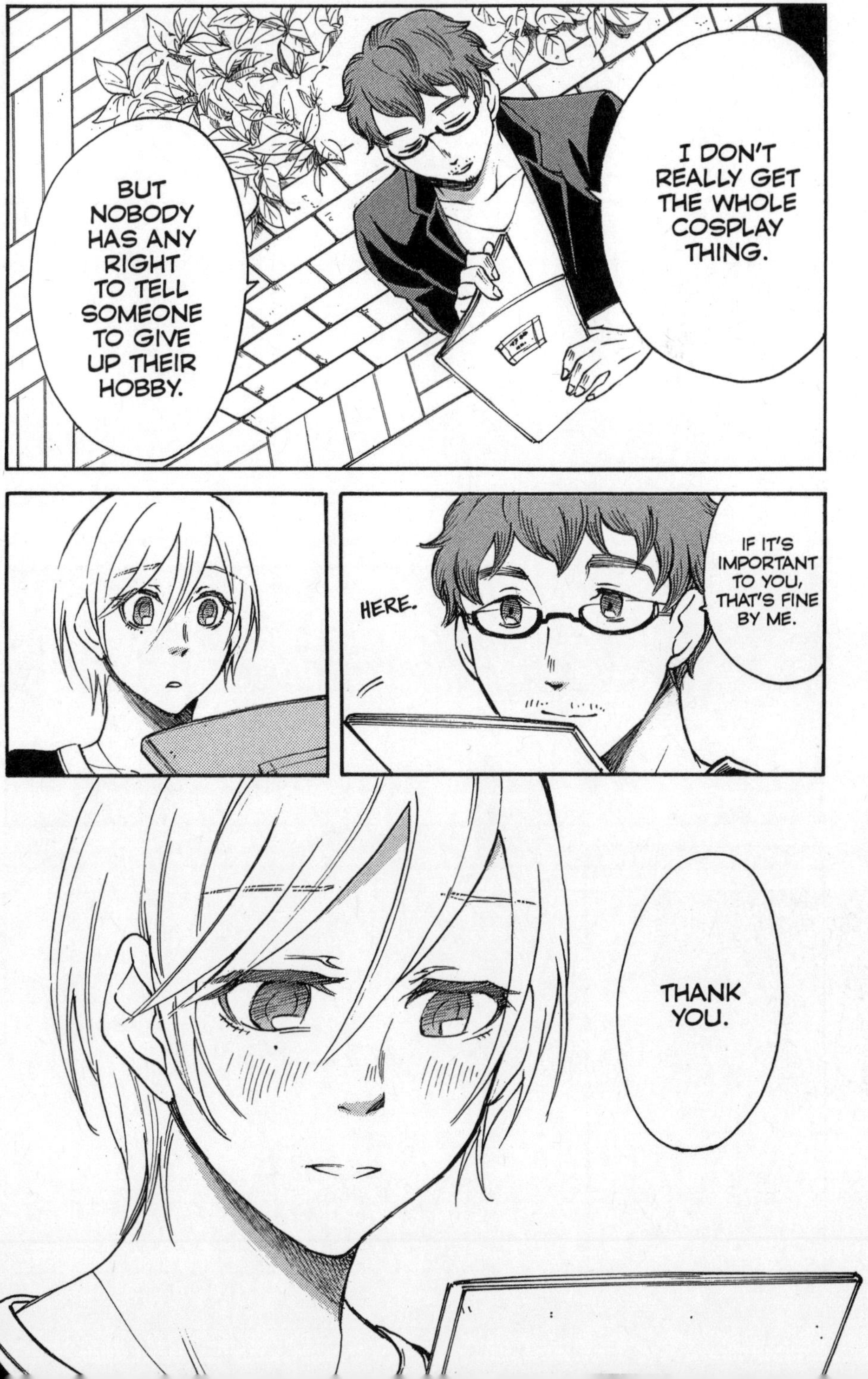
I DON'T REALLY GET THE WHOLE COSPLAY THING.
BUT NOBODY HAS ANY RIGHT TO TELL SOMEONE TO GIVE UP THEIR HOBBY.
IF IT'S IMPORTANT TO YOU, THAT'S FINE BY ME.
HERE.
THANK YOU.

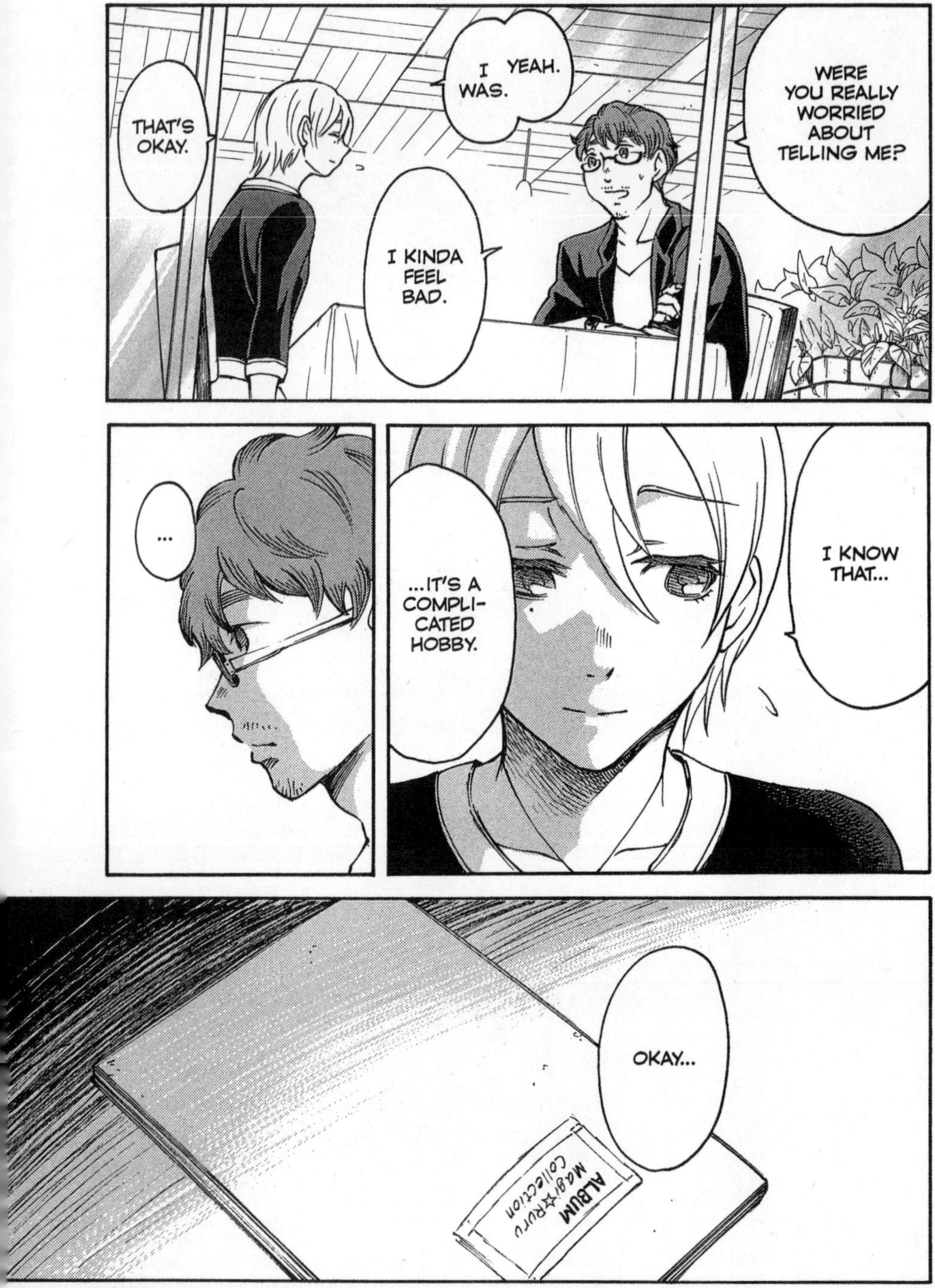
WERE YOU REALLY WORRIED ABOUT TELLING ME?
YEAH. I WAS.
I KINDA FEEL BAD.
THAT'S OKAY.
I KNOW THAT...
...IT'S A COMPLICATED HOBBY.
...
OKAY...
ALBUM Magi☆Ruru Collection

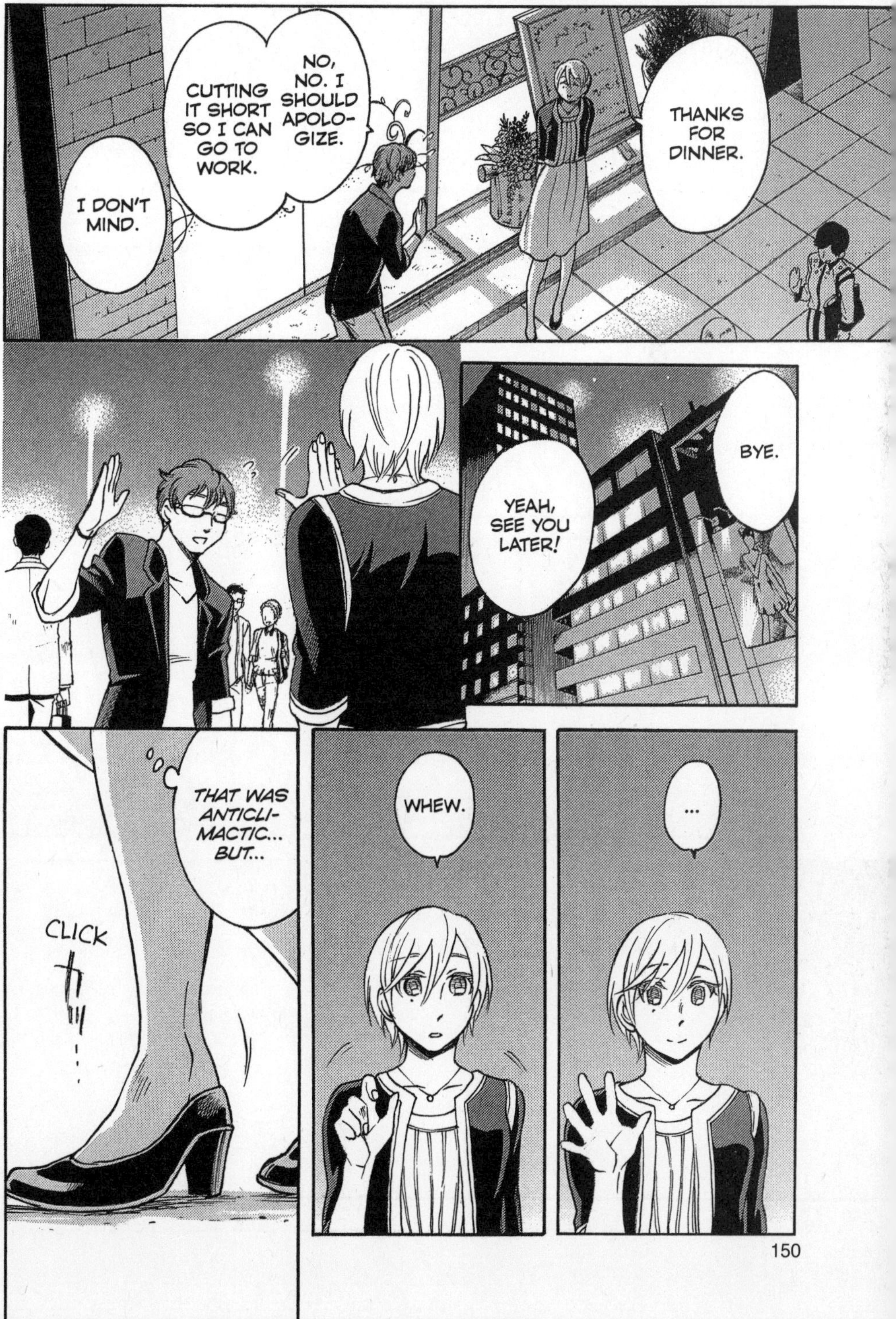
THANKS FOR DINNER.
NO, NO. I SHOULD APOLOGIZE.
CUTTING IT SHORT SO I CAN GO TO WORK.
I DON'T MIND.
BYE.
YEAH, SEE YOU LATER!
...
WHEW.
THAT WAS ANTICLI-MACTIC... BUT...
CLICK

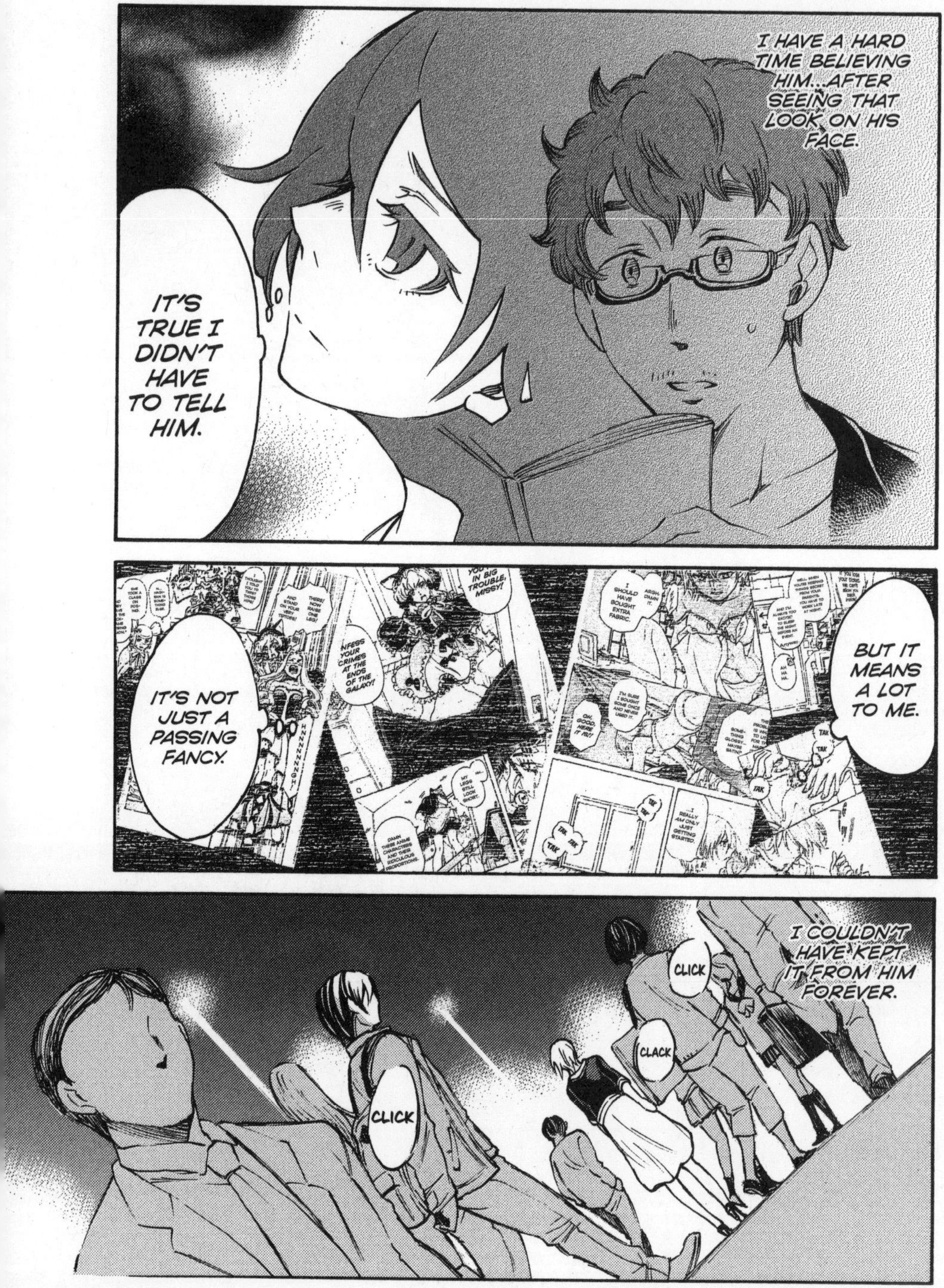
I HAVE A HARD TIME BELIEVING HIM...AFTER SEEING THAT LOOK ON HIS FACE.
IT'S TRUE I DIDN'T HAVE TO TELL HIM.
BUT IT MEANS A LOT TO ME.
IT'S NOT JUST A PASSING FANCY.
I COULDN'T HAVE KEPT IT FROM HIM FOREVER.
CLICK
CLACK
CLICK

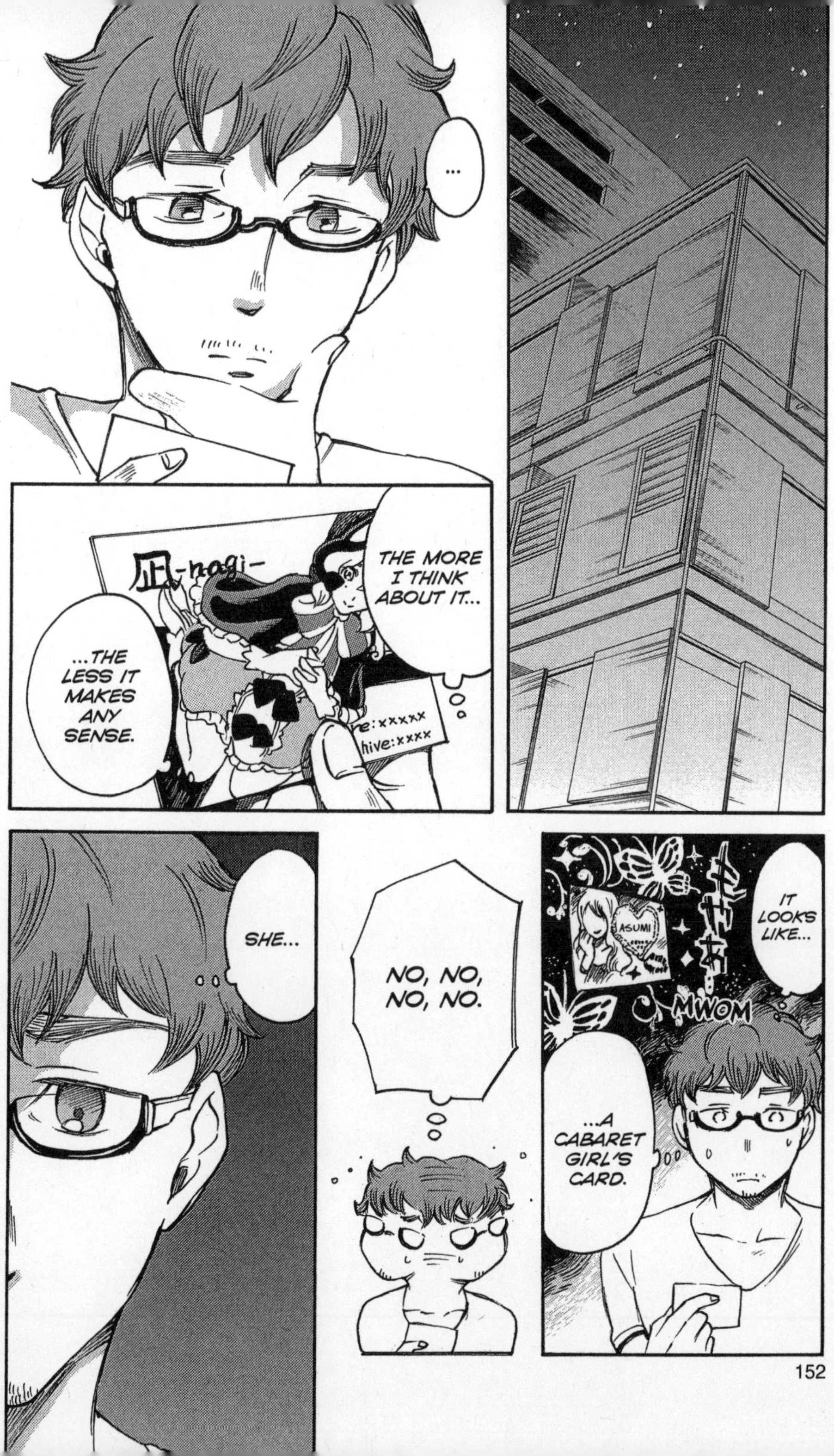

...
-nogi-
THE MORE I THINK ABOUT IT...
...THE LESS IT MAKES ANY SENSE.
ASUMI
IT LOOKS LIKE...
MWOM
...A CABARET GIRL'S CARD.
NO, NO, NO, NO.
SHE...

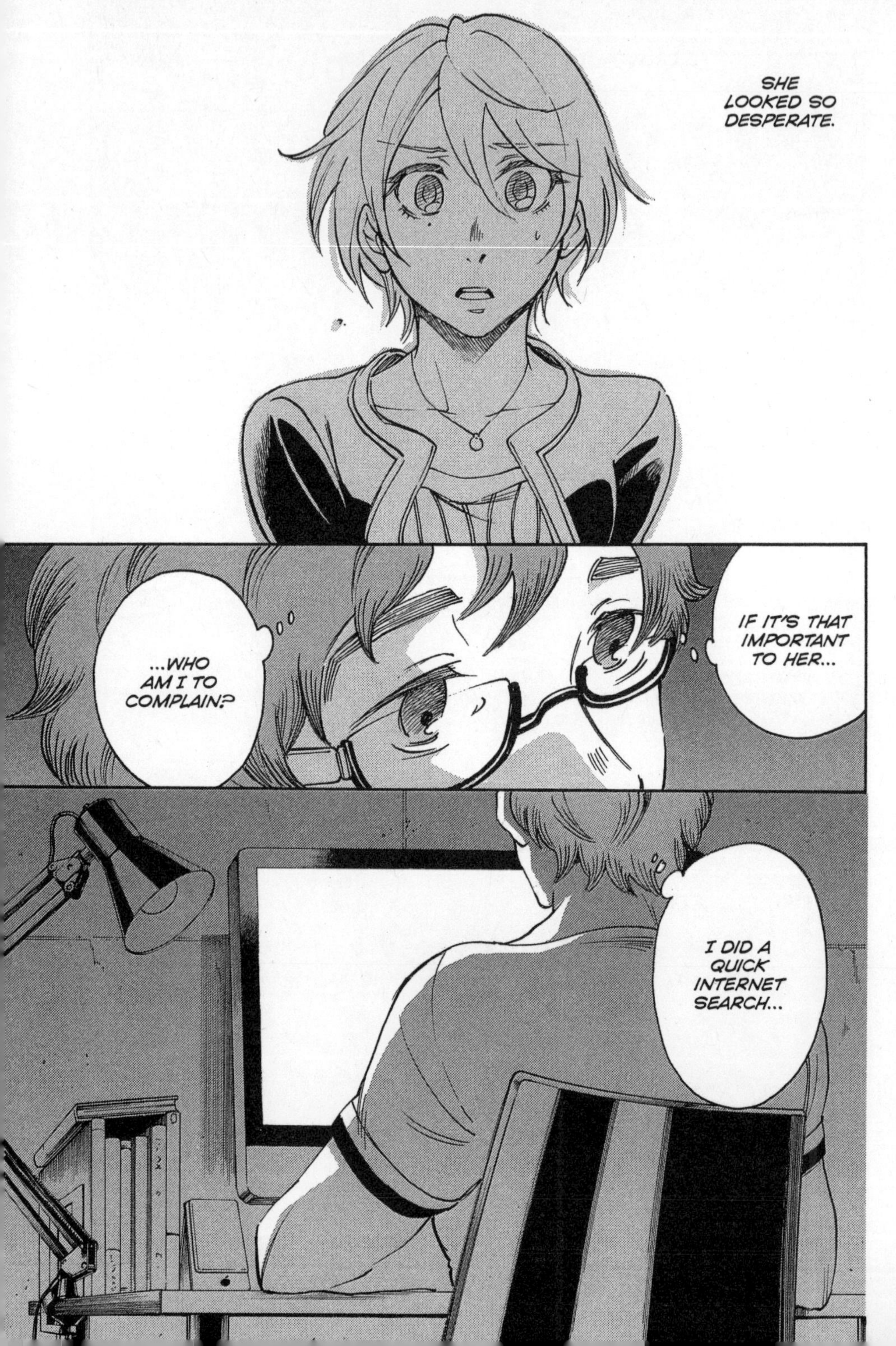
SHE LOOKED SO DESPERATE.
IF IT'S THAT IMPORTANT TO HER...
...WHO AM I TO COMPLAIN?
I DID A QUICK INTERNET SEARCH...

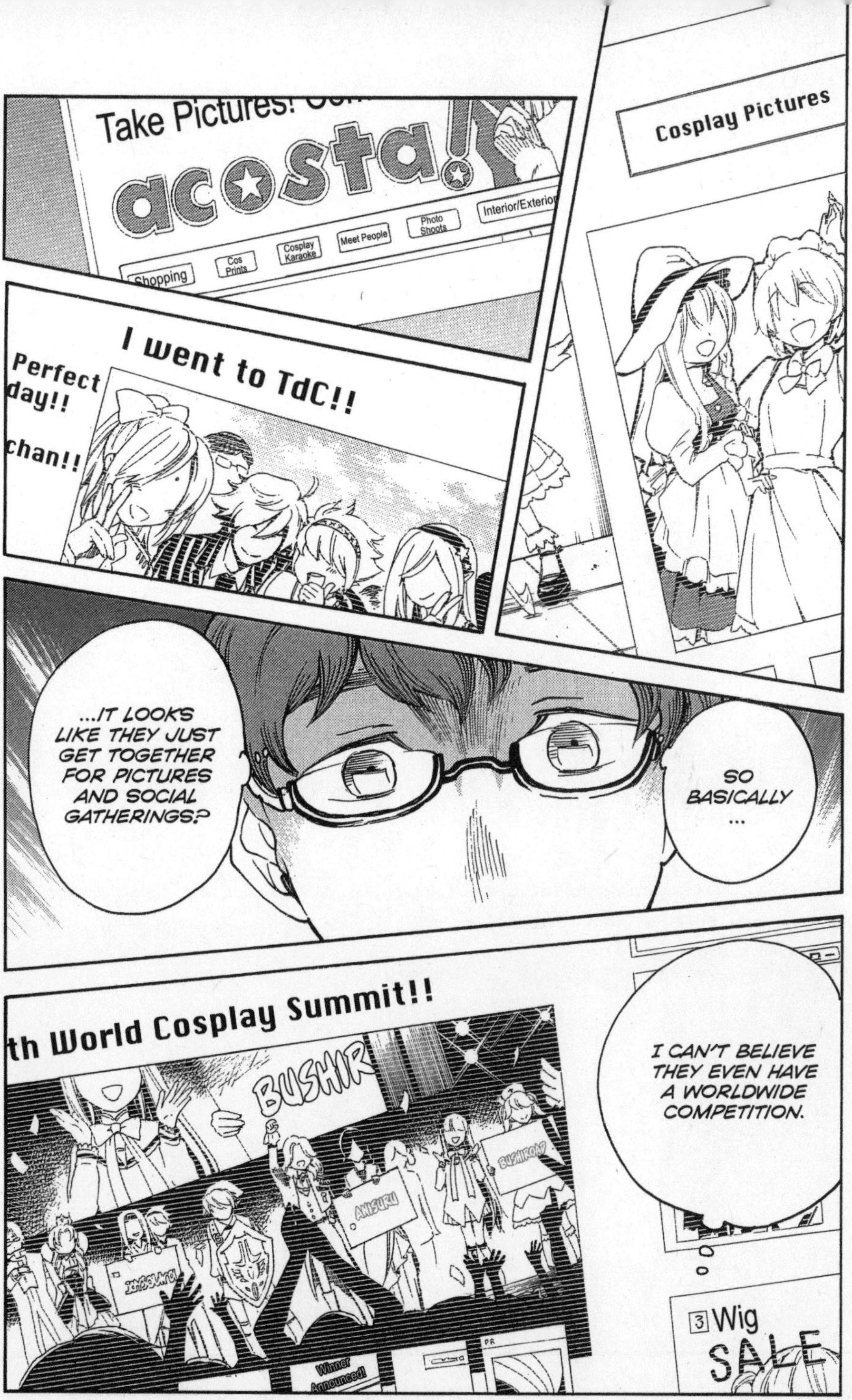
Cosplay Pictures
Take Pictures!
acosta!
Interior/Exterior
Photo Shoots
Meet People
Cosplay Karaoke
Cos Prints
Shopping
I went to TdC!!
Perfect day!!
chan!!
SO BASICALLY ...
...IT LOOKS LIKE THEY JUST GET TOGETHER FOR PICTURES AND SOCIAL GATHERINGS?
I CAN'T BELIEVE THEY EVEN HAVE A WORLDWIDE COMPETITION.
3 Wig
SALE
th World Cosplay Summit!!
BUSHIR
BUSHIROAD
ANISURU
Winner Announced!

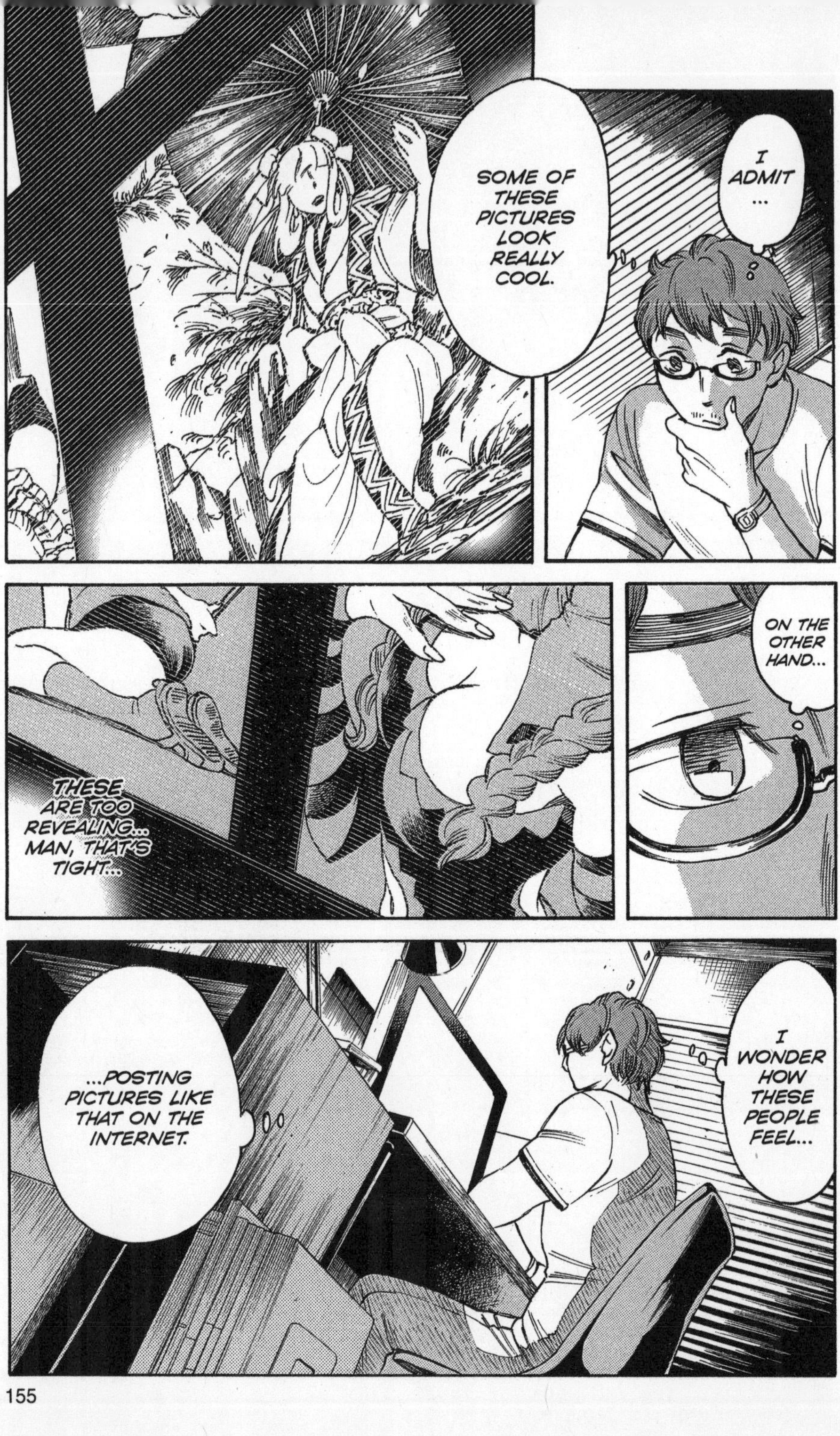
I ADMIT ...
SOME OF THESE PICTURES LOOK REALLY COOL.
ON THE OTHER HAND...
THESE ARE TOO REVEALING... MAN, THAT'S TIGHT...
I WONDER HOW THESE PEOPLE FEEL...
...POSTING PICTURES LIKE THAT ON THE INTERNET.

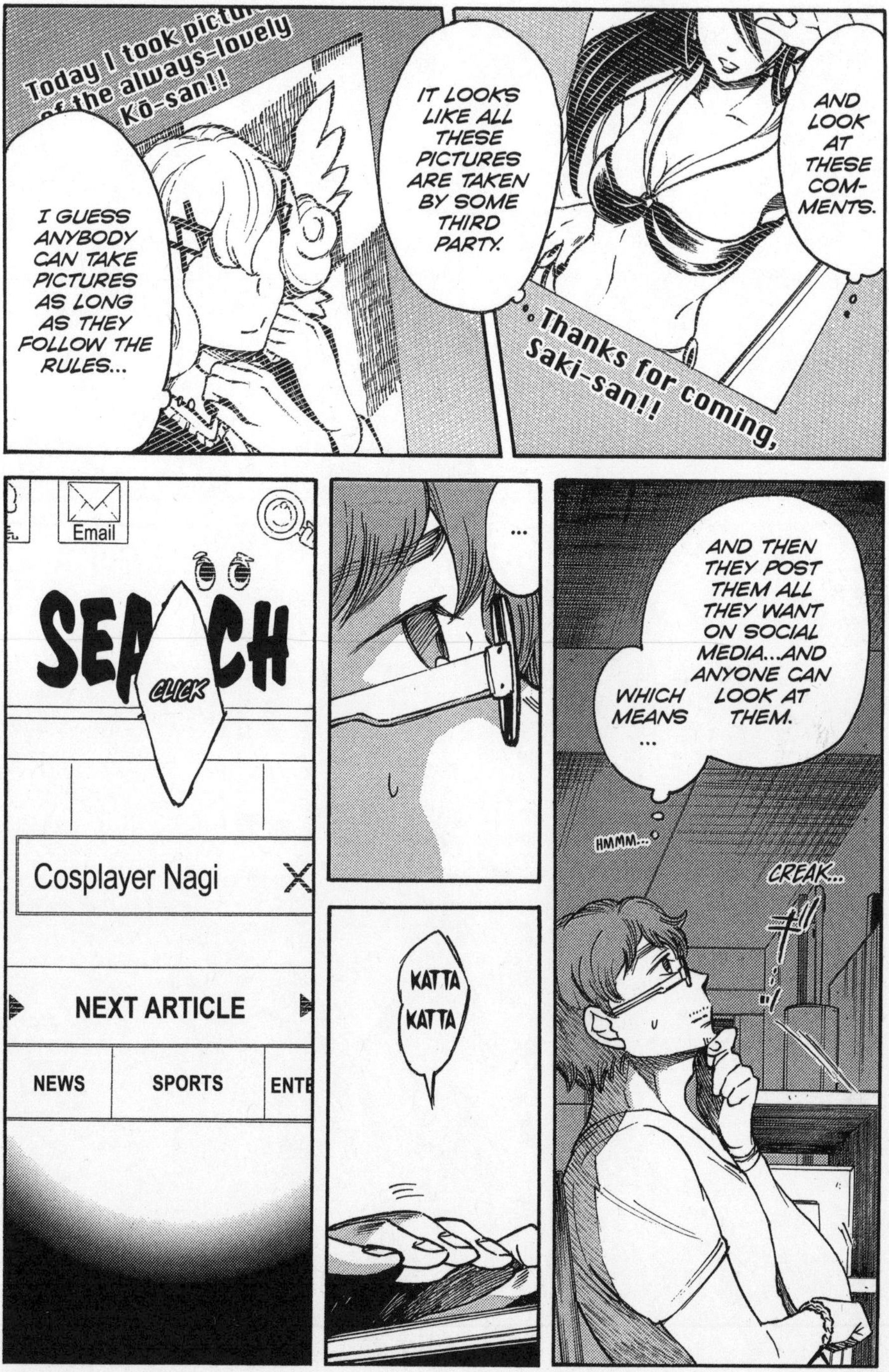
AND LOOK AT THESE COM-MENTS.
...Thanks for coming, Saki-san!!
Today I took pictur of the always-lovely Kō-san!!
IT LOOKS LIKE ALL THESE PICTURES ARE TAKEN BY SOME THIRD PARTY.
I GUESS ANYBODY CAN TAKE PICTURES AS LONG AS THEY FOLLOW THE RULES...
AND THEN THEY POST THEM ALL THEY WANT ON SOCIAL MEDIA...AND ANYONE CAN LOOK AT THEM.
WHICH MEANS ...
HMMM...
CREAK...
...
KATTA KATTA
Email
SEA CH
CLICK
Cosplayer Nagi
NEXT ARTICLE
NEWS
SPORTS
ENTE

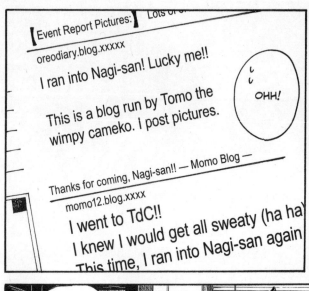

【 Event Report Pictures: 】 Lots of

oreodiary.blog.xxxxx

I ran into Nagi-san! Lucky me!!

This is a blog run by Tomo the
wimpy cameko. I post pictures.

Thanks for coming, Nagi-san!! — Momo Blog —

momo12.blog.xxxx

I went to TdC!!
I knew I would get all sweaty (ha ha)
This time, I ran into Nagi-san again

OHH!

OH!

SHE'S ON
A TON OF
PERSONAL
BLOGS.

SHE'S
PRETTY
FAMOUS.

There was
lot of Ma
this ever
But!
caught Nag
cosplaying Ururu!
She's so cute ♥♥

WHICH
MEANS...

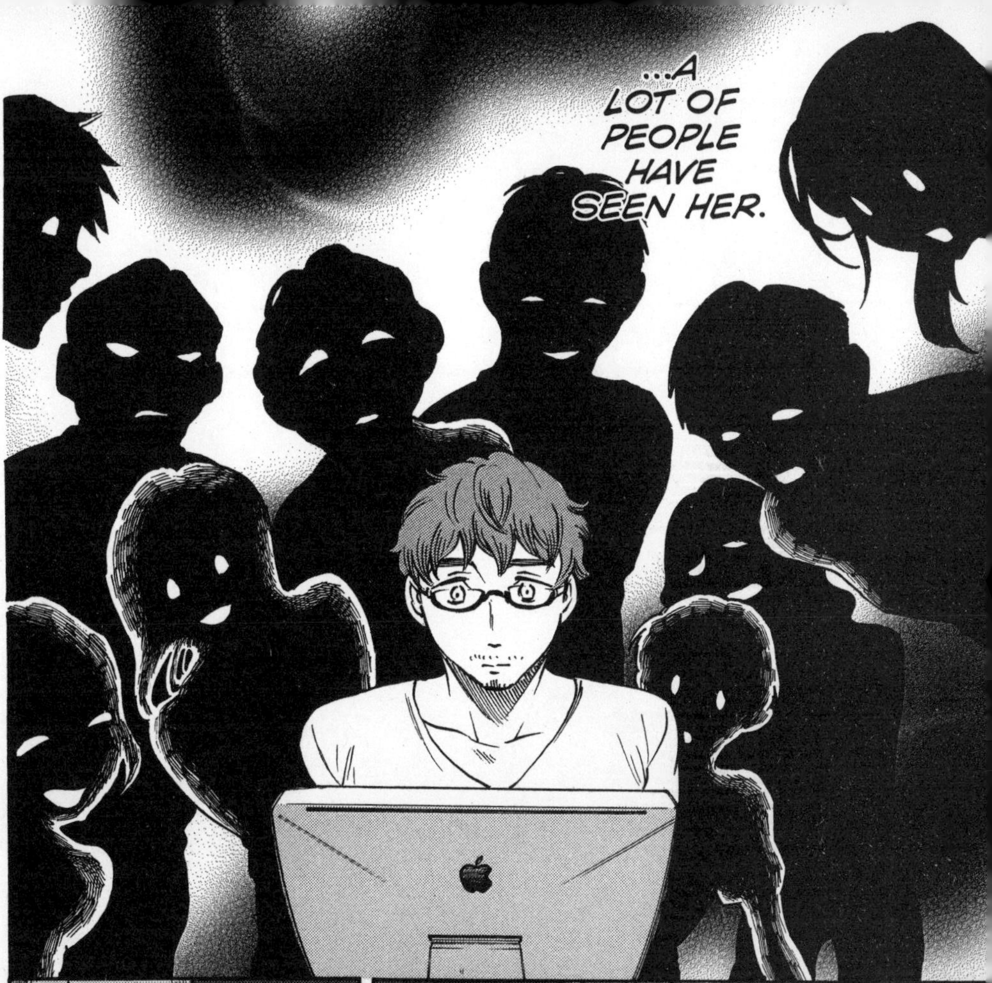
...A LOT OF PEOPLE HAVE SEEN HER.
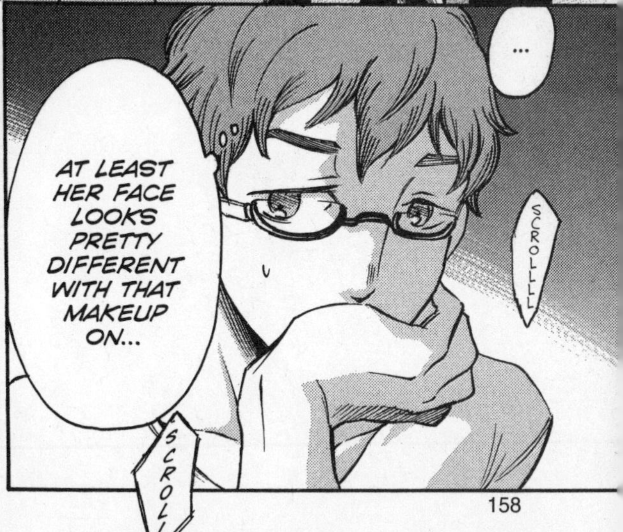
...
AT LEAST HER FACE LOOKS PRETTY DIFFERENT WITH THAT MAKEUP ON...
SCROLLLL
SCROLL
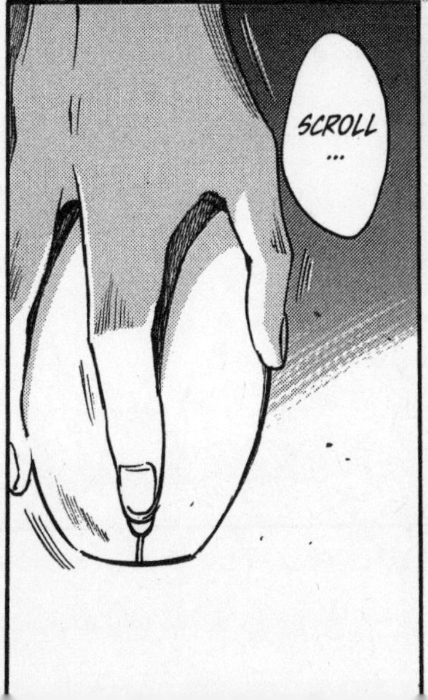
SCROLL...

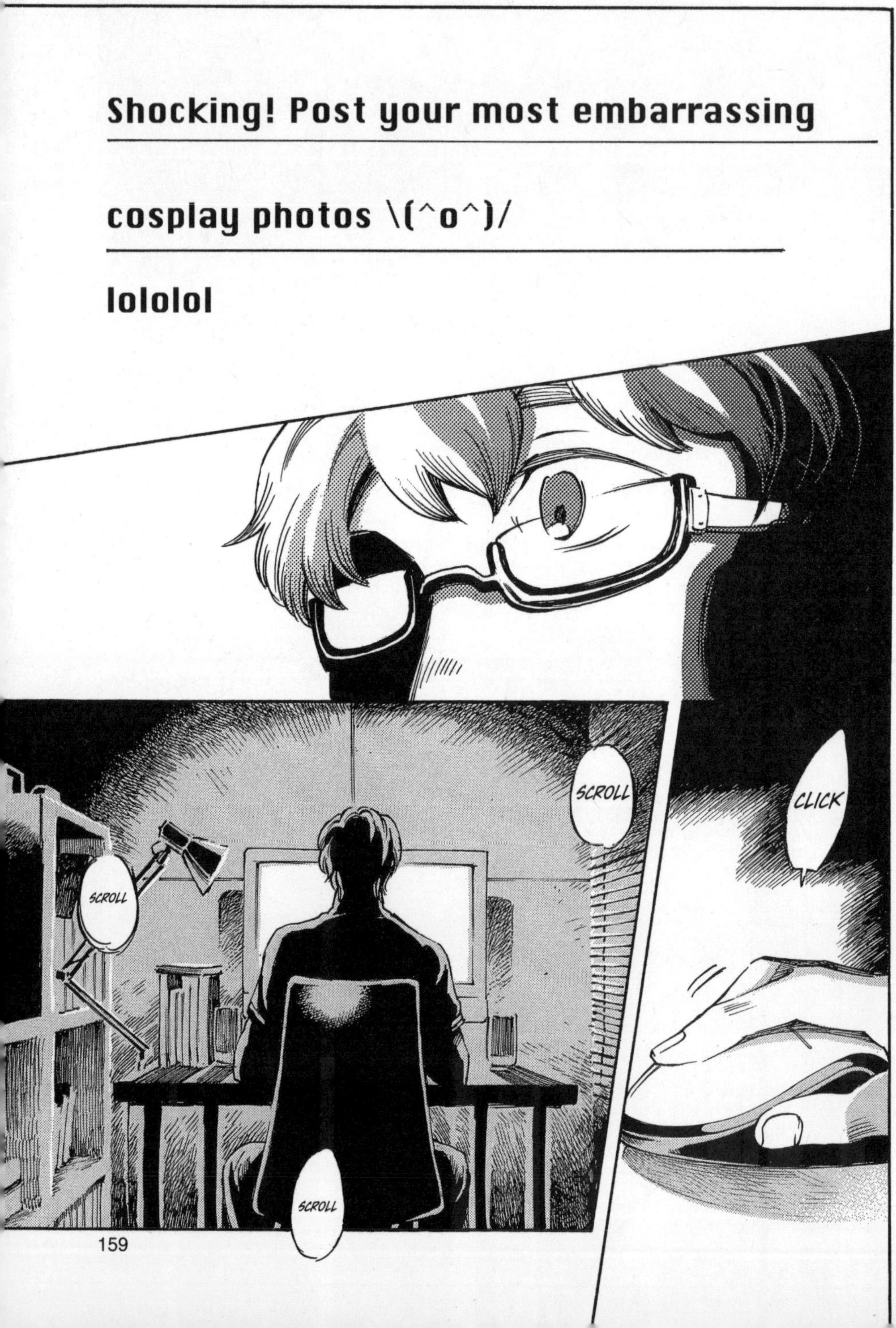
Shocking! Post your most embarrassing
cosplay photos \(^o^)/
lololol
CLICK
SCROLL
SCROLL
SCROLL

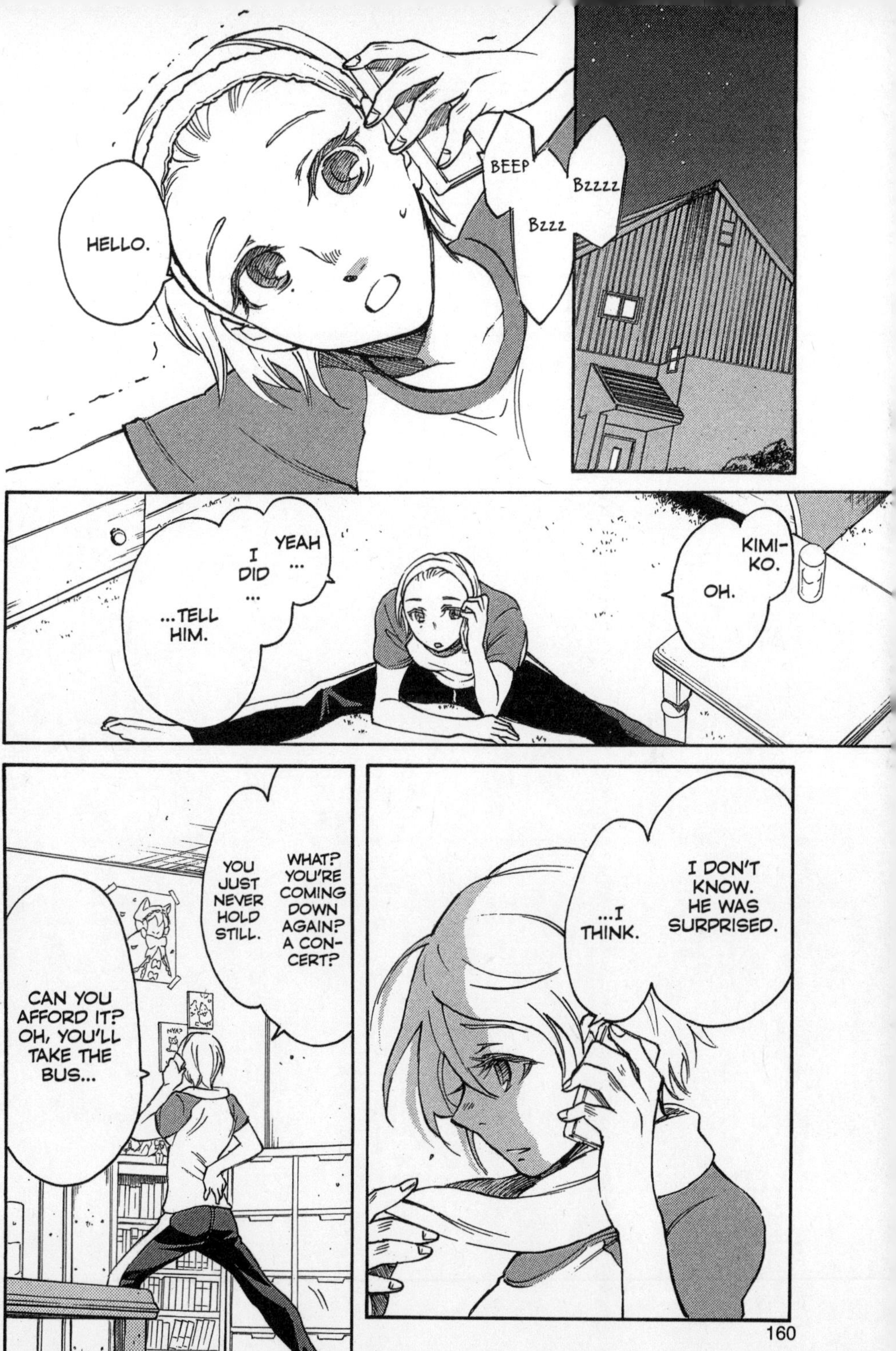
BEEP
Bzzzz
Bzzz
HELLO.
KIMI-KO.
OH.
YEAH ...
I DID ...
...TELL HIM.
I DON'T KNOW. HE WAS SURPRISED.
...I THINK.
WHAT? YOU'RE COMING DOWN AGAIN? A CONCERT?
YOU JUST NEVER HOLD STILL.
NYA?
CAN YOU AFFORD IT? OH, YOU'LL TAKE THE BUS...

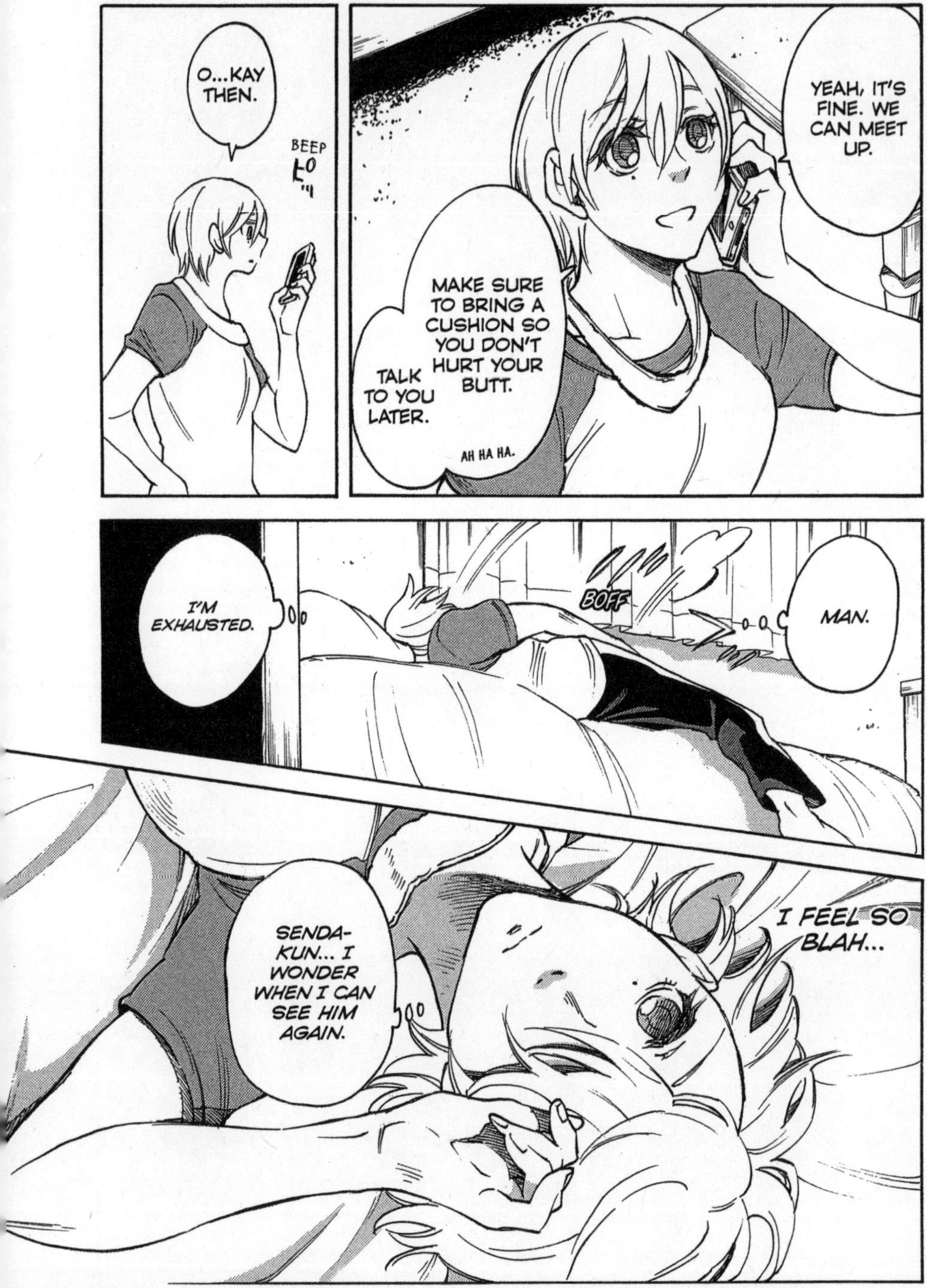
YEAH, IT'S FINE. WE CAN MEET UP.
MAKE SURE TO BRING A CUSHION SO YOU DON'T HURT YOUR BUTT.
AH HA HA.
TALK TO YOU LATER.
O...KAY THEN.
BEEP
MAN.
BOFF
I'M EXHAUSTED.
I FEEL SO BLAH...
SENDA-KUN... I WONDER WHEN I CAN SEE HIM AGAIN.

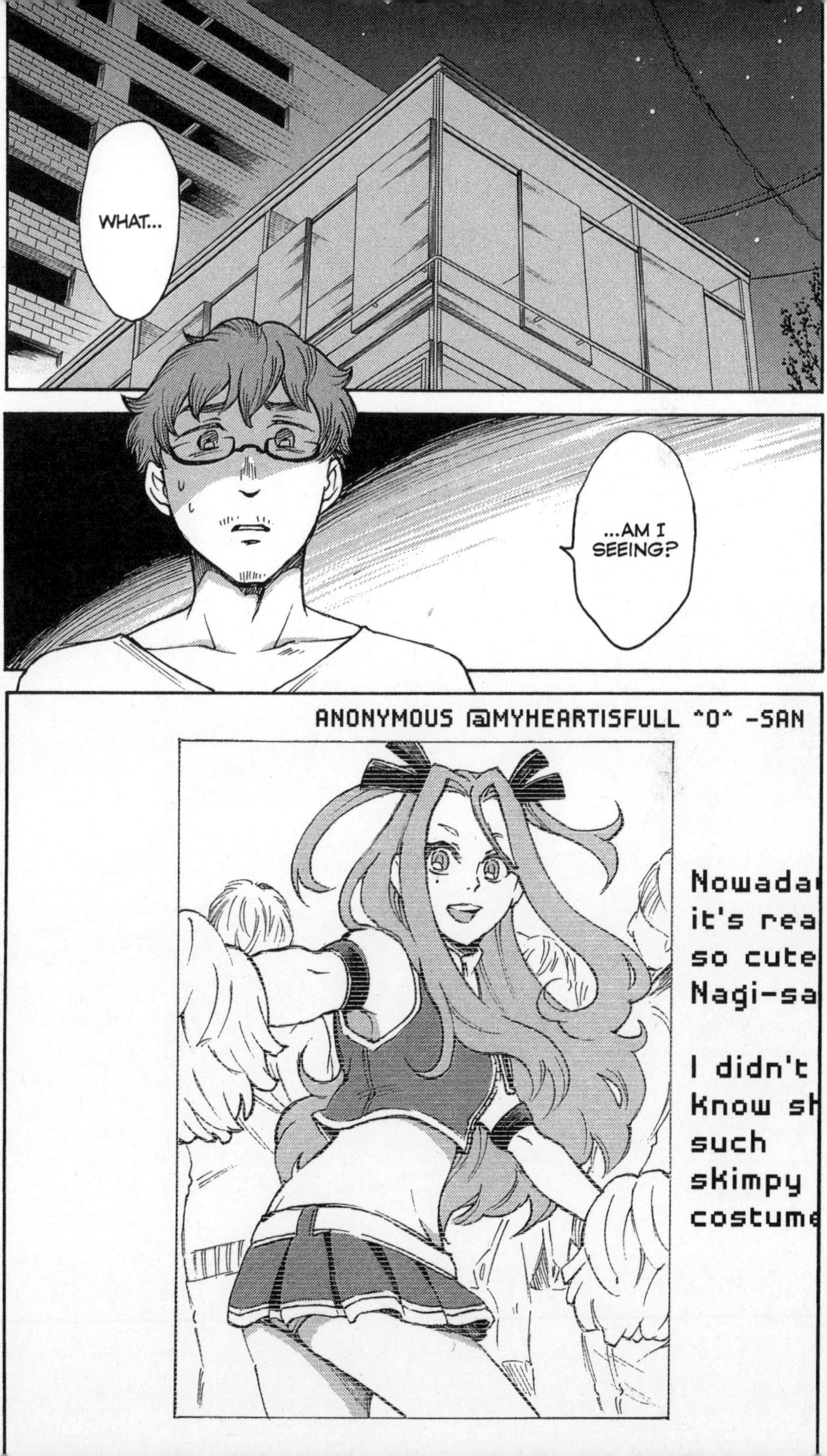
WHAT...
...AM I SEEING?
ANONYMOUS @MYHEARTISFULL ^O^ -SAN
Nowada
it's rea
so cute
Nagi-sa
I didn't
know sh
such
skimpy
costume

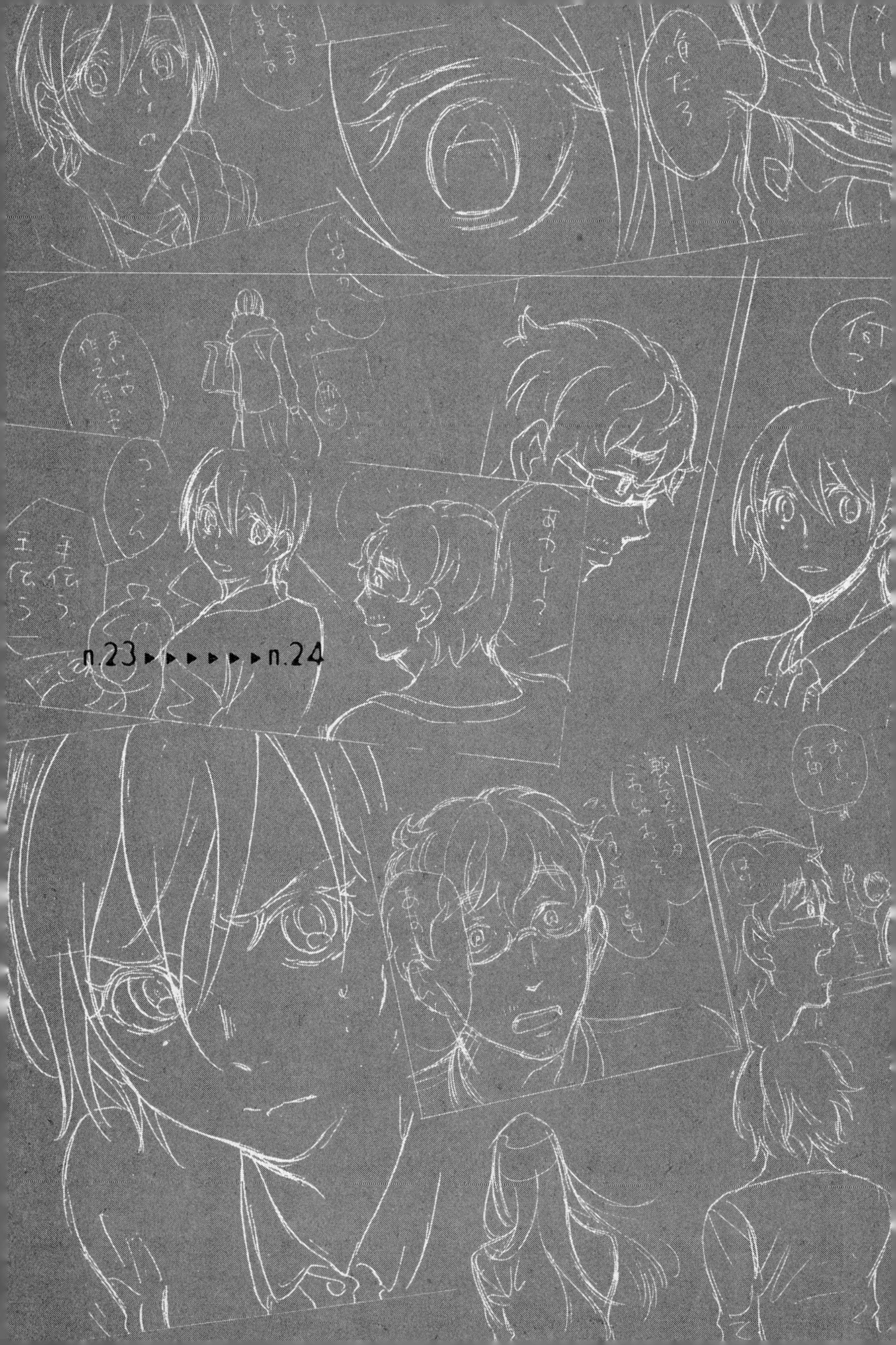
n.23▸▸▸▸▸▸▸n.24

MIKU & FRIENDS COLLABORATION 6

KAITO × NAGISA KATAURA

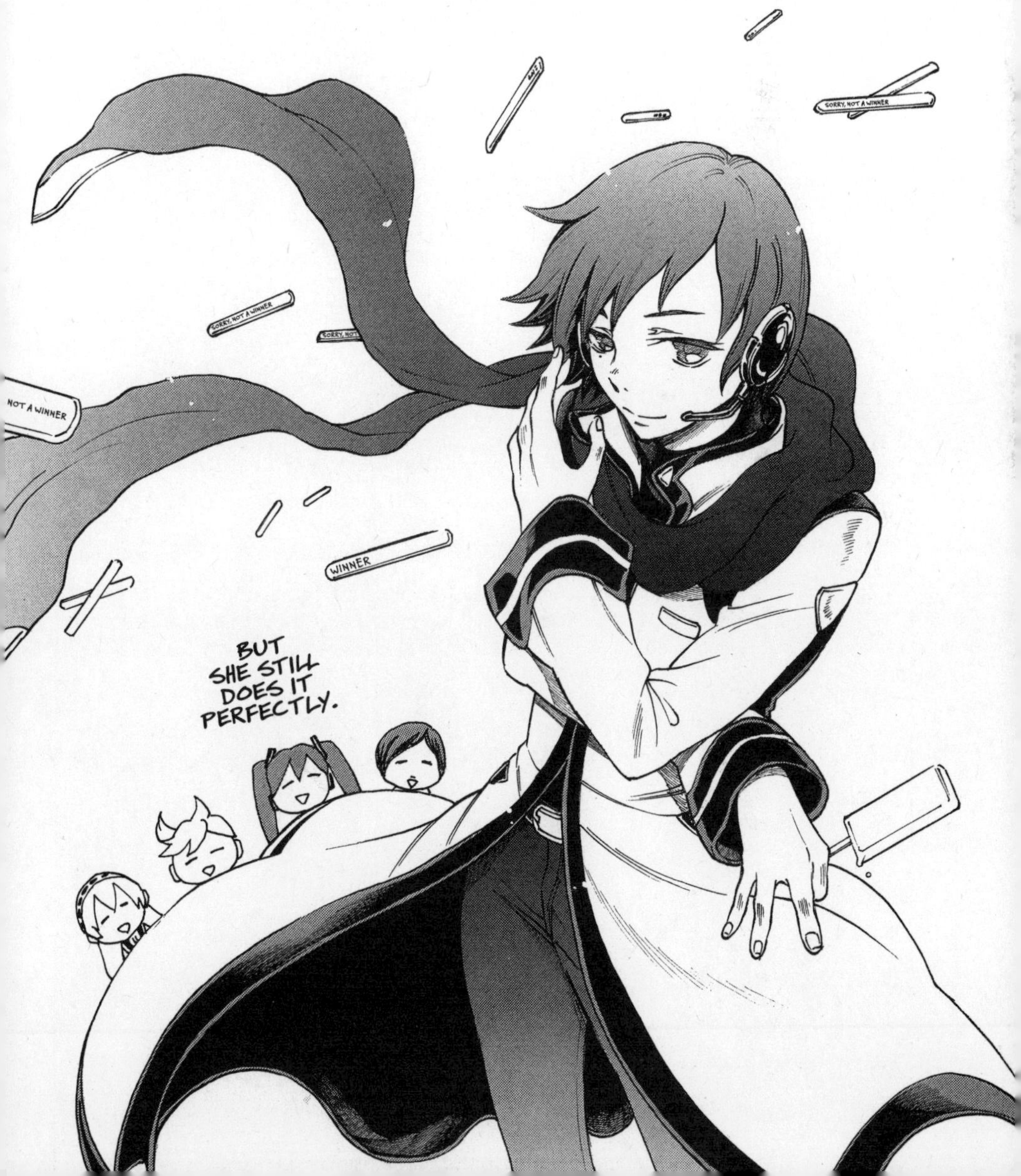
SORRY, NOT A WINNER
SORRY, NOT A WINNER
NOT A WINNER
WINNER
BUT SHE STILL DOES IT PERFECTLY.

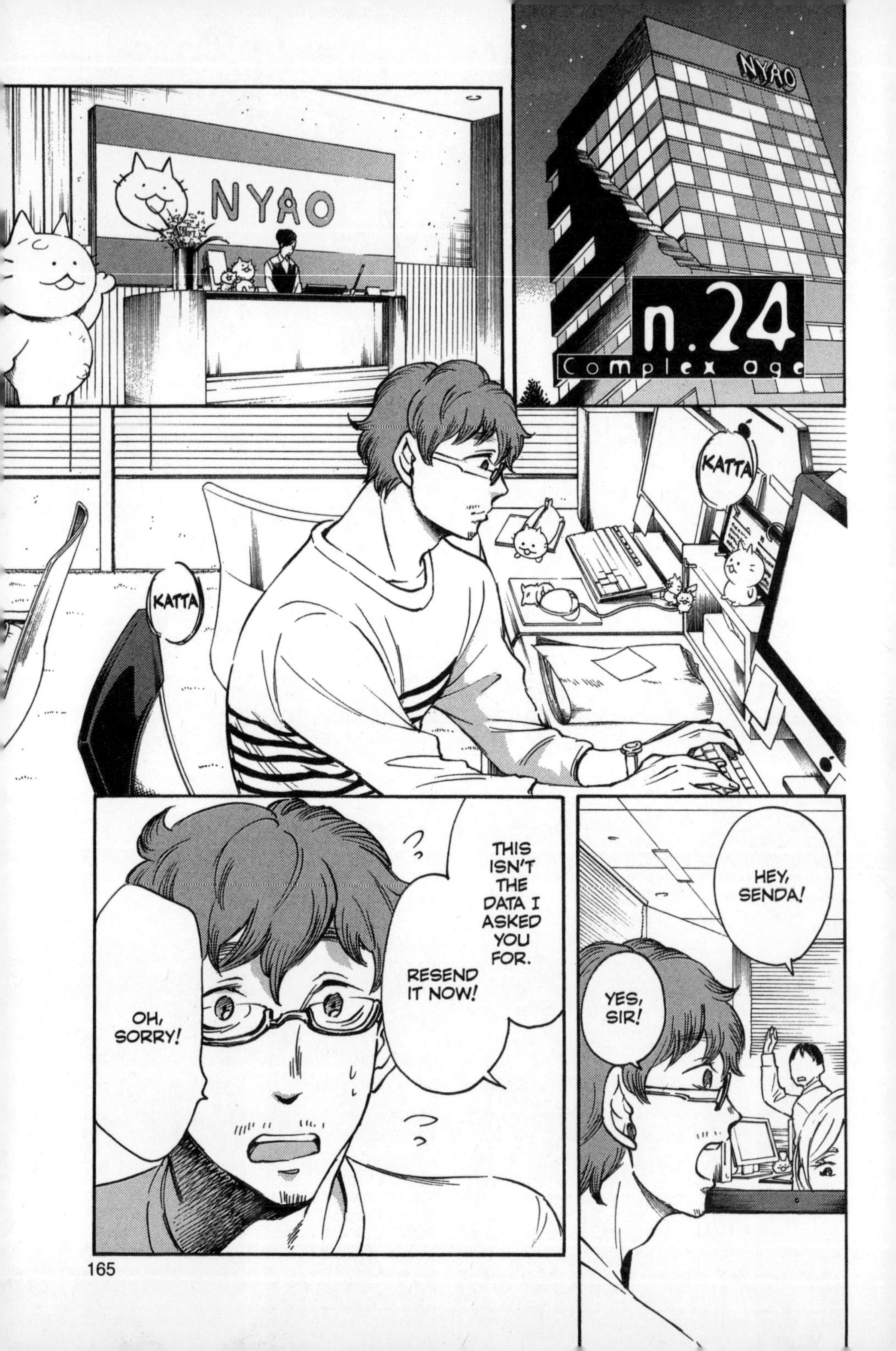
NYAO
n.24
Complex age
NYAO
KATTA
KATTA
HEY, SENDA!
YES, SIR!
THIS ISN'T THE DATA I ASKED YOU FOR.
RESEND IT NOW!
OH, SORRY!

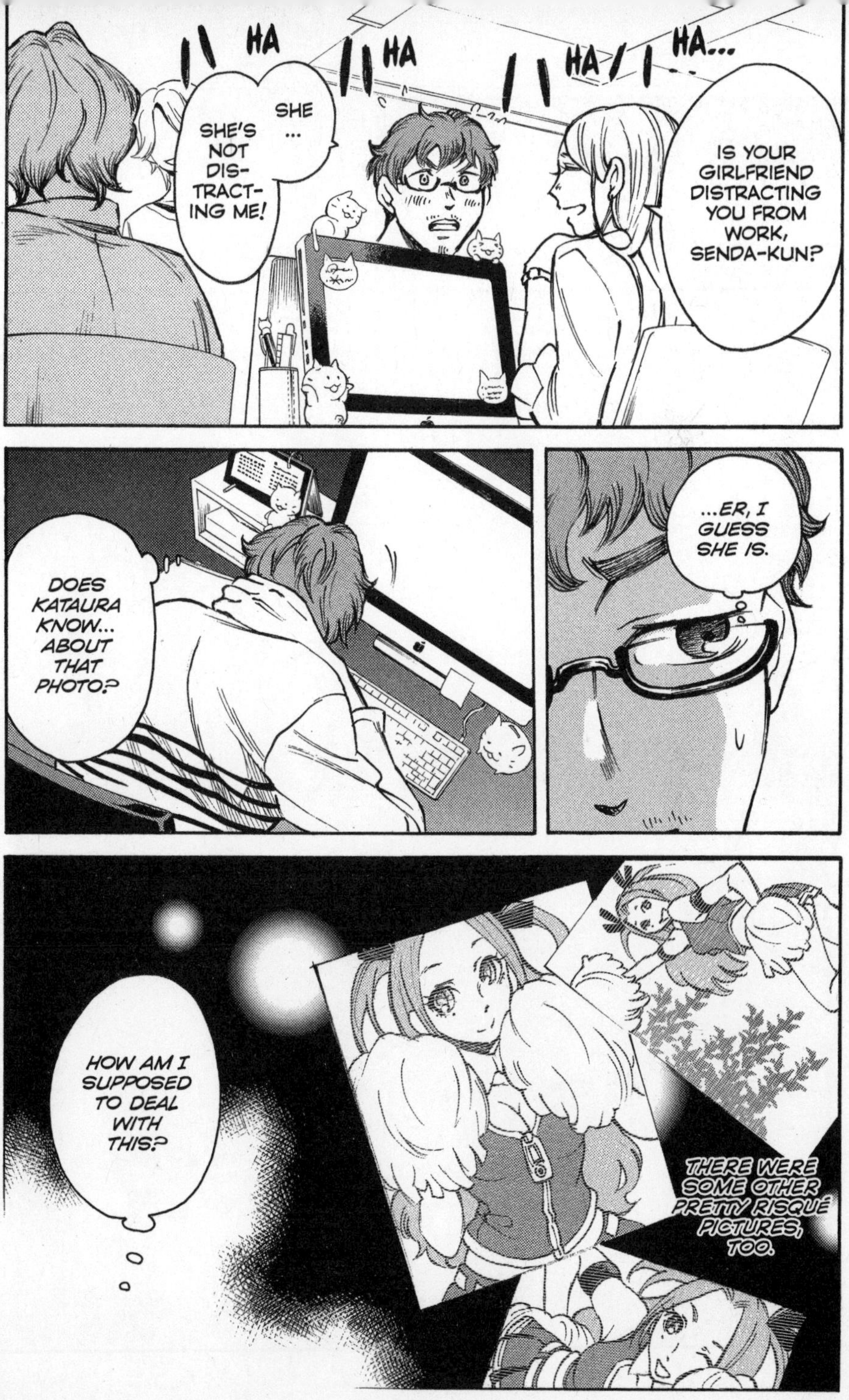
HA...
HA
HA
HA
IS YOUR GIRLFRIEND DISTRACTING YOU FROM WORK, SENDA-KUN?
SHE ... SHE'S NOT DIS-TRACT-ING ME!
...ER, I GUESS SHE IS.
DOES KATAURA KNOW... ABOUT THAT PHOTO?
THERE WERE SOME OTHER PRETTY RISQUÉ PICTURES, TOO.
HOW AM I SUPPOSED TO DEAL WITH THIS?

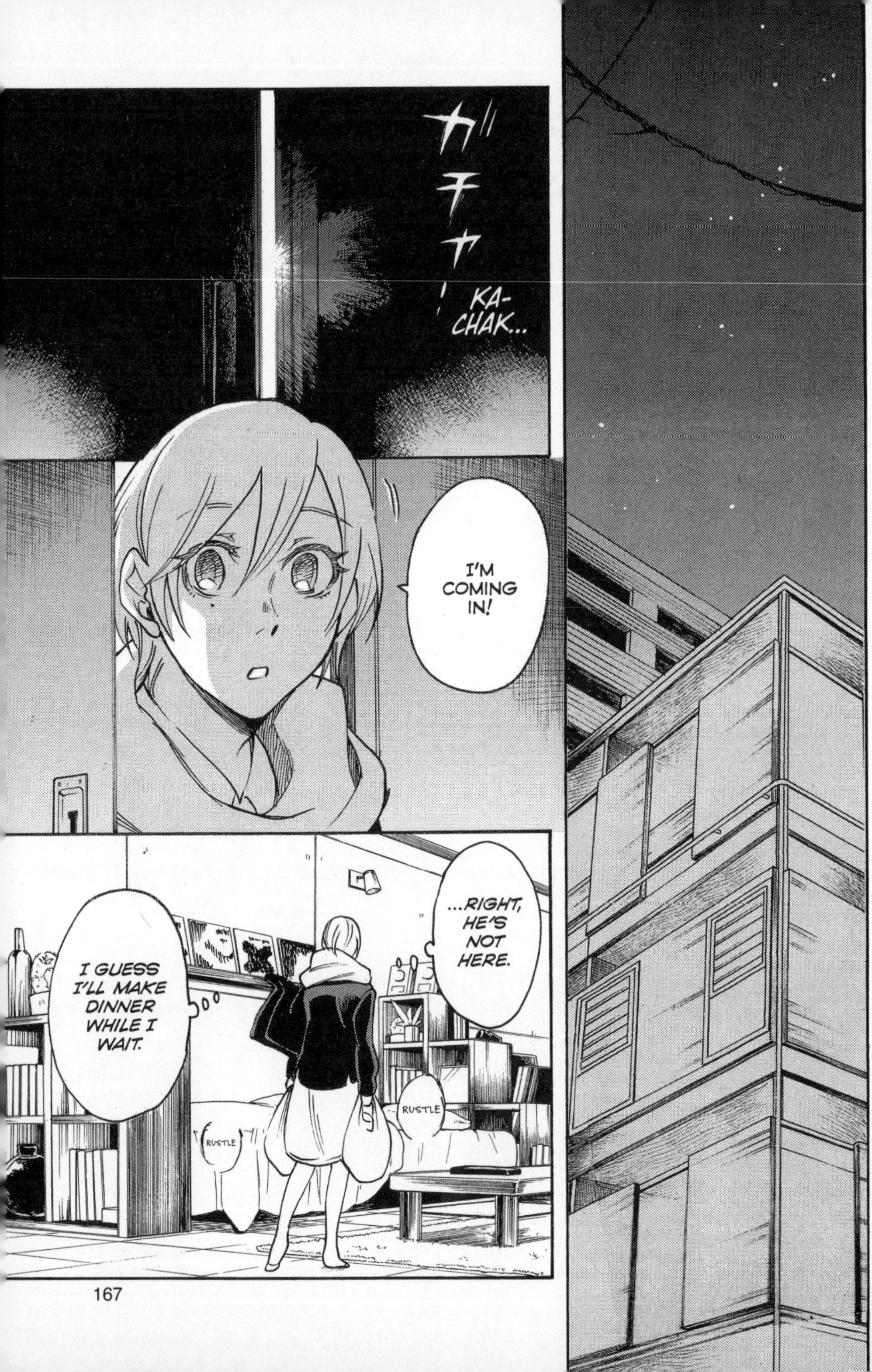
ガチャ!
KA-CHAK...
I'M COMING IN!
...RIGHT, HE'S NOT HERE.
I GUESS I'LL MAKE DINNER WHILE I WAIT.
RUSTLE
RUSTLE

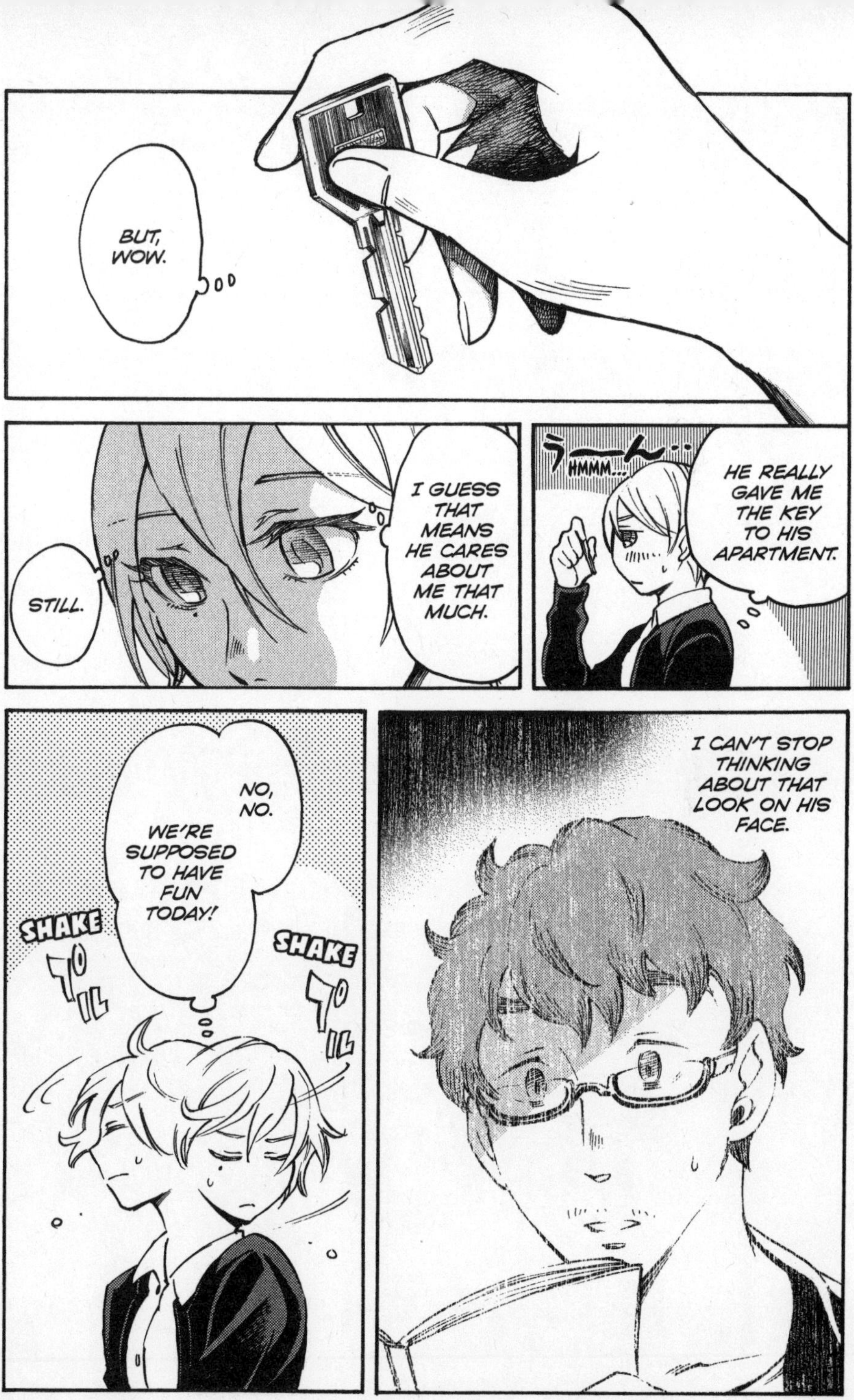
BUT, WOW.
HMMM...
HE REALLY GAVE ME THE KEY TO HIS APARTMENT.
I GUESS THAT MEANS HE CARES ABOUT ME THAT MUCH.
STILL.
I CAN'T STOP THINKING ABOUT THAT LOOK ON HIS FACE.
NO, NO.
WE'RE SUPPOSED TO HAVE FUN TODAY!
SHAKE
SHAKE

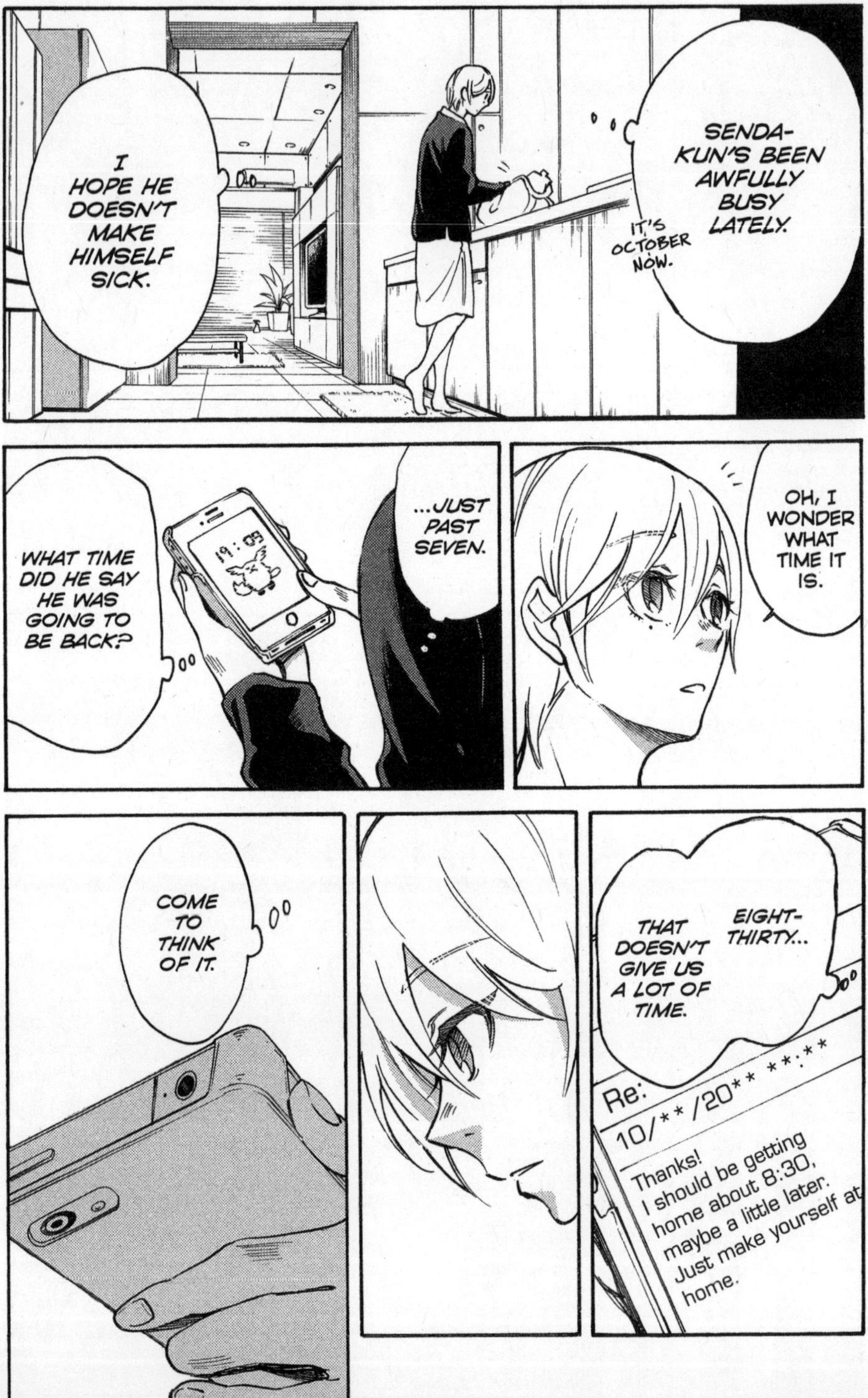
SENDA-KUN'S BEEN AWFULLY BUSY LATELY.
IT'S OCTOBER NOW.
I HOPE HE DOESN'T MAKE HIMSELF SICK.
OH, I WONDER WHAT TIME IT IS.
...JUST PAST SEVEN.
19:05
WHAT TIME DID HE SAY HE WAS GOING TO BE BACK?
EIGHT-THIRTY...
THAT DOESN'T GIVE US A LOT OF TIME.
Re: 10/**/20** **:**
Thanks!
I should be getting home about 8:30, maybe a little later.
Just make yourself at home.
COME TO THINK OF IT.

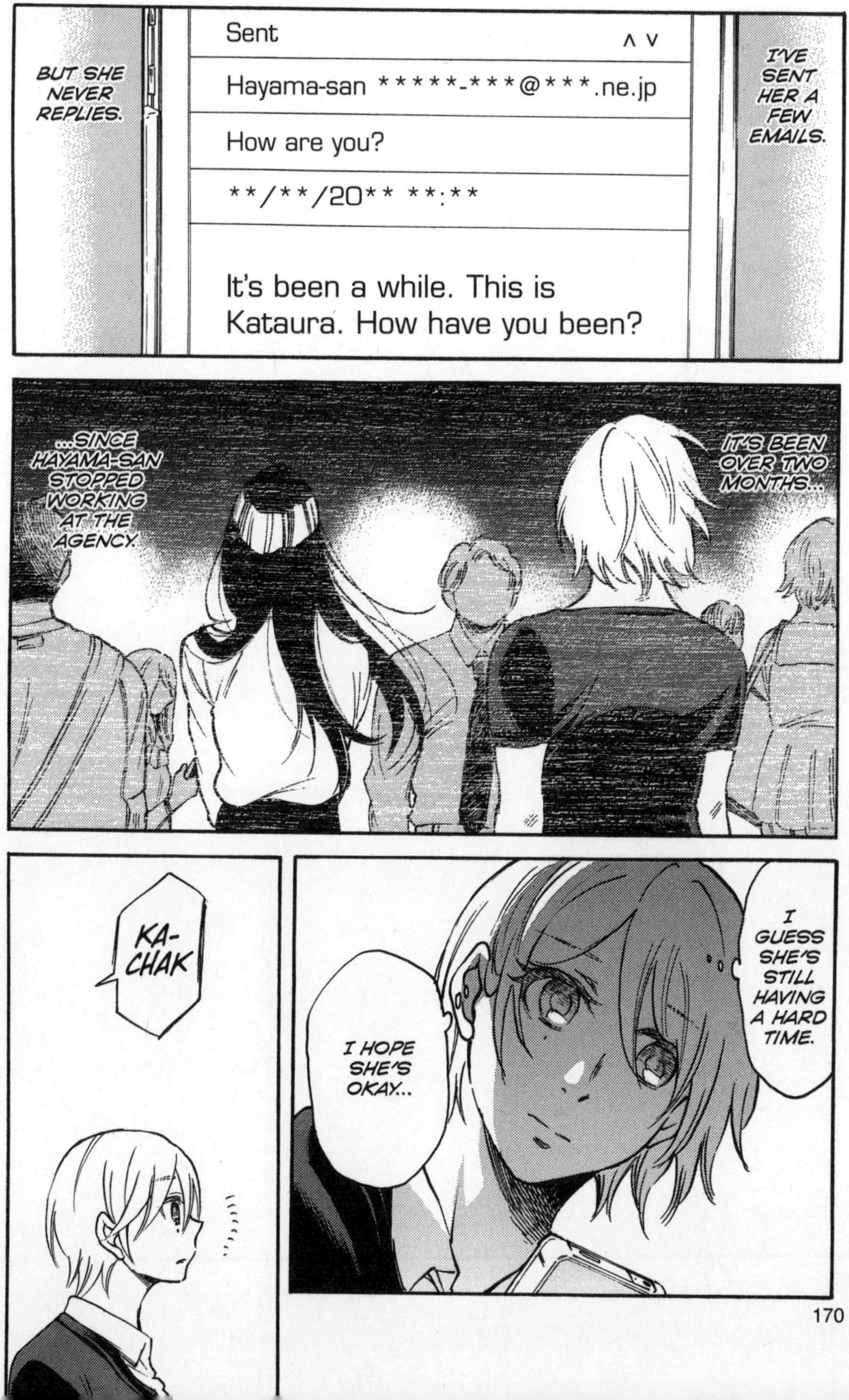
I'VE SENT HER A FEW EMAILS.
Sent
Hayama-san *****_***@***.ne.jp
How are you?
//20** **:**
It's been a while. This is Kataura. How have you been?
BUT SHE NEVER REPLIES.
IT'S BEEN OVER TWO MONTHS...
...SINCE HAYAMA-SAN STOPPED WORKING AT THE AGENCY.
I GUESS SHE'S STILL HAVING A HARD TIME.
I HOPE SHE'S OKAY...
KA-CHAK

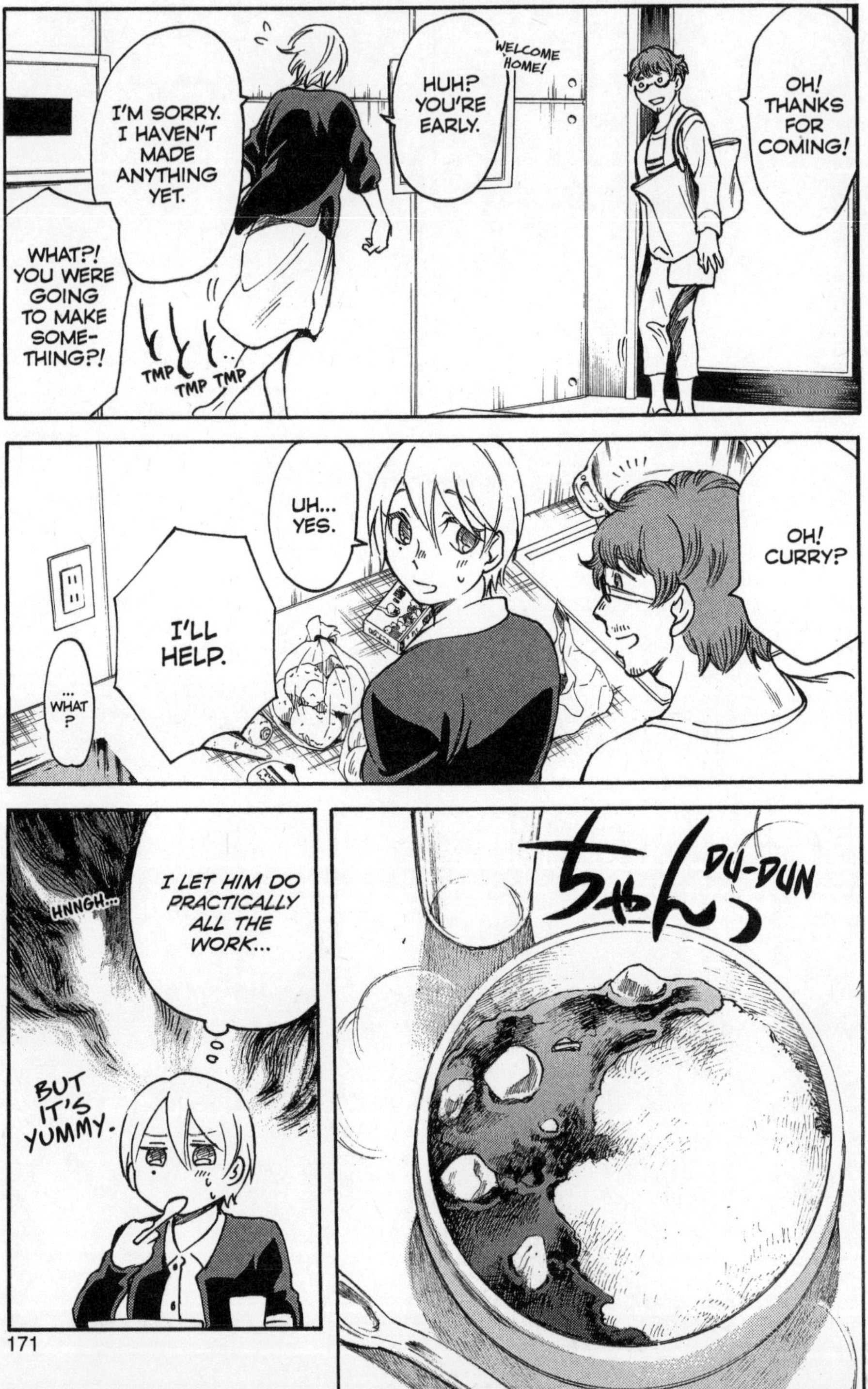
OH! THANKS FOR COMING!
WELCOME HOME!
HUH? YOU'RE EARLY.
I'M SORRY. I HAVEN'T MADE ANYTHING YET.
WHAT?! YOU WERE GOING TO MAKE SOME-THING?!
TMP TMP TMP
OH! CURRY?
UH... YES.
I'LL HELP.
...WHAT?
ちゃんっ
DU-DUN
I LET HIM DO PRACTICALLY ALL THE WORK...
HNNGH...
BUT IT'S YUMMY.

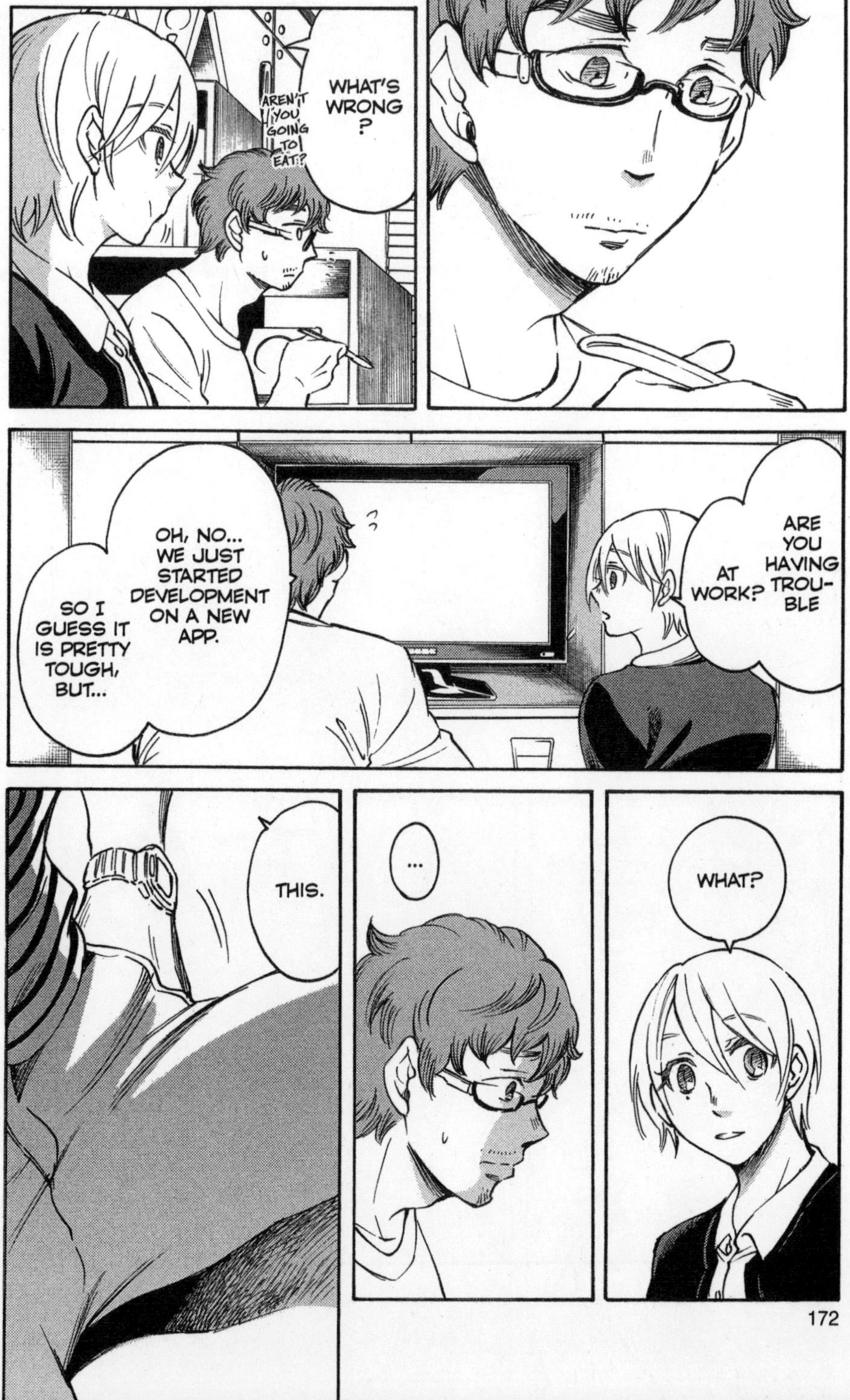

WHAT'S WRONG?
AREN'T YOU GOING TO EAT?
ARE YOU HAVING TROUBLE AT WORK?
OH, NO... WE JUST STARTED DEVELOPMENT ON A NEW APP.
SO I GUESS IT IS PRETTY TOUGH, BUT...
WHAT?
...
THIS.

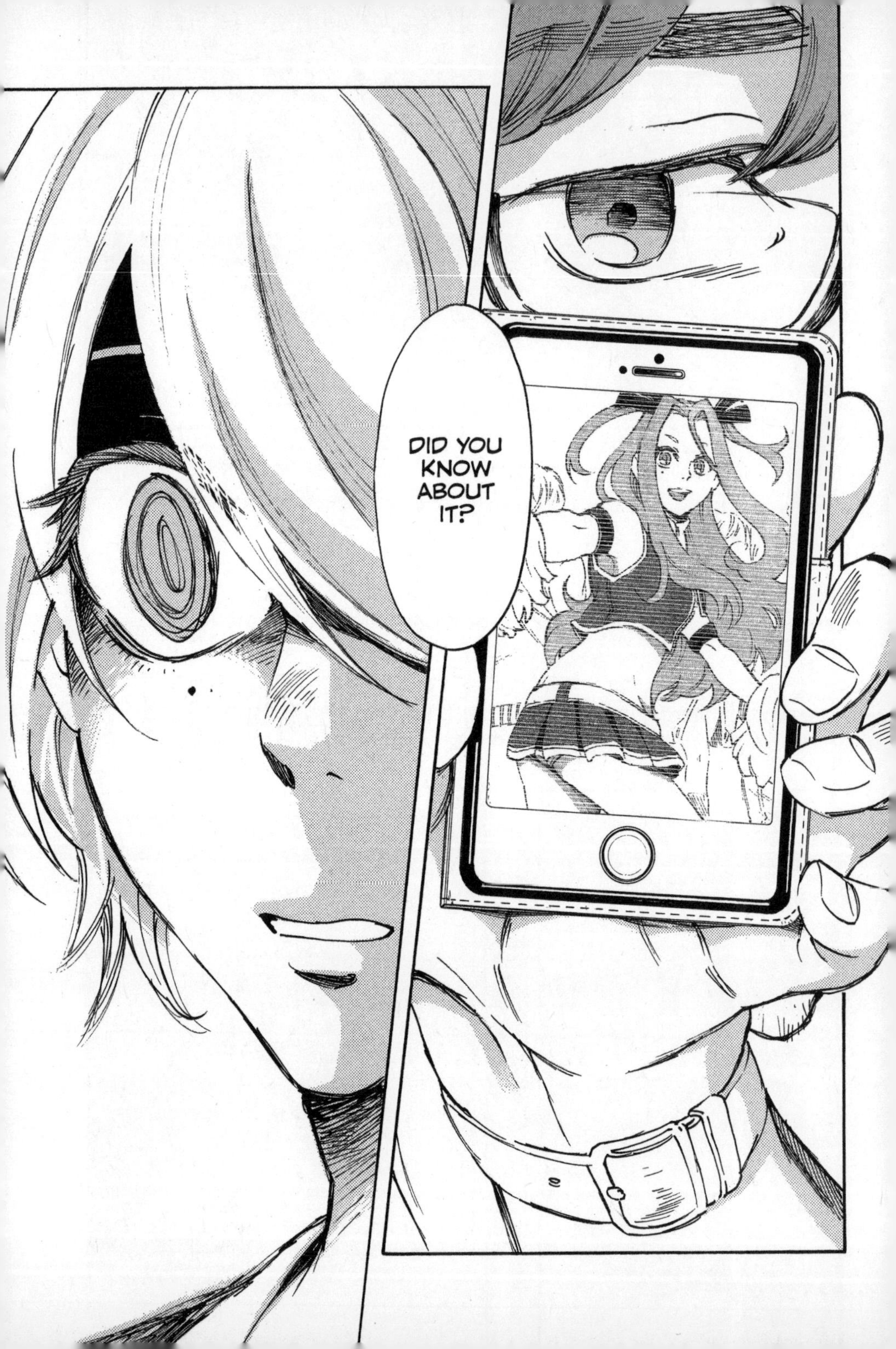
DID YOU KNOW ABOUT IT?

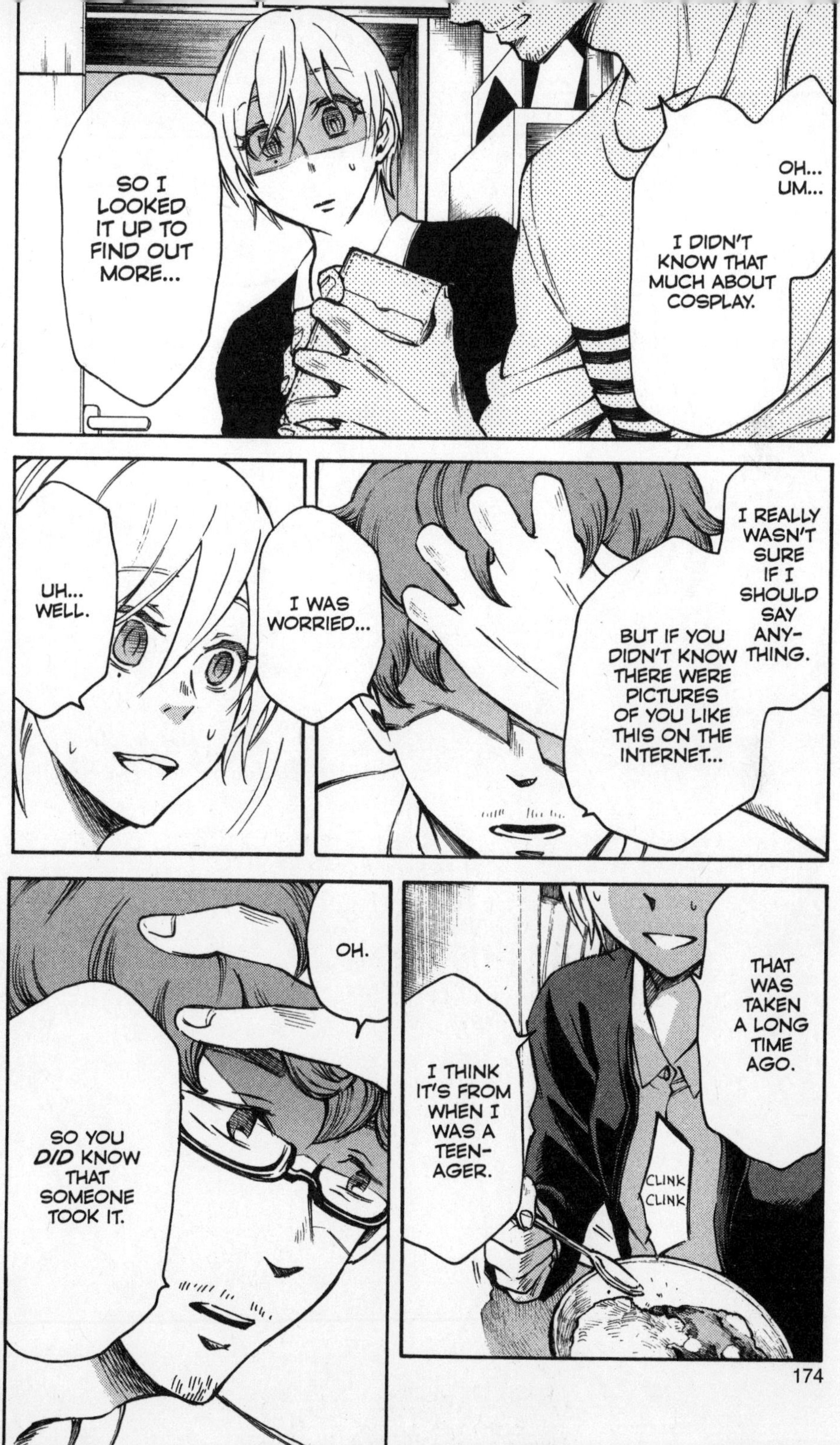
OH... UM...
I DIDN'T KNOW THAT MUCH ABOUT COSPLAY.
SO I LOOKED IT UP TO FIND OUT MORE...
I REALLY WASN'T SURE IF I SHOULD SAY ANY-THING.
BUT IF YOU DIDN'T KNOW THERE WERE PICTURES OF YOU LIKE THIS ON THE INTERNET...
I WAS WORRIED...
UH... WELL.
THAT WAS TAKEN A LONG TIME AGO.
I THINK IT'S FROM WHEN I WAS A TEEN-AGER.
CLINK CLINK
OH.
SO YOU *DID* KNOW THAT SOMEONE TOOK IT.

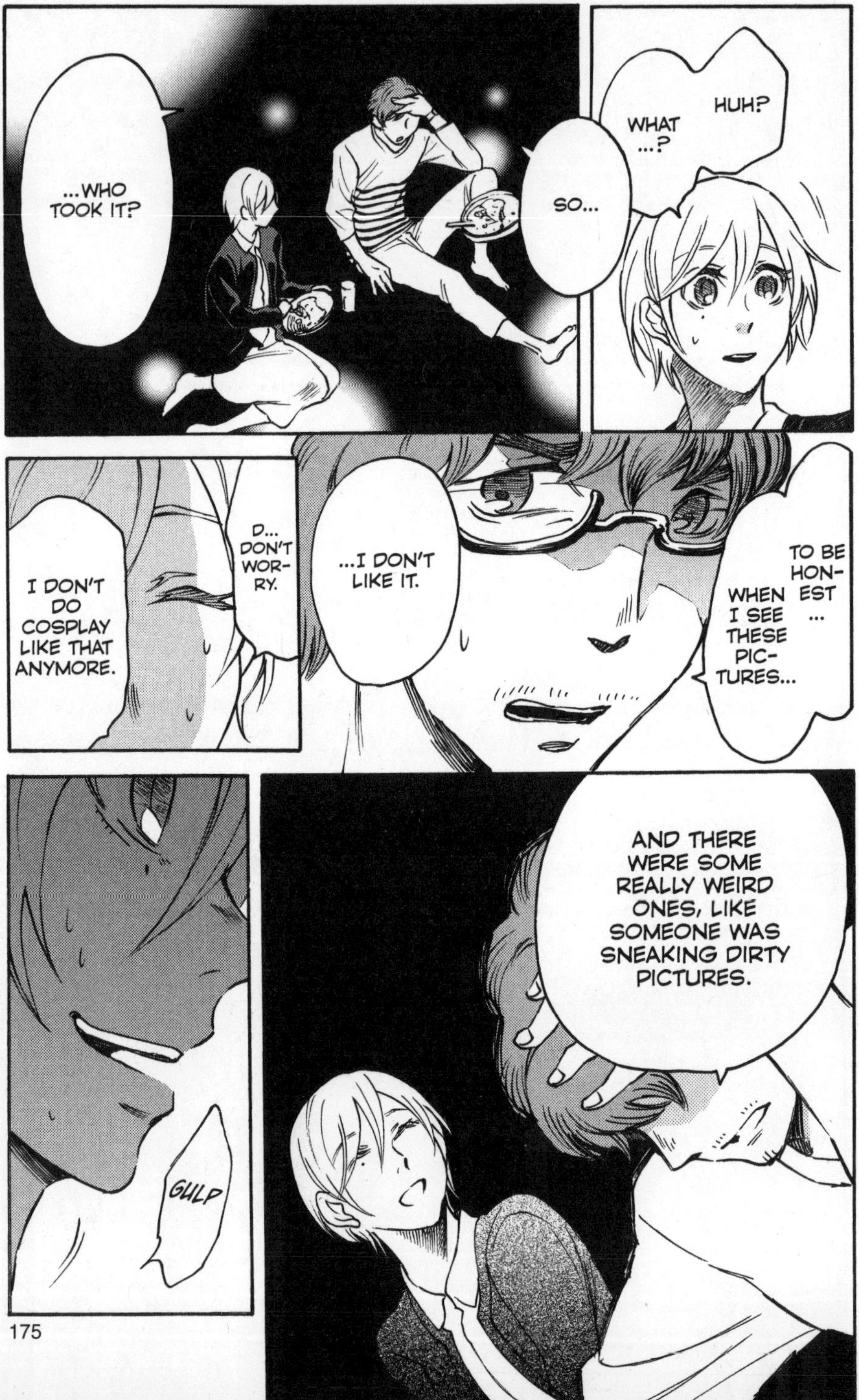
HUH?
WHAT ...?
SO...
...WHO TOOK IT?
TO BE HONEST ...
WHEN I SEE THESE PICTURES...
...I DON'T LIKE IT.
D... DON'T WORRY.
I DON'T DO COSPLAY LIKE THAT ANYMORE.
AND THERE WERE SOME REALLY WEIRD ONES, LIKE SOMEONE WAS SNEAKING DIRTY PICTURES.
GULP

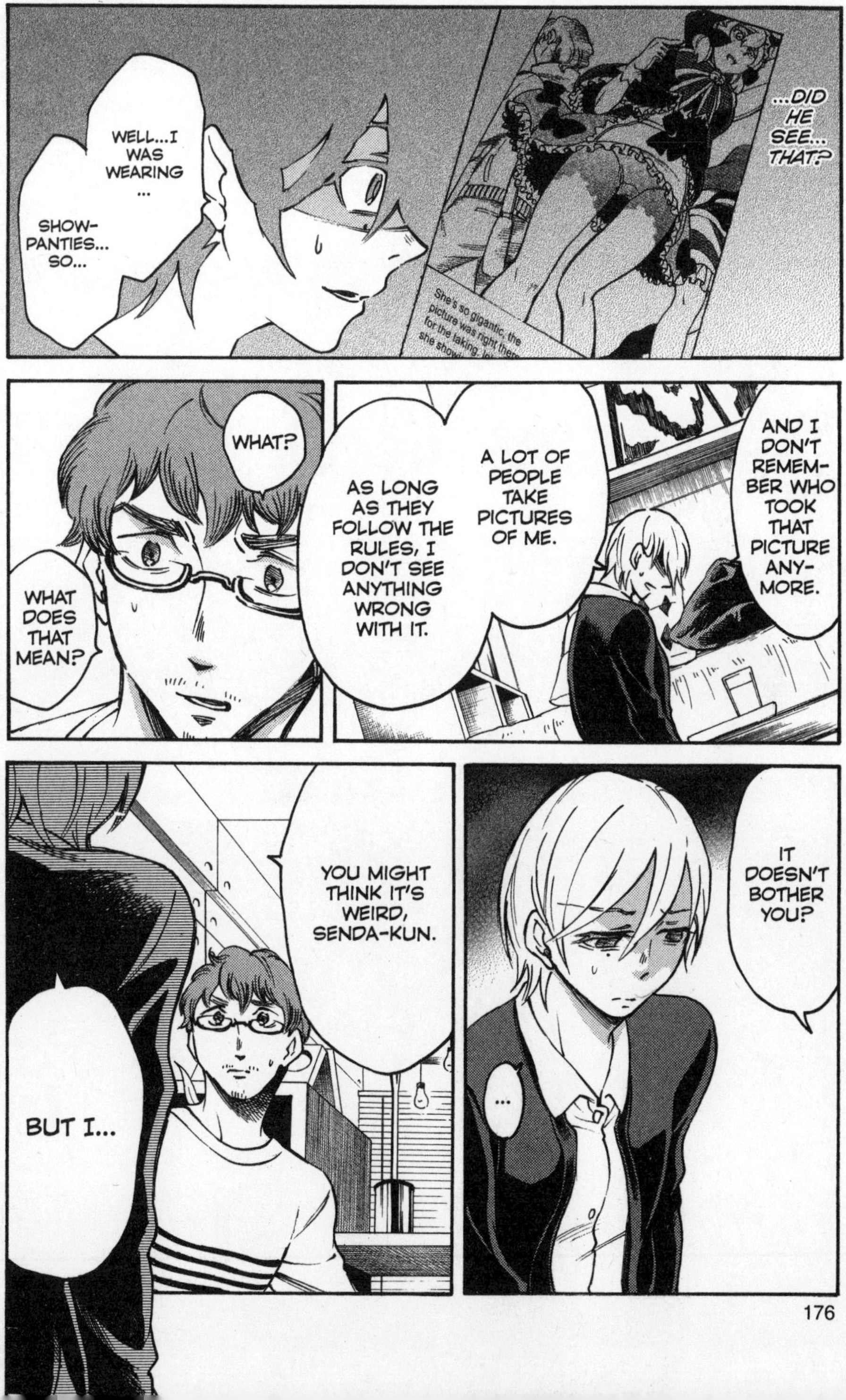
...DID HE SEE... THAT?
She's so gigantic, the
picture was right there
for the taking.
WELL...I WAS WEARING ... SHOW-PANTIES... SO...
AND I DON'T REMEMBER WHO TOOK THAT PICTURE ANYMORE.
A LOT OF PEOPLE TAKE PICTURES OF ME.
AS LONG AS THEY FOLLOW THE RULES, I DON'T SEE ANYTHING WRONG WITH IT.
WHAT?
WHAT DOES THAT MEAN?
IT DOESN'T BOTHER YOU?
...
YOU MIGHT THINK IT'S WEIRD, SENDA-KUN.
BUT I...

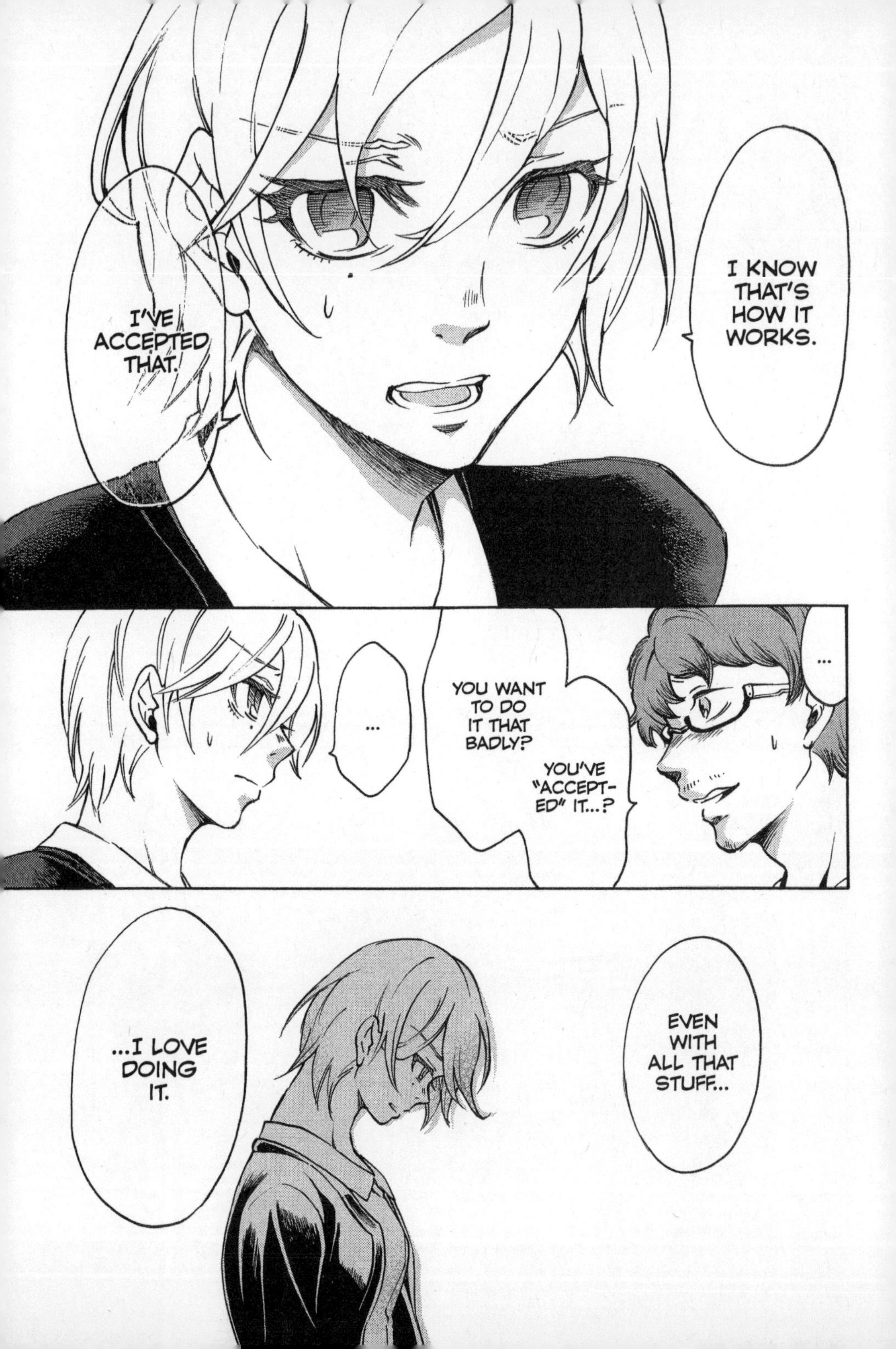
I KNOW THAT'S HOW IT WORKS.
I'VE ACCEPTED THAT.
...
YOU'VE "ACCEPTED" IT...?
YOU WANT TO DO IT THAT BADLY?
...
EVEN WITH ALL THAT STUFF...
...I LOVE DOING IT.

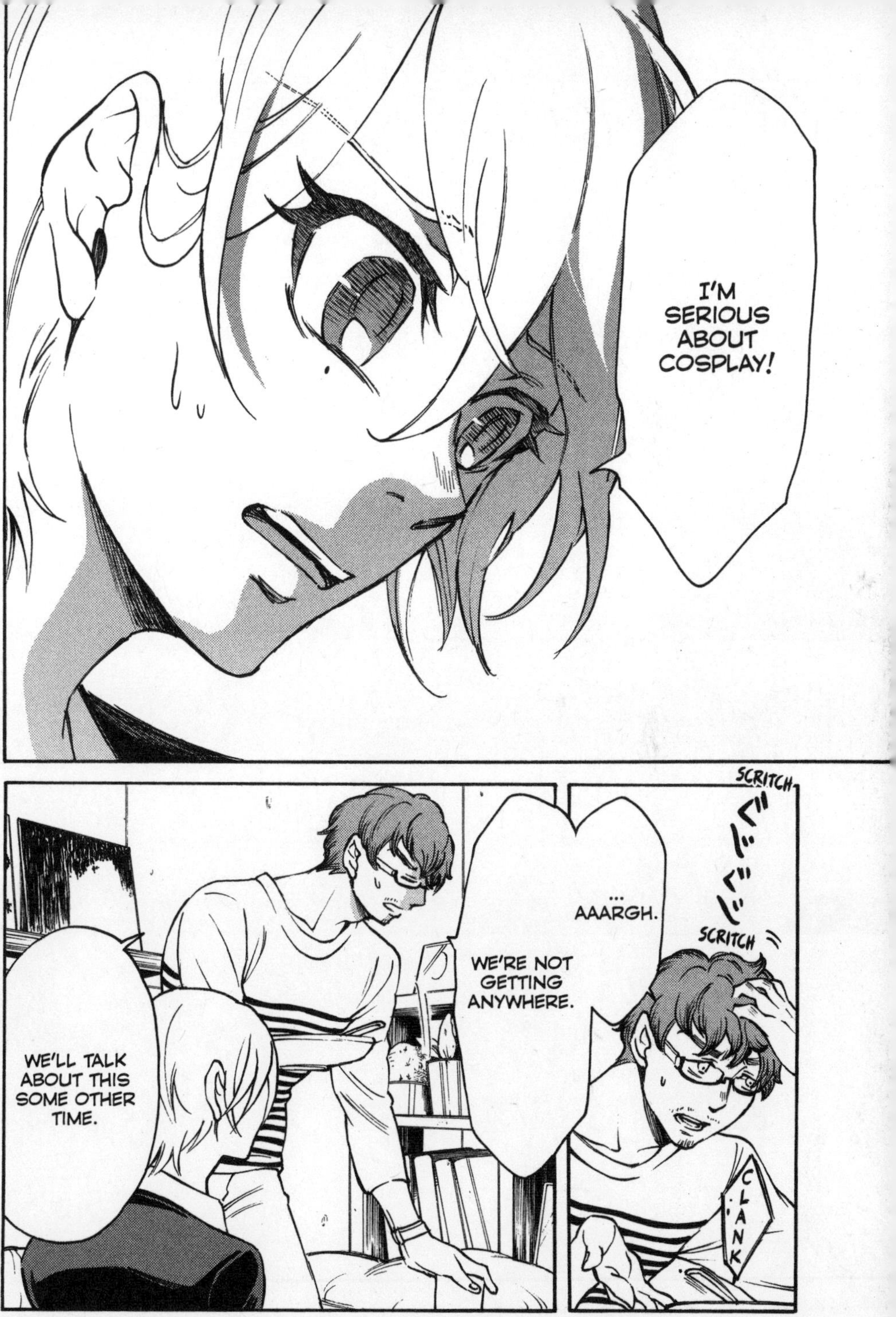
I'M SERIOUS ABOUT COSPLAY!
SCRITCH
... AAARGH.
SCRITCH
CLANK
WE'RE NOT GETTING ANYWHERE.
WE'LL TALK ABOUT THIS SOME OTHER TIME.

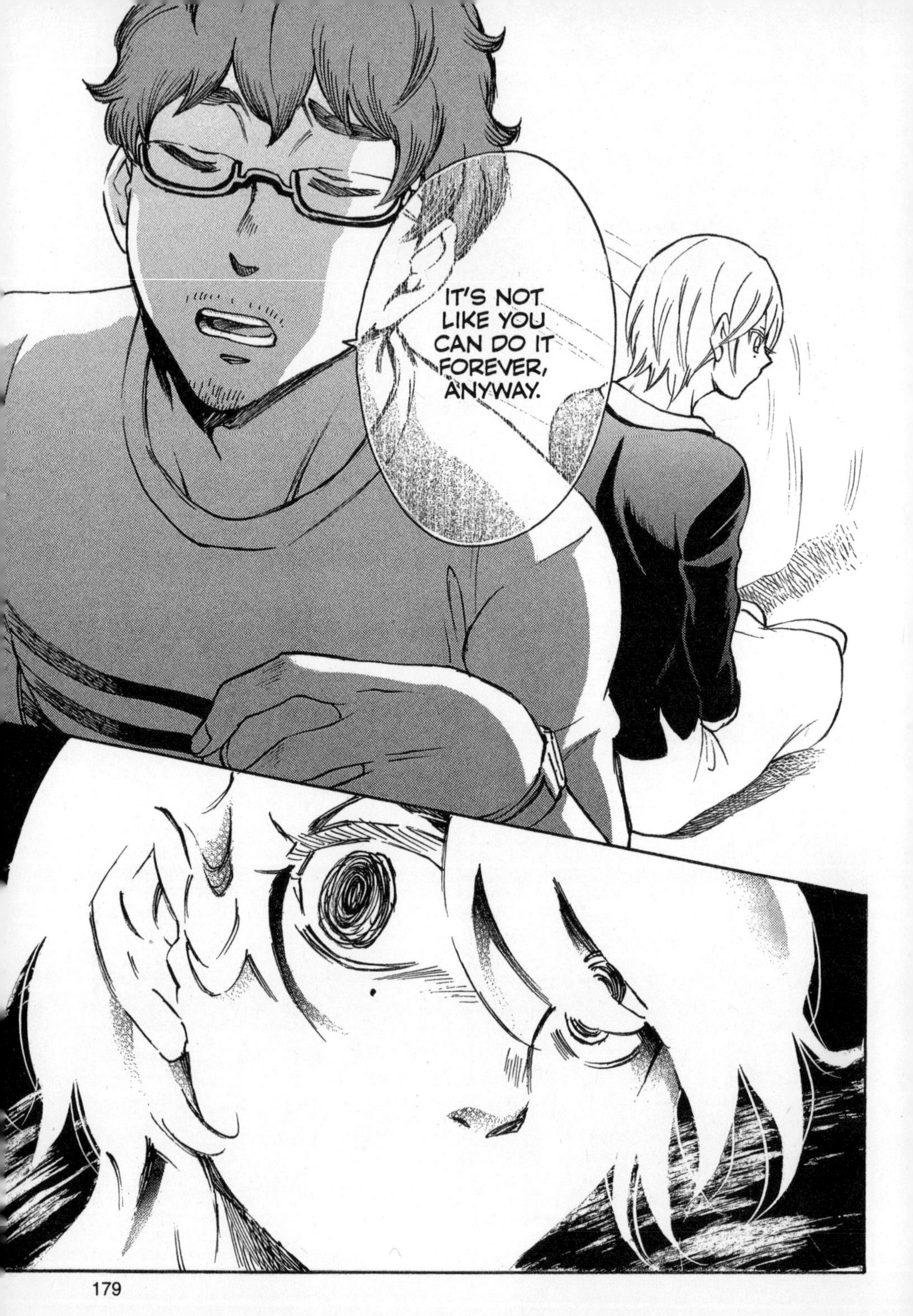
IT'S NOT LIKE YOU CAN DO IT FOREVER, ANYWAY.

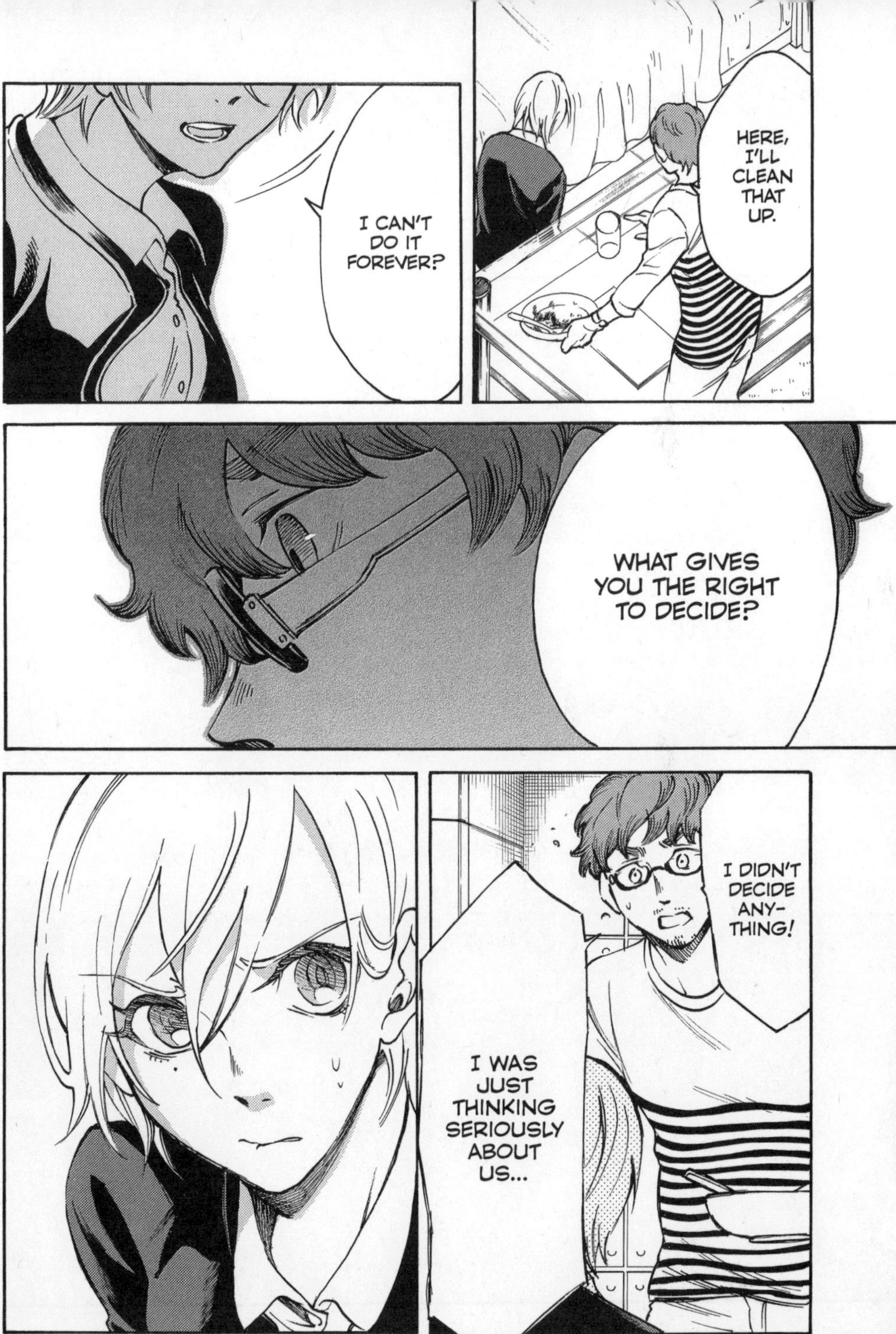
HERE, I'LL CLEAN THAT UP.
I CAN'T DO IT FOREVER?
WHAT GIVES YOU THE RIGHT TO DECIDE?
I DIDN'T DECIDE ANY-THING!
I WAS JUST THINKING SERIOUSLY ABOUT US...

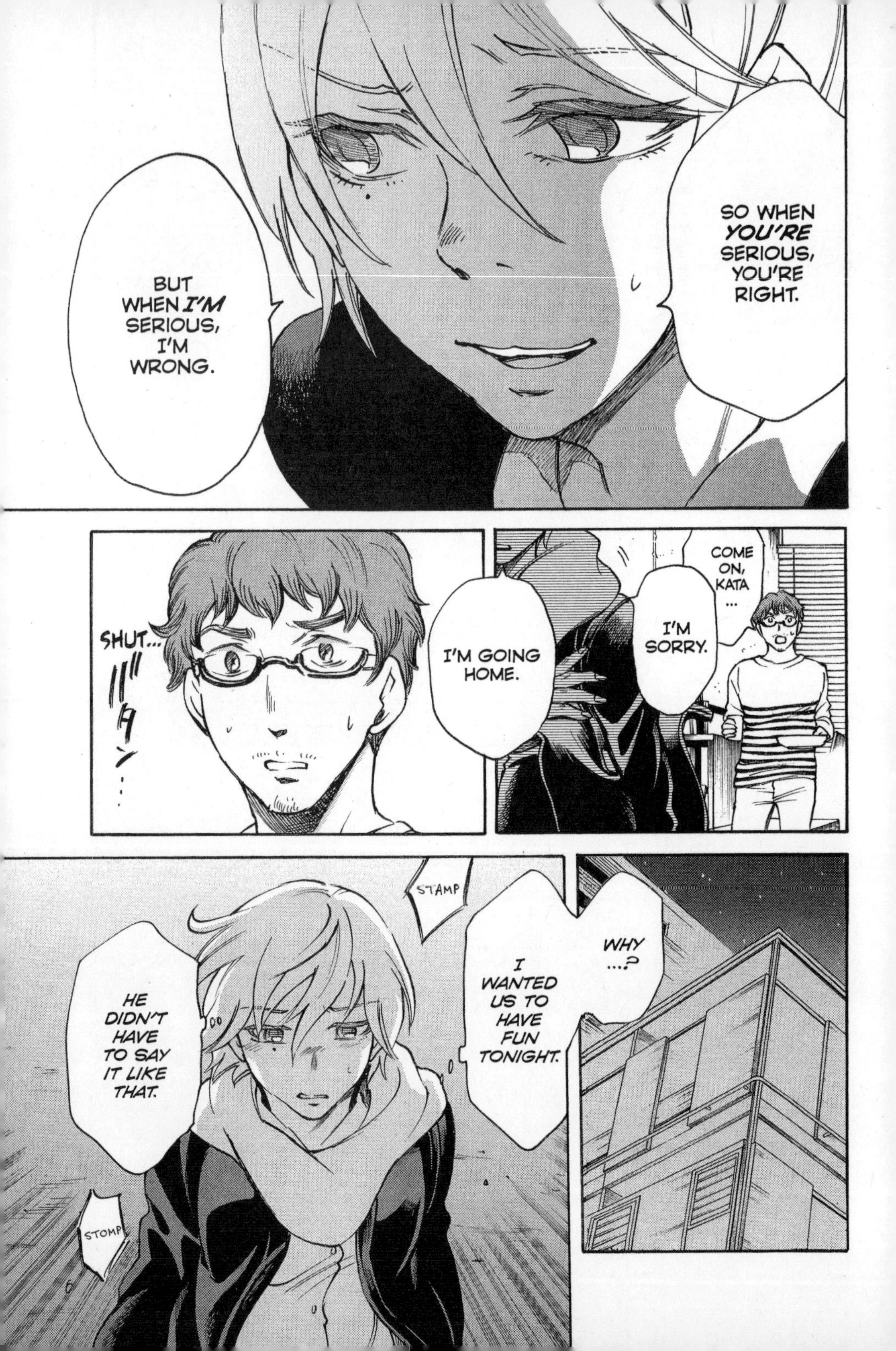

SO WHEN *YOU'RE* SERIOUS, YOU'RE RIGHT.
BUT WHEN *I'M* SERIOUS, I'M WRONG.
COME ON, KATA ...
I'M SORRY.
I'M GOING HOME.
SHUT...
WHY ...?
STAMP
I WANTED US TO HAVE FUN TONIGHT.
HE DIDN'T HAVE TO SAY IT LIKE THAT.
STOMP

AGAIN? ...CAN I FACE HIM... HOW... ...

Bzz

...I WAS WRONG.

MAYBE...

STOMP

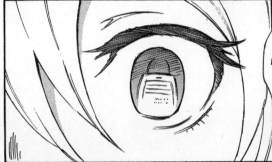

WHO IS IT?

AN EMAIL....?

○○○○   ▣

Messages   ∧∨

Hayama-san *****-***@***.ne.jp

It's been a while.

//20** **:**

Kataura-san,

This is Hayama.

Thank you for all your emails.

I'm very sorry I couldn't reply until now...

Right now, I'm

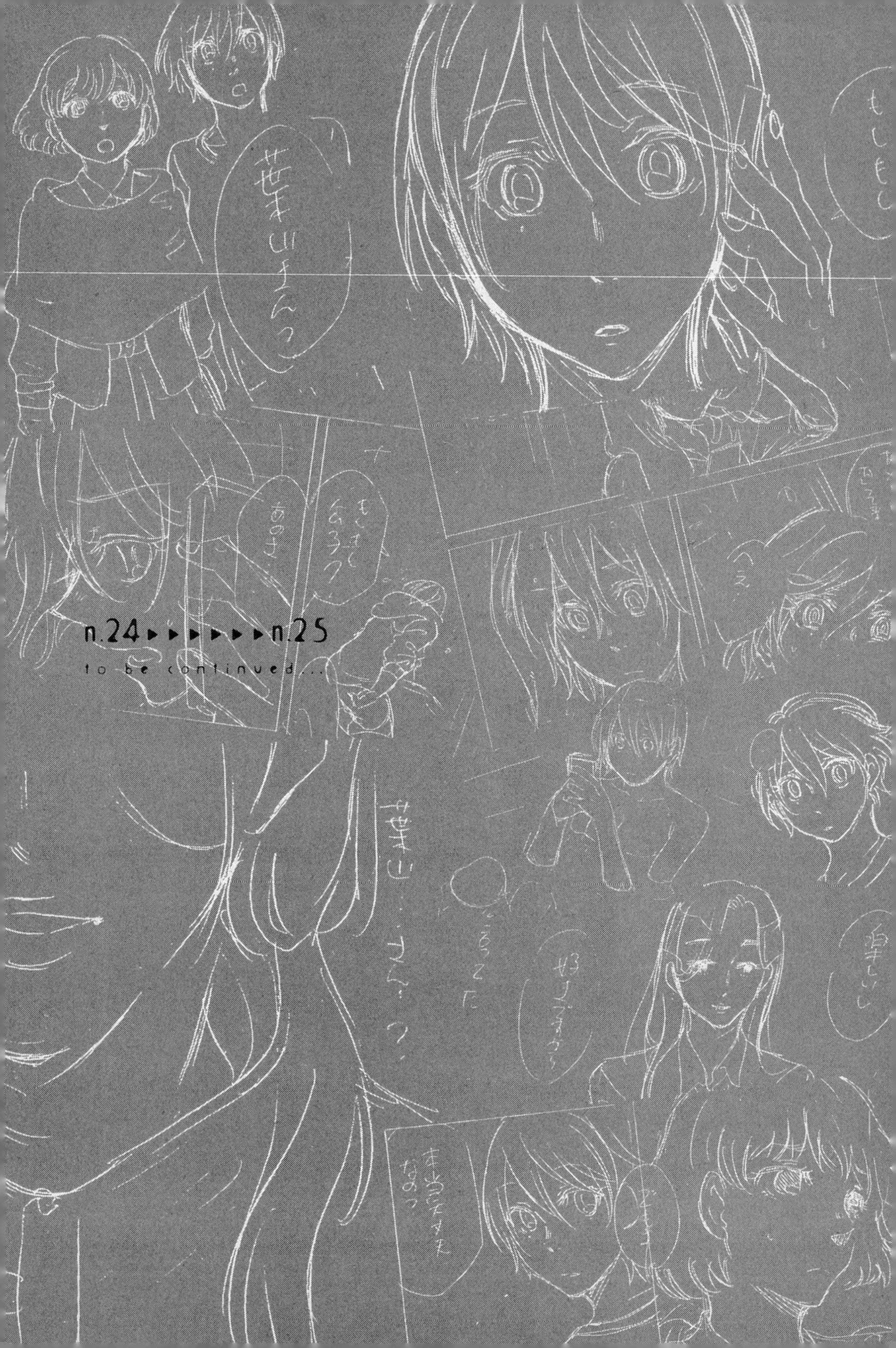
n.24 ▸▸▸▸▸▸▸ n.25
to be continued...

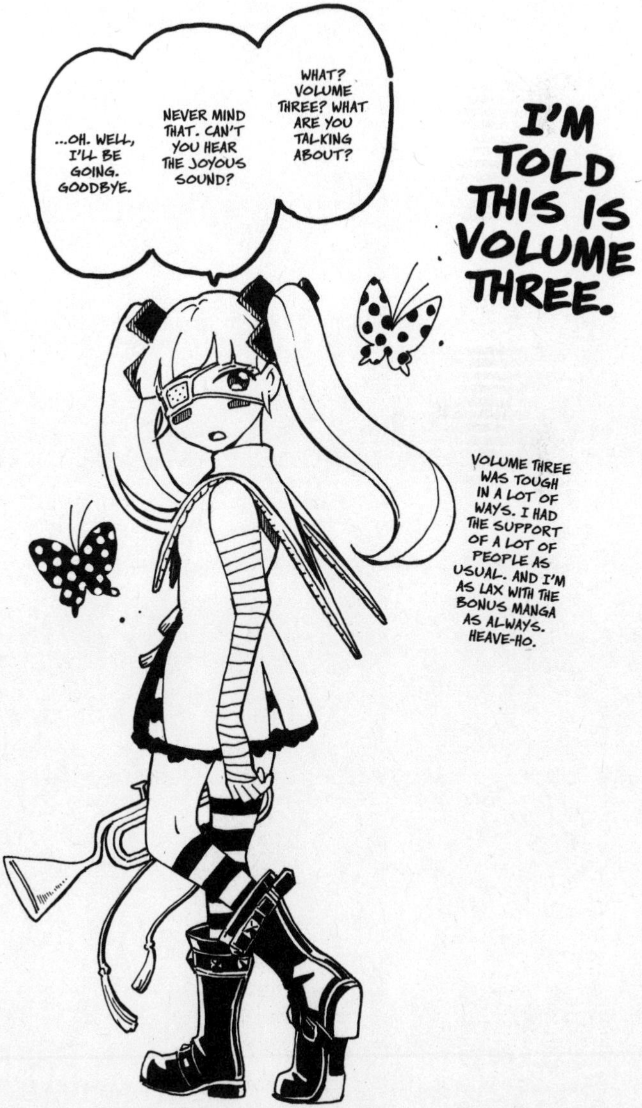
I'M TOLD THIS IS VOLUME THREE.
WHAT? VOLUME THREE? WHAT ARE YOU TALKING ABOUT?
NEVER MIND THAT. CAN'T YOU HEAR THE JOYOUS SOUND?
...OH. WELL, I'LL BE GOING. GOODBYE.
VOLUME THREE WAS TOUGH IN A LOT OF WAYS. I HAD THE SUPPORT OF A LOT OF PEOPLE AS USUAL. AND I'M AS LAX WITH THE BONUS MANGA AS ALWAYS. HEAVE-HO.

MY NAME IS MYAKO KATAURA.
SHIMMY
しゃたしゃたーっ
SHIMMY
OOOH!
YOUR CLIMBING SKILLS NEVER FAIL TO IMPRESS ME, MYAKO.
♪
COME ON DOWN NOW!
HMPH
CLANG
ガ
NNNGH... WHYYY?
SOB
SOB
YOU'LL NEVER GET HIM DOWN, DEAR.
HE HATES YOU.
COME ON DOWN NOW, MYAKO.

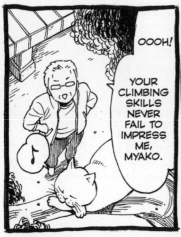

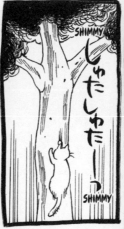

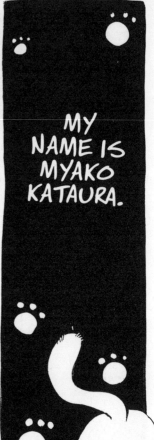

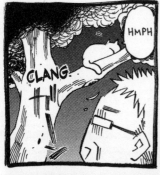

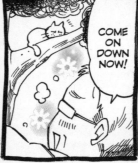

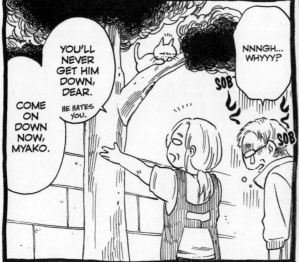

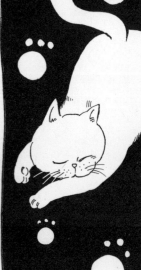

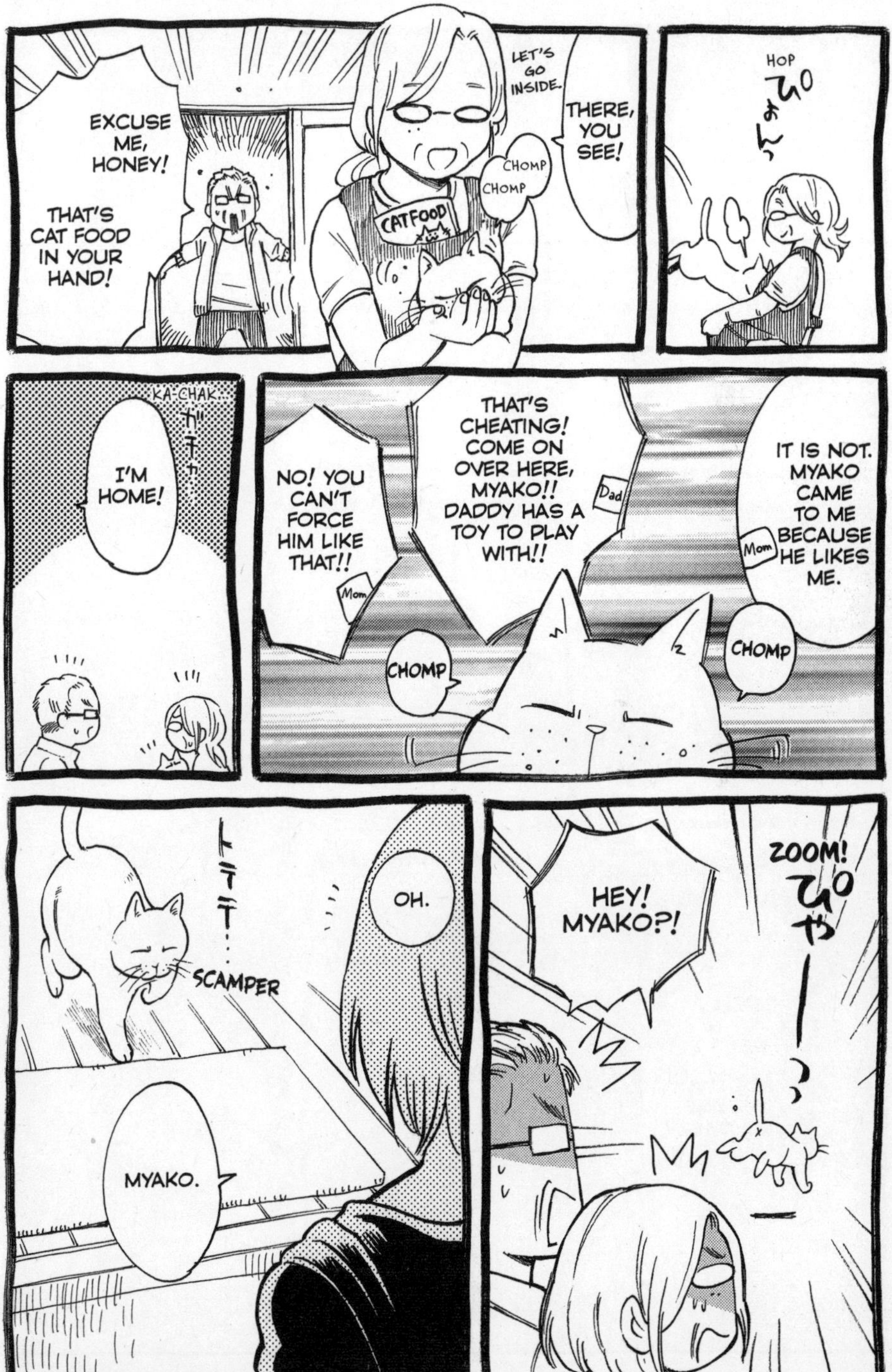
HOP
ぴょんっ
LET'S GO INSIDE.
THERE, YOU SEE!
CHOMP
CHOMP
CATFOOD
EXCUSE ME, HONEY!
THAT'S CAT FOOD IN YOUR HAND!
IT IS NOT. MYAKO CAME TO ME BECAUSE HE LIKES ME.
Mom
THAT'S CHEATING! COME ON OVER HERE, MYAKO!! DADDY HAS A TOY TO PLAY WITH!!
Dad
NO! YOU CAN'T FORCE HIM LIKE THAT!!
Mom
CHOMP
CHOMP
KA-CHAK...
ガチャ...
I'M HOME!
ZOOM!
ぴゃーっ
HEY! MYAKO?!
OH.
トテテ...
SCAMPER
MYAKO.

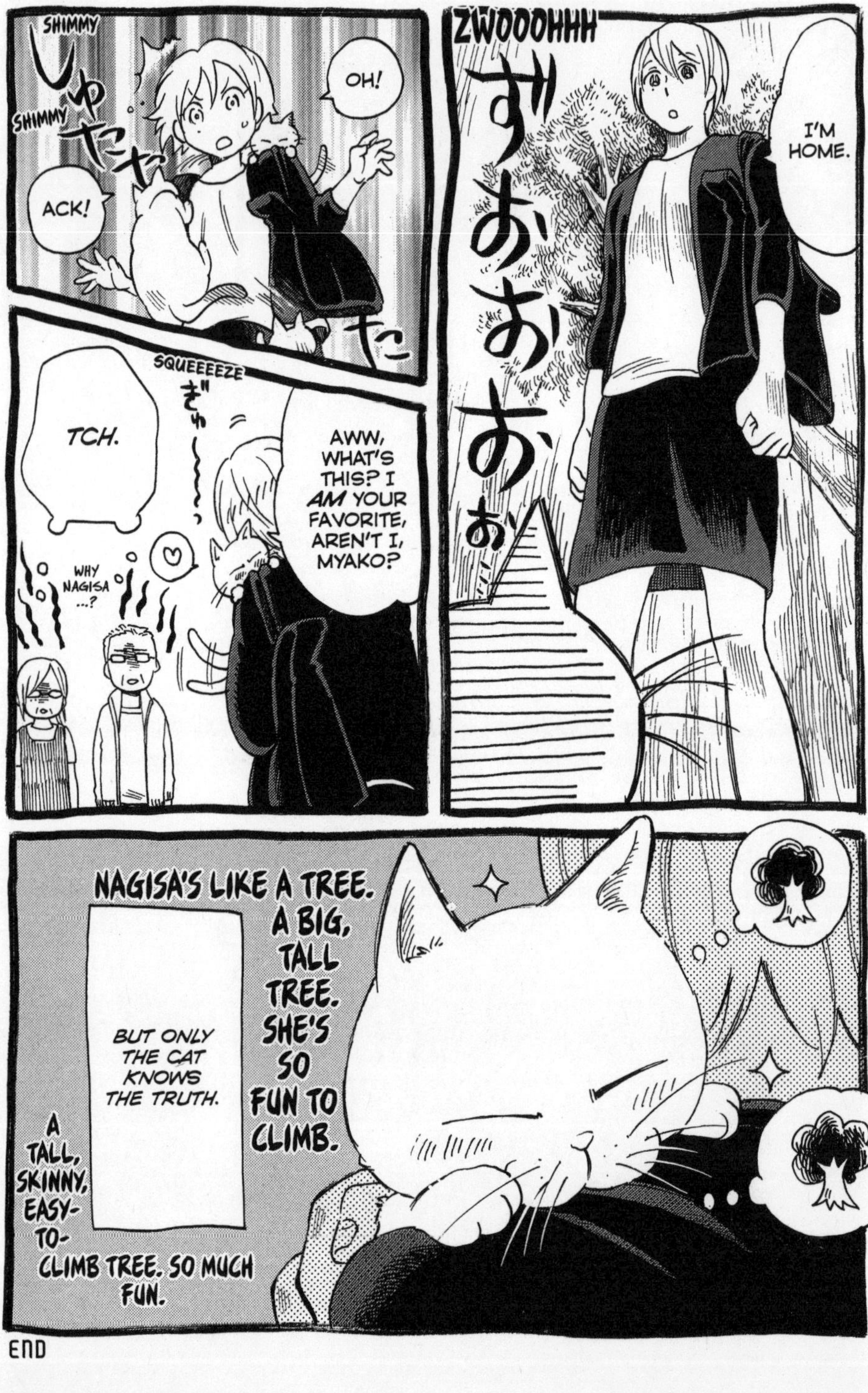
ZWOOOHHH
I'M HOME.
SHIMMY
SHIMMY
OH!
ACK!
SQUEEEEZE
AWW, WHAT'S THIS? I *AM* YOUR FAVORITE, AREN'T I, MYAKO?
TCH.
WHY NAGISA ...?
NAGISA'S LIKE A TREE. A BIG, TALL TREE. SHE'S SO FUN TO CLIMB.
BUT ONLY THE CAT KNOWS THE TRUTH.
A TALL, SKINNY, EASY-TO-CLIMB TREE. SO MUCH FUN.

END

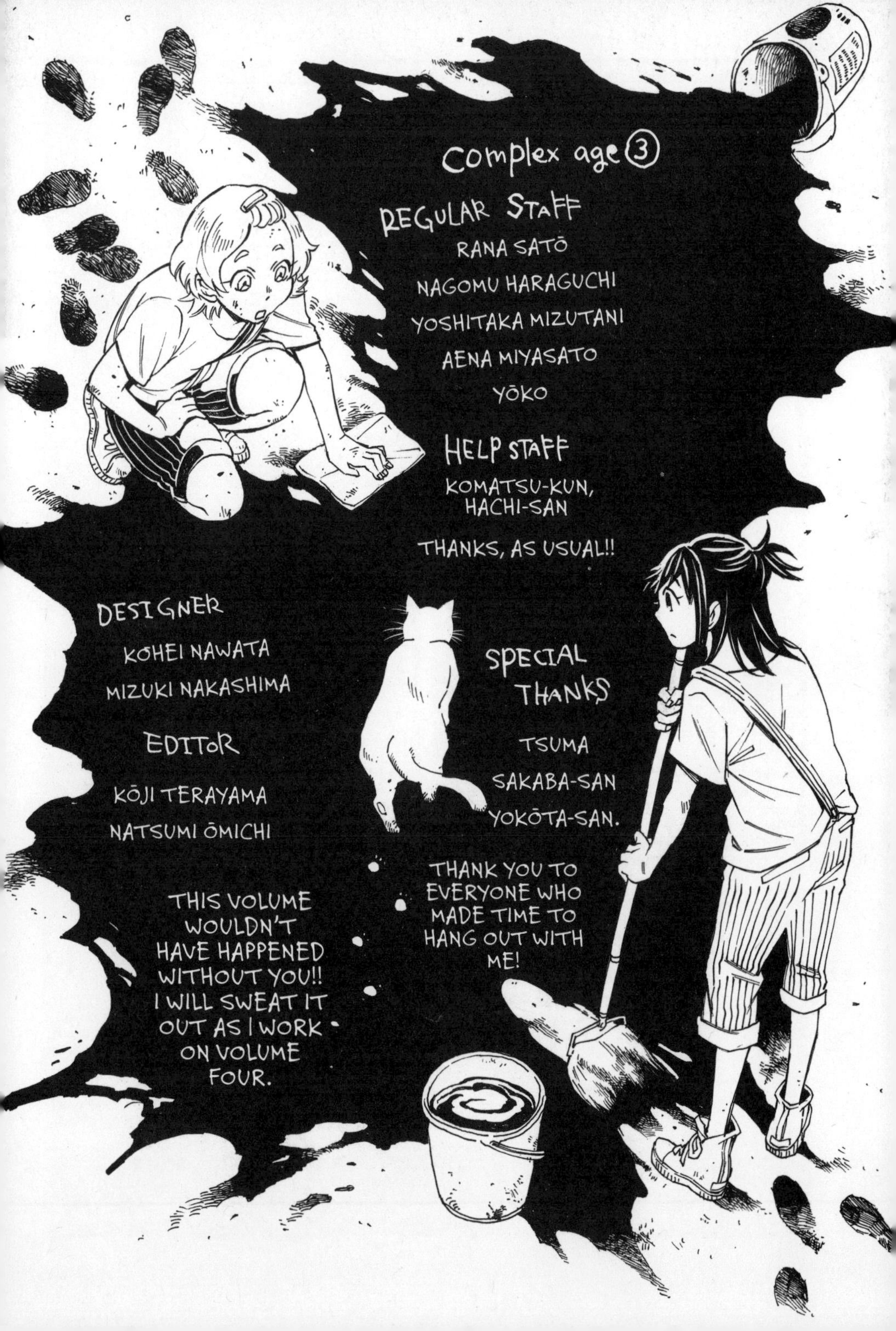

complex age ③
REGULAR STAFF
RANA SATŌ
NAGOMU HARAGUCHI
YOSHITAKA MIZUTANI
AENA MIYASATO
YŌKO
HELP STAFF
KOMATSU-KUN, HACHI-SAN
THANKS, AS USUAL!!
SPECIAL THANKS
TSUMA
SAKABA-SAN
YOKŌTA-SAN.
THANK YOU TO EVERYONE WHO MADE TIME TO HANG OUT WITH ME!
DESIGNER
KOHEI NAWATA
MIZUKI NAKASHIMA
EDITOR
KŌJI TERAYAMA
NATSUMI ŌMICHI
THIS VOLUME WOULDN'T HAVE HAPPENED WITHOUT YOU!! I WILL SWEAT IT OUT AS I WORK ON VOLUME FOUR.

Cospedia

[GLOSSARY OF COSPLAY TERMS]

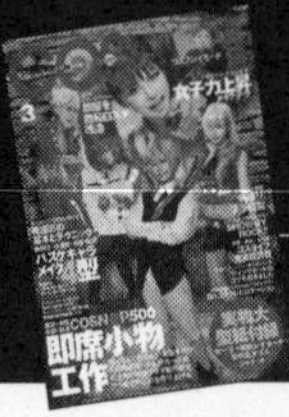

Supervisor: コスプレイモード COSPLAY MODE

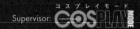

The cosplay magazine that has taken over the reins of Cosmode magazine, which ran until spring 2014. It publishes everything related to cosplay, including pinup photos, fan-submitted cosplay photos, and information on costumes, makeup, photography, armor and prop building, and cosplay culture. Released on the 3rd of every even-numbered month. (Published by Famima.com)

n.16

▶ Page 13

Album

To a cosplayer, an album isn't for one's own enjoyment so much as to show off to other people. When others see the pictures in an album, they can instantly see a cosplayer's history, and when photographing together for the first time, some layers show their albums in lieu of an introduction. Thanks to the recent spread of web services that allow for the easy production of photo books, some layers distribute their albums at *dōjinshi* fairs and other such events.

▶ Page 18

"What's a 'layer'?"

Cosplay has been around since the 1970s, but "costume player" was not generally abbreviated to "layer" until the 1990s. Until then, they were called "people who cosplay" and other similar terms.

n.17

▶ Page 27

Kagamine Rin

A character from the virtual singer software developed by Crypton Future Media, Inc. She is a 14-year-old girl who is 152 cm (5'0") tall and weighs 43 kg (94.8 lbs). Her main feature is her "strong, powerful voice." Following on the heels of the influential Hatsune Miku, she was part of the second installment of the *Character Vocal Series* of software that allows the user to synthesize a singing voice, which was released in December 2007. Her voice is provided by Asami Shimoda.

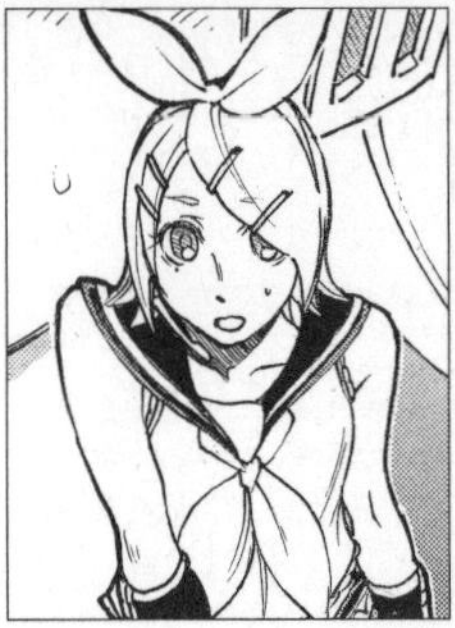

Kagamine Len

A boy character packaged along with the aforementioned Kagamine Rin software. He is 14 years old like Rin, 156 cm (5'1") tall, and weighs 47 kg (103.6 lbs). His voice is provided by the same actress as Rin, Asami Shimoda.

Lion

Short for lion board, the common name for koyo soft board. It was originally marketed as construction or packing material, but because it is durable and easy to work with, it has gained a lot of attention as a material for making cosplay props. It comes in a wide variety of sizes and thicknesses, and can be used to make swords, armor, accessories, etc.

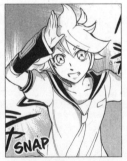

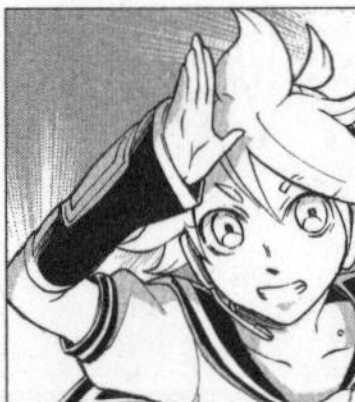
SNAP

"It's basically a sailor suit."

Kagamine Rin and Len's costumes are based on the sailor suit design. Costumes like this that are based on clothes that really exist are the best entry point for beginning costume makers. Recently, with layer popularity in mind, some anime and games have been introducing many characters wearing easy-to-construct uniforms and gym clothes.

▶ Page 28

Fusible interfacing

A material used to compensate when the outer layer of fabric is not enough to perform properly. For example, it can support the outer layer from the inside to create a beautiful silhouette, prevent a costume from losing shape or becoming loose, or enhance the thickness or hardness of the material. Fusible interfacing doesn't have to be sewn on to the fabric but sticks to it with glue, making it easier to use. It is currently the preferred type of interfacing. There are two main types—the adhesive type, and the heat-activated iron-on type.

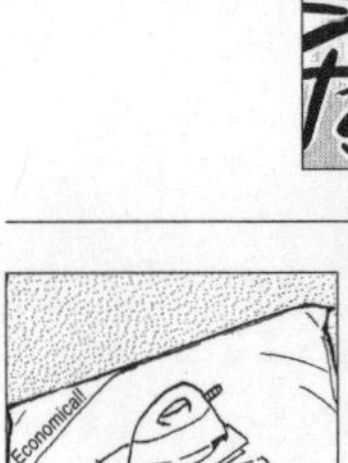
Economical!
Fusible Interfacing
Extra Stiff

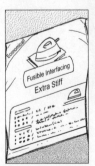

their costumes should not be restricted to officially licensed products, when the market becomes infested with unlicensed merchandise, it deals significant damage to properties that pay for production costs with sales of character merchandise, and it could even make it difficult for the series to continue. To protect the media content, it is hoped that the consumers will refuse to buy unlicensed merchandise.

▶ Page 33
Hatsune Miku
The character from the first installment of

▶ Page 30
"One of the costumes they were selling in a store."
Cities like Ikebukuro and Akihabara have several stores that sell costumes. Some of them do not get the official license to sell the costumes, and occasionally the rights holders will discover this and issue a cease and desist order (further, the act of a layer creating and wearing a costume for personal enjoyment is not illegal, but it is illegal to sell that costume). While some people are of the opinion that layers who buy

Cosplay magazines
There are several cosplay magazines with indefinite release schedules, but very few that go on sale regularly. *Dengeki Layers,* published by Asci Media Works, used to be a bimonthly magazine, but it moved to an indefinite print schedule in 2009, and is virtually discontinued. Currently, the only cosplay magazine with a regular print schedule is *Cosplay Mode,* published by Famima.com, which supervises this lexicon.

Luka-né
Megurine Luka. A character featured in the third installment of the *CV series,* following Hatsune Miku and Kagamine Rin/Len. A 20-year-old woman who is 162 cm (5'4") tall and weighs 45 kg (99.2 lbs).

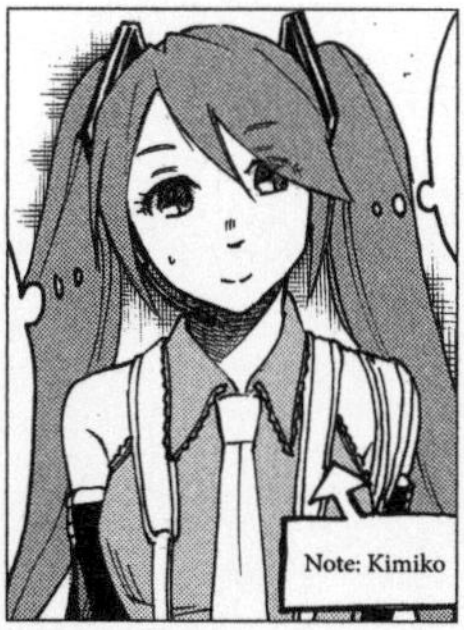
Note: Kimiko

tive works (such as nonprofit release of songs sung by Hatsune Miku), as well as the noncommercial sale of derivative works (the nonprofit sale of Hatune Miku CDs) using the Piapro Link system. Because of this, her popularity exploded among creators of all kinds of derivative works, and Hatsune Miku has grown into a national sensation.

the *CV series* that went on sale in August 2007. A 16-year-old girl who is 158 cm (5'2") tall and weighs 42 kg (92.6 lbs). Her voice is provided by Saki Fujita. This software was revolutionary because it officially recognized the creation of derivative works (publishing songs sung by Hatsune Miku and illustrations using her likeness, for example) under certain conditions. The Piapro Character License outlined at Crypton Future Media, INC.'s website, www.piapro.net, allows the creation of noncommercial, nonprofit deriva-

---

pression, so the problem is still in need of a solution.

n.19

▶ Page 65
Karaoke
In recent years, almost every karaoke machine has an *anison* (see volume 2) category. It's becoming common for not only anime fans but everyone to sing *anison,* and songs like Yōko Takahashi's "Cruel Angel's Thesis" (opening theme to *Neon Genesis Evangelion*) and Yoshimi Iwasaki's "Touch" (opening theme to *Touch*)

▶ Page 49
Sitting pose
There are some slimy photographers who try to sneak pictures of a layer's undergarments. (Note: See the note in volume 1: "The picture was right there for the taking. lolol" (unauthorized photo).) Of course, many photographers will not do this, and if a rule is put in place forbidding pictures from a low angle, it would restrict a photographer's freedom of ex-

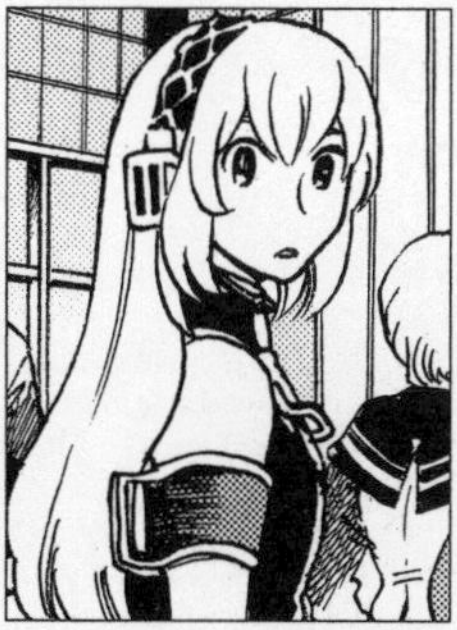

Her voice is provided by Yū Asakawa. What makes her unique is that she is a bilingual singer, who can sing in English as well as Japanese.

---

member" and referring to a fan's favorite member of an idol group. The word "*oshi-men*" became part of the vernacular with the rise to fame of the idol group AKB48. In 2011, it was nominated for U-Can's new word of the year. Now people have started using "XX-*oshi*" to refer to their favorite character in an anime.

n.20

▶ Page 87
"Re-animated scenes"
When pre-existing anime is made into a movie that recaps the series' story, scenes

are currently listing high in the rankings.

▶ Page 81
Team Ururu (Team XX)
The Japanese term, "Ururu-oshi", comes from "*ichi-oshi* member (*oshi-men*)", meaning "most recommended

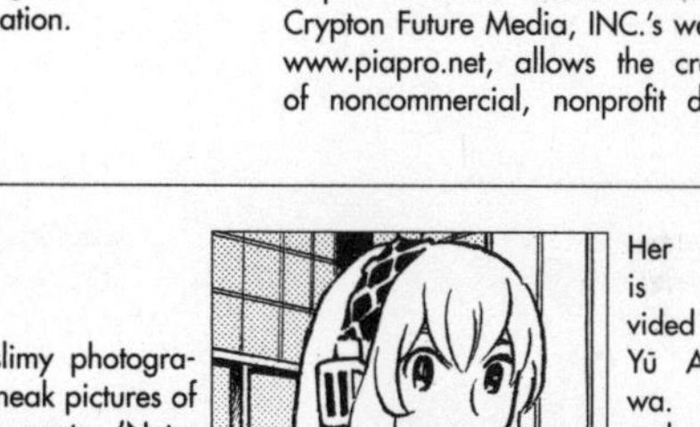
Magical Riding Hood Uru
Opening Theme Song
Ururun☆Magic

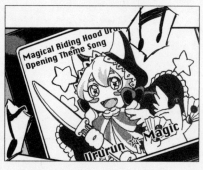

the needs of these voice acting fans. The events themselves are becoming bigger productions, and making more and more money.

▶ Page 122
Dress Form
A type of mannequin. It often refers to mannequins that are only a torso, which is why in Japan they are called *torso,* after the Italian word for "torso." On the inexpensive side, one can purchase a dress form for two or three thousand yen ($20-

and schedule permit, scenes will be redrawn just as they would be for a movie.

n.21

▶ Page 118
Voice Actor Event
An event during which the voice actors for an anime or game will appear on stage for a talk show and/or concert. In recent years, voice actors are being idolized more than ever, and more and more viewers are starting to watch an anime because they are fans of a particular voice actor. The number of voice actor events has also increased to meet

will be re-animated to make them higher quality than what the viewers saw on TV. With a TV series, a strict schedule must be maintained in order to air a new episode every week, and sometimes quality will go down as a series gets into its second half (especially bad instances of this are called "art fail"). But moving pictures can't be fixed by merely redrawing a single picture, so even revisions require an extraordinary amount of work on the part of the staff. In recent years, when a series is sold in a box set, like on Blu-ray, if the budget

---

tendance of 560,000. This number created a sensation when it was discussed in NHK's January 2015 TV program for general viewing, "The Unknown World of Comiket."

▶ Page 140
Cosplay Card
Almost every layer has made her own cards and carries several different versions. In many cases, the card will have a picture of the layer cosplaying her favorite character, and list her ID for cosplay commu-

ing dress form, which is soft enough to stick pins into).

n.22

▶ Page 137
Comiket
Short for Comic Market, the largest *dōjinshi* fair in the world. Held twice every year—in August (Summer Comiket) and December (Winter Comiket)—at Tokyo Big Sight (see volume 1). The duration of the event is generally three days. Comic Market 87, held from December 28-30, 2014, records an at-

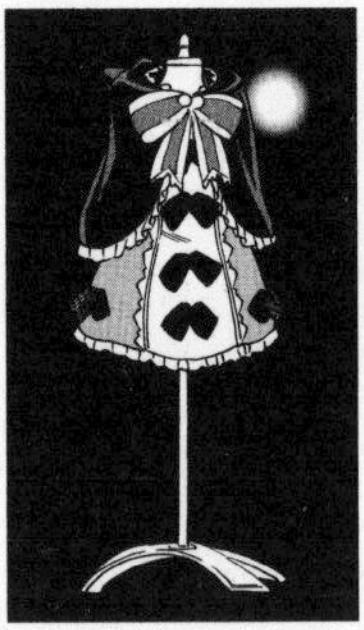

$30). Not only does it prevent the costume from losing its shape, but many layers have them for use during costume production (in those cases, it helps to have a sew-

---

Worldwide cosplay competition
The World Cosplay Summit, a cosplay event that attracts cosplayers from all over the world. In began in Nagoya in 2003 as a way to bring cosplayers together from every country, and to recognize the overseas popularity of Japan's anime and manga. In 2005, the Cosplay Championship, a contest to determine the best cosplay performers in the world, was held at the World's Fair in Expo Dome, gaining a lot

Animate, in conjunction with the cosplay photo studio, Hacostudio. At their Halloween Cosplay Fest in October 2014, they attracted ten thousand cosplayers over the course of two days.

TdC
Short for Tonari de Cosplay Haku (Cosplay Fair Nextdoor), a cosplay event held at Tokyo Big Sight's neighbor TFT (Tokyo Fashion Town Building) alongside summer and winter Comiket.

nity sites Cure and Archive (see volume 2).

n.23

▶ Page 154
Acosta!
A cosplay event in Ikebukuro's Sunshine City sponsored by Acos, the cosplay brand of the anime, comic, and game chain

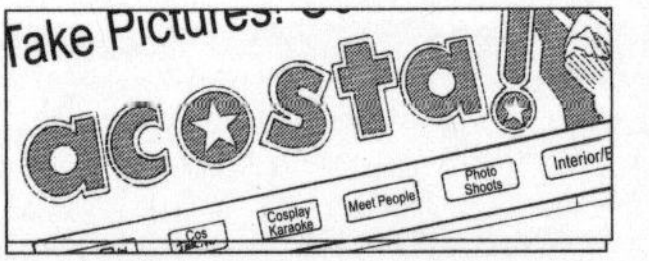
Take Pictures!
acosta!
Cosplay Karaoke
Meet People
Photo Shoots
Interior/E

▶ Page 162
Skimpy costumes
Costumes with a high degree of skin exposure are not entirely uncommon among cosplayers. Some say that their favorite character just happens to wear clothes that show a lot of skin, while others go out of their way to choose characters based on the skimpiness of their costume. (See volume 2, "High skin to fabric ratio.") The cosplay *dōjinshi* fair Cosholic is famous for attracting layers who like to show their skin. Children under 18 years of age are not allowed to attend this event.

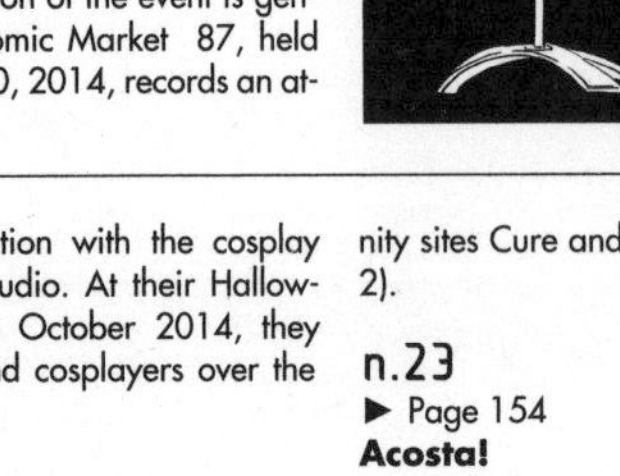
th World Cosplay Summit!
BUSHIR
Winner Announced!

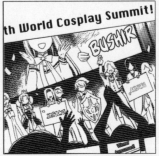

of attention for the event. More countries participate in the summit every year, with 22 countries accounted for in 2014. Performers who make it through the selection process in their various countries can participate in the contest, and are judged on craftmanship, story, and faithfulness to the source material.

Translation
Notes

PAGE 27
THE LETTER A

The note Nagisa actually wrote to herself is to think of the Chinese *kanji* character for the number eight, which looks like this: 八. The reader can see it in the sketch,

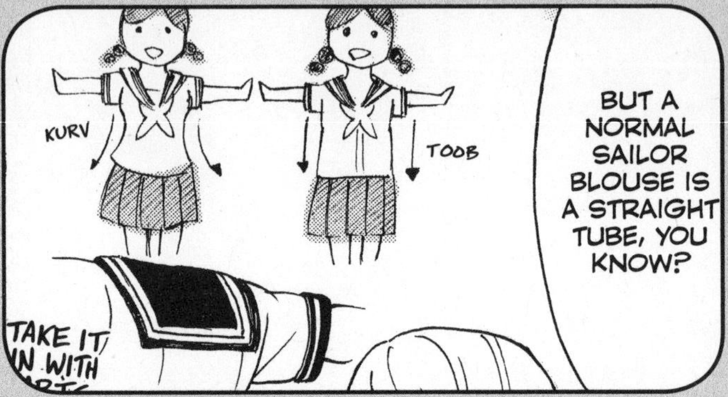
BUT A NORMAL SAILOR BLOUSE IS A STRAIGHT TUBE, YOU KNOW?
TOOB
KURV
TAKE IT IN WITH

as Nagisa has drawn arrows to show the shape of the costume. The translators adapted the note to the letter A, which readers are going to recognize more readily.

PAGE 34
DRAINED MY LYMPHS

Massaging one's lymph nodes is a way to detox and improve one's complexion, which gives one a younger look. Nagisa must have spent a lot of time rubbing her neck and face the

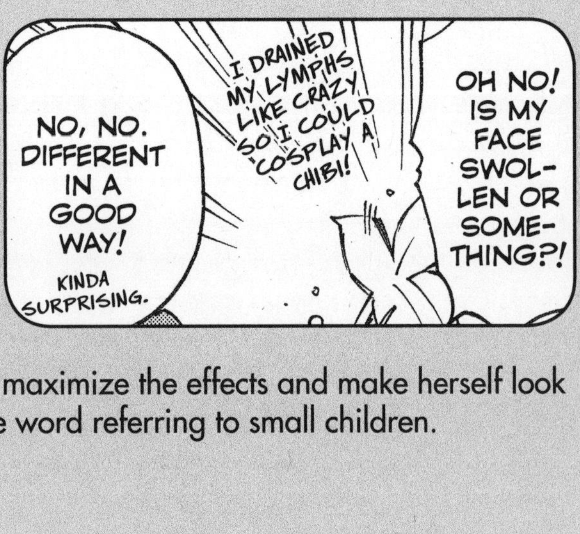
OH NO! IS MY FACE SWOL-LEN OR SOME-THING?!
I DRAINED MY LYMPHS LIKE CRAZY SO I COULD COSPLAY A CHIBI!
NO, NO. DIFFERENT IN A GOOD WAY!
KINDA SURPRISING.

night before in order to maximize the effects and make herself look more *chibi*—a Japanese word referring to small children.

PAGE 35

LUKA-NÉ

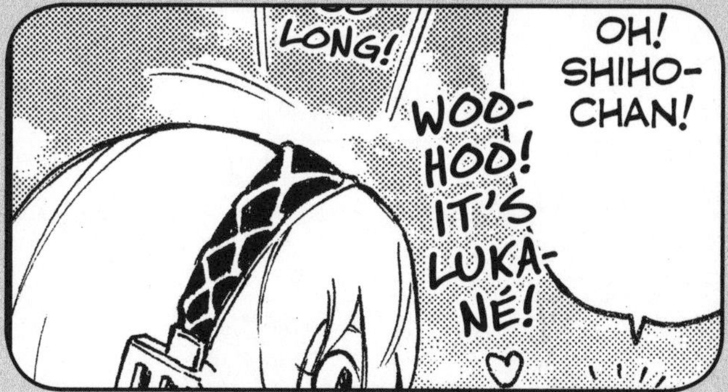
OH! SHIHO-CHAN!
WOO-HOO! IT'S LUKA-NÉ!
LONG!

Né (pronounced "nay") means older sister, and is often attached to the name of someone the speaker sees as an older, more mature type. At 20 years old, Luka is one of the older Vocaloids, so the others would see her as an older sister figure.

PAGE 89

THE GO-HOME CLUB

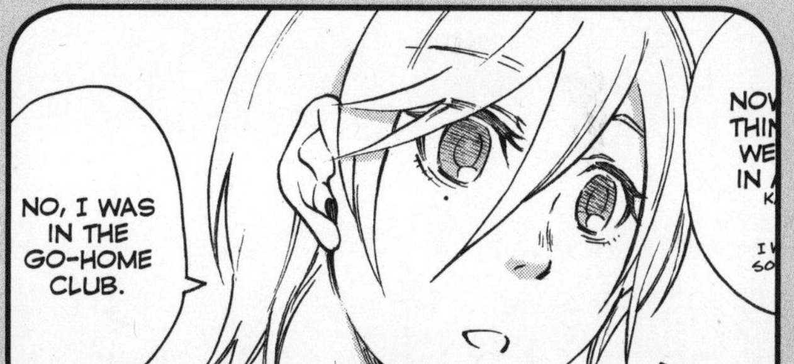
NO, I WAS IN THE GO-HOME CLUB.

In Japan, it's expected—and sometimes required—that high school students join some kind of club. Because of the ubiquity of club activities, students who were not in a club came to be known as members of a club anyway—the go-home club.

PAGE 121
TSUNDERE

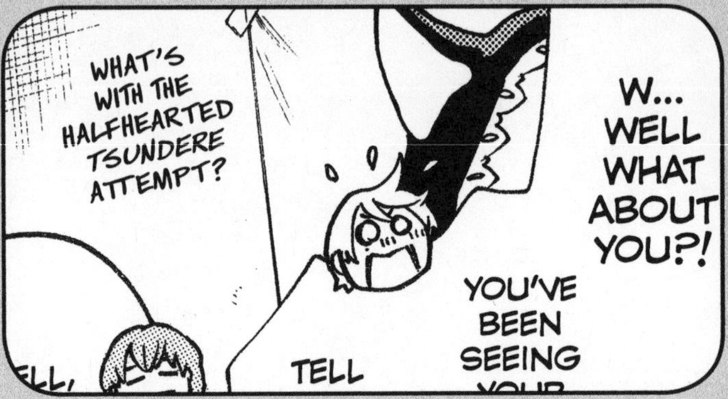
W... WELL WHAT ABOUT YOU?!
YOU'VE BEEN SEEING
WHAT'S WITH THE HALFHEARTED TSUNDERE ATTEMPT?
TELL

For readers unfamiliar with Japanese anime and manga tropes, *tsundere* comes from *tsun-tsun* (meaning prickly) and *dere-dere* (meaning lovestruck). A *tsundere* is a character whose first reaction to other people is prickly and mean, but because they care deep down, sometimes those ooey-gooey emotions will show through.

PAGE 152
CABARET GIRL'S CARD

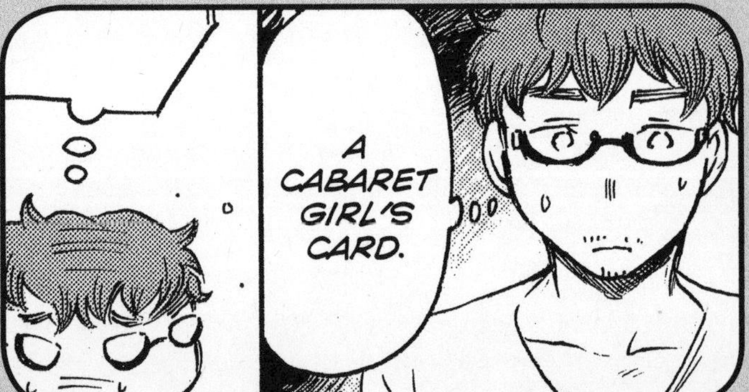
A CABARET GIRL'S CARD.

A cabaret girl is a girl who works at a type of bar called a cabaret club. These are places men can go to enjoy the company of women while they drink. For this reason, the women who entertain men at such venues can be seen as a modern form of *geisha*.

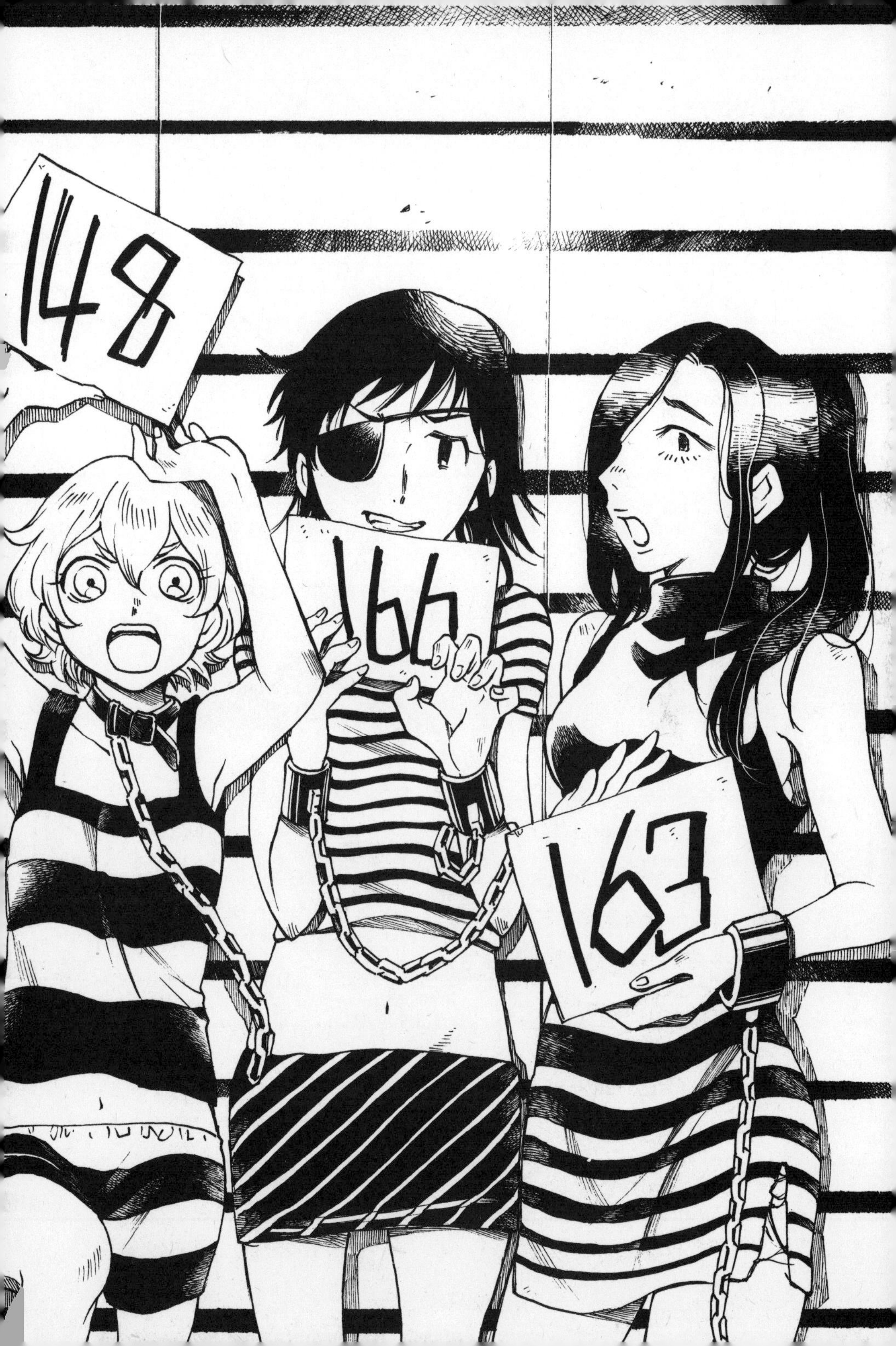
163
166
148

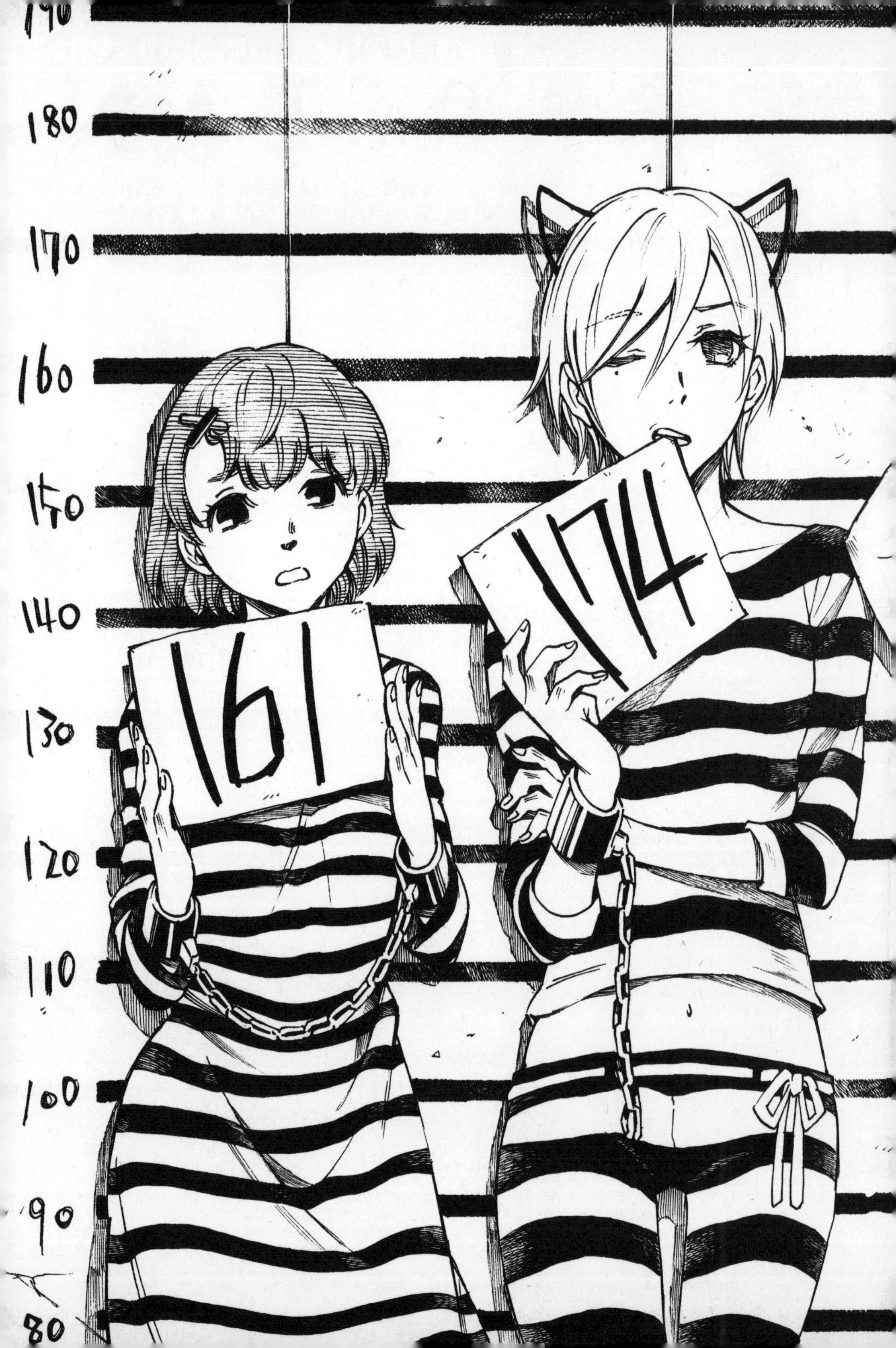
180
170
160
150
140
130
120
110
100
90
80
161
174

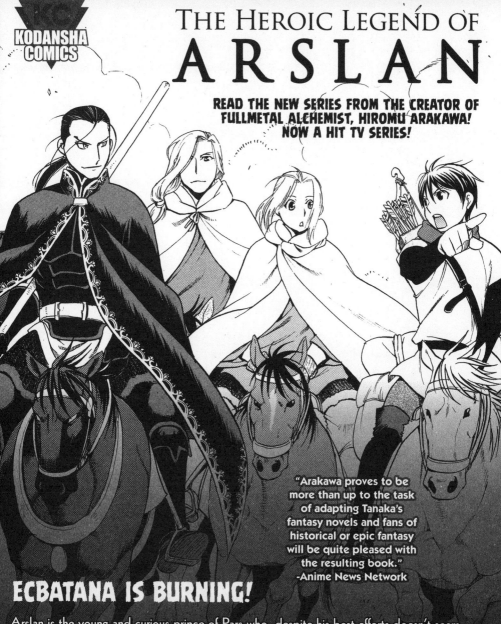

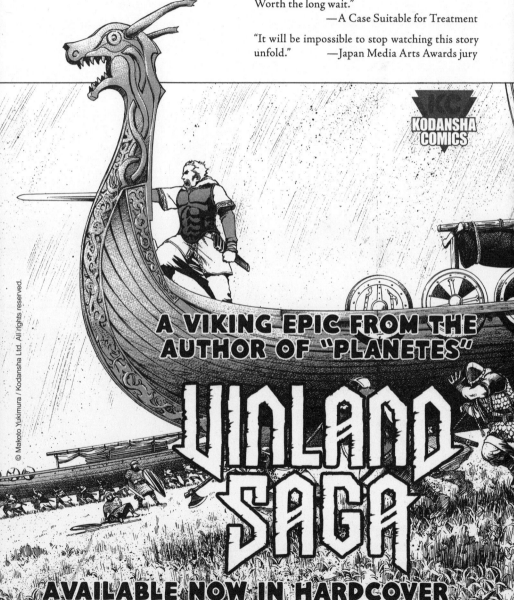

INUYASHIKI

A superhero like none you've ever seen, from the creator of "Gantz"!

Ichiro Inuyashiki is down on his luck. He looks much older than his 58 years, his children despise him, and his wife thinks he's a useless coward. So when he's diagnosed with stomach cancer and given three months to live, it seems the only one who'll miss him is his dog.

Then a blinding light fills the sky, and the old man is killed... only to wake up later in a body he almost recognizes as his own. Can it be that Ichiro Inuyashiki is no longer human?

Comes in extra-large editions with color pages!

KODANSHA COMICS

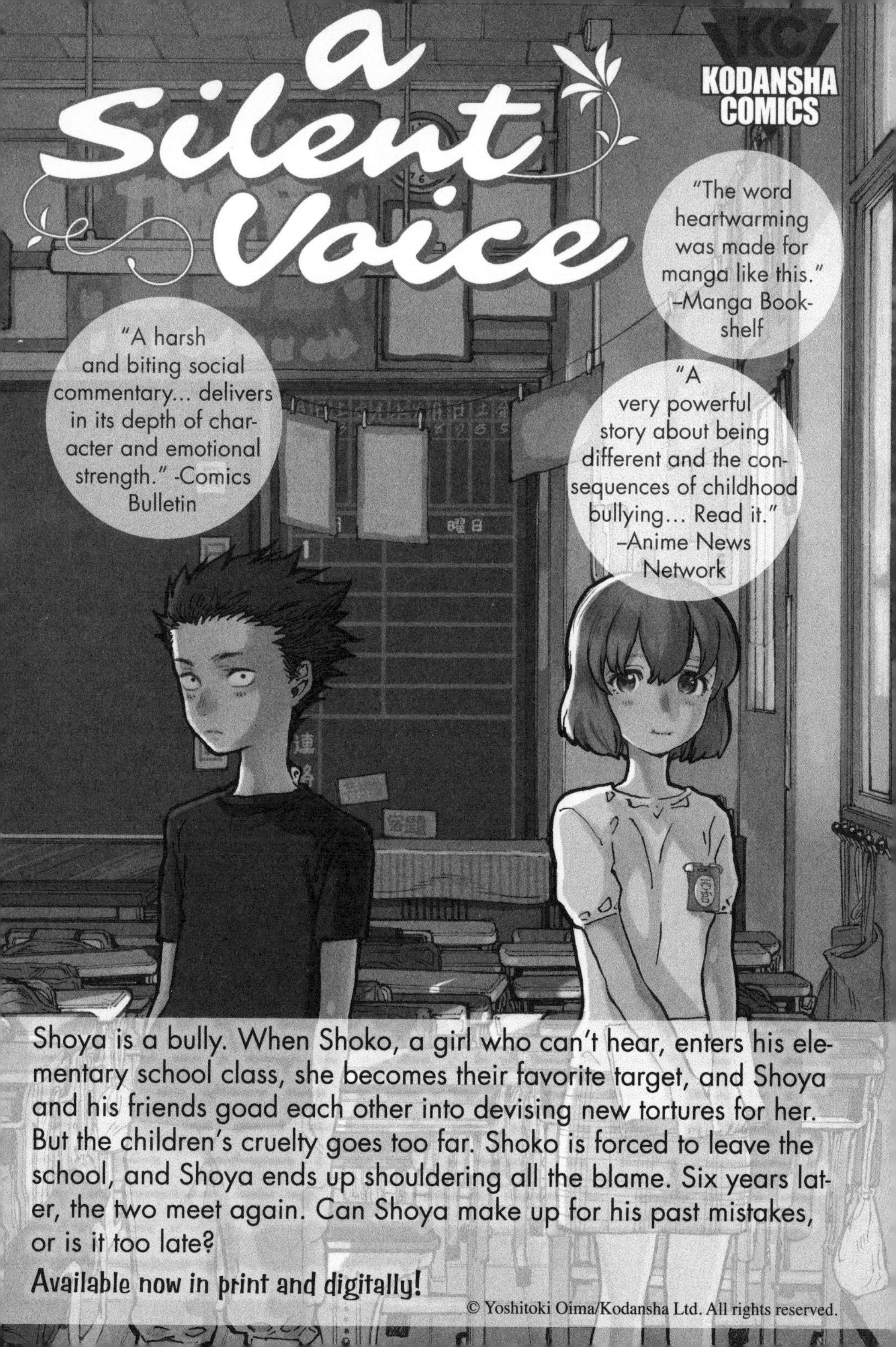
KODANSHA COMICS
a Silent Voice
"The word heartwarming was made for manga like this." –Manga Bookshelf
"A harsh and biting social commentary... delivers in its depth of character and emotional strength." -Comics Bulletin
"A very powerful story about being different and the consequences of childhood bullying… Read it." –Anime News Network
Shoya is a bully. When Shoko, a girl who can't hear, enters his elementary school class, she becomes their favorite target, and Shoya and his friends goad each other into devising new tortures for her. But the children's cruelty goes too far. Shoko is forced to leave the school, and Shoya ends up shouldering all the blame. Six years later, the two meet again. Can Shoya make up for his past mistakes, or is it too late?
Available now in print and digitally!
© Yoshitoki Oima/Kodansha Ltd. All rights reserved.

Praise for the anime:

"The show provides a pleasant window on the highs and lows of young love with two young people who are first timers at the real thing."

-The Fandom Post

"Always it is smarter, more poetic, more touching, just plain better than you think it is going to be."

-Anime News Network

Say I Love You.

KC KODANSHA COMICS

Mei Tachibana has no friends — and says she doesn't need them!

But everything changes when she accidentally roundhouse kicks the most popular boy in school! However, Yamato Kurosawa isn't angry in the slightest— in fact, he thinks his ordinary life could use an unusual girl like Mei. But winning Mei's trust will be a tough task. How long will she refuse to say, "I love you"?

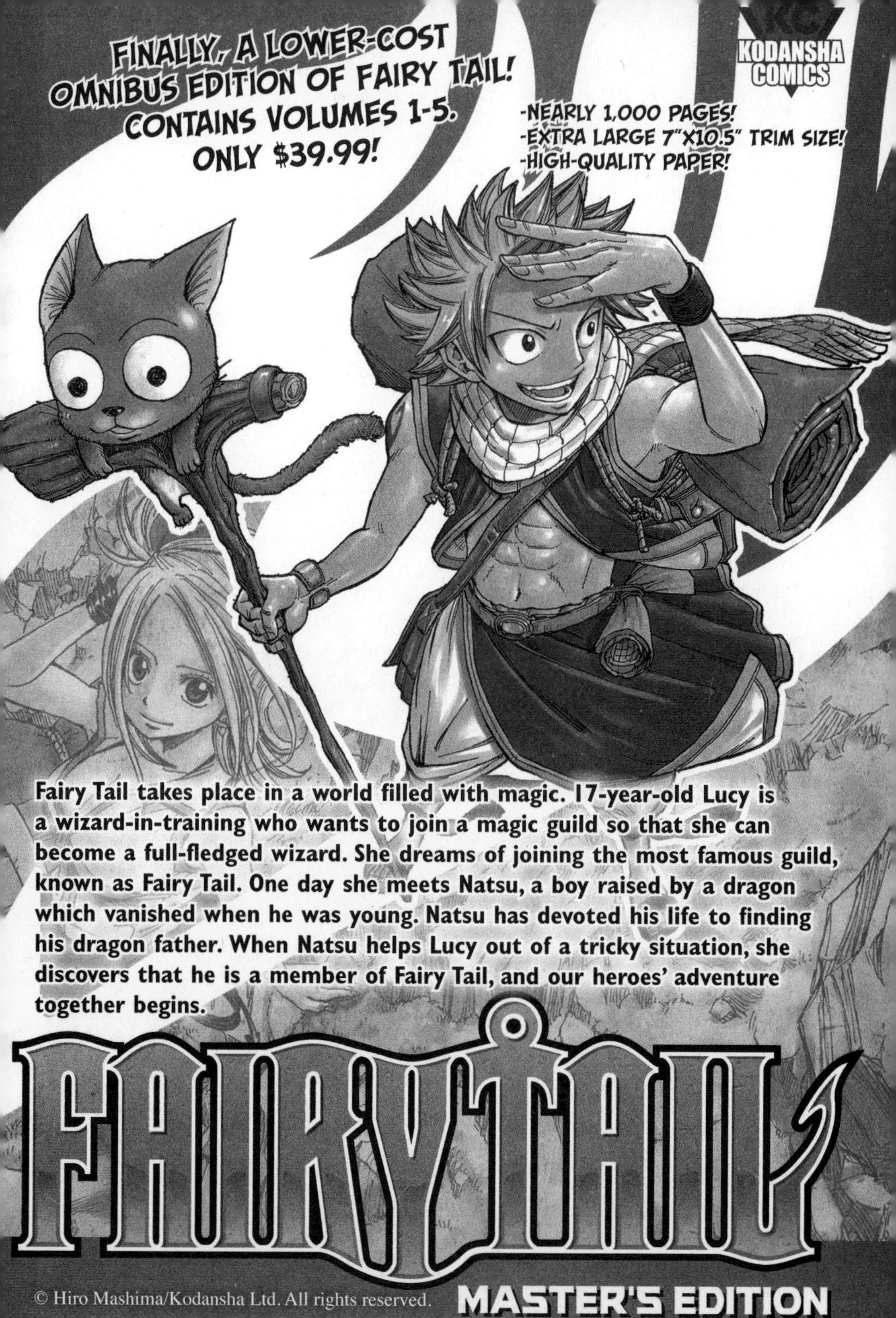
KC KODANSHA COMICS
FINALLY, A LOWER-COST OMNIBUS EDITION OF FAIRY TAIL! CONTAINS VOLUMES 1-5. ONLY $39.99!
-NEARLY 1,000 PAGES!
-EXTRA LARGE 7"X10.5" TRIM SIZE!
-HIGH-QUALITY PAPER!
Fairy Tail takes place in a world filled with magic. 17-year-old Lucy is a wizard-in-training who wants to join a magic guild so that she can become a full-fledged wizard. She dreams of joining the most famous guild, known as Fairy Tail. One day she meets Natsu, a boy raised by a dragon which vanished when he was young. Natsu has devoted his life to finding his dragon father. When Natsu helps Lucy out of a tricky situation, she discovers that he is a member of Fairy Tail, and our heroes' adventure together begins.
FAIRY TAIL
MASTER'S EDITION

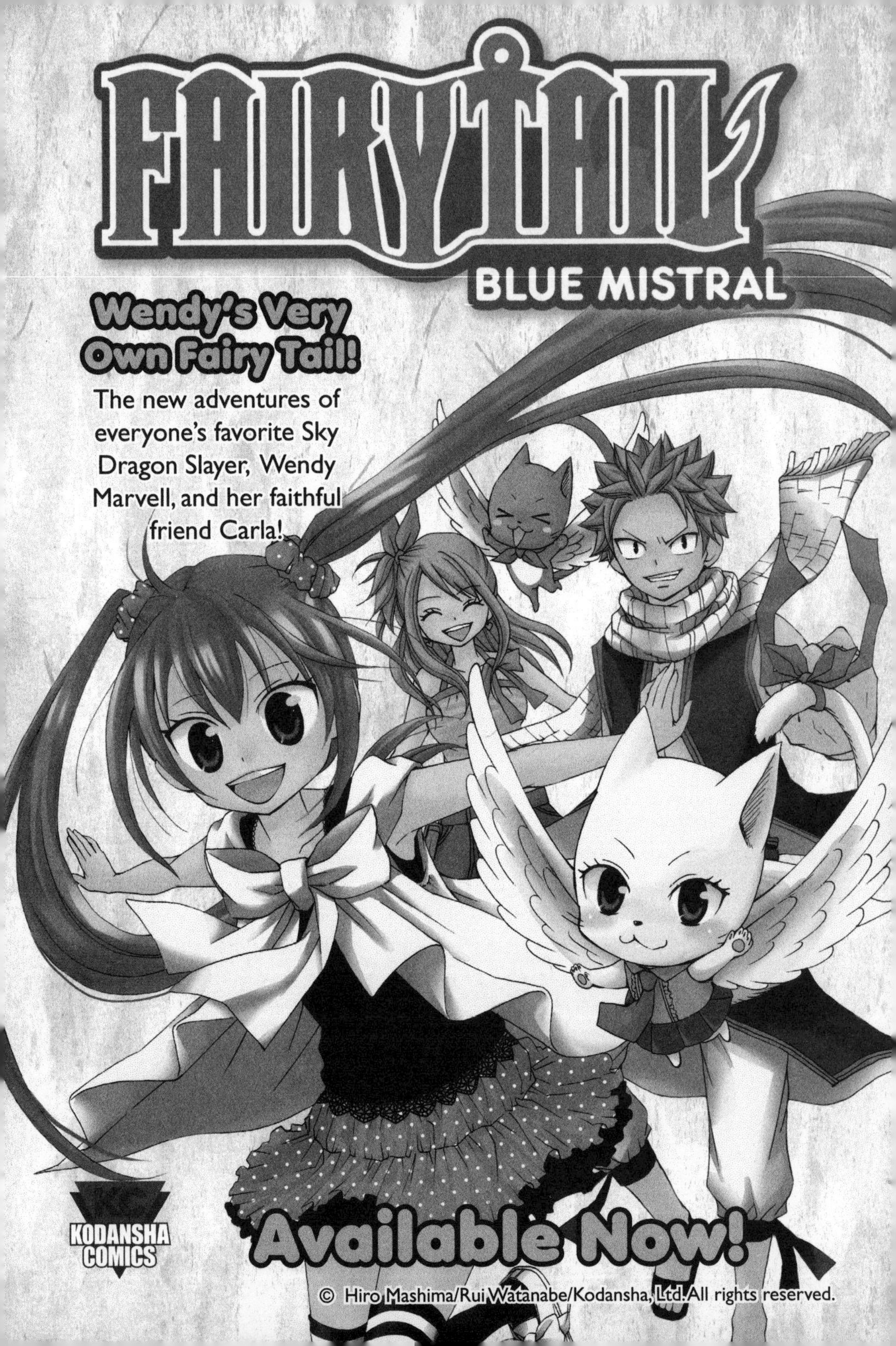
FAIRY TAIL
BLUE MISTRAL
Wendy's Very Own Fairy Tail!
The new adventures of everyone's favorite Sky Dragon Slayer, Wendy Marvell, and her faithful friend Carla!
KODANSHA COMICS
Available Now!
© Hiro Mashima/Rui Watanabe/Kodansha, Ltd. All rights reserved.

Yamada-kun AND THE Seven Witches

KODANSHA COMICS

SWAPPED WITH A KISS?!

Class troublemaker Ryu Yamada is already having a bad day when he stumbles down a staircase along with star student Urara Shiraishi. When he wakes up, he realizes they have switched bodies—and that Ryu has the power to trade places with anyone just by kissing them! Ryu and Urara take full advantage of the situation to improve their lives, but with such an oddly amazing power, just how long will they be able to keep their secret under wraps?

Available now in print and digitally!

My Little Monster

OPPOSITES ATTRACT...MAYBE?

Haru Yoshida is feared as an unstable and violent "monster." Mizutani Shizuku is a grade-obsessed student with no friends. Fate brings these two together to form the most unlikely pair. Haru firmly believes he's in love with Mizutani and she firmly believes he's insane.

KC
KODANSHA
COMICS

A Kodansha Comics Trade Paperback Original.

Published in the United States by Kodansha Comics,
an imprint of Kodansha USA Publishing, LLC, New York.

Publication rights for this English edition arranged through Kodansha Ltd.,
Tokyo.

First published in Japan in 2015 by Kodansha Ltd., Tokyo, as *Complex Age* volume 3.

ISBN 978-1-63236-250-6

Printed in the United States of America.

www.kodanshacomics.com

9 8 7 6 5 4 3 2 1

Translation: Alethea Nibley & Athena Nibley
Lettering: AndWorld Design
Editing: Lauren Scanlan
Kodansha Comics Edition Cover Design: Phil Balsman